Reconfigured Agrarian Relations in Zimbabwe

Toendepi Shonhe

Langaa Research & Publishing CIG
Mankon, Bamenda

Publisher:
Langaa RPCIG
Langaa Research & Publishing Common Initiative Group
P.O. Box 902 Mankon
Bamenda
North West Region
Cameroon
Langaagrp@gmail.com
www.langaa-rpcig.net

Distributed in and outside N. America by African Books Collective
orders@africanbookscollective.com
www.africanbookscollective.com

ISBN-10: 9956-764-21-3

ISBN-13: 978-9956-764-21-1

© Toendepi Shonhe 2018

Dedication

In Memory of David Kundishora Shonhe
My father,

and

Phillis Chihwayi Shonhe,
My mother,

Table of Contents

List of Tables

List of Figures

Chart

Diagrams

Maps

Pictures

Acknowledgements

This journey took four years of hard work, resolve, commitment and sacrifice. First, my deep appreciation and indebtedness goes to Professor Oliver Mtapuri, for the guidance, encouragement, mentorship and inspiration. I benefitted from his immense knowledge and consistent and timely feedback on all the draft chapters. His has been the guiding light for this journey. I am also greatly indebted to Professor Patrick Bond who encouraged and helped me undertake this journey in 2013. And to Professor Sam Moyo: MHSRIP - I am most grateful for the initial work in shaping the book before his departure on 21 November 2015. The long hours of debates shaped the scope of my work and deepened my understanding of core arguments of the agrarian question(s).

My gratitude also goes to Walter Chambati, Head at African Institute for Agrarian Studies; Steven Mberi, Yumi Sakata and Grascian Mkodzongi for the debates and reflections on key issues that were emerging during my work. To all my family, friends and colleagues who read sections and parts of the work and gave comments; Sandra Mutsimba, Naison Bhunu, Aaron Mushayanyama, Lawrence Paganga, Dr Emmanuel Makiwa and Chistine Jani. Caleb Maguranyanga also helped me with area Maps for Hwedza district.

I also wish to thank the many people who helped me in my fieldwork, John Chirere, Farai Chikasha and Alice Shayanewako who worked hard during data collection in Hwedza. I also thank Tendai Machemedze and Blessing Katema, Ruvimbo Shonhe and Anopa Shonhe who helped in data capturing. My deep appreciation goes to Rashid Mahiya for the help during the fieldwork and other critical stages of the study. Special thanks go to the colleagues at the Centre for Civil Society who helped with many administrative chores and providing the necessary financial support that made this study possible; Professor Patrick Bond, Hellen Poonen and Lungile Keswa.

Abstract

The aim of the study was to reveal how capital accumulation and class formation in Zimbabwe's countryside has been forged through the agricultural commodity circuits; crop financing (by commercial banks) and contract-based purchasing. The study argues that investigating agrarian change must examine the variegated nature of settlement models, agro-ecological settings, and the *re-financialisation* of the agrarian economy and how farmers have been incorporated into the global commodity circuits. The study is unique amongst post-2000 land research in Zimbabwe in placing rural capital accumulation and class formation at the centre of the analysis, and in drawing upon the nexus of capital finance and contract farming, among others, to clarify the sources of surpluses. In so doing, the study unpacked political-economic arguments within policy and political interpretations and conclusions. The research used a case study design and adopted a mixed methods approach where methodological triangulation is applied to derive maximum advantage from using both qualitative and quantitative methods (in sequence) and relying on the 'philosophy of pragmatism'. A sample size of 230 households was selected from five clusters across the settlement models and agro-ecological regions at multi-stages within Hwedza District. Data was collected using structured questionnaires and in-depth qualitative interviews – five in Hwedza and 10 in Harare, all targeting key informants.

The findings show an emerging Quadi-PMMR-model agrarian structure composed of the poor, middle, middle-to-rich peasants and some rich capitalists with a growing middle farmer base constituting two thirds of the rural population. The Quadi-PMMR model is this study's major contribution to knowledge, as well its novel link to Marxian political analysis, a rare feat. The sources of accumulation are differentiated within and across the variegated settlement sectors and agro-ecological regions. Secondly, the drivers (variables) of rural accumulation and agrarian change are connected to how *re-financialisation* through domestic and international capital has restructured resource endowment and impacted on the cropped area and crop productivity, over-time. To this end, contract farming influences resource endowment and agricultural production across settlement sectors. Thirdly, tobacco has an independent impact in a new wave of capital accumulation and class formation in rural Zimbabwe. Fourthly, changing labour relations linked to changing production patterns where peasant (including poor) farmers combine hired casual labour and family labour during critical stages of tobacco farming have changed sources of labour and incomes, providing linkages across rural sectors and urban areas. Fifth, increased prevalence of droughts has curtailed variations in agrarian change across the agro-ecological regions. Sixth, maize production has declined giving way to tobacco, which is, however, also now declining as farmers have begun shifting to horticultural crops (tomatoes and onions) due to unfavourable markets. Seventh, variations in landholding sizes across the settlement models have a narrow impact on agricultural productivity across the settlement models while there are emerging land shortages associated with vernacular land sales in the Communal Areas (CA) and population growth in the Old Resettlement Areas (ORA), reversing decongestion gains achieved through resettlement programs.

The developed model, the Quadi-PMMR model, deepens our understanding of ongoing structural transformation in the rural economy, aiding and informing theorisation, policy designing and implementation. Tobacco contract farming-led rural capital accumulation requires legislative review on how capital insertion into peasant agriculture impacts on agrarian change to protect the farmers. Beyond on-farm production dynamics revealed by this study, commodity circulation linked to contract farming purchases, further than the auction floors, through the global commodity circuits, remain understudied despite the historical significance of tobacco farming to the Zimbabwean economy. In the main, the agrarian economy remains disarticulated amidst a growing middle-class base. Further research and policy review are required. Access to capital finance remains a constraint on the rural agrarian economy across the settlement models and therefore requires policy and state intervention.

List of Acronyms

AD	Another Development
AFC	Agricultural Finance Corporation
AGRITEX	Agriculture Extension
AIAS	African Institute for Agrarian Studies
AMA	Agricultural Marketing Authority
ANC	Acting Native Commissioner
ARDA	Agricultural and Rural Development Authority
ASPEF	Agricultural Sector Productive Enhancement Facility
BAT	British American Tobacco
BSAC	The British South African Company
CMB	Cotton Marketing Board
CNC	Chief Native Commissioner
CSFS	Collective Self-Finance Scheme
CSC	Cold Storage Commission
CSO	Central Statistical Office
CTC	China Tobacco Company
DA	District Administrator
ESAP	Economic Structural Adjustment Programme
FTLRP	Fast Track Land Reform Programme
FWW	First World War
GDP	Gross Domestic Product
GMB	Grain Marketing Board
GOZ	Government of Zimbabwe
IPFP	Inception Phase Framework Plan
JOC	Joint Operation Command
LPA	Land Apportionment Act
LRRP	Land Redistribution and Resettlement Programme
LSCF	Large-Scale Commercial Farm
MCA	Maize Control Act

MDC	Movement for Democratic Change's
MTC	Mashonaland Tobacco Company
NC	The Native Commissioner
NDR	National Democratic Revolution
NLP	National Land Policy
NPA	Native Purchase Areas
NR	Natural Region
NRZ	National Railways of Zimbabwe
NT	Northern Tobacco Company
PSF	Productive Sector Facility
PWC	Price Waters Copper
RBZ	Reserve Bank of Zimbabwe
SRL	Sustainable Rural Livelihoods
SSA	Sub-Saharan Africa
SSCFS	Small-Scales Commercial Farmers
TNDP	Transitional National Development Plan
TPZ	Tobacco Processing Company of Zimbabwe
TSF	Tobacco Sales Floor
UDI	Unilateral Declaration of Independence
UN	United Nations
USA	United States of America
UTC	United Tobacco Company
VCF	Value Chain Finance
WB	World Bank
WRS	Receipt System
ZIMACE	Zimbabwe Agriculture Commodity Exchange
ZIMSTAT	Zimbabwe Central Statistical office
ZIMVAC	Zimbabwe Vulnerability Assessment Committee
ZLT	Zimbabwe Leaf Tobacco

Chapter 1

Introduction

1.1. Background

The aim of the study was to reveal how capital accumulation and class formation in Zimbabwe's countryside has been forged through the agricultural commodity circuits; crop financing (by commercial banks) and contract-based purchasing. The case site relates to the tobacco contract-farming land that structurally transformed from 2000 to 2015 in the former white commercial farms of Hwedza District, 127 kilometres east of the capital city, Harare. Whereas some studies have been carried out in Hwedza District (Kinsey 1999: Dekker and Kinsey 2011), these were confined to old resettlement areas (ORAs) and communal areas (CAs) and therefore do not reveal emerging changes in the newly resettled areas. Hwedza District is one of the sites in Zimbabwe where resettlement after 2000 resulted in a dramatically changed rural political economy with nearly two thirds of the population earning a living as communal resettled farmers (Zimstat 2013). Smallholder farmers in Hwedza are in different settings within Zimbabwe's settlement models, namely, CAs established following the Land Apportionment Act of 1930, Small Scale Commercial Farms (SSCF) established in the 1950s, ORAs established from 1980 to 1999, A1 and A2 models established under the Fast Track Land Reform Programme (FTLRP) and the remaining large-scale farms. The context for that agrarian structural transformation in Zimbabwe was far-reaching, *albeit* emerging from a politically motivated land reform, as President Robert Mugabe faced an unprecedented electoral threat following defeat in the February 2000 referendum (Raftopoulos 2003; Selby 2006).

Notwithstanding the position taken by these scholars (Raftopolous 2003; Selby 2006). Zimbabwe's FTLRP was a response to that context. Government policy stated that it was aimed at land redistribution, poverty alleviation, food security, economic development and the decongestion of communal areas (GoZ 2001a).

1

Amid extreme local, regional and global pressure levelled against Robert Mugabe, the FTLRP was no easy feat, notwithstanding the urgency with which it was initiated. The forces in favour of the FTLRP included war veterans and other political nationalists and anti-colonial radicals who felt the 1979 Lancaster House Agreement and the 1990s Economic Structural Adjustment Programme (ESAP) had empowered Large Scale Commercial Farmers (LSCFs) (Moyo 2001) in that such a neo-liberal policy required co-existence with capital stalling land redistribution and giving a reprieve to the white farmers.

This research was more than merely an outcome of academic curiosity. The economic context was therefore vital. Firstly, the FTLRP coincided with a poorly performing national economy in which, over the previous years, labour had become more militant (especially with public sector strikes beginning in 1996), growth had reversed (1997 onwards), war veterans had demanded and won generous new pensions (1997), the stock market and currency had crashed (1997), urban protests demanding economic justice had begun (1997), exposure of the national army in a war associated with minerals extraction in the Democratic Republic of the Congo (1997-99), and Zimbabwe had been unable to repay its foreign debt (since 1998). In early 1999, an opposition front emerged at the Working People's Convention, which led to the formation of the Movement for Democratic Change (MDC) that September.

Then followed 'eight consecutive years of negative economic growth in Zimbabwe; from 1999 there had been a total fall of nearly 50% gross domestic product (GDP), coupled with significant capital flight and reductions in private sector investment' as most investors, both domestic and foreign ceased making new investments during the 2000s resulting in scarce foreign currency inflows and a tight exchange rate regime (Kamidza 2013, 1). Consequently, there was a decline in the country's 'manufacturing capacity utilisation from 35.8% to between 4 and 10% by 2008' and the country 'increasingly became a shadow of its past well diversified industrial and export base' (Kamidza 2013, 3 citing Nyakazeya 2009). Thirdly, economic policies zigzagged; there was dollarization and the re-introduction of liberal policies in the marketing of agricultural produce and other

2

non-agricultural produce from 2009, and smallholder farmers were forced to diversify into export-oriented cash crops (mainly tobacco and cotton) and other off-farm income generating activities. Drought reappeared, shortages of basic inputs were common, and there was hostility to the FTLRP by most white farmers who faced dispossessions. Despite rising levels of food aid from Western donors, there was food insecurity after 2000.

What then is the problem? The Zimbabwean agrarian economy is in crisis, particularly because of capital flight experienced from 2000 (Scoones *et al.* 2010), and this has negatively impacted on both the supply and demand side of the economy. Efforts for agricultural recovery have been militated against by continued economy-wide challenges despite economic liberalisation from 2009. These difficulties impact negatively on the economy, as some studies (Zimstats 2011; Zimvac 2013) show. For instance, the two studies show that 76% of the rural population is poor while another 22.9% is extremely poor. In terms of food insecurity progression, the Zimvac (2013) reveals that 85% of Zimbabwe's rural population remains vulnerable after considering own food production and stocks. To aid the resolution of this problem – the agrarian crisis - its negative impact on the rural community and on the larger economy, it is crucial to reveal and conceptualise capital accumulation and class formation processes in Zimbabwe's countryside. On its part,

> The GoZ has insisted that the root cause of poor performance in land use today has been the external sanctions imposed on Zimbabwe, combined with three droughts (in the 2001 to 2008 period) and "sabotaged" by various actors (remaining white farmers, commercial banks through their reluctance to fund farmers, some input suppliers with an interest in profiteering, etc.) (Moyo, Chambati, Murisa, Siziba, Dangwa, Mujeyi, and Nyoni 2009).

The redistributive FTLRP has since 2000 acquired over 10 million hectares of freehold large-scale commercial farm (LSCF) land and redistributed it to over 146 000 households under the A1 model farms and 30,000 households in the A2 model farm units (Moyo, 2011a). This resulted in relative decongestion in some parts of rural

Zimbabwe. However, the highly variegated settings in which the FTLRP unfolded, the economy-wide challenges and repeated droughts make drawing conclusions problematic. As a result, the implications of the FTLRP for rural accumulation, class formation and their linkages with capital (emergent international commodity and finance markets) have not been fully revealed.

While some studies (Moyo and Nyoni 2013; Moyo and Yeros 2005) provided a macro-level investigation concerning the interface of rural capital accumulation and class formation in Zimbabwe, micro-level research to reveal these dynamics remains underdeveloped. Similarly, some scholars (Arrighi 1967; Ranger 1977; Phimister 1977; Selby 2006; Hodder-Williams 1983) acknowledge the role of capital in pre-independence agrarian processes in the then Southern Rhodesia, despite intermittent resistance by the indigenes in differentiated forms. Micro-level studies on agrarian change (see Marongwe 2008; Zamchiya 2012; Alexander 2006) have tended to eschew the role of capital and instead focus on power, politics and state practice which poses the danger of missing the major driving force to agrarian capital accumulation and class formation, thereby misinforming policy on agrarian development in a country where, according to Zimstats (2011), over 60% of the population reside in rural areas and directly rely on agriculture for a living in an agro-based economy. The study was opportune and helped reveal emergent linkages of rural capital accumulation and class formation by comparing patterns of agricultural productivity, rural capital accumulation and class formation among smallholder farmers in CAs, ORAs, small-scale commercial farms (SSCFs) and in the FTLRP (A1 and A2 models) at a micro-level.

Since the late 1990s struggle for a new constitution included liberal elements demanding 'rule of law' and respect for property rights, the land issue began to be mixed up with politics and became a contested terrain within the ruling ZANU PF party, within civil society and the academia. Some scholarly proponents of redistributive politics suggest that the FTLRP was both crucial and successful, citing the large number of resettled households since 2000 and accumulation from below in some key sites, including Masvingo

(Scoones *et al.* 2010), Shamva and Zvimba (Matondi 2012), Moyo *et al.* (2009) survey in six districts of Kwekwe, Goromonzi, Zvimba, Chipinge, Mangwe and Chiredzi. Hanlon *et al.* (2013), who did some qualitative studies in Mazowe, Goromonzi and Chimanimani, also concluded that accumulation from below is taking place. Moyo *et al.* (2009) acknowledge the government position that the FTLRP could have achieved more were it not for sanctions, sabotage and frequent drought conditions experienced in some years after 2000. Some scholars (see Marongwe 2008; Alexander 2006) prioritised democracy, human rights and liberal values, in their critique of the land redistribution process, overlooking its impact on social differentiation and agrarian change.

The study derives conclusions and adds to existing knowledge on the emergent agrarian structure, agricultural productivity, capital accumulation and class formation with this reconsideration of the way capital has begun to flow again in Zimbabwe after the *"jambanja"* (violent and chaotic land repossessions) of 2000. Furthermore, drawing from Moyo's (2011b; 2013) tri-modal agrarian structure and capital accumulation model, the study develops a model/framework of Zimbabwe's agricultural productivity, capital accumulation and class formation resulting from emerging farming practices in the post-FTLRP Zimbabwe. Moyo's (2011; 2013) tri-modal structure borrowed extensively from Lenin (1964), de Janvry (1981) and Kausky (1988) who conceptualised agrarian accumulation paths and class formation in Europe. Using de Janvry's (1981) uneven development thesis, this study reveals how capital has been re-inserted into Zimbabwe's agrarian productivity, accumulation and class formation processes. The secret to the *re-financialisation* associated with Zimbabwe's land reform which is consistent with global agricultural neoliberalism is contract farming and the emerging global commodity circuits. Neoliberal *re-financialisation* therefore has a specific form of agrarian accumulation and class formation in Zimbabwe, whose model/framework this study utilises. To achieve this, clear research objectives aimed at addressing this problem were set from which several research questions were derived as is fully elaborated below.

1.2 The Context of the Study

This study is evaluative in nature. It sought to reveal the qualitative impact of the FTLRP by studying rural capital accumulation and class formation dynamics using Hwedza district as a micro-level case study. As Moyo (2013, 29) remarks, only a 'few studies have examined the qualitative character of this outcome' and, as such, the full impact of the FTLRP consequently remains unclear. The stated objectives of the government's FTLRP were to:

- Restore racial balance in land ownership by removing the racial inequalities created by colonialism;
- Decongest the over-crowded communal areas whose economic and environmental value continued to decline precipitously;
- Tackle rural poverty and improve food security at national and household levels;
- Broaden and diversify the agricultural production base by ensuring greater and wider access to, greater efficiency and utilisation of, the finite land resource; and to
- Develop commercial agriculture within the indigenous community (GoZ 2001a, 6-7).

These objectives have been met in varying degrees, but with surprising outcomes in terms of their impact on Zimbabwe's agrarian economy and society. The conditions in Hwedza provide an especially exciting site for considering the role that international and domestic capital and global commodity circuits play in restructuring and transforming rural relations.

With regards to the role of capital, Malaba (2014: 7-8) acknowledges that the most important challenge facing agricultural recovery is the 'imperative that agriculture be adequately resourced' with appropriate financing and this must be viewed 'in the context of the broader economic situation prevailing in the country characterized by serious liquidity constraints, declining economic activity, low domestic demand and a widening current account deficit'. To this extent, Hwedza's farmers have grappled with liquidity constraints and the limits of the domestic market, understanding of which requires a full study to reveal the solutions that they have adopted and to establish how these are linked to capital accumulation and class formation.

Whereas politics and state practices affected accumulation and social differentiation within the agrarian economy (Alexander 2003: 2006; Zamchiya 2011, 2012), insufficient attention has been given to the changing levels and availability of agricultural finance, as well as how such finance is linked to international commodity markets through contract farming. Undoubtedly, the poor performance of the Zimbabwean economy since about 2000 resulted in reduced investment in agriculture (Scoones, Marongwe, Mavedzenge, Mahenehene, Murimbarimba, and Sukume, 2010). For instance, Malaba (2014: 2-3) observes that banking credit for agriculture declined from 80% of commercial banks' lending in 1997 to 15.68% in 2014, even though 70% of the population derives sustenance and livelihoods from this sector. This study therefore focuses on financial and commercial capital because understanding the Hwedza farmers' recovery from the immediate post-2000 capital strike (Murisa and Chikweche 2015) enables an investigation into Hwedza's multi-variegated settlement system with a much clearer sense of how the various parts fit together, and how the agrarian economy may be revived. Even if the impact of politics, state practice and patronage on access to land, farming inputs and markets as advanced by some scholars (Alexander 2003, 2006; Zamchiya 2012; Marongwe 2008) was to hold, the differentiated settlements and agro-ecological settings would result in distinctive trajectories on rural capital accumulation and class formation post the FTLRP.

Malaba (2014: 2-3) observes that besides the macro-economic policy shift, a raft of changes to the financing and marketing of tobacco resulted in increased production and funding as 55.3% of total agricultural lending of $620 million in 2014 supported farmers in this sub-sector. He further observes that for many agricultural commodities, the focus has shifted to 'value chains and increased role of merchants in crop financing', following dollarization and changes in marketing policies, even though 'there appears to be marginal

7

benefits being accrued by farmers with more of the benefits accruing to contractors' (Malaba 2014: 2-3).

This Book argues that an investigation into agricultural productivity, capital accumulation and class formation must consider the variegated nature of settlement and agro-ecological settings, and the *re-financialisation* of the agrarian economy and how farmers have been incorporated into the global commodity circuits. The study relies on works by Luxemburg (1968), Harvey (2005) and Bond (1998) on uneven development based upon primitive accumulation, de Janvry's (1990) agrarian structure and Moyo's (2011) adaptation of this as a trimodal agrarian structure.

1.3 Research Objectives and Questions

1.3.1 Objectives
The objectives of this study are:

1. To assess the role of capital in rural accumulation and class formation in the variegated farming sectors in Hwedza district.

2. To analyse emerging local-national-global linkages within the agrarian economy (capital, social and labour relations, land use, commodity markets, climate change).

3. To develop a model/framework of Zimbabwe's agricultural productivity, capital accumulation and class formation resulting from emerging farming practices in post-FTLRP Zimbabwe.

1.3.2 Research questions
The broad research question to be answered is: What explains accumulation and class formation for smallholder farmers in Hwedza in post-2000 Zimbabwe, particularly in terms of land reform and contract farming? In search of answers to this question, other questions must be answered as well. These are as follows:

1. How have land reform and contract farming changed the financing of the agrarian economy, and affected production patterns, accumulation and class formation for communal and resettled smallholder farmers in Hwedza District?

2. Which financial and commercial circuits of capital accumulation have emerged to extract surpluses, from transnational corporate tobacco merchants and commercial banks to small vegetable vendors?

3. What are the agrarian classes emerging in Hwedza District in Zimbabwe since 2000, and how do these relate to land reform opportunities as well as the new contract-farming regime?

4. What explains accumulation and class formation for smallholder farmers in Hwedza in post-2000 Zimbabwe, particularly in terms of land reform and contract farming?

5. How have accumulation and class formation affected broader social relations in Hwedza District, and are these patterns likely to prevail more generally in Zimbabwe?

6. What model/framework of Zimbabwe's agricultural productivity, capital accumulation and class formation can be developed as a consequent of emerging farming practices in post FTLRP Zimbabwe?

1.4 Study Justification and Contributions to Knowledge

This Book contributes to the burgeoning literature on the Zimbabwean FTLRP, but extends it with focus on capital accumulation and class formation processes which are undergirded by the *re-financialisation* (re-insertion of capital after 2009) of the agrarian economy, resulting in structural agrarian transformation. The study also examined production relations, agricultural productivity, and global commodity circuits (mainly for tobacco as well as other crops and in one case international tourism and game farming). The study is unique amongst post-2000 land research in Zimbabwe in placing rural capital accumulation and class formation at the centre of the analysis, and in drawing upon the nexus of capital finance and contract farming to clarify the sources of surpluses. This research therefore helps reveal roles of financial and commercial capital in accumulation and class formation in the variegated settlement models and across different agro-ecological regions. It helps to interpret whether Hwedza's unique configuration of class, race and party-affiliated social relations can explain accumulation, alongside the relationships between Hwedza's agrarian economy to larger national and global circuits of capital.

However, the vastly variegated circumstances in which FTLRP unfolded make sketching deductions problematic. Most creatively, Moyo (2011a) suggests that a trimodal agrarian structure has re-emerged based on large-, medium- and small-sized landholdings. Moreover, while there is a great deal of literature on the impact of the FTLRP, and while the tri-modal structure operates in various places, no scholars have done a comparative analysis of agrarian change for smallholder farmers in the variegated settlement models. Dekker and Kinsey's (2011) conclusions on resettled farmers *vis-a-vis* those in the CAs are based on old data complied before the FTLRP and is therefore less informative (see Zamchiya 2012). The process by which trimodality emerges is not yet fully understood, and hence it is difficult to project whether the historical trends of agricultural centralization and concentration will re-emerge. Similarly, the implications of the FTLRP for rural accumulation and class formation have not been fully revealed.

What is the significance of this study? Whereas the trimodal structural *outcome* is undergirded by capital accumulation (and class formation) processes which are supported by local-national-global linkages within the international agrarian economy, there is need to unpack and to draw policy and political conclusions from political-economic argumentations, to aid the development of an agrarian model for Zimbabwe and beyond. In this respect, one gap in Moyo's (2011) trimodal structure is its emphasis on size of land *holdings* among other factors, but Hwedza's land *utilisation* records also have a story to tell about rural accumulation processes. A study that reveals emergent linkages by comparing patterns of agricultural productivity, capital accumulation and class formation among smallholder farmers in CAs and in resettled areas (RAs) at a micro-level with the objective of modelling agrarian structural transformation in post-2000 Zimbabwe was therefore opportune. Revealing these dynamics deepens our understanding of ongoing structural changes and therefore aid theorisation, policy designing and implementation.

1.5 Scope and Limitations of the Study

This research is conceptualised under agrarian political economy to assess 'the agrarian question in the international political economy' (Moyo and Yeros 2005) using 'variations of specific processes of agrarian change and the circumstances of different rural classes' (Bernstein 2010) and investigates emerging social relations, dynamics of production and social reproduction and politics using historical and contemporary empirical data. However, in seeking to reveal the role of capital in agrarian change, this research only focuses on the role of contract farming in export crops with specific focus on tobacco farming, even though information was collected on all agricultural commodities, to aid comparison. The research case study is in Hwedza District to take advantage of the researcher's social networks since he did his higher-level studies within the district. The researcher is affiliated to a reputable agrarian research organization, African Institute for Agrarian Studies (AIAS), to tap from their research experience and networks on the ground.

In part, limitations were faced regarding data collection in some A2 farms where farmers are not necessarily resident on the farm. To this end, the targeted number of respondents of 50 could not be attained. Instead, data was collected from 32 respondents. In addition, the timing of the study coincided with crop harvesting as well as grading and marketing of the tobacco crop which led to repeated visits to some respondents. Securing gatekeepers approvals in rural Zimbabwe poses a constraint. However the researcher secured these well in advance of the pilot study to circumvent the challenge.

1.6 Structure of the Book

Chapter 1: Background, Context and Methodology of the Study
This chapter gives the background, context, objectives, research questions and methodology of the study. The chapter sets out the research setting.

Chapter 2: Conceptual and Theoretical Framework: Uneven development and primitive accumulation

This chapter presents the uneven development and primitive accumulation conceptual framework deployed in this study. In addition, the chapter also presents the definition of concepts and terms.

Chapter 3: Conceptual and Theoretical Framework: Class formation and tri-modal agrarian structure

This chapter discusses the conceptual framework centring on theories of class formation and the tri-modal agrarian structure.

Chapter 4: Research Methodology

This chapter outlines the research methodology and design, sample selection and data collection and analysis. It also introduces the research study site.

Chapter 5: Literature Review: Historical Background – from colonial to independent Zimbabwe

This chapter presents the historical background of the study, covering different debates on ideology, land use, accumulation and social differentiation as part of the land and agrarian development in Zimbabwe. It also introduces the debate on the role of capital and the state from the 1890s to 1980.

Chapter 6: Literature Review: Historical Background, 1980 - 2000

This chapter introduces the debate on the role of capital and state from 1980 to 2000. The chapters analyse land reform initiatives and agricultural policy in early independent Zimbabwe.

Chapter 7: Literature Review: Historical Background, from colonial to independent Zimbabwe

This chapter presents some historicity, ideological perspectives, matters of accumulation and agrarian reforms which shape and reshape the current landscape in terms of land development in Zimbabwe. It also introduces the debate on the role of capital and the state from 2000 to 2015.

Chapter 8: Hwedza's Socio-Economic History and Tobacco Production

This chapter presents results of the agrarian structure emerging in Hwedza, as well as the production trends and relations and reproduction processes in the study area. It presents Hwedza's accumulation and class formation processes from 2000 to 2015, relying on the collected data.

Chapter 9: Sectoral Commodity Production in Hwedza, 2000-15

This chapter presents empirical data on production patterns on food crops, cash crops and export crops, and how the production trends are influenced by, and influence, social relations of production, capital and labour relations.

Chapter 10: Capital and Commodity Markets

The chapter presents data on the different circuits of capital and market relations and how these mediate accumulation processes for smallholder farmers. It focuses on contract farming, credit, remittances, off- and on-farm income, government support programmes and state practice, and how these impact on differentiation. Local, national and international commodity circuits and linkages are also revealed and analysed.

Chapter 11: Hwedza's Agrarian Capital Accumulation Model

This chapter develops the capital accumulation model emerging in Hwedza, with focus on the role of domestic and international capital involved in the tobacco contract farming system, in marketing of local produce and to some extent in game farming.

Chapter 12: Conclusion

This chapter presents the conclusion of the Book. It summarises the results linking them to theory and literature review. The realisation of the objectives, how the research questions were addressed and the contribution to knowledge are also presented in this chapter. The theoretical frameworks are subjected to critique versus empirical data to confirm their suitability in explaining production patterns, capital accumulation and class formation in communal and resettled areas, before drawing the conclusions and recommendations.

1.7 Conclusion

This introductory chapter provided the context of the study, contemporary debates, identification of knowledge gaps and set the objectives of the study and the research questions. The chapter justified the study and articulated the contribution of the study to knowledge. Hwedza District was also introduced as the case study area of the research. The chapter confirmed the merits of a comparative study in the variegated settings of Hwedza to establish lessons on capital accumulation and class formation.

Chapter Two

Conceptual and Theoretical Framework: Uneven Development and Primitive Accumulation

2.1 Introduction

This study focuses on policy outcomes of the FTLRP implemented in Zimbabwe since 2000. Studies of the agrarian question reveal that the 'double dialectic processes' between 'production and circulation' and between the 'centre-periphery' structure under the laws of motion of capital in the world economic systems 'moulds the external necessities of the periphery into possibilities for the centre to overcome its barriers of accumulation and growth' (de Janvry 1981: 26). The contradictions in the world economic systems yield an 'articulated' pattern of accumulation at the centre and a 'disarticulated' pattern of accumulation in the periphery (Amin 1976: de Janvry 1981; Shivji 2009: Moyo and Yeros 2005) as the dialectical organic totality provides a scientific basis for uneven development between firms, sectors, regions and countries fostering the development-of-underdevelopment in the periphery. Tied to this setting is the latest weapon of historical capitalism accentuated by Amin (2015): the 'generalized – monopoly capitalism', highlighted in three ways - 'strengthened centralization of control over the economy by the monopolies, deepening of globalization (and the outsourcing of the manufacturing industry to the peripheries), and financialization'. Again as Amin (2015) puts it, smallholders have been reduced to subcontractor status where monopolies provide inputs and financing upstream and marketing chains downstream using price structures that wipe out income from the farmers' labour. In this context, 'contemporary financialisation and globalized capitalism' have eliminated national self-determination (Moyo and Yeros 2005, 11) as disorder is replaced by chaos (Amin 2015). This chapter presents this theoretical grounding as it relates to this study.

2.2 The Laws of Uneven Development

Scholars on the agrarian question have generally relied 'on the methodology of dialectical and historical materialism to develop a dynamic theory of society' as opposed to the modernist and the monetarists approaches (de Janvry 1981: 7-8; Shivji 2009: 19). It is argued that the modernisation school, rooted in the neo-classical theorisation, tends to avoid and negate the relevance of social science, the power relations, gender, ecology as well as 'exploitation, racism, sexism, militarism and imperialism' (de Janvry (1981: 7) and the 'history and specificity of the less developed countries'. The neo-classical approach presents development simply as 'normal patterns of growth' temporarily located at varying stages (Chenery 1960). Marx (1977: 91) therefore concludes that 'the country that is more developed industrially only shows, to the less developed, the image of its own future'.

For Luxemburg (1968), the world expansion of capitalism is derived from contradictions of accumulation between the centre and the periphery and as Marx (1977) posited, relies on the failure of capitalism to self-sustain and therefore the need to continuously expand its sphere of circulation by incorporating additional pre-capitalist areas in which part of the surplus production of commodities can be realised and from which cheap raw materials can be imported for the production of capital goods. In this regard, therefore, the periphery is fertile ground for capitalist expansion given its less developed conditions. As Bond (1998) notes, from a Marxist perspective, the process of uneven development is unavoidable in that the relation of production produces both wealth and poverty because the relations have both forces of production and repression, and produce bourgeois wealth for the bourgeois class by annihilating the membership of this class, creating an ever-growing proletariat (See also Marx 1967: 15).

As Bradby (1975), puts it, this is achieved through the 'destruction of pre-capitalist spheres' by merchant capital under primitive accumulation, bringing about uneven development. Some scholars (Shivji (2009; Rodney 1972; Samir Amin 1990), relying on the *dependencia* school, argue that organic centre-periphery dialectic results in the development-of-underdevelopment in the periphery. For instance, Shivji (2009: 58) argues that the 'periphery is the site of generating surplus; the centre the site of its accumulation'. Beyond the centre–periphery dynamism of uneven development, such as the one between the developed world and the Third World, Africa included, Arrighi and Saul (1973b: 145) presents a similar dynamic within Africa, where there is prevalence of *uneven development* created by capitalist penetration in Africa. For the underdevelopment of Africa relative to the industrial centres of the West has been accompanied and mediated by uneven development as between regions, states, tribes, and races *within* Africa itself, and this fact adds important dimensions to the class struggle in Africa and to the character of the resistance of progressive African forces to contemporary imperialism.

To begin with, some scholars like de Janvry (1981: 11; and Lenin and Bukharin (1973), following Luxemburg (1968) and Marx (1977), assert that the origins of the limit of capitalist accumulation is its 'overripe' status of capitalism in some countries in the centre whereas in the periphery viable investment opportunities do not exist because of backwardness. Alternatively, the end of capitalism can originate from the accumulation of enormous masses of capital that derive down rates of profit and needing "young areas" capable of low prices for land, low wages and cheap raw materials. For Patnaik (2014), therefore, uneven development has been promoted by 'the acquisition of non-increasing prices' of primary commodities from the periphery to the centre, such as oil among other minerals, tobacco, cotton and sugar, as capital seeks new areas with low prices, low wages and cheap raw materials to make greater profits.

Secondly, the accommodating features of finance have the effect of ameliorating developmental stagnation, yet its control and speculative functions accentuate uneven development in the productive circuit of capital. Some scholars (Lenin 1964; Amin, 2015; de Janvry 1981; Foster 2015; Bond 1998) suggest that the export of industrial and finance capital under monopoly capitalism helps the centre overcome its contradictions of accumulation. Over accumulation has very important geographical and geopolitical implications in the uneven development of capitalism, as attempts are made to transfer the costs and burden of devaluation to different regions and nations or to push overaccumualted capital into "built environment" (Bond 1998: 7) as a last-ditch speculative venture. Moreover, the implications of over accumulation for balance in different sectors of the economy - between branches of production (mining, agriculture, manufacturing, finance, and so forth.), between consumers and producers, and between capital goods (the means of production) and consumer goods (whether luxuries or necessities) can become ominous. Indeed, because the rhythm of over accumulation varies across the economy, severe imbalances between the different sectors and 'departments' of production (sometimes termed 'disproportionalities' or 'disarticulations') emerge and introduce threatening bottlenecks in the production and realisation of value, which further exacerbate the crisis.

Thirdly, as Aglietta (1979: 232) observes, the process of uneven development can be ameliorated by credit finance through its role in absorbing the divergence between the rhythm at which income is received and the rhythm at which it is spent. However, the process of eliminating the contradictions in the centre causes various negative developments in the periphery. The use of finance capital to ameliorate the effect of uneven development leads to increased subjugation of the reproduction processes by finance (Bond 1998: 14). Some scholars suggest that this process enhances 'rapid development of capitalism in the West' (Kuusinen 1928) and the development of underdevelopment, unequal exchange and dependency in the periphery (de Janvry 1981). The next sections assess the dialectic relations of production and circulation, articulations and disarticulations, primitive capital accumulation, monopoly capital finance, functional dualism in greater details and in that order.

2.2.1 The Dialectic between production and circulation

The contradictions of capital accumulation within the world economic system are a consequence of the heterogeneous structure of global capitalism. Taking from Marx (1967), de Janvry (1981) advances the view that the dialectical unity of production and circulation explains the contradictions of capital that originate from the unplanned nature and class, create growth and barriers to growth and the historical specificity of the recurrent crises that define the historical capitalist development. The contradiction emanates from the relationship between production and circulation, where 'circulation is the negation of production and production is the negation of circulation'. The production and circulation contradictions emanate from the 'class nature of capitalism' which imply 'interclass conflicts regarding the generation and distribution of the economic surplus', particularly regarding how generated economic surplus is to be distributed between profits for capital and wages for labour (de Janvry 1981).

The quest to increase profits means the introduction of new technologies or the new rationalisation of the work processes to increase labour productivity or alternatively, holding back wages (de Janvry 1981). These two possible initiatives will trigger different responses; increased labour productivity, which implies increased 'production capacity of the economic system' and restricted wages and labour-saving technology, which implies decreased consumption capacity of the economic system (de Janvry 1981). This follows the logic that 'in the capitalist mode of production: the labourers as buyers of commodities are important for the market' yet capital seeks to keep the cost of labour power low. These contradictions also arise from the established tendency of capital to fall resulting in stagnated accumulation, triggering a set of reactions intended to overcome the barriers within the heterogeneous world economic system.

As de Janvry (1981, 25) argues, uneven development is the source of the heterogeneity as industrial development is at different stages of progress within the world capitalist system as well as the centre-periphery dynamics. Such uneven development, as manifested by the centre-periphery relationship, 'creates the necessity for external relationships' between the two poles as capital seeks to eliminate the contradictions of accumulation in the centre and vice versa (de Janvry 1981). However, because the centre dominates the periphery, it then moulds the latter to the possibilities and 'requirements of the resolution of its own contradictions', furthering uneven development, confining development to the centre and underdevelopment in the periphery (de Janvry 1981).

2.2.2 Accumulation patterns in articulated and disarticulated economies

An articulated economy is sectorally articulated and has linkages between productive sectors whereby an 'increase in the production of consumption goods creates an increase in derived demand for capital goods' (de Janvry 1981: 27). Under articulated conditions and sectoral linkages create the necessary inducement for development and allocate labour among sectors of production, creating *social articulation* in which the essential relation between the development of production and consumption exists between capital and labour (de Janvry 1981). Uneven development creates an articulated economy in the centre and a disarticulated economy in the periphery. The organic dialectical relationship of centre-periphery relationship generates a disarticulated economy in the periphery due to varied reasons. For Shivji (2009: 58), disarticulated economies are characterised by unsustainable development due to failure of self-regenerating development leading to uninterrupted backwardness.

Firstly, structural disarticulated economies are mainly because of 'colonial, extraverted, vertically integrated economy dependent on primary commodities, both agricultural and mineral', responding to the crises and needs of the centre resulting in acute distortions in developing countries (Shivji 2009, 58). One source of disarticulation is that what is produced is not consumed by the domestic market and what is consumed is not produced locally, in the periphery (Shivji 2009, 59). Consumption goods are imported by the urban elites while a majority rely on own production yet peasantry labour faces competition with cash crops and agro-fuel crops; threatening food security (Shivji 2009, 60). Secondly, the disarticulation between agriculture and industry creates similar distortions. Scholars such as de Janvry (1981: 34) posit that under *sectoral disarticulation* there are no 'forward linkages in the production of raw materials (plantation and mining) and backward linkages in industrial production (outward- and inward-orientation)'. As a result, conditions are created where agriculture is de-linked from industry, yet both are linked to global circuits (Shivji 2009: 60-61) that are skewed in favour of the centre. In cases where industrial capacity is developed within the periphery, production patterns are perverse and centred on consumer and intermediate goods for the few elites, produced using capital and not labour-intensive technology (Rweyemamu 1973) where sectoral under development persist.

Thirdly, the few existing cases of agro-industrial processing are extroverted and not intended for domestic markets and often accompanied by an 'influx of supermarkets that import processed foods and other agricultural products' (Shivji 2009: 62). This negates development because industrial development is critical for the total transformation of the society (see Amin 1990). As de Janvry (1981), concludes, peripheral export-enclave economies where the modern sector's production capacity is a function of return to capital, itself derived from export demand, such return sustains the import bill for consumptions goods for the few elites. This is unlike in the import-substitution economies, where the modern sector's capacity to produce is created by the return to capital derived from home market demand generated from consumption of part of the surplus value.

Fourthly, intra-sectoral disarticulation in peripheral industries and among productive sectors such as infrastructure creates distortions where there is a dislocation between the source and location of industrial units (Shivji 2009: 62). In this regard, Amin (1990) used a schematic analysis to highlight the dislocations through a four-sector model centring on: a) production of means of production, b) production of goods for mass consumption, c) luxury production and consumption and d) exports. The articulated model is privileged of 'a' and 'b' while the disarticulated periphery suffers from 'c' and 'd', leading to conditions of increased productivity in the centre and leading to increased wages and peasant income whereas, in the periphery there is a delink between productivity and wages (Amin 1990: 7-8). In this regard, de Janvry (1981: 34) concluded that where 'the relation between production and consumption capacities does not imply a relationship between return to capital and return to labour: the economy is *socially disarticulated*'.

In the end, the centre-periphery distortions lead to conditions where peasants and semi-proletarian labour bear the 'brunt of exploitation of surplus' (Shivji 2009: 66) and as such subsidize capital through primitive accumulation or accumulation by dispossession (Harvey 2005). Peasants are dispossessed of their ability to reproduce themselves and become a 'reservoir of cheap, seasonal, casual, forced, and child labour under various disguises' (Shivji 2009: 67), and in many cases resort to struggles for survival under super-exploitation by capital through other activities such as petty trading, construction, craft making, gold panning, quarrying and so forth (Moyo and Yeros 2007a: 84). Such super-exploitation of peasants and semi-proletarian labour by dominant capital through cheap food and cheap labour is at the heart of a disarticulated economy in the periphery (Shivji 2009: 67).

According to de Janvry (1981), the disarticulated economy relies on reduction of labour costs by perpetuating the subsistence economy where the cost of maintaining and reproducing the labour force is partially assumed by the peasants and semi-proletarians. This is achieved through *functional dualism,* a concept that shall be fully interrogated below, suffice to say at this point that it exists between the modern and traditional sectors of the economy whereby the modern sector is enabled to maintain wages below the cost of maintenance and reproduction of the labour force through self-exploitation of the semi-proletarians in the traditional sector and therefore provides the structural framework for meeting the requirements of cheap labour derived from the laws of accumulation under social disarticulation (de Janvry 1981).

However, de Janvry (1981: 37) makes a wrong conclusion to the effect that peripheral capitalism is a 'historically specific stage in the development of capitalism in the periphery' set to disappear with the eventual decomposition 'while sustaining rapid accumulation in the modern sector'. As Amin (1990: 185) puts it that, 'contrary to the orthodox view, the world expansion of capitalism is accompanied by increasing inequality in social distribution at the periphery' and, in any event, countries that were in the periphery a century ago remain so to date. This is primarily because the peripheral state 'does not control local accumulation' and is 'objectively- the instrument of "adjustment" of local society to the demands of worldwide accumulation, whose changing directions are determined by changes at the centres' (See also Amin 1990: 206).

Is there a possibility of an internal dynamic capable of triggering an escape from the development of underdevelopment in periphery?

Some scholars have sought to advance Eurocentric modernity and economistic approaches arguing that industrialization is key to overcoming backwardness and as such resolve the agrarian question (see Moyo *et al.* 2013: 94), despite the genocidal and militaristic propensities of monopoly capital. Moreover, some scholars have further suggested that the agrarian question is resolved. For instance, Byres (1991b: 12) concludes that the agrarian question is resolved to the extent that 'capitalist industrialization is permitted to proceed, then, as the social transformation comes to be dominated by industry and urban bourgeoisie'. A counter argument is presented by Amin (1990: 206-208) who posits that even though semi-peripheries do emerge, this does not show the true nature of the dialectic governing this movement, 'the convergence, or conflict between the (favourable and unfavourable) internal factor and the (unfavourable) external factor', but only goes to the extent of explaining the non-static nature of the world system and the crystallization process of the centres. Amin (1990, 206-208) further elaborates that it is becoming more and more difficult for the centre to emerge as 'obstacles represented by the external factors are increasingly difficult to overcome'.

The semi-peripheries have therefore predominantly remained so for the past "four centuries", post the imperialist cut-off point (Amin 1990: 206-208). As for semi-periphery states such as Brazil, India, South Korea, South Africa and China, it remains to be seen if these countries will be able to 'succeed in building the bourgeois national state capable of controlling internal accumulation and subjecting their external relations to this accumulation, that is, to escape the heavy constraints of "adjustment" to the demands of the expansion of central monopoly capital". For Shivji (2009: 67), the 'devaluation of peripheral labour and resources is the lynchpin in the exploitation and transfer of surplus from the periphery to the centre' as shall be fully revealed in the next sections.

2.2.3 Primitive capital accumulation
The basic definition of capital accumulation is the generation of wealth in the form of 'capital' which is applied to produce commodities for exchange, for profit, and as such for self-expansion of capital (Bond 1998: 4). Whereas there are various strands of

primitive accumulation, Marx (1977)) applies a conception that illustrates how capitalism utilises 'extra-economic' force such as violence and war to separate peasants from means of production; land, and commodities to capital's advantage. Marx (1977) accentuates how the capitalist system persists to deploy various invisible means to 'exploit labour power beyond the labour time' (Moyo *et al.* 2012) essential for the social reproduction of labour. Arendt (1968) argues that this is 'the original sin of simple robbery' or 'the original accumulation of capital' or 'primitive' accumulation (see also Moyo *et al.* 2012).

Some scholars (Luxemburg1968; Lenin 1996; Harvey 2005; Moyo *et al.* 2012; Bond 1998; de Janvry 1981) argued that primitive accumulation configures capital accumulation and class formation in the periphery in a manner that resolves contradictions in the centre. For Luxemburg (1968), primitive accumulation manifests in two organically linked processes. On one hand, capital accumulation is the commodity market and the production site where surplus value is produced (the factory, the mine, the agricultural estate) concerned with the economic process and therefore the relationship between the capitalist and wage labour. On the other hand, it is concerned with the relations between capitalism and the non-capitalist mode of production, relying on colonial policy, the international loan system, war and monopoly capitalism.

As Moyo (2011: 6) and Moyo *et al.* (2012: 185) observe, argumentations by Lenin (1996) and Luxemburg (1951) were in response to 'the new wave of militarism and colonial expansion at the turn of the twentieth century that were led by large monopolistic firms and major capitalist states in the classic scramble' as 'a result of monopoly capitalism (in the case of Lenin), or an inherent need in capitalism to plunder non-capitalist societies as a means of overcoming a chronic problem of 'underconsumption'. A third strand was posited by Moore (2003: 33) who applies the classical and modernization theoretical farming of primitive accumulation to analyse the 'violence-ridden and economically devastating' crisis faced by Zimbabwe since 2000. The strand proposed by Moore (2003) agrees with Marx (1967) that primitive accumulation, just like capitalism emerges and often leaves 'blood dripping from every pore'. There are two worldviews on the origins and manifestation of primitive capital accumulation; from a post-structural pre-disposition, it is expressed as the crisis tendencies of capitalism by Harvey (2005: 138), undergirded by underconsumption or overaccumulation at the centre.

On one hand, as Harvey (2005: 142) posits, imperialist expansion was 'touched off by a curious kind of economic crisis, the overproduction of capital and the emergence of 'superfluous' money, the result of oversaving, which could no longer find productive investment within the national borders'. In this instance, low wages result in low disposable income and therefore low demand for finished goods, necessitating capital to 'reinvest rather than consume' through trade and with 'non-capitalist social formations' in a bid to secure a systematic way to close the gap on effective demand. In this regard, therefore, lack of sufficient effective demand is bridged by reinvestment through spatio-temporal fixes—the geographical expansion of capitalism to non-capitalist social formations, where 'cheap labour power, raw materials, low costs land, and the like' is found in abundance, (Harvey 2005, 139). On the other hand, a structured approach from the world systems theory (historical-structural theory), Moyo et al. (2012: 186) argues that primitive accumulation must be understood from a centre-periphery dialectical analysis. In their view, Moyo et al. (2012, 185), the Western monopolies overall exploit the peripheries 'either directly or indirectly, the net being a systematic transfer of surplus value, far beyond the initial investment' through repatriation of profits, interest payments, and dividends, monopoly rents, as well as unequal exchange'.

Through these processes, the centre can displace its own contradictions of accumulation, to the periphery (Moyo et al. 2012, 185) setting in motion a permanent wave of 'semi-proletarianization' (Moyo and Yeros 2005). This is an important dimension in that semi-proletariats are known to engage in a process of self-exploitation and super-exploitation, an extra-economic aiding of capital. Capitalism has maintained the imperative to create 'conditions for the perpetuation of non-remunerated labour outside the market and the displacement of most costs of social reproduction onto labourers

25

themselves' (Moyo *el al.* 2012: 187). In Amin's (2011: 52) view, broadly speaking, primitive accumulation is rarely financed by the rich, but by the poor majority, for the benefit of the few rich and ', this primitive accumulation has not exclusively taken place in the bygone and outdated capitalism. It continues today'.

On the contrary, Marx suggests that primitive accumulation was crucial and progressive and an ugly stage through which social order needed to be changed. For Marx (also see Harvey 2005: 169), some paths must be destroyed and disrupted, for; 'to make some omelette some eggs must be broken'. Moyo *et al.* (2013) urges 'conceptual retrospective' of Marx's writings on primitive accumulation which they suggest were 'more descriptive than systematic' since his objective was to illustrate how capital uses *extra-economic* force to separate peasants from the means of production (land) and transform labour into capital to be exploited in less transparent ways, appropriating labour power beyond labour time necessary for the social reproduction of the workforce. Luxemburg (1968 cited in Harvey 2005: 176) agrees and maintains that capital accumulation is crucial in providing the nexus between the expanded reproduction and accumulation by dispossession, through a dialectical relation within the anti - and alternative globalization agenda and movement. However, Amin (2011: 72) presents vicious strictures to this view, and suggests that the "Extrication from capitalist/globalization (what I call delinking) is a first condition for extrication from peripheral capitalist status (in vulgar terms, getting out of underdevelopment or of poverty)".

However, for Luxemburg (1968), if the two aspects of expanded reproduction and accumulation by dispossession are organically linked, dialectically intertwined, it follows that the two struggles must be seen in a dialectical relationship. If the current period has seen a shift in emphasis from accumulation through expanded reproduction to accumulation by dispossession, and if the later lies at the heart of imperialist practices, then it follows that the balance of interest within the anti-and alternative globalization movement must acknowledge accumulation by dispossession as the primary contradiction to be confronted. But it ought never to do so by ignoring the dialectical relation to struggles in the field of expanded reproduction, as argued by Luxemburg (1968). Harvey (2005: 179) agrees with Luxemburg and suggests that the dialectical relation 'must assiduously be cultivated', while Amin (2011: 53) suggests that there is no serious difference between the two but prefers to use the latter. For Harvey (2005), 'primitive accumulation that opens paths for expanded reproduction' is different from 'accumulation by dispossession that destroys and disrupts' such paths, as posited by Marx (1967).

Some scholars (Harvey (2005 and Bernstein 2010) agree that primitive accumulation carries with it high levels of exploitation of labour power and abundant cases of abusive practices. For Bernstein (2010), such exploitation of labour is driven by the need to expand the level of production and increase productivity to make profit. These negative tendencies of capital accumulation results in a class of landless labour, necessary *proletarianisation*, a source of cheap labour and cheap raw materials (Beckman 1977) feeding the underdevelopment of peasant agriculture, through super exploitation and primitive accumulation. Under these conditions, capital does not meet the full cost of peasant labour reproduction (Bernstein 1977) under semi-proletarianism (Moyo and Yeros 2005).

In Africa, primitive accumulation has been shaped by 'its pre-colonial integration in the world economy as a slave reserve, it's relatively recent history of colonialism, and its settler experience' and 'accumulation by dispossession' (Harvey 2005). In this regard, Harvey (2005) suggests that primitive accumulation is permanent and subsists beyond the establishment of 'expanded reproduction'. Beckman (1977) posits that capital subject peasants to extraverted production relations under monopolistic relations of exchange. The re-conceptualised primitive capital accumulation therefore provides scope for the re-visitation of our understanding of accumulation and class formation by incorporating the role of the capital in agrarian processes, including semi-proletarianisation and emerging social relations among the rural peasantry. The following section focuses on 'the new imperialism' as we seek to reveal how financialisation and export of finance capital continue to institute primitive accumulation through super-exploitation of the labour power in the periphery thereby undermining social reproduction.

2.2.4 Monopoly- finance and export of capital

Bond (1998: 4) defines financial capital as the 'totality of financial institutions and instruments which advance money (and credit and other financial paper) for gaining a return (interest, dividends, increases in value, and so forth).' Citing Marx, Bond (1998) notes that 'credit "interest-bearing money capital" lubricates (or "accommodates") capitalist production and commerce.' The scramble for resources from the periphery by capital has been in a constant process of evolution from the 1890s to the current phase characterized by intensifying dispossession of reproduction capacity through increasing integration into global circuits (financing and marketing of commodities). This new phase, currently in full swing (Moyo 2011c; Moyo, Jha & Yeros 2012) is characterised by concentration and centralisation of capital, which in turn gives rise to monopoly capital in the centre (Shivji 2009). For Moyo, Jha, Praveen & Yeros. (2013), the new scramble consists of the geopolitical and the ongoing escalation of the process of primitive accumulation characterized by highly financialised accumulation emanating from monopoly capitalism, the entry of the non-Western semi-peripheral, relatively autonomous capitalist states in the continent, a result of the anti-colonial struggles of the twentieth century.

As Bond (1998: 29) emphasises, what was 'Of profound importance was the way in which control of space passed from merchants, miners and farmers into the hands of foreign capital, landed speculators and financiers' through facilitating payments, facilitating capitalist production and centralization of investment funds and the hiring of workers. In Bond's (1998: 5) view, such processes also promoted the emergence of the controlling characteristics of finance, as financial, industrial and commercial capital, mediated through banks and its speculative nature increases with capitalist crises, turning credit and money into financial capital playing less of the lubrication role. For Amin (2015), the three epochs of crises of capitalism (1870s, 1875-1945 and 1975 to date) have been characterised by the concentration of capital's control, deepening of uneven globalisation and financialisation of the system's management leading to the nineteenth century formation of the monopoly capital – the generalised – monopoly capitalism. Even

28

though, according to Foster (2015), imperialism evolves changing form and 'phenomenology', as elaborated by Boron (2005); the fundamental parameters of imperialism, the historical materialist classical works remain relevant today, aiding our in-depth understanding of these classical accounts and epochs.

In this new phase of imperialism, as Amin (2015) argues, all facets of production are controlled at a certain level by capital. For instance, smallholder farming (peasantry) is controlled upstream by monopoly capital through input financing and downstream through global commodity chains which are structured to wipe out profits from the peasants. In this event, generalised monopoly capitalism or global monopoly finance capitalism secures the power to manage the means of production; new wars and tendencies are emerging. Contributing to this debate, Foster (2015) identified seventeen constellations of categories of imperialism employed by Marxian theorists and thinkers which are summarized as follows:

(1) monopoly capital/finance capital; (2) surplus monopoly profits; (3) the international division of labour and internationalization of capital; (4) the division of the world among the great powers; (5) nation-states as promoters of the global interests of their monopolistic firms; (6) inter-capitalist competition; (7) currency and trade wars; (8) colonies, neo-colonies, and dependencies; (9) economic crisis and imperialist expansion; (10) export of capital; (11) the search for new markets; (12) the struggle to control key raw materials; (13) integration of non-capitalist areas; (14) international wage inequality; (15) labour aristocracy in the imperialist core; (16) militarism and war; and (17) international hegemony.

To capture the evolving tendencies of imperialism, classical theorists applied the lenses of historical materialism. To begin with, Lenin (1964) advanced the theory of monopoly stage of imperialism and its attendant accumulation processes, then Luxemburg (1968) subsequently advanced the concept of accumulation of capital and how capital penetrates the disappearing non-capitalist areas. Bukharin (1973) was to follow with the theory of 'international division of labour' – and the 'internationalization of capital' advancing that surplus value is derived from high level of 'exploitation of cheap labour in the periphery'. For Foster (2015), therefore, Lenin's theory was based on the hypothesis that uneven development of monopoly capitalism is a result of rivalry of various world powers for geopolitical hegemony (conquest of [or ascendancy over] territory), not so much directly for themselves but in some cases just to weaken the opposition and reduce its perceived or real hegemony. Under these rivalry conditions, monopolistic corporations lead the building of the dependency syndrome in the global south, propelling uneven development and its accompanying destabilisation and weakening.

Some post-modernist scholars such as Hardt and Negri (2000) argue that the achievement of the global market necessarily brings about the end of imperialism. In support of this thesis, Robinson (2004) and Sklair (2001) have argued for Kuatsky's (1988) ultra-imperialism dominated by transnational capital and a transnational state, devoid of the nation-state. However, Harvey's (2005) accumulation by dispossession thesis counters these views and instead asserts that the crisis of over accumulation and falling profits in the centre forces capital to focus to non-capitalist areas as part of the spatio-temporal fixes, involving 'force, fraud, predation and the looting of assets'. Moyo and Yeros (2012) agree that capital has a negative role on the peasantry, but they, however, concur that the 'spatio-temporal fixes' approach by capital as suggested by Harvey (2005) is devoid of the necessary structural analysis.

A new development in accumulation trajectories, from a Marxian approach, under the ongoing monopoly-finance capitalism has been the shift of the manufacturing industry in recent times from the developed world to the global south, under historical centre-periphery conditions (Foster 2015) except for China. Prospects for an immediate remedy are slim, with valid fears that the developing countries (outside China) could take up to three decades to catch up with the centre, mainly due to these recent developments, marked by growing outsourcing of industrial production by multinational corporations which seeks to exploit inequalities in the world economy, focusing on labour (Foster 2015).

For Foster (2015), the outsourcing of labour costs, the global low-cost labour arbitrage – (Non-Equity Modes of International Production) - keep wages in the periphery well below the average value of labour power worldwide (see also Baran and Sweezy, 1969: 107-8) with profits extracted back to the centre, under multinational corporations' terms. Labour costs for Apple iPhones produced in China are as low as 1.8% of the retail price of same in the United States of America while garment exclusively produced in the global south under subcontracting arrangements are at as low as 1-3% of the final retail price (Foster 2015). As Foster (2015) further observes, countries such as China, India, Indonesia, Vietnam, Cambodia, Bangladesh, South Korea, Thailand and Philippines produce garment for large multinational corporations such as Nike, Hennes & Mauritz among others at below 1.6% of retail prices. Foster (2015), taking a cue from Robinson (2004), therefore surmises that the enormous cost savings in production for monopolistic enterprises, result in the increase in profit margins, enhancing outflow of imperial rent from the periphery to the centre through extraction of surplus disguised by complex global commodity circuits, trade exchange and hidden accounts. The little in imperialist rent that remains in the periphery only serves as payment to the local ruling classes for their roles in global manipulation.

This financial superstructure of the capitalist economy has three major effects on development trajectories: first, it uncouples asset accumulation from actual investment creating distortions in the centre; second, enhanced by the communications and digitalization technology, it results in the deepening and broadening of commodification, with the centre retaining financial and asset accumulation control; third, it leads to the fragility of the entire capitalist world economy. Screpatni (2014) therefore concludes that internationalisation of production under multinational corporations result in decentralized production but centralised control of production and circulation in a way that facilitates extraction of profits from the periphery to the centre. This is achieved through processes that advance the interests of the imperial powers of the capitalist core through political, economic, and military means as evidenced by numerous destabilised situations in many parts of this

31

super-exploitative and expansionist imperialist world economic system today (Foster 2015).

2.3 Functional Dualism

The establishment of the peasantry as a ready source of semi-proletarian labour under capitalism, promotes the creation of functional dualism. According to de Janvry (1981: 84), such dualism consists of an agricultural sector made up of a capitalist sector which produces commodities relying on hired semi-proletarian labour and the peasant sector, producing use value and petty commodities relying on family labour thereby delivering cheap wage labour for capitalist expansion. Whereas, in the central economies, social articulation of freed labour provides the basis of relative surplus value and its transformation into profits through the expansion of wage goods markets, in the periphery, social disarticulation for the proletarians results in the value of commodities being unrelated to workers' wages (de Janvry 1981).

As was the case in Latin America, 'free semi-proletarians' who settled in *minifundistas* outside *latifundio* but provide cheap labour and cheap food to capitalist farmers and the modern sector promote increased levels of exploitation in the periphery to levels higher than that of the centre (de Janvry 1981). As such, de Janvry (1981: 262) observed, primitive accumulation allows for wages to be driven below social reproduction of labour, and 'functionalizes peasants to the needs of disarticulated capital accumulation and negates their reproduction as agriculturists' by turning them into labour, thereby contributing to poverty. Absolute poverty and its dialectical counterpart of disarticulated growth results in a dual structure that symptomises and embodies the contradictions of peripheral capitalism as epitomised by the proletarianisation and impoverishment of the rural masses with increased domination of capital over peasants, trigger a fight for survival and competition for wages and product sales among the peasants. (de Janvry 1981).

To this end, de Janvry (1981) adds that the determinants of such extreme poverty are found in the contradictions of disarticulated accumulation and functional dualism. The contradiction is inherent and evidenced by the fact that semi-proletarianization of the peasantry is functional in ensuring the sustenance of peripheral accumulation patterns but also results in resource base depletion for the peasants as well as ecological and demographic contradictions that lead to the overall underdevelopment of the peasantry in the periphery. Such disarticulated peripheral accumulation patterns generate poverty on the back of cheap labour and cheap food delivered to the centre by the peasants. Ultimately, such contradictions lead to rural impoverishment that eventually eliminates the peasantry within the rural sector.

The peasants are tied to small plots that are insufficient for family subsistence, creating conditions for the proliferation of semi-proletarianisation that serve as a purveyor of cheap labour. Stavenhegen (1996) observes that on one hand the peasant economy provides minimum subsistence income to its members at little cost to the national economy and on the other hand, it is unable to improve the standards of living for poor peasants due to limited resources available to them, forcing them to seek complementary sources of income in the commercial farms and the modern sector. In de Janvry's (1981) view, this is a global tendency that results in uneven development of the productive forces and massive rural poverty. For Moyo and Yeros (2005: 19-20), functional dualism remains to this day and ensures the persistence of semi-proletarianisation in the countryside of the periphery. To the extent that capital does not need to realise its profits nationally, semi-proletarianisation and poverty will remain functional to its reproduction, ensuring that 'functional dualism' between the capitalist and non-capitalist sectors (not necessarily a rural affair but artisanal sector in the urban areas as well) remain in place, necessitating a political and economic transformation programme, capable of reversing uneven development in disarticulated economies.

2.4 Extraction of Surplus Value

The logic of primitive accumulation (brought in through plunder and looting – expropriation of values without exchange) (Lenin 1964:

Shivji 2009), though historical, continues to shape the dialectical relations between the centre and the periphery, production and exchange in the contemporary global south. For Shivji (2009: 56), to the extent that the producer has not been fully separated from the land, primitive accumulation remains incomplete while for Harvey (2005), accumulation by dispossession remains prevalent in the periphery. Shijvi (2009) asserts that the introduction of commodity exchange and production of values in the periphery integrates the peasantry into the global commodity circuits, enabling the co-existence of expanded reproduction and primitive accumulation.

This co-existence is evidenced through the prevalence of contradictions between the capitalist and territorial logic in the periphery, which is reliant on the 'contradiction between accumulation by dispossession and accumulation by expanded reproduction on one hand (capitalist logic), and the contradiction between nation and imperialism (territorial logic) on the other'. Authors such as de Janvry's (1981: 50) therefore argue that surplus is transferred from the periphery to the centre through industrial and financial loans and through international trade; through unequal exchange in trade, unequal trade and unequal rewards, in the formation of international prices as the centre and periphery is integrated into the world economic system under relations of production and circulation. The extraction of surplus value from the periphery through industrial and financial imperialism is triggered by the prevalence of disarticulated economies which infer super profits on foreign investment through; the joint occurrence of high productivity and low wages, secured though suppression of workers' demands, functional dualism (cheap semi-proletarian labour), the internationalization of value (imports of cheap wage foods) and efficient production of wage goods (de Janvry (1981: 51) in the developing countries.

These mechanisms that are used to extract profits from the periphery to the centre are fully discussed below. Before these arguments are presented, it is worth revealing the tendency for surplus value extraction in some detail. As Bond (1998: 5) notes, profits correlate with surplus value 'generated through exploitation of labour in production'. This happens because capital 'cannot "cheat in exchange" – buy other inputs, especially machines that make other machines, from each other at a cost less than their value – the increases in value that are the prerequisite for production and exchange of commodities must emanate from workers' (Bond 1998). In simple terms, opportunities for exploitation, for surplus value extraction and profits, fall as mechanisation and automation increase, a reflection of falling scope for labour exploitation due to their falling proportional contribution in production and circulation of commodities (Bond 1998). Therefore, core to primitive accumulation is the extraction of surplus at the level of production and circulation, as the next section will reveal.

2.4.1 Extraction through the third form of surplus value

Lenin (1964) observed that the imperialist stage of capitalism results in concentration of capital, the rise of finance capital, its oppression and its predation over weak nations and its unrelenting militarism through two defining processes; monopoly and export of capital. This is often achieved through the third form of surplus value extraction. To begin with, as Smith (2015) observes, neoliberalism has caused an expansion of a large pool of poor people through exploitative labour relations in southern nations. The International Monetary Fund (IMF) (2007) observes that a global pool of labour is accessible by the developed nations through imports and immigration, what Roach (2004) referred to as the global labour arbitrage – the substitution of high-wage workers in the centre with like-quality, low-wage workers in the periphery. According to Roach (2003), this is achieved through the maturation of offshore outsourcing platforms such as e-based connectivity and cost control that is underpinned by lower wages as a catalyst.

To this end, labour is the new source of industrial efficiency. For Shivji (1992: 129), therefore, the peasant is integrated into the international division of labour, producing export crops for the centre and 'answering to the needs of capital' and 'chaining the peasant into the world market', whereby the peasant depresses his requirements to subhuman level, yet supplying superhuman labour at the level of production. Lenin (1966)), figured this out far earlier and noted that the peasantry exists not because of technical superiority in

35

the capitalist society but because its requirements are reduced to levels below that of wage workers while they are taxed far more than workers situated in the centre.

Marx (1967: 430-1) dwells on the theory of the third form of surplus value and agrees with this observation and therefore asserts that capitalism increases its rate of exploitation by: firstly, 'lengthening the working day', thereby increasing 'absolute surplus value' and secondly, by 'reducing necessary labour time by increasing the productivity of workers producing consumption goods, thereby increasing 'relative surplus value'. Thirdly, capital achieves exploitation by 'pushing the wage of the worker down below the value of his labour-power', enabled by rising unemployment and harsher labour regimes in low-wage countries in the global South today. Today, 'A combination of monopoly ownership and/or control of land through the state, control over the market, and deployment of extra-economic coercion enabled the colonial state to maintain and reproduce a system of super-exploitation' (Shivji 2009: 66).

Higginbottom (2009) therefore concludes that super-exploitation is the hidden common principle that defines imperialism in which workers are exploited more, under the global labour arbitration rather than new technology – a predominant capital-labour relation in developing countries. Higginbottom (2009) and Marx (1981) give us a point of departure of analysis of today's global financialised monopoly capitalism. As Shivji (1992: 130) observes, at the stage of monopoly capitalism, capital is no longer satisfied with average profits and in its bid to secure high profits, finance capital is deployed all over the world where the peasants are chained to the chariot wheel of capital while retaining ownership of the means of production. Capital can make super profits without being responsible for the reproduction of labour (Shivji 1992: 130). The wage worker therefore become a semi-proletarian who straddles between town and rural areas (Shivji 2009: 66) in such a way that peasant combines both land ownership and labour but earns nothing from both as labour power is undervalued (Shivji 1992: 2009).

In a way, this is achieved through the imposition of cash crops for export through contract farming, as the peasantry is integrated into the global markets by way of production and reproduction. Watts (1994: 254) suggests that subcontracting to capitalist and peasant out growers is a risk reduction mechanism adopted by agribusinesses to 'exploit cheap and "self-regulating" peasant farmers', under what Buraway 'calls despotic and hegemonic production politics'. Grossman (1998) adds that contract growers marshal the household labour (family members, relatives, and friends) in complex ways relying on low-cost social networks in ways that Lahmann (1986) confirms are not available to larger capitalist firms. In this instance, the production management contract farming agreement has 'substantive implications on peasant labour processes' (Grossman 1998: 22). As some researchers (Davis 1998; Clapp 1988, 1994; Watts 1994a; Little and Watts 1994) observe, peasants under contract farming should be viewed as 'disguised' or 'concealed' wage labour' or 'propertied proletarians', 'hired hands on his own land' more comparable with wage labour than independent farmers. In Clapp's (1994: 81) view, contract farming creates 'disguised proletarianisation' whereby the contractor (read capital) secures 'control of the land and labour of the peasant while leaving him with formal title of both', under his illusory control. Reardon and Berret (2000, 200) also noted contract farming 'typically displaces decision making authority from the farmer to downstream processor or distributer, turning farmers into quasi-employees', what some scholars (Clapp 1988; Watts 1994; De Schutter 2011) describe as 'proletarianisation' of small farmers without dispossession', in a 'win-lose' situation for agribusiness and smallholder farmers respectively. However, some scholars (Mann 1990; Baxter and Mann 1992 cited in Grossman 1998) suggest that since farmers can withdraw from the contract farming agreement, then they still have control over the land and therefore are not 'free wage labour'.

In the case of Zimbabwe, Arrighi (1970, 2010 citing Bettison 1960) noted that the level of wages for the African worker was customarily fixed in such a way that it could only allow for the subsistence of a single person. The persistence of this custom meant that African wageworkers continued to rely on their tribal economy for support from their families and for themselves during periods of old age, sickness and unemployment (Arrighi 1970; 2010). This situation also meant that the workers had to remain engaged in the rural tribal social system by retaining cultivation rights and that they had to be able to claim support and succor whenever it became opportune. These conditions could not create 'stabilized labour' but brought about a semi-proletarianised peasantry that straddle from rural to urban and urban to rural in search of livelihoods. Extraction of surplus value also takes place at circulation level as will be revealed in the next section.

2.4.2 Extraction through market integration

The internationalisation of value through the import of cheap raw materials by the centre from the periphery under terms that favour the former is the origin of surplus extraction carried out through three possible processes: unequal exchange, unequal trade and unequal rewards. According to de Janvry (1981), this is achieved through the setting of equilibrium production prices allowing for transfer of value from the disarticulated to the articulated economies, unequal trade based on taking advantage of the material discrepancy between production and market prices and unequal rewards emanating from differences in labour productivity in traded commodities, respectively.

Unequal trade or non-equivalent exchange rely on surplus extraction to the centre through trade transactions as monopoly capital exploits on the centre's power to distort prices on the world market using tariffs on imports from the periphery, capturing increasing volumes of exports at lower (than production costs) market prices (ibid; See also Shivji 1992: 133). For instance, smallholder farmers have been inserted into contract farming by domestic and international capital resulting in intensified integration into world commodity circuits (Glover 1990 cited in Masakure and Henson 2005) that are potentially exploitative and are part of capitalist accumulation model (see Watts 1994). For Gibbon and Ponte (2005), agribusiness discovered that control over the plantation system was less important compared to processing, packing, trading, transport, branding and distribution nodes of the commodity circuits, as is obtained under contract farming. Bijman (2008) therefore posits that international finance capital introduces middle and poor peasantry to a sophisticated and exploitative system that reduces the small farmers involved in contract farming to even greater misery, dependency, subordination and proletarianisation, to the benefit of international capital. Grossman (1998: 7) suggests that the contract relation is based on unequal terms where bargaining power is asymmetrical, and peasants serve as a tool for extraction of surplus and labour control. In this regard, the contracts are a 'breeding ground for intense struggles, conflicting interpretations, manipulation, and dishonesty'.

The dependency theory sees international capital, working in cahoots with the comprador bourgeoisie and the state, extracting and repatriating the economic surplus from the periphery. Under this arrangement, 'contract forms of vertical integration are of undoubted and increasing importance among other things because contract farming is less risky for the foreign investor compared to direct ownership of the plantation' (Grossman 1998: 7). According to Glover and Kusterer (1990: 134), 'Transnational corporations may prefer peasants because they are less powerful and more easily controlled than are the large-scale landowners' (cited in Grossman1998: 6) resulting in classic peasant subsidy to capitalism through 'self-exploitation' of their household labour and ability to supplement income through food production, thereby guaranteeing labour reproduction.

For Watts (1994), manipulation of producers by contractors results in an unequal relationship and skewed distribution of income, pervasive indebtedness, familial tensions, food insecurity, and enclave development among other ills. Primitive accumulation is fostered by the exploitation of monopoly capital through contract farming to extract surplus value through labour exploitation at production level and unequal exchange at circulation level. It is therefore opportune that empirical studies be carried out to establish how the interface of the peasantry and capital has shaped peasant struggles, politics and state approaches, reconfigured rural accumulation and class formation in the aftermath of the FTLRP.

2.5 Schematic Conceptual Framing

The conceptual framework links primitive accumulation in the periphery to worldwide uneven development favouring the developed centre and supported by the world economic systems. Within the periphery, surplus value extraction is enabled through the re-financialisation of peasant agricultural production through contract farming, the schematic diagram 2.1 shows.

Diagram 2.1: Schematic presentation of the conceptual framework

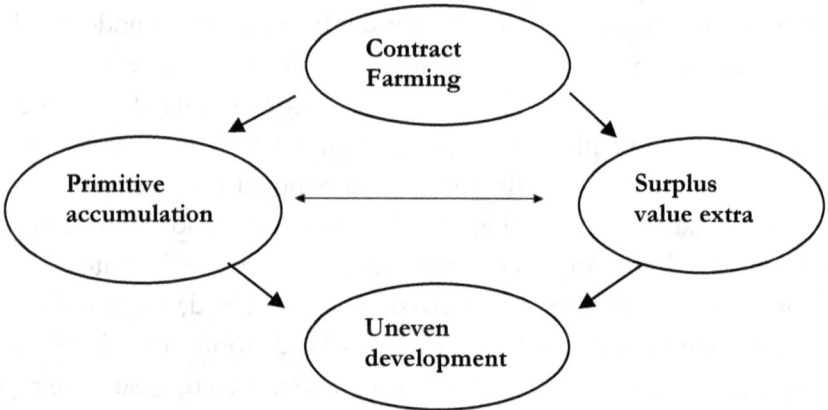

Source: Author

The extraction of values takes place at two levels; the production level and at the circulation level. To this end, global capital finds its way through the introduction of contract farming and the establishment of global commodity circuits where extraverted economies in the periphery support and aid the resolution of the crisis of under production and over accumulation in the centre. This conceptual framework therefore provides lens through which to analyse how structural changes in the input and output markets have impacted on capital accumulation for the smallholder farmers 15 years after the FTLRP.

2.6 Conclusion

This chapter presented one of the conceptual frameworks for this study. A discussion on the theoretical framework based on the world systems theory was presented. The concepts included uneven development, primitive accumulation, surplus value extraction and contract farming. To set the stage for the contextual background, the Zimbabwean setting on accumulation paths and peasants struggles against global monopoly capital will be presented in the next chapter. overall, these concepts provide lens for ease of interpretation of the ongoing agrarian transition in post-fast track land reform Zimbabwe. Empirical chapters will revisit these concepts, providing evidence of sustained peasant exploitation through export finance and commodity exports.

Chapter Three

Class Formation and Peasant Struggles

3.1 Introduction

In response to global monopoly capital, peasants within the periphery constantly engage in class struggles thereby defining accumulation trajectories. There is extensive literature on capital accumulation and class formation in the colonial periphery. The conceptual framework used in this study in part applies paths of accumulation and unequal exchange under the agrarian question. The chapter presents arguments that uneven development propelled by primitive accumulation and exploitative extraction of surplus value (de Janvry 1981; Luxemburg 1968; Amin 1976; Lenin 1964) shape accumulation and class formation that Moyo (2011) and Moyo *et al.* (2012) have identified as the trimodal agrarian structure in Zimbabwe. The different manifestations of primitive accumulation (Kausky 1988; Max 1977; Harvey 2005; Luxemburg 1968) have resulted in differentiated paths of accumulation in the periphery (de Janvry, 1981; Byres 1991) which have combined in various ways (Moyo and Yeros 2005) under the trimodal accumulation model as will be critically assessed in this and subsequent chapters. The Zimbabwean setting is applied to these concepts to reveal the ongoing accumulation paths.

3.2 Class Formation

Bernstein (2010) defines differentiation or class formation in class terms as the tendency of petty commodity producers to divide into classes of capital and labour that are also shaped by gender relations and capital accumulation as expanded reproduction where accumulation of profit to invest in production (or trade, or finance) is driven by the desire to make more profit. Beckman (1977: 1) asserts that external forces such as capital and the state shape peasant differentiation and class formation where the 'neo-colonial state continues to serve as a vehicle for the subordination of peasantry to capital accumulation at a world scale', through bureaucracy-led state appropriations and price suppressions, at times leading to stagnation in petty commodity production and peasantry development. Saul and Woods (1971) give an African perspective and suggest that notwithstanding some pre-figurings of a peasant class in the pre-colonial period, the interaction between an international capitalist economic system and traditional socio-economic systems brought about the African peasantry.

Arrighi (1967: 38) posits the view that colonial capital interests occasioned the emergence of accumulation patterns and differentiation comprised of five classes in pre-war Rhodesia. The classes included, the white rural bourgeoisie working in mining and agriculture, international capital working in transport (railways) and power (coal), and involved in primary production and speculation in land, the white wage, and white petty bourgeoisie working in all sectors of the economy, particularly in trade and the African peasantry and wage-earners. With regards to sources of social differentiation or class formation, Tshuma (1997: 22-23) asserts that metropolitan capital and European settlers benefited through the reconstruction of traditional land tenure systems and alienation of land in two ways. Firstly, it ensured the creation of conditions that undermined indigenous producers, forcing them to sell labour to mining and agrarian capital. Secondly, it availed land to the settlers through land grants thereby promoting better conditions for capital accumulation in favour of the whites.

Palmer (1977a) notes that various vices were applied to ensure the domination of blacks by white capital. Put succinctly, as Palmer does, African farmers were disenfranchised through land dispossessions, increased competition with heavily subsidized white farmers, reduced access to markets and imposition of costly dues such as taxes, rents, dipping and grazing fees, to the effect that Africans could no longer sustain themselves through purchase of their needs from sale of agricultural proceeds and ended up being wage labourers in the white farms, mines and the emerging industry. In theoretical terms, Lenin (1967) focused on the tendency to social differentiation among peasants and petty commodity producers arguing that class differentiation arises from 'the peculiar combination of the class places of capital and labour in petty commodity production' (see Bernstein 2009, 30). In this regard, Cliff *et al.* (2011) assert that the new structure emerging in the aftermath of the FTLRP must be understood as 'involving class reformation'. Cousins (2013: 118) concurs and adds that 'The dynamics of class differentiation are a key feature of debates on the "classic" agrarian question'. For Beckman (1977), capital and state are a source of differentiation and class formation as peasants' access to state bureaucracy and merchant capital is differentiated. As such, the neo-colonial state continues to subordinate the peasantry in capital accumulation within the world economy (Beckman 1977).

According to Bernstein (2010), differentiation is driven by random factors that impact on the relations of production. The factors include 'size and composition, soil fertility, access to irrigation and transport, remittances and reinvestment in agricultural production' and these lead into class formation where the 'tripartite classification of the 'poor', the 'middle' and 'rich' peasants emerges. The *poor* peasants are unable to reproduce themselves and end up turning into a *rural proletariat* owning a small plot for cultivation subsidizing their wages. The *middle* peasants can reproduce themselves through family labour and combine farming with other forms of production. The *rich* peasants or kulaks operate as a commercial farmer employing labour and sometimes rents out farm equipment, operates local trade shops, lends out money for capital, purchase farm produce, engage in rental business, transport and in some cases, engage in productive small-scale processing and manufacturing enterprises, operating within their localities. The study adopts these typologies in its analysis, before developing its own in chapters to follow. This places both Communal farmers and resettled farmers in the peasant category.

As Lenin (1967 [1899] cited in Cousins 2013 and Bernstein 2009), puts it, the middle peasants can meet the exigencies of simple reproduction from their efforts, poor peasant are unable to secure simple reproduction and resort to squeezing their capital and/or their labour, and in some cases, they may end up relying on the sale of their labour only for survival. The rich peasants engage in expanded reproduction and often transform themselves into capitalist farmers. However, as Bernstein (2010) argues, the exchange of labour power is not a sufficient ingredient for class differentiation, because some peasants buy and sell labour power at different periods of the annual economic cycle. It is therefore vital that we look at other sources of differentiation in class terms, such as the intensification of commodity relations where labour power becomes a commodity also exchanged, just like farm produce, within the real economy (Ibid). In this regard, Dekker and Kinsey (2011: 1017) suggest that differentiation processes are not entirely clear and are not only a result of participation in the cash crop markets, migration processes and livestock ownership in the late 1990s, such that a full understanding of differentiation processes can only be secured through further analysis.

For Cousins (2013), class formation emerged from differentiated processes involving diversification of livelihoods and class stratification caused by differences in land holdings, cattle holdings and ownership of productive implements. Hart (1994) and Ellis (1998: 10) posit that non-farm income was critical in shaping accumulation trajectories for farming households in the periphery, as farmers progress in capitalist farming, and invest in ancillary activities such as crop trading, processing, rural retail trade and transport, advancing credit, supply of animal and power driven draught power. The emerging capitalist farmers begin to invest in urban business investments and send their children to better schools, creating diversified capital accumulation trajectories.

Cousins' (2011a) proposes a typology where distinct classes are established, constituted of 'supplementary food producers, allotment-holding wage workers, worker-peasants, petty commodity producers, small-scale capitalist farmers and capitalists whose main income is not from farming' and suggests that such a schema of defined classes does not exist. Bernstein (2010) had earlier proposed an approach where it is accepted that a general tendency to class differentiation exist, but class formation is always mediated by other determinants in given any circumstances, and a wide range of locally specific dynamics, including intersections and combinations of classes, including social differences such in gender, age, ethnicity, race, religion and caste. It is therefore noteworthy that the tendency to class differentiation of peasants is beset with its own contradiction and complexities. Globalisation is one such factor shaping and contributing to incomes and the reproduction of the poor and middle peasants, accelerating tendencies to class differentiation, wherein the current phase of imperialism results in poor peasants being confronted by increasing simple reproduction 'squeeze' (Bernstein 2009).

Scholars on Zimbabwe's colonial era (Phimister 1977; 1986: Moyana 1984; Cheater 1990; Bond 1998; Palmer and Parsons 1977) have underscored the significance of capital and geopolitics in explaining capital accumulation and class formation in pre-independence Zimbabwe. For instance, Cheater (1990: 192) asserts that the Shona had identified a '*hurudza*, a large-scale agricultural entrepreneur, representatives of which category had, by the turn of the century, expanded and 'mechanised' their production, selling the output to white and Indian traders, farmers and miners'. Class differentiation was also perpetuated by the state from 1980-2000 through its support for small-scale farming in the former reserves as that created new opportunities for petty commodity producers. As Cousins *et al.* (1992: 18–20) observe, 'Income from wage-labour facilitated investment in farming, so that worker-peasants as well as petty commodity producers contributed a significant proportion of the crop surpluses' produced in the rural areas.

To this end, Bernstein (2015: 103) concludes that specific forms of 'existing capitalism' in history, including the colonial period have produced fragmented classes of labour in the countryside and not peasants and a few farmers. In Bernstein's view, the countryside is made up of petty commodity producers and some small-scale capitalist producers - members of classes of labour with a rural base, an existing reality that must guide the analysis of the rural economy and its changing nature. This conclusion however contradicts his earlier view (shared by this study) that 'as a result of class formation there is no single "class" of "peasants" or "family farmers" but rather differentiated classes of small-scale capitalist farmers, relatively successful petty commodity producers and wage labour' (Bernstein 2010: 4). The diverse combinations of farming and other off-farm activities structured by class relations result in complex situations where poor peasants are most likely to engage in wage-labour and other more marginal and 'crowded' branches of non-agricultural petty commodity production.

Under these circumstances, some poor and middle peasant households sell and buy labour power such that the boundaries between the poor peasantry and the rural proletariat are often blurred, as the paradoxical term 'landless peasants' suggests (Bernstein 2010). The confusion about peasantry for rural Africa requires a clear analytical approach which will be less easy to derive (Bernstein 2010), as attempted by Moyo (2011a). To fully unpack class formation for peasants in this neo-liberal period, the concept of paths of accumulation must be assessed in greater detail, as the next section attempts.

3.2.1 The accumulations paths

The underdevelopment school, as posited by Amin (1976) and de Janvry (1981), underscores the disarticulated pattern of accumulation whereby, the home market in the periphery continued to subsidize capital in its role in exporting wealth to the centre, under functional dualism between capitalist and non-capitalist countries, sectors beyond rural and urban areas. The existence of a semi-proletarianised state was first postulated by some late nineteenth century theorists of the agrarian question (Kautsky 1988; Lenin 1964) who observed that the phenomenon in Europe did not conform with Marx's (1973) deterministic formulations regarding transition to capitalism in agriculture (see also Moyo and Yeros 2005). They observed that primitive accumulation does not render petty commodity production archaic; instead, small peasants farming existed alongside large capitalist farming, with the former serving the interest of capital, subsidizing the reproduction of labour through lower wages (Moyo and Yeros 2005).

Moyo (2015) identified the impossibility of a historically deterministic, Eurocentric and linear logic of Europe and North America being reproduced in Africa. Firstly, the nature of capitalist transformation on a world scale is both uneven and intertwined (Moyo and Yeros 2011) as finance capital is concentrated in a few developed nations (McMichael 2012). Secondly, experiences in Europe and America were influenced by colonialism and its vices in the periphery, including transfer of raw material, which fuelled industrialisation thereto (Patnaik 2012). Marx (1973) had identified the emergence of a rural bourgeoisie following dispossession of peasant by large capitalist tenant farmers under a trinity arrangement where the landlords earned rent, the farmers a profit and the workers a wage, in England (see also de Janvry 1981 and Pierre Jailee 1968). However, Marx (1973) concluded that such a trajectory would predominate only in those countries that dominated the world market during the transitional period from the feudal to the capitalism. Lenin's study of the Russian pre-revolutionary development identified two paths – the Junker road of the Prussian landlords and the American road constituted of small farms, what Kautsky (1988) called 'production sites' – where the capital–labour relations are sustained.

According to de Janvry (1981), the *Junker road* leads to the massive dispossession of peasants of their land transforming the peasants into semi proletarians, landless workers or rural proletarians under pauper standards of living. For Moyo and Yeros (2005), this path was witnessed in Latin America and Asia, with a white-settler variant in Southern Africa but matured in the twentieth century and culminated in the green revolution. This path is mainly constituted of large-scale commercial farms who work in alliance with transnational capital, and at times expand into agro-tourism (Moyo and Yeros, 2005) and more recently land deals have seen their expansion into agro-fuels through a new scramble for land in Central, Western and Southern Africa (Moyo, Yeros and Jha 2012).

Scholars such as Lenin (1964) and Kautsky (1988) did not foresee the enduring nature of semi-proletarianization within the centre-periphery structure brought about by colonialism, and therefore concluded that the ***American path*** – of broad-based accumulation by petty commodity producers would subsist, only temporarily. For de Janvry (1981), following the argumentation by these scholars, capitalist agricultural development via the farmers' path results in far reaching class formation in the countryside, based hard work, resource endowment, as some farmers accumulate land, capital and

49

hire wage-labour, while its negative effects convert most of the farmers into proletarians. Resultantly, differentiation leads to an insignificant minority of small producers getting wax rich and getting on in the world, turning into bourgeoisie, while the overwhelming majority are utterly ruined and become proletarians eternally eking out a pauper life (de Janvry 1981). The farmer road is deemed as more economically and politically superior to the Junker path since it is more democratic and results in the enlargement of the domestic market that give space for the creative nature of masses, as Lenin (1964) posits.

The **merchant path** denotes the existence of modernised, medium sized farms characterised by absentee management who double up as petty bourgeoisie of professionals, military personnel and technocrats who bought and own land (de Janvry 1981). To this end, Moyo and Yeros (2005) added that these could also include bureaucrats who could have accessed land through freehold, via the state, the market or land reform. The merchant road relied on wageworkers and fully proletarianized social relations of production, non-rural, merchant, financial and industrial capital. The farmers are fully integrated into exports markets and the global agro-industry. de Janvry (1981: 109) also identified a **capitalist path**, also found in Latin America where contract farmers or other types of lease arrangements are established. These arrangements involve multinational agribusiness firms who establish contracts with local landowners to produce specified crops under stated technology at an agreed final price and quality. Whereas this path was confined to highly modernized farming through medium and large-scale farms; in the periphery it cuts across the peasantry. For instance, in Mexico, contract farming has tended to encourage the production of food crops, while in Zimbabwe, cotton, sugarcane and tobacco crops are produced mainly to satisfy the export market. Soya beans and seed maize are also produced under contract farming in Zimbabwe.

Beyond Lenin (1964) and the work by de Janvry's (1981), Moyo and Yeros (2005: 30-31) identified the accumulation paths to be as follows:

- A **state path** - land is appropriated by states as part of nation building, which is common in the periphery.

- A limited *middle-to-rich peasant path* of petty-commodity producers, a result of generic tendencies to rural differentiation and active state policies in the post-World War period. These peasants have been affected by neo-liberalism as the farmers have accessed insignificant state support resulting in them diversifying into "off-farm activities, such as transport, trading and small-scale hospitality services" and "may also include 'contract farming', whereby transnational capital contract petty-commodity producers directly, controlling their conditions of production (providing inputs, standards and output markets) but without taking title of the land or becoming embroiled in labour issues."

- A *rural poor path*, involving the masses of fully proletarianized and semi-proletarianized peasants relying on a retained or acquired family plots used for "petty-commodity production and social security (consistent with functional dualism)", but the peasants may also "migrate within rural areas, from rural areas to urban centres, and across international boundaries; it enters the informal economic sector, both rural and urban, through such activities as petty trading, craft-making and flexibilized employment; and it struggles for re-peasantization, sometimes successfully." Neo-liberalism has resulted in growth in peasants reliant on this path as retrenched workers from mines, farms and urban industries have joined, and often get involved in social movements from below.

3.2.2 The tri-modal path and structure

Moyo (2011c) has identified the emergence of a *trimodal path* where the peasantry, middle-sized farmers; large-scale capitalist farmers; and agro-industrial estates, plantations, and conservancies co-exist. These classes and accumulation paths are based on differences in land ownership, land tenure systems, social status of landholders and smallholders' capacity to hire labour (Moyo 2011c), agro-ecological potential and technical capacity (Moyo and Yeros 2005). In this regard, Moyo (2015), following Amin (1974), also observed that the accumulation path for Sub-Saharan Africa (SSA) includes petty commodity production and large capitalist farming, differentiated by processes of land alienation and world market integration. Some scholars (Mamdani 1996; Moyo 2008; Moyo 2015) observe that there is limited scale of plantation enclaves alongside dominant peasantries in most of the SSA countries. Moyo (2015) therefore suggests that the agrarian path for most SSA countries appears to be shaped around the tri-modal structure comprised of small-scale family farms which pre-dominate but often expanding into LSCFs and plantations.

However, the agrarian restructuring is currently under threat from land grabs by large monopoly capital from all parts of the world in many parts of Africa, under the hyper-speculative logic of capital (Moyo, Jha and Yeros 2012) and from a new dynamic of world agricultural and financial markets (Moyo 2015). The expansion of LSCFs in SSA is driven by non-rural domestic capital, which emerged from the public service, industrial workers and professionals and capitalist in trading, processing and manufacturing since the 1970s (Mkandawire (2013) under leasehold tenure (Moyo and Moyo 2015). For Moyo (2015), the emergent trimodal accumulation trajectory is driven by the integration onto the world market of various sectors of farmers. The peasants are generally stratified according to organic tendencies towards economic differentiation even through some are more integrated due to superior resource endowments or their accumulated benefits from past government support. In addition, the locational situation of peasants is a source of differentiated access to markets, because some areas have high infrastructure deficits and limited access to motorised vehicles (Moyo 2015). Such varied endowments are also affected by differentiated social, agro-ecological and economic conditions (Moyo and Yeros 2005) where about 20% of small-scale peasants in SSA are market-oriented producers of both food and cash crops while the middle farmers are the semi-subsistence producers focused mainly on producing food crops (Moyo 2015).

According to Moyo and Yeros (2005), in Zimbabwe, the 'middle-to-rich' small-scale peasants - the 'market-oriented' and 'semi-subsistence' commodity producers emerged through government policy from the 1950s. This category, according to Moyo (2011c), is constituted of peasants, whose agrarian relations are defined by self-employment of family labour working towards producing foods for self-consumption and selling the surpluses. The category also engages in various non-farm work and short-term wage labour, with differentiated capacities to hire limited labour, and to be hired out by others. Generally, all the categories rely on land that is held under customary rights for the communal areas and state permits for A1 farms/plots in the newly resettled areas. They produce for domestic and export markets through independent and/or contract farming and are therefore linked to international and domestic capital and world markets differentially. The second mode of accumulation within the trimodal path is that of the middle-scale and large-scale capitalist farmers. According to Moyo (2011c), these households rely on relatively larger numbers of hired labour than they rely on family labour (see also Chambati 2011), with a few hiring farm managers (AIAS 2007). These farmers hold land tenures which are amenable to market transactions, mainly through leases, and freehold title (2011c). Some of the capitalist farmers are middle class constituted of formerly employed professionals, small non-farm capitalists and rural 'elites', traditional chiefs, some better-off peasants, and some working-class people (AIAS 2007).

The *better-off* (*market-oriented* or *capitalist peasants*) occupy mostly the SSCFs under title deeds and A2 farms in newly resettled areas under the 99-year leases, employ more hired labour than family labour power, sells larger quantities of produce to markets and are therefore connected to the world market in the agricultural input and output matrix (AIAS 2007). The third category is made up of agro-industrial estates mostly owned by large-scale (Moyo 2011b) under freehold title and is vertically integrated enclaves, including tourism conservancies and state estates (Moyo 2011c). They hire large amounts of permanent and seasonal labour (Chambati 2011) and rely on an increasing number of out-growers (Moyo 2011c) under contract farming. With regards to capital accumulation, the differentially market integrated farmers endure differentiated levels of surplus extraction through super exploitation by capital, as shall be fully explored in the next sections.

3.3 Contemporary Peasant Struggles

The prevalence of independent peasant movements since colonial times and more recently in Brazil, Colombia, Ecuador and Mexico is illustrative that struggles over control of the means of production and labour persist. The contestation for the control of the means of production and circulation continue to shape peasant struggles (see Shivji 1992), mould politics and moderate state intervention. Petras and Vetmeyer (2001) argue that peasants and rural proletarians are currently engaged in struggles to resist the exigencies, pressure and demands of the financial and commercial capital, free market policies and external orientation that threaten the success of the small local producer, rural workers and their communities.

For Moyo and Yeros (2005), the last quarter-century has witnessed profound socio-economic and political changes in the countryside of the periphery whereby the weight of structural adjustment programmes under globalisation and neo-liberalism on peasants and workers is resulting in a deterioration in their conditions of social reproduction. This has been underway and has seen the rise of new and militant rural movements from Brazil and Mexico to Zimbabwe and the Philippines. In this regard, Mkandawire (2013) notes that the persistence of struggles over land and agrarian markets in colonial and post-independence states, as neo-liberal agricultural policies lead to reduced government support and increased exposure to greater risks of land alienation for the peasants.

In the main, poor peasants are engaged in struggles for land and a living *vis-s-vis* the better-off peasants, and LSCFs, as well as other employers who hire them at wages below the cost of social reproduction (Mkandawire 2013). Contributions by rural peasants to agricultural employment and the creation of livelihood opportunities are being thwarted by land shortages, labour constraints, and limited access to agricultural resources and world markets. As a result, the most popular progressive and militant movements have emerged from the countryside in the world today (Moyo and Yeros 2005). For Zimbabwe, peasants engaged in these struggles against capitalism under colonialism and today, have no choices other than participating

54

in the struggle against neo-liberal policies that are impacting on agricultural production, labour relations and commodity markets. To this end, peasant struggles are paradigmatic and as such are shaped by state and capitalist tendencies and vice versa, shape policy designing and approaches.

3.4 Structure and Agency – A paradigmatic debate

There is extensive debate on the viability, nature and significance of contemporary peasants and landless workers' movements interlinked to social change and development. A paradigmatic debate on the structural approach and non-structural forms of analysis, including postmodernist sensibility is reshaping contemporary thinking on the agrarian question. To begin with, the postmodernist approach is based on three major dimensions: economic (progress and prosperity), political (individual freedom protected by democratic institutions) and social (equality, justice and equity), and as such requires the institutionality of capitalism, protection of property rights, wage labour, the market and the state and re-orientation towards modern values such as universalism and individual achievement (Petras and Veltmeyer 2001: 85). This modern system is 'multidimensional but takes the form of capitalist development, rural outmigration and urbanization and unequal and inequitable property relations in land and access to other means of social production' as opposed to equity and social inclusion and systemic transformation and social revolution propounded under Marxism and Neo-Marxist Political Economy (dependency theory and so forth.) in the 1970s (Petras and Veltmeyer 2001: 85-86).

However, the search for Another Development (AD), grassroots development, small-scale, community based, participatory, dynamic and generated from below and from inside rather than from above and outside, resulted in Kitching's (1982) 'economic populism' (see also Petras and Vetmeyer (2001: 86). For Marxism, this entailed the fight against modernism under capitalism; urbanisation, industrialisation and proletarianisation (see de Janvry 1981), albeit in a somewhat ambiguous manner. In the 1990s, other formulations emerged, including the sustainable rural livelihoods (SRL) (Barkin

1998) that acknowledged the imperative for analytic focus of the community structural context aimed at engendering democratization to enlarge the participation space for the local, community-based and people-centred and people-led development. Kay (1999) focused on the multi-faceted process and social conditions of agrarian change and development centred on the modernist search for economic prosperity, justice and freedom, which sought to avoid exclusion of peasants from forces of change and modernisation which lead into a permanent semi-proletariat peasantry. Other structuralist and modernists such as Hobsbawn (1994) foresaw the death of the peasantry despite the resistance by peasants to forces of social change and development.

However, the crescendo of the epistemological crisis and theoretical impasse of structural and materialist paradigm, led by Post-Structuralist/Marxist/Modernist analysis, was reached in the 1980s (see Booth 1985; Munck and O'Hearn 1999) following that of the 1930s, 1940s and 1970S by exponents of critical theory. Some poststructuralists and postmodernists in social and development theory reject the Marxist perspective on the basis that it focusses on the cause and not the meaning of observed phenomena and reduces all phenomena to matters of class and modes of production, yet class has neither empirical referents nor material basis in the immediacy of lived or experienced reality. As Petras and Vetneyer (2001: 102) elaborate, the 'post-structuralist discourse is predicted on the notion that meanings expressed therein have no theoretical representations of the real world' and as such they are mere social constructions. The structuralist discourse analysis assumes a relation of correspondence or truth between categories of analysis and the real world. Structuralist view class to have referents and the structures to which they refer to theoretically as real and be a basis of causally operating forces.

Whereas Kay (1999) argues that modernisation had made the whole concept of radical agrarian reform irrelevant and anachronistic in the face of global changes, a new economy, market demands, and imperatives for global competitiveness that have eroded the possibility of peasant based agrarian reform, Petras and Vetmeyer (2001) insist that peasant-led social movements of modernist character still represent the peasantry itself and therefore these can be characterised as agency of change. Petras and Vetmeyer (2001) suggest that as agency of change peasants are affected by economic and political structures that constrain them and by their consciousness in their struggle to create a just and better society in an ongoing modernisation process, as was the case in Colombia, Brazil, Ecuador and Zapatista uprising in Chiapas.

All these developments point to a growing peasantry rather than a disappearing one, outside the pigeon holes presented by Hobsbawn (1994) and others, themselves based on a flawed demographic deduction. Petras and Vetmeyer (2001) therefore contend that class analysis under the Marxist theory provides superior understanding of the fundamental dynamics of rural development and the related pursuance of systemic social change in a modernist struggle to secure social-economic improvements within a modern economy, dominated by capital. The materialist approach places social class struggles and contradictions as the basis for change and gives us the 'big picture' by assisting in 'discovering, understanding, and identifying the movements of social reality embedded in historical materialism' (Shivji 2009: 22; Marx 1971 [1859).

Scholars such as de Janvry (1981: 8) argue that this approach focuses on the emergence of contradictions emanating from production and circulation of material goods as a framework for understanding the social system, revealing how patterns of accumulation of capital driven by the exploitation of labour by capital results in uneven development. In this regard, the peasantry must therefore be viewed as neither pre- nor postmodern, instead, they highlight modern social class struggling for anti-systemic change as a dynamic force in a persisting and continuous modernisation process, seeking a just and better society freed from oppression and where members of the society enjoy their dignity and cultural values. To this end, organised peasants/masses exercise power through grassroots mobilisation.

3.5 A Mixture of Normalisation and Redicalisation Politics

Peasant struggles in Zimbabwe have been shaped by both radicalisation and normalisation of state-capital relations, underpinned by peasant agency. According to Moyo and Yeros (2007), the failure by peripheral states such as Zimbabwe to resolve the agrarian question and as such the national question as illustrated by recurrent economic, social and political crises leads to escalation of a revolutionary situation. In the case of Zimbabwe, the pre- and post-FTLRP economic crisis is due to falling rate of profit – due to over accumulation; social crisis related to labour's inability to reproduce itself as evidenced by high infant mortality, prevalence of chronic malnutrition, increased vulnerability to preventable disease, and predominance of low life expectancy (Moyo and Yeros 2007).

In a chicken-and-egg conundrum, postmodernists insist that the FTLRP has been chaotic and violent resulting in the economic downturn, while structuralists argue that while violence was unavoidable, it is the economy-wide crisis from 1997 onwards that has crippled productivity post 2000. Consequently, different interpretations on legitimacy that reached its peak in 2000 led to divergent views on its extent and effect, resulting in calls for 'regime change' politics that triggered resistance by the government. In response to escalating resistance from below, the government in Zimbabwe increased its interventionist role in the economy from 1997 onwards, leading to the suspension of the structural adjustment program and commencement of state-led violent expropriation of farms (Moyo and Yeros 2007).

On one hand, democracy and liberties advocates increasingly mobilised opposition aligned to workers, and the urban centres became restless, while on the other hand, the periphery state went beyond revolution to become radicalised – rebelling against neo-colonialism (Moyo and Yeros 2007), as contestation for political power became the central agenda. However, the government of Zimbabwe has sought to infuse normalisation through restoration of economic and political order on the back of a consolidated and emerging black agrarian bourgeoisie class with strong ruling party links after realising the need for order and capital accumulation

58

(Moyo and Yeros 2007), yet the state remains radicalised and interventionist as evidenced by the introduction of state policies such as the indigenisation and empowerment policy in 2012. However, these contradictions brought to the fore the ideological contestation between elitist and mass based development paths and struggles, as shall be fully dealt with in the next section.

3.6 Ideological Contest: Neo-liberalism vs Redistributive Policies

Petras and Vetmeyer (2001) observe that some structuralists from both the Marxist and liberal ideological inclination view modernisation as a version of development whereby a new economy and the demands of the market as well as the pre-requisite for global competitiveness have eroded possibilities of effective peasant-led agrarian reform. To this end, the emergence of globalisation brought about sustained ideological assault on historical materialistic analysis to the classical agrarian question (Moyo and Yeros 2005). The globalisation claim assumed two varieties: that the periphery has entered a period of industrial transition where nationhood is to be achieved through foreign direct investment and export orientation; secondly, that rather than targeting industrial development in the periphery, it would be opportune to secure comparative advantage in the global market as a sufficient ingredient for national development.

This later view is supported by Kay (1999) who suggests that radical agrarian reform is irrelevant and anachronistic; instead, neo-liberal approaches that lead to elite hegemony through exclusion and displacement of peasants and rural workers, benefitting large scale exporters, big land owners and multinational businesses must predominate. The view posits that the struggle in the countryside is beyond tradition and modernity, elitist and exclusionary and the landless workers and peasants; instead, it is over the means of production and state support. For neo-liberals the only path of development is one based on export markets and large-scale farming where the struggles by landless peasants and landless workers is not an alternative to modernisation (Key 1999). In this regard, contradictions between tradition and modernity are based on neo-liberals' thinking that the techno-economic and modernisation approach undergirded by the achievement of huge export surplus, high returns for big investors – with access to financial markets and export markets and underpinned by labour oppression are key to capital accumulation, investment and development.

Relying on this optic for analysis 'overlooks the class relations that define land tenure, access to credit, technical assistance and choice of markets' and eschews 'routes, agencies and property forms within which modernization could occur' (Petras and Meyer 2001: 95). For the peasants, such an approach represents retrogressive de-modernisation where peasants face displacement from their markets, are forced into subsistence farming as they are denied or dispossessed of means of production; land, technology and credit, and become rural refugees contributing to the swelling of the low-income and low productivity sectors of the disarticulated economy (Petras and Veltmeyer 2001). The notion of peasantry as anachronism, or as backward in material, cultural or political terms is not supported by evidence because some peasants reproduce themselves within the economic spaces for agricultural petty commodity production in the divisions of labour of capitalism resulting in class differentiation. For Moyo and Yeros (2005), what is central is that the principle of national self-determination is affirmed, importantly, without obscuring both unequal development and a state-system that is threatened by imperialism and globalisation.

Bernstein (2009: 40) posits that globalisation and imperialism have introduced re-peasantisation in the imperialist periphery, through 'structural adjustment, lending and trade liberalization' that have put pressure on 'industrial and urban employment' (see also Moyo 2011a). In this regard, re-peasantisation as a 'concept implies that the peasant grammar is further articulated, in a more coherent and far-reaching way, while it materialises, *in practice*, in stronger, more convincing and more self-sustaining constellations' *(emphasis in original)* (Ploeg (2008: 35). This study sought to uncover these dynamics through in-depth analysis of the classical agrarian question and the accumulation trajectory emerging in Zimbabwe.

3.7 The Zimbabwean Setting

Some scholars have placed emphasis and debate on the end of the peasantry in relation to the advent of capitalism, colonialism and imperialism in Zimbabwe. Scholars who studied the historiography of Zimbabwe's colonial era (Phimister 1977; 1986: Mtetwa 1975; Moyana 1984; Cheater 1990; Bond 1998; Palmer and Parsons 1977) have underscored the significance of capital and geopolitics in explaining capital accumulation and class formation in pre-independence of the country. Take for instance, what Ranger (1977) noted, that notwithstanding the possibility of the pre-colonial existence of the peasantry, the insistence on a particular point in time as the peasantisation moment and on the impact of the international capitalist system on that 'moment' confuses the entire historical development. Phimister (1977) makes a clearer observation that the Ndebele and Shona people were so experienced that at the advent of colonialism they were swift in taking advantage of the new markets, supplying food to the Europeans even though the Europeans' quest for food was quickly replaced by the want of labour (Ranger, 1977), resulting in changed priorities from peasantisation to de-peasantisation and to proletarianisation.

However, some writers tend to link the 'moment' of, 'areas where, and periods' when peasantry emerged to the advent of capitalism in Southern Africa. For instance, Beach (1977: 37) suggests that the capitalist economy was only established in 1890 and was based on 'farming, mining, and manufacturing' leading to massive transformation from the 'traditional economy' to a dual economy where capitalism deliberately triggered the expansion of African peasantry but later legislated against its success to secure cheap labour from the 'African labour Reserves'. Parsons and Palmer (1977: 5) emphasise the interconnectedness between the 'pre-colonial relations of productions, the colonial undermining of self-sufficiency and the process of peasantization' as capitalism prompted the development of underdevelopment in the periphery, Africa included. As Arrighi (1967: 36) puts it, in the case of Rhodesia, now Zimbabwe:

International capitalism was represented mainly by the British South Africa Company which, apart from its control over the railways, the bulk of gold production and coal mining, also owned land in part exploited for productive purposes (maize, cattle, citrus, and so forth).

In the case of Southern Africa, 'international financial power thus helped to establish a terribly uneven form of sectoral and spatial development', with the BSAC securing substantial control over mining, railway line, citrus plantations, timber, banking and insurance and as well as vast tracks of land (Bond 1998: 35). Despite this historicity, some scholars (Alexander 2006; Marongwe 2008; Zamchiya 2012 and McGregor and Alexander 2013) argue that neo-patrimonialism explains productivity, accumulation and differentiation patterns in resettled areas. This analytical framing is based on a somewhat narrow view of the state, wherein corruption is placed at the fore, eschewing the transformative role of the fast track land reform program. While some scholars (Zamchiya 2012; Alexander 2006 and Marongwe 2008) conclude that politics, state practice and power, respectively, influenced productivity, capital accumulation and class formation; no connection is made between the political positioning and social network's impact on access to resources and marketing of crops to that of capital in the variegated settlement settings.

Yet the various forms of capital, either through government assistance to farmers, off-farm income and through political and social networks impact on agricultural productivity and class formation. To be sure, Moyo (2011: 961) argues that the emerging 'agrarian labour relations are now more dominated by self-employment in diverse farming and non-farming activities, and part-time wage-labour is more common, prevailing wages and income remain repressed by low productivity, exploitative commodity markets and slow recovery of production in other economic sectors'.

Similarly, these conclusions elude findings by many researchers and scholars who have concluded that the FTLRP broadened participation resulting in accumulation from below. For instance, Cliff *et al.* (2011) concludes that 'there has been major transformation of the agrarian structure in Zimbabwe since 2000, and that the central characteristic of that outcome is that smallholder production now predominates. Moyo and Yeros (2013) content that land alienation under the new tri-modal agrarian structure has succeeded in ensuring that the Junker path in Africa, through foreign capital and its domestic allies replace the merchant path. Moyo (2011b: 527) therefore concludes that:

> Moreover, since capital was not totally ousted in Zimbabwe's land reform and alternative sources of financing Zimbabwe's agrarian reform have been limited, internal class contradictions have enabled (politically unaccountable) international capital to reinforce the emerging unequal agrarian relations, using deregulated market mechanisms tied to the unequal world trade regime.

Over the past three and half decades, Zimbabwe has gone through three phases of land reform (state-led market sales, up to 1985, expropriation and market sales from 1986 to 1999 (including under ESAP), and fast track; involving land invasions, expropriation until today) (Moyo 2011). According to Bernstein (2009), the advent of globalisation has ushered in the liberalization of international and domestic agricultural commodity markets, new patterns of corporate and agribusiness investment, and technical advancement in primary production in farms and value addition through food processing, manufacturing and distribution. The production and distribution patterns create new opportunities and challenges for agricultural petty commodity producers located differentially within the global commodity chains as ensuing chapters will reveal.

3.8.   Conclusion

This chapter presented a discussion on the theoretical framework pertaining to class formation, peasant struggles and re-peasantisation. This has neatly tied up with the previous chapter which presented such concepts as uneven development, primitive accumulation, paths of accumulation and surplus value extraction. These concepts are revisited in later chapters where empirical evidence is used to reveal new waves of class formation that are underpinned by the *re-*

63

financialisation of Zimbabwean agriculture through contract farming. And to set the stage for the next chapter that focuses on the contextual background, the Zimbabwe setting was also presented. The next chapter focuses on the historical context of the study and will shade light on the economic and social history and changes in agrarian relations in Zimbabwe.

Chapter Four

Research Methodology

4.1 Introduction

The purpose of this chapter is to address the methodological issues of the study. A comparative study of agrarian change dynamics in five settlement sectors and four agro-ecological regions required information from varied sources for triangulation. An in-depth understanding of role of capital in capital accumulation and class formation in rural Zimbabwe requires information that captures the historicity, complexity and their changing nature through quantitatively and qualitatively rigorous methods. The reliance on archival sources, case study field work in differentiated and contiguous settlement sectors; and content analysis reveals the changing agrarian dynamics in capital accumulation and class formation through a deeper understanding of the role of capital in rural Zimbabwe.

The study does not exclusively focus on tobacco farmers in the variegated settlement sectors but on food and export crops and other sources of income, even though the role of contract farming on tobacco farming forms the basis of evidence, as the research sought to reveal how capital impacted on capital accumulation and class formation in rural Zimbabwe. Information on other crops and in all settlement sectors helped in providing a holistic view of the changing rural dynamics. Besides archival work on the historicity of tobacco production and Hwedza District's social and economic history, the study also relied on literature reviews, content reviews of AIAS district survey reports, a case study of five sites in Hwedza District, through a structured questionnaire and in-depth interviews, both of which were administered and conducted respectively by the researcher and some research assistants. This chapter provides the setting of the study and describes the procedures followed in the study. The research design, sample design and population sample procedure, data collection procedures and data analysis are also presented. Finally, the chapter presents data analysis strategies and the study organisation.

4.2 Background to the Study Area

The study applies a case study approach to shed light ongoing agrarian change through evaluation as propounded by Diang'a (2011). A case study is defined as 'an in-depth investigation of an individual, group, institution or phenomenon (Mugenda and Mugenda 1999) and can be located and viewed as an example of events or group of individuals (Diang'a 2011) that can permit for generalisation of findings (Patton 1987) using quantitative and qualitative data for rich learning about issues of central importance. This study was carried out in Hwedza Communal Area (CA), which is situated 127 kilometres in the southern part of Harare and has a total population of 70,968. Hwedza District is predominantly situated in NR IIa, IIb, III and IV which has sandy loam soils, suitable for tobacco and cereal crop farming. It is one of the sites in Zimbabwe where resettlement after 2000 resulted in a dramatically changed rural political economy, with nearly two thirds of the population earning a living as resettled farmers (Zimstat, 2013).

Out the 102,329ha previous under Large Scale Commercial Farms (LSCFs), only 400ha remained under this sector in 2015. The case study site straddles four of Zimbabwe's agro-ecological regions, thus providing varied climatic conditions and differing agricultural potential (Dekker and Kinsey 2011: 998). Hwedza District was chosen as the study area, firstly, because the district has a high number of people who were resettled after 2000 and rely on farming for their livelihoods. Secondly, despite the high number of resettled households, rural poverty remains high at 79.4% in the CAs and 76.4% in fast track areas, while inequality in Hwedza stands at 0.63 (Zimstat 2013). The settlement patterns in Hwedza District depict a historical account on land and agrarian reform and how capital accumulation and class formation were shaped by capital, state practice and policy from 1890.

4.3 Research Design

This research used a case study design and relied on the mixed methods research (see Guba and Lincoln 1994; Schwandt 2000 and 2006) where methodological triangulation is applied to derive maximum advantage from using both qualitative and quantitative methods (in sequence) (Morse 1991), relying on the 'philosophy of pragmatism' (Johnson et al. 2007).

According to Cresswell and Clark (2007), the use of the mixed method allows for use of both qualitative and quantitative methods in tandem, giving greater overall strength to the study. The research also relied on archival data, government reports and AIAS Survey Reports and research findings on rural accumulation in post-2000 Zimbabwe. The study, therefore, relied on both post-positivist and social constructivist worldviews/paradigms as this allows for researchers to make careful observation and measurement of the objective reality existing in the world and to learn about the individuals and the subjective meanings of their experiences (Creswell 2009). Writers such as Rossman and Wilson (1985) offer three reasons why a combination of the two methods (qualitative and quantitative) is helpful. It enables confirmation and collaboration of each other, provides thicker, deeper and richer data analysis, derives deeper meaning through, as Denzin (1978) observes, dealing with emerging and uncovered convergences, inconsistencies, and contradictions.

Greene et al. (1989) add complementarity and expansion to the rationale for the mixed method. The qualitative element of the mixed method, was utilised to ensure subjectively lived experiences, meanings and perceptions constructed when people engage with the marginalised groups and individuals in the community, help to understand the multiple perspectives in an interpretive research (Kitchin and Tate 2000; Mottier 2005). The research questions require data on households' perspectives, experiences, responses to, and interpretation of the impact of fast track programme on production patterns, capital accumulation and rural class formation processes for small scale farmers in post-2000 Zimbabwe (see Table 7-1). The mixed methodology which was used provides relevant data through deeper probing on the 'why' and 'how' of the issues under study, aiding a deeper understanding of people's life experiences, beliefs and attitudes (Ulin, *et al.* 2002), giving a structuralist-critical view of the research process (Johnson *et al* 2007).

4.4 Population and Sample Selection

Given the geographically dispersed population in the study area, cluster sampling was applied in carrying out the study. Hwedza District was selected as the big cluster in stage 1 of a three-stage sample selection process (see Neuman 2006), as it presents a unique case study due to its distinct characteristics. The second stage in the multi-stages involved randomly selecting five small clusters within the big cluster before randomly selecting sample elements within the selected clusters, as the last stage of the sampling process. The use of clusters selected in Hwedza District reduced the cost and time for the study while ensuring that all the settlement sectors and agro-ecological regions were represented. The household was the unit of observation. 'A household was defined as a single person or a group of people, who usually live, cook and eat together, related or not related' (GoZ 2003; see also Mtapuri 2008: 11), and living in the same unit of habitation sharing the basic expenses of provisions (Muanamoha 2008).

For resettled areas, the ward population for each small cluster was the universe, the resettled households within the selected cluster were then randomly sampled; while for the CA, the ward population was the universe for the small cluster while two villages and households within the villages were also randomly sampled. The head of the household in all the clusters was targeted to ensure effective collection of historical data on key issues. An unweighted sample of about 50 households was randomly selected from each small cluster as respondents for the study. Given that Hwedza district has five settlement sectors; the CA, SSCF, ORA, and A1 and A2 (under the FTLRP), clusters were purposively selected to ensure representation for each sector to enable the collection of accurate data for comparative analysis on capital accumulation and class formation within the changing agrarian structure. Overall, there are 930 households under SSCA, 943 households under ORA, 2,861 households in the A1 and 303 households under A2 farms, giving a total of 5,037 resettled households, with a total of 12,491 households residing in the CA, studied wards had lower number of households, as Table 7.1 shows.

Table 4-1: Hwedza Multi-Stage Cluster Sampling Source

Ward	13	4	3	1	5	
Settlement Type	Settled Clusters				Communal Cluster	
Targeted sector	SSCF s	ORAs	A1	A2	CAs	Total
Populations size	2423	3198	2983	4813	6664	20081
Ward households	533	722	627	1136	1625	4643
Households sample size	53	46	46	32	53	230

Source: compiled from CSO census data, Ministry of Agriculture, 2015

However, the targeted wards have varied population sizes as follows: Ward 13 in Zviyambe, under the SSCF has 533 households and a total population of 2,423 (See also Map 7.1)

Similarly, Ward 4 targeted for ORA has 722 households and a total population of 3198; Ward 3 has 627 A1 farmer households and a total population of 2,983; Ward 1 has 1,136 households A2 farmers and a total population of 4,813; Ward 5 has 1,625 CA households and a total population of 6,664. In all, the five clusters have a total of 4,643 households and a total population of 20,081. Hwedza District has a total of 17,147 households in fifteen wards and a total of 70,068 in population. A sample size of 230 households was selected during multi-stages within Hwedza District. As depicted in Map 7-1, the SSCF are in Zviyambe in agro-ecological region IIIa and IV, about 60 kilometres south of Hwedza Centre. Most of the area is under agro-ecological region IV, which is suitable for cattle ranging, even though small-scale farmers in this area also engage in crop farming.

Map 4-1: Hwedza District - Agro-ecological Regions and Settlement Sectors Studied.

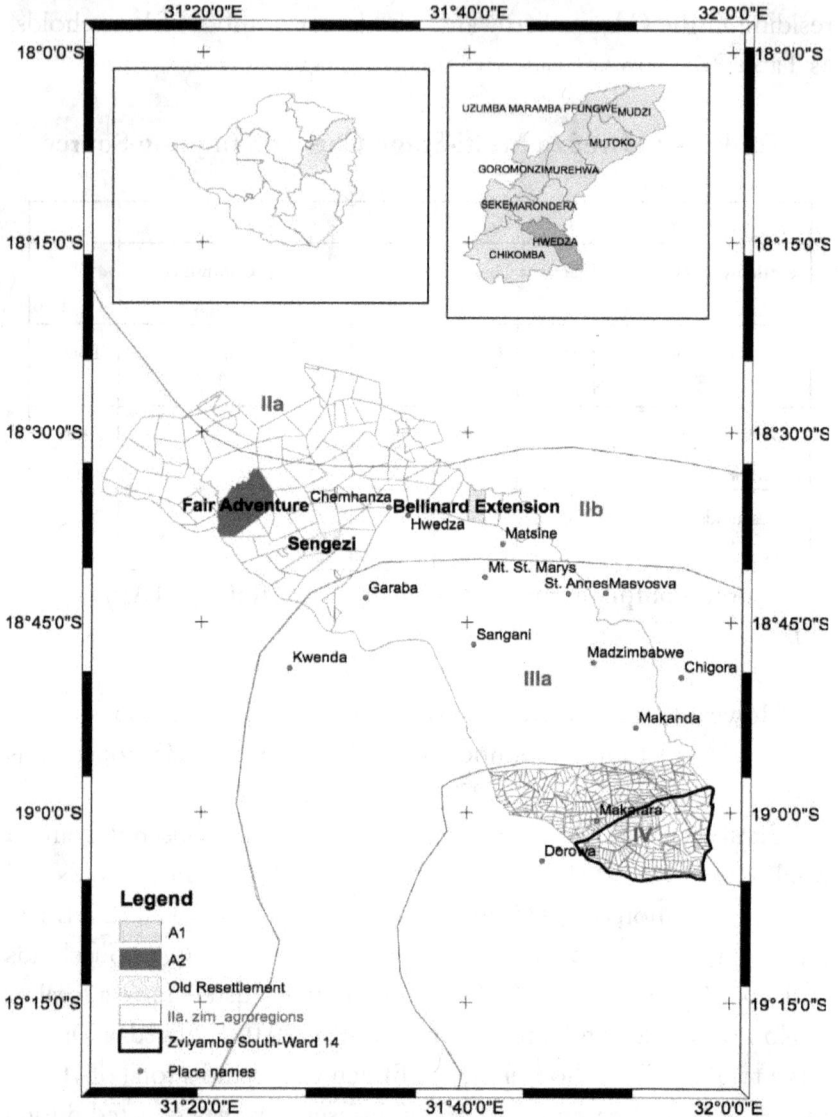

Source: Author, using data from the Ministry of Lands, 2016

The farm sizes in Zviyambe range from 2.4 hectares to 325.3 hectares and are mainly constituted of red loamy soils. The CA is in agro-ecological regions IIb and IIIa and is situated between the SSCA, to the South partly ORA to the north and resettled areas (RAs) partly to the north east. The CA is suitable for maize, tobacco production and some small grains. The historiography of settlement of the Svosve people in this area is fully explained in Chapter 8, suffice at this stage to observe that this history is characterised and epitomised by land dispossession from NRII to NRIII and NRIV, during the colonial period. Most of the households (69.3%) residing in this Hwedza district rely on agricultural production of cash and grain crops for their livelihoods (CSO 2012). To capture data within this sector, respondents were randomly selected from Mutambirwa village in Makwarimba ward (5) situated contiguous to A1 farms, ORAs farms and Hwedza Growth Point. The ward also falls under NRIIb and therefore agricultural production and social reproduction patterns are comparable to those in the RAs.

There are three ORA sites in Hwedza, being Zana, Tongogara and Sengezi, all located in NRIIb. Most of the people settled in these areas originally came from the CAs within the district, and produce maize, tobacco and livestock, mainly cattle. Sengezi was selected as a sector site for the ORA given that it is situated contiguous to Fast track farms sites and CA sites. The A1 sector respondents were selected from Mtokwe, farm located in NRIIb, grows maize and tobacco and rears livestock. The site is contiguous to the CA site and the ORA. The A2 cluster, which is in NRIIa, at Fair Adventure Farm is located along the watershed. Within this agro-ecological region, there is one diversified white commercial agro-estate involved in eco-tourism, tobacco farming and horticultural production as well as three black-owned commercial farms resettled before the FTLRP.

The five clusters are located within varying distances from Hwedza centre, they are variably connected to the centre through the finance markets, input and output markets. As such, this investigation reveals and analyses emerging local-national-global linkages within the agrarian economy (capital, social and labour relations, land use, commodity markets, climate change based on data collected in Hwedza District. The selection of households within each site was simple random, whereby, in resettled areas, plot numbers were used to identify the households, while in rural areas each household was allocated a number for identification purposes. The sample selection process involved placing the numbers in a jar from where a number was picked per turn, repeatedly, without replacement, until on average, 50 households were selected per study site. The collected information on capital accumulation and class formation assists in analysing and developing a model of Zimbabwe's agrarian change post the FTLRP.

4.4.1 Sample design

The targeted number of respondents per cluster enabled effective comparative analysis for CA, SSCF, ORA and FTLRP farms (A1 & A2) sectors. For the quantitative survey, random sampling was used to select about 50 households in each cluster in the five wards targeted for this research. However, the study relied on purposive sampling technique to identify one key informant from each of the five clusters in the five wards to help gather historical data on productivity, capital accumulation and class formation processes.

Twenty respondents from local traditional leadership, government institutions and departments were sampled purposively for interviewing to elicit for the official government positions. Careful contact and references were used to ensure that the few people identified have detailed knowledge (Nigel, 2008), through other members of the Hwedza community. Purposive sampling is appropriate for identifying uniquely informative members for the subject under investigation to get detailed historical knowledge of the area under study. Secondary data was collected from baseline surveys, media articles, farmers' association reports, marketing boards and government documents such as ward, district, provincial and national land allocation, farm productivity and household livelihoods reports. Quantitative data was collected on household housing, assets, crop and livestock productivity, income, and expenditure, farming input support and labour utilization. Data on political and social networks, access to education, health services and household vulnerabilities was solicited from households/respondents.

4.5 Fieldwork

4.5.1 Pilot data collection

The questionnaire was developed by the researcher in August, September and October 2015. A pilot study was carried in mid-March 2016 as part of the study area familiarisation process to aid with the cluster sampling within the district, to test the effectiveness of data collection tools and to familiarise the interviewers with the research tools,. The pilot study was useful for time allocation for travel and intervals and to help in budgeting for the main fieldwork. After pre-testing the data collection instruments, improvements (clarifying questions) were made before the main fieldwork was carried out from end of March to May 2016. The clarification of questions was crucial in eliminating potential errors by interviewers during the main fieldwork.

4.5.2 Main data collection

The main fieldwork was conducted over a period of two and half months by the author with the assistance of three trained interviewers. These field assistants were identified from within Hwedza District during the pilot survey and were partly involved at this early stage of the fieldwork. Prior arrangements and appointments with the respondents ensured success during the fieldwork. Table 7-2 presents the linkages between the objectives, research questions, data requirements, data sources as well as the data collection methods.

4.5.3 Structured questionnaire

The fieldwork was carried out with the assistance of the three trained fieldworkers according to the initial plan. Besides the training carried out during the pilot fieldwork, the fieldwork assistants were carefully selected based on their accumulated experience in carrying out similar tasks for other students and some ongoing household surveys in Hwedza District. For instance, two of the assistants had been involved in the ongoing Bill Kinsey Household Survey in Sengezi, while the third one was involved with another student, also during our pilot field work. The amount of time taken to complete a questionnaire and errors encountered reduced with time as the fieldworkers gained experience and became more familiar with the questionnaire. The researcher also carried out fieldwork and was accessible to the fieldworkers to deal with any challenges that occurred and checked the questionnaires at the end of the day's work. To reduce costs and increase coordination and supervision, the whole team carried out fieldwork in one cluster at a time and only moved to the next after accumulating 50 questionnaires as per research cluster.

Table 4-2: Linking Study Objectives, Questions, Data Requirements and Sources

Objectives	Research questions	Data requirements	Sources of data	Collection methods
❑ To assess the role of capital in rural accumulation and class formation in the variegated farming sectors in Hwedza district.	• How have land reform and contract farming changed the financing of the agrarian economy, and affected production patterns, accumulation and class formation for communal and resettled smallholder farmers in Hwedza district?	a. location and identification details b. land holding c. asset ownership and investments d. land use, agricultural production and food security e. Sources of funding	i. smallholder farmers ii. Ministry of agriculture (agritex officers) iii. TIMB iv. Tobacco companies	• Administering questionnaires • In-depth interview schedules
❑ To analyse emerging local-national-global linkages within the agrarian economy (capital, social and labour relations, land use, commodity markets, climate change).	• Which financial and commercial circuits of capital accumulation have emerged to extract surpluses, ranging from transnational corporate tobacco merchants and commercial banks to small vegetable vendors	a. agricultural inputs b. agricultural markets c. financial markets	i. Smallholder farmers ii. Agritex officers iii. Ministry of Agriculture iv. TIMB v. Tobacco companies vi. Banks	• Administering questionnaires • In-depth interview schedules
	• What are the agrarian classes emerging in Hwedza district in Zimbabwe since 2000, and how do these relate to land reform opportunities as well as the new contract-farming regime? • What explains accumulation and class formation for smallholder farmers in Hwedza in post-2000 Zimbabwe, particularly in terms of land reform and contract farming?	a. agricultural labour b. land use, agricultural production and food security c. food consumptions d. income e. productive capital assets	i. Smallholder farmers ii. Traditional leaders	• Administering questionnaires
❑ To develop a model of Zimbabwe's agricultural productivity, capital accumulation and class formation as a consequent of emerging farming practices in post FTLRP Zimbabwe.	• How have the accumulation and class formation affected broader social relations in Hwedza district, and are these patterns likely to prevail more generally in Zimbabwe? • What model/framework of Zimbabwe's agricultural productivity, capital accumulation and class formation can be developed as a consequent of emerging farming practices in post FTLRP Zimbabwe.	a. agricultural labour b. land use, agricultural production and food security c. food consumptions d. income e. farmer organisation and networks f. challenges facing the farmers. g. Asset ownership and	i. Smallholder farmers ii. Ministry of Agriculture iii. TIMB iv. Traditional leaders v. Shop traders	• Administering questionnaires • In-depth interview schedules

Source: Author

4.5.4 Constraints on fieldwork

A potential constraint was related to the issue of securing political and administrative approvals. However, the researcher had secured these well in advance, before the pilot survey. During the pilot fieldwork, the researcher and the field assistants took time to introduce themselves to the gatekeepers. Using letters from government officials and local agricultural extension officers which ensured cooperation from the communities involved. However, the cost of travelling was high given that the researcher resides in Arcturus, approximately 110 kilometres from Hwedza and the clusters were in some cases as far apart as 70 kilometres.

The field team needed accommodation and food for the duration of the fieldwork as it was going to be more expensive to travel back to their rural homes daily. Such an arrangement would have also caused logistical difficulties resulting in delayed completion of the fieldwork. Carrying out the research fieldwork during March, April and May presented challenges in that the auction floors were open, and farmers were involved in grading and the transportation of their tobacco to the auction floors. In some cases, interviews and questionnaire administration were carried out whilst the farmers continued with their tasks, where possible, to reduce the inconvenience. Nevertheless, ensuring prior contact with the farmers usually made the task more convenient for the farmers.

4.5.5 In-depth Interviews

In-depth qualitative interviews were also carried out in Hwedza and Harare (see Picture below). In Hwedza, the interviews targeted traditional leaders, war veterans, agricultural extension officers and some selected farmers. In all, ten (10) interviews were conducted in Hwedza District (see schedule of interviewees – Appendix 3). In Harare, 10 in-depth interviews were carried out with key government officials knowledgeable with tobacco farming and trading, mainly in the Ministry of Agriculture, government parastatals such as the TIMB and tobacco contracting companies and auctions floors. In Harare, emphasis was put on the value chain; processing, manufacturing and pricing of tobacco products and labour issues while in Hwedza District, emphasis was put on production patterns, capital accumulation and class formation patterns.

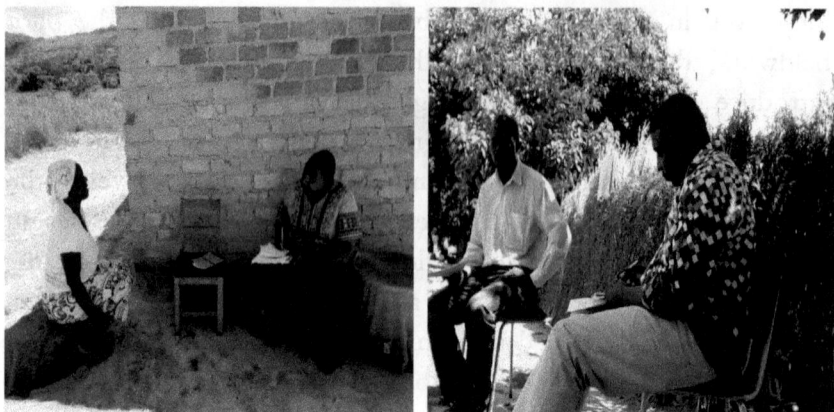

Picture 1 and 2: In-depth interviews in Hwedza CA and district centre, 2016

The researcher carried out all the interviews and relied on references to get more contacts (snowballing), especially in different companies where a lot of secrecy is maintained. The in-depth interviews were used to fill the gaps observed during quantitative data collection. The gaps included data on wage hours taken by households per cropping area, local linkages in marketing of grain and horticultural crops and on cost of production, processing and manufacturing at various levels of the tobacco commodity circuits. All names used in this study are fictitious to protect the privacy and confidentiality of the respondents.

4.5.6 Observations

The researcher made observations during the research period as part of data collection and evaluation to establish how respondents within the research area were engaging in farm and non-farm activities within Hwedza District and at the various input and output levels (See Pictures 3 and 4). Observations were therefore made on ownership of productive assets, production levels and ongoing non-farm activities on the farms.

Pictures 3 and 4: Observations in (a) Zana A1 Farm in Hwedza Communal Area and (b) Tobacco Sales Floor, Harare, 2016

At input level, observations were made on-farm shops, local trading shops, at Hwedza Growth Point and at the tobacco auction floors. At the output level, observations were made at the vendor markets, trading shops and tobacco auction floors in Harare. By merely watching at these various trading and on the farms, the researcher was able to learn and explore on developing market linkages and production capital accumulation, labour relations, food security which aided analysis and drawing of conclusions. Reliance on observations may disadvantage the research process in that respondents may change behaviour when they realise that they are under observations. This was however mitigated by engaging in repeated observation processes at similar and differing places.

4.5.7 Qualitative data limitations

In Harare, access to key informants from companies involved in tobacco processing and cigarette manufacturing proved significantly challenging. The information is kept with high levels of secrecy due to cut-throat competition in the tobacco business. It was, therefore, very difficult to collect information relating to employment statistics, cost of production, pricing and export amounts and destinations. However, due to the depth of the interviews and the complimentary data secured through the quantitative instruments, sufficient data was captured to enable a full analysis of the issues under research.

4.6 Data Analysis

A structured questionnaire was used to collect pre-coded data while an interview schedule was used during in-depth qualitative interviews by the researcher (see Appendices 1 and 2 respectively). The collected data was then captured using CS pro data package. The data was cleaned to eliminate errors and essure internal consistency through logical checks before transfering into SPSS for analysis. The cleaning process invloved clarifying with respondents where errors in data collection were suspected. The computed database was then organised into forteen sections in relation to the questionnaire, as follows; (a) location and identification details (b) social-economic and demographic data (c) land holding (d) asset ownership and investments (e) land tenure issues (f) land use, agricultural production and food security (g) agricultural inputs (h) agricultural labour (i) agricultural markets (j) food consumptions (k) farmer organisation and networks (l) income and (m) challenges facing the farmers. Qualitative data was coded by the interviewer after collection.

As such, the data collected through the 250 structured questionnaires was analysed using Statistical Package for Social Science (IBM SSPS) Statistics version 20 while frequency tables and bar graphs were developed for presentation of summary statistics to enable cross tabulation for exploration of relationships in the data from the five settlement sectors. The use of Dey's (1993) model of interpreting qualitative data was applied to derive themes. This involves the creation of category sets through a disciplined and systematic approach, by sifting through ideas, assessing their relevance, guided by initial qualitative research and emerging questions. The process of developing category sets for onward data analysis inevitably reflected the type of data being used, aims, inclination and conceptual inclination of the study. The process begins with more 'broad categories and their interconnections' before detailed analysis and refinement through subcategorisation and putting up sets of 'bits of data' from the transcribed data, as Dey (1993: 110) explains. A total of 20 in-depth interviews were carried out. Further analysis of the data involved qualitative interpretation of data through proper coding, description, classification, identification and exploring interconnectedness of themes and concepts (Babbie 1995 and Kitchin and Tate 2000). The analysis of transcribed data was based on pattern matching logic, comparing an 'empirically based pattern with a predicted one' (Yin 2003: 116).

Dey (1993: 232) observes that 'Qualitative data is typically of uneven quality—and hence the importance of taking quality into account'. Neuman (2006) states that reliability and validity are central to establishment of truthfulness, credibility, believability, transferability and confirmability of both quantitative and qualitative research data and outcomes. In his view, reliability refers to dependability and consistency while validity means truthfulness – resembling reality. The challenges in maintaining reliability, efficiency and flexibility of qualitative data is in that the development of few categories which ensures flexibility but results in high efficiency, while too many categories enhance efficiency at the expense of reliability and later flexibility. In Dey's (1993) view, reliability is not simply an empirical issue at all, but a conceptual one as well. To achieve reliability, a care balancing act was carried out and was aided following a crucial procedure in categorizing or linking data, summarizing data, splitting and spicing categories and making connections, following Dey's formulation. Such a procedure ensures that conceptualization closely relates to available data by testing these against a variety of data sources.

According to Dey (1993: 261), validity refers to data analysis 'which can be defended as sound because it is well-grounded conceptually and empirically' based on acceptance of basic cannons governing rational inquiry as a basis for arriving at reasonable conclusions. This study ensured that evidence was not pushed to conform to the researcher's wishes and prejudices and that the possibility of an error was accepted – as such judgment was suspended for as long as possible, different interpretations of the data was considered while refraining from making judgment on rivalry interpretations until it has proven beyond reasonable doubt. This helps in keeping an open mind, allowing for the development of alternative accounts, and consideration of alternative interpretations. Prior to presentation of the qualitative data, the validity of the data was established through peer debriefing and prolonged engagement

(Lincoln and Gobi 1985). With regards to credibility, the research achieved this by ensuring internal coherence of explanations, the empirical scope and completeness of explanations and the practical significance of explanations (see Dey 1993). Member checking also ensure the validity and credibility of the findings.

In the case of quantitative data, triangulation and cross-checking primary data with other secondary sources helped validate collected data. All the research processes were cross-checked by my supervisor who is competent in qualitative and quantitative research methodologies. As for the data which were gathered, the settlement sector settings allow for effective comparison of productivity, capital accumulation and class formation to decode changing agrarian relations and class dynamics in rural Zimbabwe.

4.7 Analytical Approach

4.7.1 Indicators for Classification

As observed by Haroon Akram Lodhi (1993), Lenin's (1964) attempts at classification had emphasised sizes of land holdings, which Haroon Akram-Lodhi (1993: 562) believes 'could shroud important differences in the distribution of productive assets, in the method of production and indeed the purpose of production'. Patnaik (1987) therefore proposes reliance on economic strength where size is just one of the factors considered important. In this regard, Haroon Akram-Lodhi (1993: 563) considers 'area cropped, amount of rented land, number of animals, availability of water, quality of soil, quality of seed and fertilizers, degree of mechanisation and availability and use of labour' as crucial for classification of the farmers. For Lenin (1968; See also Haroon Akram Lodhi 1993: 564), therefore, the three indices for assessing farm class status are the extent of possession of land and other means of production (tempered with for knowledge that land ownership and tenancy does not define class on its own), basis of production (household labour vs non-household labour) and ability to generate surplus to satisfy consumption needs, depreciation and investment. Whereas Patnaik (1987) chooses to apply the basis of production as a tool of analysis, whereupon household status in labour exploitation is the criterion

80

and applying typologies as appropriate classification criterion (see Chart 1), this study will rely on the means of production that considers the cropped area and yield per unit, food security and generation of surplus for consumption, depreciation and re-investment.

CHART 1
PEASANT CLASSES: A TYPOLOGY

Class	E=X/F	Reason	Primary characteristic
Landlord	$E \to \infty$	F=0, X>0 & large	No manual self-employment and large hiring-in of labour.
Rich peasant	$E \geq 1$	F>0, X>0, $X \geq F$	Employ others at least as much as self-employed.
Middle peasant	$1 > E > 0$	F>0, X>0, X<F	Employ others less than self-employed.
Small peasant	$0 \geq E > -1$	F>0, $X \leq 0$, $\|X\| < F$	Others not employed; work for others less than self-employment.
Poor peasant	$E \leq -1$	F>0, X<0, $\|X\| \geq F$	Work for others more than self-employed.
Landless labourer	$E \to -\infty$	F=0, X<0 & large	Work only for others.

Notes: **(E)** is the ratio of net surplus labour appropriated through labour hiring to surplus labour in self-employment, where **(X)** is net labour hired-in through labour markets and **(F)** is agricultural self-employment.
Source: Patnaik [1987].

The study uses the cluster classification methodology, adopts and revises typologies and schemes proposed by Patnaik (1976) which also coincided with those identified by Lenin (1964), Mao (1967), Bardahan (1982) and Roemer (1988). The means of production and ability to generate income are tied to resource endowment which is itself linked to capital resources, either in the form of finance capital, fixed assets, productive assets and the ability to hire labour. All these impact on the area cropped and the yield per unit, which in turn determines the surplus available for consumption, re-investment and to cater for depreciation. This study therefore argues that ultimately capital finance is at the heart of class formation because it enables the acquisition of all other assets that are critical for the productive capacity of the farms. However, as Mast (1996) notes, to establish the capital finance available, the whole range of sources of income and credit must be established, which may be problematic? To go around this, while Patnaik (1987) chooses to rely on labour use to derive the basis of production, this study uses yield per unit area and cropped area for peasant classification. The reasoning behind this approach is that yield per unit is a derivative of resource endowment, labour regime, and access to capital, as such, it is all-encompassing.

This study reveals farmers' views on the issues impacting on productivity and accumulations, and these included sources of finance (access to credit, contract farming, non-farm and off-farm income, diaspora and local remittances, personal savings from outside agriculture, government support, working capital, access to green revolution inputs such as fertilizers, chemicals and certified seed, land access, utilisation and security, draught power (ownership of cattle and tractors), drought and access to commodity markets, food security, labour utilisation and agricultural productivity and surplus attainment. The statistical clustering methodology streamlines these variables, a process which enables confirmation of the importance of the identified variable for clustering analysis. The clustering analysis or segmentation analysis is an explorative analysis applied to identify structures and classes within the data.

Cluster analysis therefore seeks to identify homogenous groups of cases –which we refer to as classes- among the study respondents. Moyo et al. (2009) applied cluster analysis in the AIAS Interdistrict Survey carried out in 2005/6 although prior to applying the cluster classification methodology, households were requested to describe the classes that they perceived to exist in the six districts surveyed and these were proffered as summarised in Table 4-3. This study relied on the statistical clustering approach for classification relying on revealed evidence on sources of income, agriclutural productivity and capital accumulation patterns established on the households in Hwedza Didtrict, but will also apply findings from other contemporary studies in post 2000 Zimbabwe. The clustering aanalysis or segmentation analysis is an explorative analysis applied

82

to identify structures within the data. Cluster analysis therefore seeks to identify homogenous groups of cases among the study respondents. In this sequence, factor analysis is used to reduce the dimensions and the number of variables, minimizing multicollinearity effects, whereas the cluster analysis identifies the groups and the discriminant analysis, through tests of the significance, verifies the correctness of the model developed by the cluster analysis.

Table 4-3: Description of Farmer Classes According to the Beneficiaries

Distinguishing attribute	Distribution of class in community		
	Low class	Middle class	High class
Land	Have small plots	Large plots	Big plots>20ha
Livestock	Have no or very few cattle (2), Have 0-2 goats, Have poultry, Little draught power	Have some cattle, Have draught power	Have herd of over 40 cattle, Have draught power
Housing	Poor housing, Dagga houses and huts,	Good houses, Flat houses	Asbestos roofed houses, Decent accommodation
Farm equipment	No farming equipment, No irrigation equipment, Have few hand tools and depends on borrowing	Have few farming equipment and machinery, Have few irrigation equipment, Have average farm tools	Have irrigation equipment, Own tractor and tractor drawn implements, Have hand tools
Access to capital	Lack finance, Limited sources of income, Poor	Have average farm capital, but still needs assistance, Have some money to hire equipment.	Earn forex and own companies, Finance from high salary, Saves money
Ability to hire labor	No hired labor force, Resource-poor.	Medium hired labor force	High production and can hire a lot of labor,
Food security	Doesn't produce enough to meet households needs, Buys food throughout the season.	Produce food for consumption, Don't have excess output to sell,	Produce enough for the household, Have surplus food to market
Household assets	No shoes and don't have decent clothing	Decent clothing, Few have cars,	Have cars
Social relations and habits	Attend church services during weekends, Always drinking beer, Belong to traditional and church groups, Political party supporters	Always drink beer, Participates in politics, Church groups and services,	Drink clear beer; Attend church services and hold own meetings, Members of parliament

Source: AIAS Household Baseline Survey (2005/06)

To establish the link between access to capital and resources to emerging classes, factor, cluster and regression analysis were carried out to aid data analysis and establish emerging classes.

4.7.2 The Two-Step Clustering Analysis

This study relies on the SPSS Two-step cluster analysis. Broadly, of the three methodologies that can be used to establish class formation relying on the Marxist class analysis, which Patnaik (1988) notes; resource endowment; nature of labour utilization, and surplus appropriation, this study preferred to use the nature of labour utilization, after applying conscious reductionism. Maast (1996) applies surplus appropriation (total cash income) to derive stratas in rural Zimbabwe on the basis that the '*level of cash income* is the most important single factor stimulating peasant differentiation, since it determines not only the households' scope for consumption and non-agricultural investments, but also their capacity to utilize their agricultural land productively'. Mueller (2011) also proffers this methodology as an option for class analysis, among others. Adjustment is then made for differing household levels and differences in household's levels of subsistence production. Detailed analytical procedures and methodologies are applied in Chapter 11, where capital accumulation and class formation are fully revealed, suffice to note at this stage that this study will borrow and apply the approach advanced by Patnaik (1988), Mueller (2011) and Maast (1996), with some amendments.

The SPSS package applies three classification methods, the K-means, hierachical and the TwoStep cluster methods. This study applies the Two-Step cluster method which combines the first two methods. Based on literature review and on-site data gathered and analysed in this study (multionomial logistic regression analysis), indicators were established and applied. The Two-Step clustering technique allows for both auto-selection and presetting of the number of clusters, either using the log likelihood which relies on chi-square with degrees of freedom. The Two-Step clustering method also applies Akaike's Information Criterion (AIC), on the complete data, encompassing 230 respondents from the five study areas located in Hwedza's five setlement models and is repeated on selected data for each settlement model to establish sectoral membership composition within each cluster. For each settlement model, the two-step clustering processes identify the key indicators and these differ per cluster, as is fully demonstrated in the followings sections.

4.7.3 Factor Analysis

Factor analysis is used to summarise and uncover patterns in a set of multivariate data by reducing the complexity of the data (Landau and Everitt 2004). Factor analysis or exploratory factor analysis is 'concerned with whether the covariance or correlations betweena set of observed variables can be explained in terms of a smaller number of unobservable constructs known either as *latent variables* or *common factors*' (Landau and Everitt 2004, 289). The analysis involves establishing the number of common factors required to describe correlation between observed variables and estimating how each is related to each observed variable and trying to simplify the initial solution through a process called factor rotation. The process can be handled through SPSS, in which case the SPSS cluster analysis process can rank the inputed indicators according to importance, allowing for the inclusion and exclusion of some factors. The Two-Step cluster analsysis provides scope for ranking indicators/variables according to their importance. This study also adopted the multinomial logistic regression analysis and analysis of variance (ANOVA) processes to establish the significance of the variables to be applied in class analysis, as shall be fully revealed below.

4.8 Conclusion

This chapter presented the methodological framework for the study. The design of the study, background of the study area, sampling approach and the data collection procedures were described. A justification for the study approach was also made, while data coding and analysis processes and procedures were explained. The analytic framework was presented, in brief. The next chapter discusses the study area's socio-economic history, with special focus on tobacco production.

Chapter Five

Agricultural Development (1890-1980)

5.1 Introduction

This chapter provides a historical assessment of the development of agriculture from settler agriculture to independence and assesses the changing roles of capital and the state within the context of changing agrarian relations, focusing on how this has impacted on class formation among the smallholder farmers for over a century and a decade, beginning with the period immediately before the arrival of Rhodes and the pioneer column in 1890. This historicity will show how capital has remained inserted in rural and agrarian change, with short and intermittant periods of stoppages, interchangeably in coalition and confrontation with the State (see Arrighi 1973). Capital has both impacted upon accumulation processes and has been impacted upon by the same processes; through differentiated access to finance: credit, contract farming, state support, remittances and through income from the sale of agricultural commodities.

The argument presented in this chapter is that colonialism brought about suppression and domination of the African peasantry through primitive dispossession of land and capability as the colonial State represented by capital, in the form of the chartered companies such as the British South African Company (BSAC) as set out by Rhodes (Palmer 1977; Phimister 1986), sought to adavnce their imperial interests. The chapter examines the changing roles of capital and the changing state policy in the context of peasantisation of the Africans before their proletarianisation as wage workers for white commercial farmers, commerce and industry. This chapter therefore examines the processes of peasantisation and proletarianisation and reveals how the state and capital have interfaced, thereby impacting on the peasantry during the pre-independence period.

5.2 Evolving State-Capital Complex under Colonialism

The convoluted and interlocked state-capital complex remained emmensed in the land question ever since 1888. Cecil Rhodes recognised the need to make money to advance his political schemes in Southern Africa, and therefore proceeded to register a company charged with mining diamonds and 'acquisition by concession, grant, purchase, barter, lease, licenses or otherwise, of any tracts of country in Africa or elsewhere and the expenditure of moneys on railways, telegraphs, wharfs and harbours' in March 1888 (Rhodesian Authority 1920). However, effectively, the role of capital in land dispossession became elaborate by 1892. Besides correcting crises of accumulation in the United Kingdom (Bond 1998), geopolitical and capital interests also undergirded Rhodes' occupation of Southern Rhodesia. As Selby (2006: 34) observes, Southern Rhodesia was occupied as a commercial enterprise within Rhodes' wider imperial vision, in which mineral resources were expected to finance an extension of the British Empire'. The discovery of gold would have secured a power balance with Afrikaners control of the Witwatersrand while that of diamonds would have ensured De Beers' monopoly, with agriculture playing only a secondary role.

Pursuant to this, the arrival of the Pioneer Column and the conquest of the black indigenous people (Cheater 1984), pursuant to the Berlin Conference of 1884 gave an impetus to the 'alienation of land to European settlers as their exclusive private property' (Tshuma 1997, 13). The concrete starting point was when Rhodes secured a Royal Charter for the BSAC on 12 September 1890, as it enabled him to administer Mashonaland, with the main purpose being to 'make money and lose no time about it' (Palmer 1977 citing the Bulawayo Sketch Plan dated 20 July 1895). The proposed objects of the occupation were to encourgage development through extending the railways and telegraph inftastructure northwards in the direction of the Zambezi, encourage emigration and colonisation, promote trade and commerce and to develop and work mineral and other concessions (Tshuma 1997). In pursuance thereof, the signing of the Lobengula Treaty and the Rudd Concession, later on to be signed by the imperial powers as well, transferred ownership of all metals and minerals to the BSAC.

For Bond (1998: 30) and Lenin (1986: 75), relying on Rhodes' utterances of 1895, the United Kingdom needed to acquire lands to settle the surplus population in colonial states to avoid a bloody civil war and to provide new markets for commodities produced in factories and mines. In light of this, the Chartered Company purchased the Edouard Lippert Land Concession sold to him by Lobengula in 1891 through a 'defective and fraudulent' process (Tshuma 1997: 15). The concession granted the company the 'sole and exclusive right, power, and privilege for the full of 100 years to lay out, grant, or lease farms, townships, building plots and grazing areas; to impose and levy rents, licenses and taxes thereon, and to get in, collect and receive the same for his benefit, to grant certificates for occupation of any farm, townships, building plots and grazing areas' (Tshuma 1997: 15; Palmer 1977: 27). The concession heralded the Capital-State convolution aimed at advancing white settler political and economic interests.

In essence therefore, as observed by many scholars, the search for gold and other mineral reserves in the last decade of the nineteenth century was a precursor to land dispossession, alienation, domination and repression of the indigenous people by settler capital (Mamdani, 1996; Alexander, 2006). However, the BSAC overestimated the mineral reserves in the country and ended up overcommitting developmental resources in the construction of railways (Loney 1975). The Charter Company subsequently conveniently and wrongfully deemed Lobengula to be the sovereign authority over land comprising Matebeleland and Mashonaland (Tshuma 1997). This allowed Rhodes political and economic control over both Matebeleland and Mashonaland, deceitfully taking over from traditional leadership in the country. Yet, the absolute limit of the Ndebele state were in fact the Zambezi in the North-West, the Hunyani in the North east, and the Mutilikwe in the east-north of the Sabi as the Europeans and the Ndebele themselves often claimed (Palmer 1977).

Even though challenges around the 'sovereign authority' technicalities emerged prior to the invasion of Mashonaland in 1889, the settlers ignored these on the pretext that Queen Victoria had by 1888, already 'recognised Lobengula as the sovereign on both peoples' (Tshuma 1997: 14). Consequently, as Cheater (1984: 1) asserts, 'individual members of the Pioneer Column claimed large tracts of potential farming land promised to them by Rhodes, while a chartered company, BSAC laid general claim to both mineral and land rights in Mashonaland and Matabeleland, in terms of the Rudd and Lippert Concessions'. However, many of these settlers ended up selling their land for as low as £100 each to speculators such as Frank Jonson and John Willoughby as they marched to Salisbury by 1891 (Tshuma 1977). Besides, a large amount of land was parcelled to larger companies such as Willoughby consolidated, as the BSAC sought to raise capital (Tshuma 1997) for subsequent investment in mining and farming.

As a result, 'more than half of all pioneer land rights were owned by speculators', many of whom were 'connected to the British aristocracy and floated land companies in London, generating an estimated £20 million of speculative capital by 1896' (Selby 2006: 32-33). Furthermore, 'by 1899 more than half of the alienated 16 million acres was owned by companies' (Palmer 1977: 36; see also Figure 5-1).

Figure 5-1: Large Companies Land Ownership and Use by 1899-1926

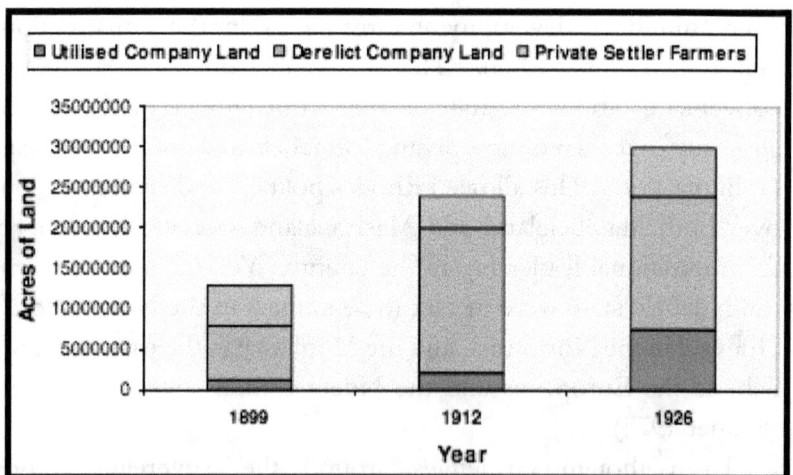

Source: **Palmer (1977: 36 and 86; Rukuni (1994); Selby (2006)**

As soon as the Company realised that both Mashonaland and Matebeleland did not have the 'Second Rand', following the striking of a refractory sulphide zone that made it more expensive to extract gold, frustration set in and 'both the Company and the settlers turned to looting the Shona and Ndebele economies' (Phimister 1988a: 16; see also Tshuma 1997). Arrighi (1967: 36) puts it more succinctly; 'The desire to recover the original heavy outlays induced the Chartered Company to foster the formation of a white rural bourgeoisie' and reckoned this could be achieved though developing the country and raising the value of its assets (the railway system, the mine claims, and land) in Rhodesia.

Bond (1998: 31) also observed that 'Once the mistake was realised in 1894, Rhodes resorted to rampant looting, and ordered the conquered people of Matabeleland and Mashonaland to surrender as many as 200,000 cattle outright, to pay taxes (in the form of crops, cattle and goats), and to submit to forced labour.' In the case of Insiza District in Matebeleland, as Alexander (2006: 18) reveals, by 1893, the Company had established 60 000 claims of mines, looted cattle and forced conscription of labour. Whereas Phimister (1988) suggests that the parceling of land was partly in reward to BSAC settler workers who were becoming redundant and companies that were suddenly finding themselves out of business due to poor economic performance, the net result was that such alienation of land dispossessed Africans of their land. Indigenous Africans either ended up with decreased and inadequate land or they, together with their chiefs, were forced to 'squatter' on land that once belonged to their forefathers (Cheater 1984).

As Selby (2006) puts it 'the impact of colonial occupation on land rights and access for blacks was significant'. According to Tshuma (1997: 1), the 'alienation of most of the fertile land to European settlers and the adoption of discriminatory agricultural policies resulted in oppression, marginalisation and impoverishment of indigenous producers'. Land alienation and the creation of private property in favour of settlers, which was juxtaposed with the restructuring of land tenure systems of indigenous people led to the enhancement of 'colonial accumulation' processes and deprivation of the Africans.

In spite of the clauses inserted in the Charter to guard against introduction of discriminatory legislation, settler farmers successfully campaigned for the imposition of segregationist policies, including elimination of competition from African producers (Tshuma 1997). Settlers also questioned the 'right of Africans to acquire, hold, encumber and dispose land of the same conditions as the Europeans and demanded division of the colony into separate white and black areas' (Tshuma 1997: 17). The period from 1891 to 1896 was dominated by land alienations through various invasions in Matebeleland and Mashonaland, by the settlers. The invasions were subsequently aided and consolidated by the Native Reserve Commission of 1914/5 which designated the fertile 'white highlands' to the settlers and confined blacks to marginal areas (Palmer 1977). This land ownership model overwhelmingly shaped the pattern of political and economic development henceforth (Selby 2006: 33). For the period up to 1923 when a colony state was established through a referendum, the BSAC became both the state and capital and ensured that accumulation favoured its interests. In any event, the settler authorities from 1923 perpetuated and consolidated subjugating and segregatory policies in favour of settler capital during the entire period of the colonialism, eventually attracting the war of liberation from the black Africans in Zimbabwe, as the next sections will reveal.

5.3 Agricultural Financing under Colonialism

An important aspect on the role of capital in imperial capital accumulation was raised by Bond (1998: 42) when he asked; Was the relationship between finance and imperial accumulation accidental ('conjunctural') or structurally-determined ('organic')? Rhodes was clear on this matter, as he retorted, 'If we get Mashonaland, we shall get the balance of Africa' (see Bond 1998: 30). For some scholars, geopolitical interests (Bond 1998) and capital interests (Phimister 1977) undergirded settler and international capital effort, setting the path for native social and economic domination in pre-independence Zimbabwe. It is crucial to track capital insertion into rural Southern Rhodesia during the colonial period to uncover its role in rural accumulation over that period. In the case of Southern Rhodesia, as

Bond (1998: 40) noted, 'geographical and sectoral flows of finance would play first accommodating, then determining, then rigourously delimited, roles in this process if uneven development'.

Yet settler farming only emerged as the BSAC directors turned to agriculture in response to failed mining in 1907 before subsequently turning to speculation, through the lunching of an official 'white agricultural policy' (Tshuma 1997: 23). This shift in interest resulted in changed priorities, with the company expanding farming interests from 1907. Agricultural finance is one area that reflects the changed settler capitalist priorities. As Bond (1998) noted, the 'control of space passed from merchants, miners and farmers into the hands of foreign capital, landed speculators and financiers' while at the global level, the flows of capital finance were backed and often heightened the numerous processes at the domestic level. To this end, as some scholars (Rubert 1998; Palmer 1977 citing National Archives of Zimbabwe records (CNC, 3 September 1926), observe that the government set up a Land Bank which was capitalised to the tune of £250 000 in 1912. However, as Bond (1998: 34) notes, spatial capitalist expansion avoided rural areas. In any event, financiers such as the Standard Chartered Bank and the Land Bank were generally reluctant to extend agricultural credit on a medium and long term basis. According to van Onselen (1976: 41-2), 'commercial agriculture was sufficiently profitable to draw capital previously employed in mining' by 1912, while after this time, 'most of the mines' food requirements were met by European commercial agriculture'.

Bond (1998: 42) captures this conjectural moment when he observes that finance was at the switch point of the various circuits of local capital accumulation and poses a critical question 'Was the relationship between finance and imperial accumulation accidental ('conjunctural') or structurally-determined ('organic')?' The infusion of international capital into Southern Rhodesia established uneven spatial and sectoral development and a sustained accumulation favoured the imported bourgeoisie which was undergirded by BSAC administrative rights granted to them by the British government from 1890 to 1923 (Bond 1998: 34-35). In this regard, as Selby (2006: 43) noted, 'The 1923 referendum on responsible government has been seen as a different opinion between land speculators and mining companies (promoting union with South Africa) and settler farmers and traders (calling for autonomy'. Tobacco growers also supported a self-government on the basis that it would further their European market, following their disagreements with the South African based United Tobacco Company (UTC) in the 1921/22 season, even though others differed (Selby 2006: 44). In essence, therefore, the 23 October 1923 power shift to self-government had economic interests considerations at the core and, as such, the administration set up was tailored to advance capital for the sectoral interests of farmers, emerging imported bourgeoisie, larger landholding speculators and the BSAC.

With regards to the relations between the state and the white-settler farmers, the formation of the Rhodesian Tobacco Association (RTA) in 1929 completed an equation where 'Commercial agriculture had achieved its hold on the state, whilst the settler state secured its hold on the farmers through control and regulation', and indeed, the 'mutual strenghtening between the settler farmer institutions and the state continued for decades to come' (Selby 2006: 47-48). As a result, as Selby puts it, 'Every Rhodesian Prime Minister after Coglan was a farmer and during the first decades of self-government and most MPs were graduates of farming politics' (Selby 2006: 49-50). These farmer MPs and Prime Ministers started pushing for what Hodder Williams (1983: 226) concluded was 'the racially discriminatory legislation of the 1930s [which] owed as much to economic requirements as to racial bigotry', in support of white settler producers, undermining black producers.

Bond (1998: 41) also concludes that banks' involvement in provision of currency, savings and other roles (as will be elaborated below) impacted negatively resulting in uneven spatial development in Southern Rhodesia. To begin with, in the early 1910s, Standard (and later Barclays) had established a wide branch network which provided bills of exchange — and thus stimulated much broader economic activity — for various small trading posts and mining centres, the branch networks were expanded to other mining towns during the 1930s. In the second place, Bond (1998) notes that the colony's 1933 purchase of the BSAC mineral rights was supported by a £2 million overdraft from Standard Bank, a first clear indication of what was to emerge as a symbiotic financing relationship with the local State. Thirdly, the banks assisted in the establishment of a monetary system, initially based on their own notes and then through supporting a new local currency in the late 1930s. As Bond (1998) observes, Southern Rhodesia was forced to maintain 100% foreign exchange cover for its local currency in London, using accounts at Standard and Barclays, which in practical terms meant that financial considerations now more directly shaped uneven development at the British colonial scale.

The banks were involved in the financing of long term State debt and supplying money as a means of payment, accentuating business successes and failures, even though this was terminated by 1930 (Bond 1998: 42). As such, 'as the Southern Rhodesian economy matured during subsequent decades, geographical and sectoral flows of finance would play; first accommodating, then determining, then rigorously delimited, roles in this process of uneven development' as finance capital linked to multinational corporations rose in its prominence, with increasing specultive impulses (Bond 1998: 43). Notwithstanding the surge in financial importance, the world system's uneven development was to be witnessed during the 1930s-40s as the two banks operating in Southern Rhodesia responded to the war situation and the quest to make profits by exporting increasingly more 'excess reserves' from peripheral Southern Rhodesia to their London Headquarters in the centre, as noted by Barber (1961: 166-167).

As Bond (1998) observes, in 1936, the two banks (Standard and Barclays) held just 50% of their assets in local short-term credit for trade purposes, which declined to 41% in 1940 and 20% in 1945 even though local deposits increased from £8 million to £22 million over the same period. Consequent to this, the amount of funds that accumulated in London increased from 49% in 1939 to 74% in 1945, reaching an amount of £16.5 million. The wartime instability inhibited the banks from engaging in the scarce opportunities that existed at the time, as observed by the Central Statistical Office (CSO) (1947: 9). The situation was reversed such that in the 1950s, 'two-thirds of the total domestic investments of nearly £300 million during those years was derived from international sources', including the World Bank whose fund stood at US$140 million partly lent towards Kariba dam construction at a total construction cost of £114 million, the Rhodesian railways and the implementation of the Land Husbandry Act of 1951 which brought about another threat to the balance of payments in the form of loan repayments' (Bond 1998: 56).

According to Stoneman (1981), available credit was mostly directed towards white farmers such that at the end of the Second World War, 'short-term credit to 6200 white farmers exceeded $R150 million, whereas credit to 685 000 black farmers barely exceed $R1 million' resulting in white farmers increasing their share of marketed crops from 30% in 1960 to 75% in 1978. Similarly, the average real earning for black farmers decreased by at least 40% between 1948 and 1970, even though other factors such as overpopulation, land degradation, overgrazing and economic marginalization came into play (Riddell 1978a). Moyo and Nyoni (2013) sum this up, positing that Rhodesia's agricultural transformation strategy entailed state support targeted at large- scale white settler farming with an average land size of 2,000 hectares; some foreign and some domestic estates, holding well above 5,000 hectares of land. As Rukuni *et al.* (2006) observes, state support to large-scale irrigated estates through constriction of essential infrastructure such as dams, rural electrification among others, aided the white capital progress (see Stoneman 1988). The government proceeded to create state-owned farm estates, including through the Agricultural and Rural Development Authority (ARDA), which took over from the Tribal Trust Lands Development Authority and the Cold Storage Commission (CSC), among other parastatals by 1970.

According to Chimedza (1994), the successive colonial government ensured the exclusion of majority of the rural population in favour of the LSCFs. A variety of schemes and programs were developed in support of this policy. To begin with, a Land Bank was established in 1924 which eventually became the Agricultural Finance Corporation (AFC) in 1978; the establishment of plot holders in the 1930s, before its expansion into drylands in 1956; the establishment of the Agricultural Loan Fund in 1964; the use of agricultural service cooperatives and the extension of medium-term and long-term loans from 1945 to 1968 all ensured biased facilitation of economic development for the whites. For Bond (1998), therefore, in cases where the credits were extended to the rural peasantry, the 'availability of credit assists in drawing small farmers into tightly-structured capitalist markets, and therefore credit programmes will invariably emerge from the state, development agencies and capitalist interests (even if vast market distortions, high interest rates and the like subsequently force out the least productive of these farmers)', and subsequently African farmers were either left out or they ended up being squeezed by credits, undermining their capital accumulation trajectory. According to Chimedza (1994), however, real effort at incorporation of the farmers in the communal areas was initiated in 1979 in response to the changing political environment.

5.4 Agricultural Productivity and Peasant Colonial Subjugation

There is vast literature on the advent of capitalism upon the arrival of settlers, the invasion of both Matabeleland and Mashonaland provinces, their impact on the stimulation of peasantisation and subsequently its suppression through undermining peasantry productivity and accumulation capabilities in Southern Rhodesia. Although different sub-regions in Africa have peculiar historicity of the agrarian question, the Sub-Saharan Africa situation has mainly been that of injustices associated with land alienation and its consequences of domination and oppression on the nationalities. Some scholars (Mamdani 1987; Neocosmos 1993) argue that the Sub-Saharan Africa agrarian question has not been mediated by economic and legal issues of ownership; instead, it is essentially concerned about 'oppressive relations between the state and the peasantry' where social domination and exploitation are unmediated and are experienced as state domination and exploitation of agricultural producers through extra economic methods such as extraction of surplus through marketing boards. This is in sync with our own observations that the state-capital matrix is viewed as both a complicated and interlocked coalition working against the peasantry.

The 'White Agricultural Policy' defined the agricultural production pattern for the colonial period in Southern Rhodesia. The policy was promoted during a tour of the BSAC directors in 1907 who decided that it was time to end the myth of the 'Second Rand' by diversifying from minerals and by encouraging European farming (Palmer 1977). As the author elaborates, the company began to develop an interest in the production of tobacco, citrus and ranching, which was carried out at central farms established in many parts of the country. Whereas European farmers were opposed to the emergence of an African landowning class of commercial farmers, as the writer argues, agricultural production patterns are dependent on access to productive land among other factors. This author therefore, argues that the starting point was to dispossess the Africans of more productive lands and take over the production of the key crops. However, a compromise was reached resulting in the Land Apportionment Act (LPA) of 1930, setting aside 7.5 million acres of land under the Native Purchase Areas (NPA) where only Africans could buy the land.

As Phimister (1986) notes, on their own, Africans were also progressing well and were quick to take advantage of emerging opportunities in producing and marketing their produce and were willing and able to pay rents for alienated land in areas with ideal natural farming ecological conditions, but great effort was made to undermine this for social and economic reasons, by rural bourgeoisies, using acquired economic and political powers. However, African farmers made great progress following the end of the first uprising as they were freed from war and focused on agricultural production (Palmer 1977). As the author noted, another rise was noted during the First World War period as Africans were able to sell crop produce and cattle at rising prices. Palmer notes that Africans sold 198,000 bags of maize at 10 shillings per bag in 1920, 20,000 head of cattle at £7 to £8 each but their position in the Rhodesian economy changed dramatically for the worse from 1920 as they only sold 43,600 bags of maize at 5 shillings per bag in 1921 resulting in a drop in income from £100,000 to £10,000. They were unable to sell any cattle at all, as Palmer (1977) observes. With regards to total agricultural sales during the period from 1965 to 1980, a steady increase in all the sectors, even though the AC sector secured less volumes, AS Table 5.1 reveals.

However, such efforts to undermine the success of the Africans were not without resistance. As Palmer (1977: 235) observes, the intended domination of Africans by the European settlers continued to be undermined by an 'old Cape clause introduced in Rhodesia at the insistence of the British in 1894' which stipulated that 'A native may acquire, hold, encumber and dispose of land on the same conditions as a person who is not a native'. The effect of this clause was to slow down settler domination. Coincidentally, the settlers were not vehemently opposed to this clause, and knew that 'wholesale segregation of the natives was an impossible proposition, because it would affect the labour supply and labour was essential for the development of the country' (Palmer 1977: 235). The resilience by Africans in agricultural production meant that more tools had to be deployed in a bid to undermine progress among Africans.

In the early settlement period, European farmers' agriculture remained hugely subsistence with many of them cultivating as little as 6 acres, in the period before the turn of the century (Arrighi 1970). European settler-farmers agricultural production rose under the 'White agricultural policy' and was only affected by the First World War (FWW) as many of the settlers were on active service but a post-war boom was experienced when the war ended, and the new settler government took keen interest in advancing agriculture from 1923 onwards (Palmer 1977). However, there was an increase in the number of European farmers from 324 in 1911 to 2355 in 1921 and increased government financial support from £33,468 during the period from 1918-19 to 1922-23 to £75,636 in the period 1923-24 to 1928 -29, as Palmer (1977) further observes. Maize, tobacco and cattle farming dominated European agriculture, even though maize production fluctuated by a huge margin. An enormous increase of European-owned cattle from 394,856 in 1915 to 1,006,086 in 1925 compared favourably with an increase in African owned cattle, which rose from 445,795 to 1,095,841 during the same period, resulting in intensified racial competition for grazing lands (Palmer 1977, 146).

Table 5-1: Sectoral Agricultural Sales (1965 -1980)

Year	LSCF and SSCF Sectors Z$ Million	Communal Sector Z$ Million
1965	98.1	2.3
1966	83.7	3.9
1967	87.4	5.4
1968	64.9	1.3
1969	92.0	5.0
1970	80.9	2.7
1971	106.1	6.1
1972	129.5	12.6
1973	124.9	8.2
1974	200.4	15.3
1975	224.2	14.2
1976	225.4	18.2
1977	228.6	15.6
1978	237.0	17.1
1979	249.2	12.2
1980	350.0	22.2

Source: Sachikonye (1989) from CSO

The total contribution to agricultural sales per sector shows that from 1965 to 1980, LSCF and SSCF sales increased from Z$98.1 million to Z$350 million while the Communal sector increased from Z$2.3 million to Z$22.2 million (Sachikonye 1989). However, over the 15-year period, the communal sector never rose beyond 8% of total agricultural sales. The obvious stage from which to undermine Africans was one at which the produce was being marketed. The LSCF and the SSCF made the biggest contribution to agricultural crop sales except in commodities such as groundnuts, sunflower and oriental tobacco, ensuring that capitalist agrarian sector maintained the overall strength of the sector through its export capacity and food self-sufficiency.

5.5 Marketing of Agricultural Produce

African peasants progressed well in the post war period of 1896 to 1908 due to favourable marketing conditions. However, according to Tshuma (1997: 230), the period beginning the first decade of the first century saw the colonial government implementing agricultural marketing policies that favoured settler agriculture. As Palmer (1977: 195) noted, the policies were 'aimed at establishing white hegemony across the economy' and promoting settler accumulation by limiting the competitiveness of African agriculture. Settler agriculture benefitted from government subsidies and cheap labour from the Africans. The settlers were given agricultural support to entice them into farming while limiting indigenous peasants' competitiveness. As such, it is in the marketing of the produce that Europeans ensured Africans' effort was curbed the most. Having replaced Africans as the major producers of tobacco, maize and cattle, the settlers using both political and capital power went on to undermine the pricing of the produce.

As Moyana (1984: 15) explains, the Grain Marketing Board (GMB) bought produce from Africans at lower prices than that for European commodities. One of the reasons given was that it is not possible for Africans to produce grain of the same quality as that of the Europeans because they (Africans) are settled in poor ecological regions. As the writer observes, the GMB levied maize to reduce income for the Africans, by reducing the purchase price and income accruing to the African farmers even though the quality of produce would have been as good. The colonial government also enacted the Maize Control Act (MCA) of 1931 amended in 1934, which 'undermined the terms of trade for producers in favour of settler agriculture accumulation by imposition of taxes on African producers to subsidize settler farmers' (see Mosley 1984). The policy created two pools for the purchase of grain, with one for the white farmers at 40% higher than world market prices, less export costs (Rukuni 1994: 23; Selby 2006: 50). The 1930 (LAA) became the *Magna Carta* for the Europeans as it guaranteed the previledged status and blocked Africans advancement through exclusion from the highveld and agricultural markets and forcing it into proletarianism. The marketing

101

system extracted surplus of peasant labour through the purchase of their produce at low prices by the state.

Financial power was also asserted at a microeconomic scale as a means to sustain cheap labour supplies, itself achieved through a repressive compound system based on workers debt trap to the farm and mine store for basic needs such as food and clothes (see Van Onselen 1976: 162 -166). The LAA institutionalised the dualistic agricultural system in which, as Brand (1981: 54) noted, the 'white had a floor which they couldn't drop through while blacks had a ceiling which they could not exceed'. Phimister (1977: 260) elaborates on the problems related to marketing mechanisms involving traders who were dotted in many parts of the country, which, while making markets more accessible to the peasants, created yet other challenges in that the traders began to control the whole process from availing credits, supplying inputs to purchasing the produce and becoming vendors of consumption goods. The use of levies on maize and cattle sales and indeed other approaches, such as the use of these Trade Stores to buy grains at lower and non-economic prices and at times through goods exchange, angered Africans. The Native Commissioner (NC) for Mazowe reports of one European who retorted, on 12 July 1934, that 'Never before during my 30 years service in this department have I heard natives express themselves so strongly or so openly display such spirit of antagonism to any law as they did to the Maize and Cattle Control Levy Acts'.

It is therefore clear that capitalism, as represented by the Trade Stores, reaped off peasants by exploiting the absence of transport to markets, thereby becoming the only source of credit, agricultural inputs and became vendors of consumption goods. Besides, Trading Stores also had the effect of undermining pre-colonial income sources and accumulation processes for Africans as modern goods supplied by the emerging traders, replaced local products produced by the peasants. Phimister (1986: 246) confirms this point when he observed that by 1908, stock-in-trade comprised of 'ploughs, trek-chains, yokes and skeys, plough-shares, hoes and picks, carpenters' tools, cooking utensils, enamelware, crockery, boots and shoes, ready-made clothing of all descriptions, hats, shirts, drapery, coffee, tea, jams, sugar, salt, flour, candles [and] paraffin', which had the effect of replacing locally produced goods. In any event, the accumulation trajectory of the Africans was further undermined by the fact that Africans were deliberately settled further away from the railway stations, only 30 in every hundred 'of the land assigned to Africans, as against 75% of that alienated to Europeans ... was within 25 miles of a railway' (Arrighi 1970).

Selby (2006) observes that economic self-interest also influenced the white farmers' response to the Unilateral Declaration of Independence (UDI)-linked sanctions threat and as a result, the tobacco industry (tobacco buying companies and mostly international capital) were vehemently opposed to its implementation. The imposition of the sanctions by the United Nations (UN) in 1965 resulted in stoppages of tobacco purchases by the UK, Germany and Japan impacting negatively on national revenue as the crop was contributing more than 50% of foreign currency for the country. For Mbanga (1991 cited in Selby 2006), despite reliance on organised cartels of smugglers of the crop to varied destinations, production fell from 100 000ha to 50 000ha and export earnings fell from $75 million to between $25 and $35 million per year, from 1965 to1980. Figure 5-2 shows the related changes in number of farmers growing tobacco and the cropped area for the crop. White farmers were therefore encouraged to diversify into other crops such as maize, cotton and livestock farming, and to cattle, presenting direct competition with the black farmers who were participating in these enterprises, until then. According to Selby (2006: 69), the UDI period also heralded the promulgation of policies targeted at centralising control and protecting key strategic sectors to ensure domestic dominance and protection through state institutions such as the Agricultural Marketing Authority (AMA). This policy was skewed in favour of the white interests, as a result, as Phimister (1988: 8) demonstrates, the burden of UDI was carried by black peasants, as illustrated by 'a subsidy disparity of $8 000 per white farmer versus 60 cents per peasant.'

Figure 5-2: Impact of UDI on Tobbaco farming

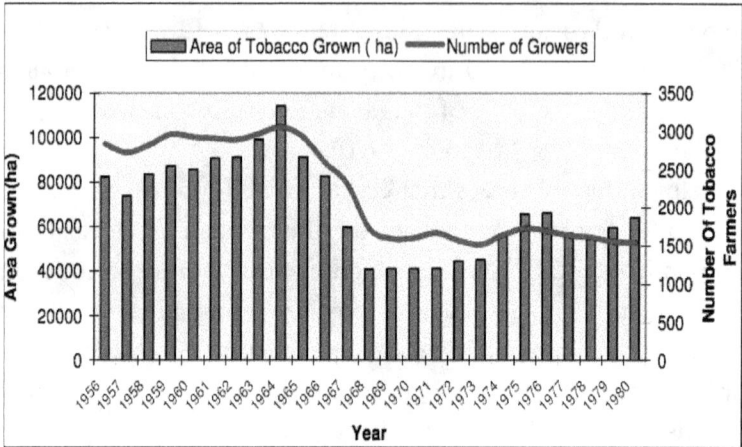

Source: Selby (2006) and TMB

Essentially, a 'long association between international capital and settler colonialism at strategic levels' (Hatendi 1987) only began to faulter during UDI as domestic capital gained prominence and dominance, with Tiny Rowland's Lonrho becoming the 'face of capitalism' (Selby 2006: 70). The undermining of the productivity of the Africans and unequal exchange of agricultural produce ultimately impacted negatively on their accumulation and class formation among them, as shall be fully revealed in the next section.

5.6 Accumulation and Class Formation under Colonialism

Evidence from corpus literature show that the agrarian question in Southern Africa had its origins in accumulation strategies and land policies adopted in most colonial states whereby colonized states ended up integrated into the global economy (Tshuma 1997; Phimister 1977; Palmer 1977; Ranger 1978; Alexander 2006). The state was a productive force in the form of metropolitan capital responsible for 'extraction of surplus value through the purchase of the labour power of migrant workers below its value' (Tshuma, 1997: 24). Even though international capital was keen to uplift Africans and create a market for its domestic agricultural and industrial output, white settlers saw it fit to under-develop Africans by undermining its productive potential, its mining and agricultural potential as a way of advancing its own capitalists interests.

Capital was responsible for only part of the social reproductive needs of the workers' households, with their families responsible for the remaining part of their needs through peasant agriculture under semi-proletariat conditions. More broadly, as Phimister (1977), Bundy (1977) and Arringi (1970) put it, the creation of the African peasantries as well as the differentiation among them was a result of the interaction between an international capitalist economic system and a traditional social economic system. As capitalism further developed, it had begun to eat into the peasantry it first defined and created. To this end, Phimister (1988a: 68) argues that the effect of the various measures adopted by the colonial state on class formation, was mediated by existing pre-colonial processes that were underpinned by already existing commodity exchange in rural areas. For Palmer (1977: 71), peasant farmers in Rhodesia seized opportunities presented to them between the period 1896 to 1908 by venturing into new markets, setting off 'on the high road to prosperity' with more freedom in the post 1895/6 war situation working on the land and selling their produce to the settlers.

However, as Phimister (1986: 241) observes, before the turn of the century, 'The looting carried out by settlers and the British South Africa Company, as well as the devastation caused in the Risings of 1896-97 and by rinderpest, had disturbed and in some cases destroyed patterns of indigenous accumulation, but had not arrested the process of commodity production. On the contrary, it was accelerated both when people tried to recoup their losses and by the proliferation of trading stores throughout the territory'. Zamchiya (2012: 12) agrees with this view and observes that colonialism heightened class formation among the Africans but did not stimulate it. As such, Mtetwa (1975) observes that commodity production and class formation were already in existence in the pre-colonial period, with *vapfumi* (the rich, in Shona language) and *varombo* (the poor) following his research of Duma society. By the turn of the twentieth century, the African large scale agricultural entrepreneurs and traders (*vapfumi or hurudza*, in Shona language), selling their outputs through 'white and Indian traders, farmers and miners', had emerged, demonstrating pre-colonial Zimbabwe's inter-connectedness to international capital and its markets (Cheater 1990; Ranger 1985). Other writers have noted that at the turn of the century, Africans were already regarded as agriculturists... '[who] do not view the prospect of becoming miners with any enthusiasm. Their present occupation ...pays them better and is a more pleasant life' (Phimister 1977: 255). This is collaborated by Phimister (1986: 244) who cites the CNC's memorandum to Private Secretary of the Administrator (1904):

Although administrative measures oppressed all blacks, the processes of differentiation and stratification already well under way in rural areas mediated their impact. Capitalism's uneven development since 1890 had encouraged peasant production to the point where in 1903 Africans received an estimated £485,000 from the sale of grain alone. If other sources of income such as 'the Sale of Hides... and the Sale of Market Produce near the towns', as well as the natural increase in livestock numbers, were counted, their annual aggregate income approached £600,000... By 1904 black cultivators produced over 90 per cent of the country's total marketed output, and as the reconstruction of the mining industry proceeded, so they helped to supply the hundreds of markets, which sprouted across the countryside.

However, some scholars have argued that the collapse of African agricultural economy and the emergence and domination of European settler agriculture began in 1908 with the setting up of the Estates Department whose mandate was to promote European settlement, the reorganisation of the Department of Agriculture and the appointment of the first director of agriculture (Palmer 1977: 232). Because of these initiatives, Europeans overtook Africans in production of key crops, ranching and the growing of citrus. For instance, as argued by Palmer (1977, 232), European settlers had earmarked tobacco to ultimately develop into the pillar of white settler farming and the Rhodesian economy was, just like maize, widely grown by Africans peasants, had been before land alienation. It is further argued that before subjugation of the African peasantry, grain was already traded into the drought-ridden northwest against tobacco exports, and in the central region, the commoditization of iron tools was an important means of capital accumulation, which was mainly represented by livestock. Ranger (1985) confirms that Africans were settling in areas close to transport routes possibly in anticipation of trading opportunities associated with access to markets, which facilitated trading and accumulation from agricultural activities.

A combination of those pockets of pre-colonial accumulation which had survived the violence of the 1890s, and the productive reinvestment of income earned in wage labour, gave rise to a distinctive pattern of rural differentiation. Palmer (1977: 72) made the observation that, 'Indeed, some Shona near Salisbury were at this time employing other Africans as wage labourers for 10/- per month' illustrating an upward mobility. On this basis, in Victoria, 1898 reports by the Civil Commissioner to the BSAC dated 31 March 1898, also cited by Phimister (1986: 245), observed that the natives had done better than the Whiteman and the natives had traded their surplus to their advantage and had also done well in sheep and cattle. Furthermore, the report noted that the demand for food at Selukwe mines had begun to place the whites on the high road to prosperity. The prosperity was collaborated by the Mining Commissioner for Bulawayo who reported on 31 December 1907 that it was beyond doubt that the local natives were getting rich:

> It is beyond doubt that the local native is getting rich, and he sees the day not far distant when he need not work at all. Many have already reached it. One can hardly see the smallest kraal without its accompaniment of a herd of 20 to 50 head of cattle, plus sheep and goats; and I am told that some kraals possess hundreds - up to 600 head of cattle - a good sign so far as the welfare of the native is concerned, but not encouraging from a labour point of view (MB/1/3 1907).

Despite improved contributions by settler agriculture to the economy following a boom in tobacco in the 1940s, the state continued to promote better conditions for settler accumulation by suppressing the African peasants (Tshuma 1997: 24). During the colonial period, tobacco production grew to be a major contributor to industrial growth, employment creation and foreign currency earnings. The BSAC became interested in tobacco production in 1909/10 farming season, producing a total of 132,310lb which increased to 3,061,750lb by 1912/3. However, Shangwe people of Mapfungautse in Gokwe are known to have traded in tobacco with the Ndebele people before 1870. Phimister (1986) cites both Arrighi (1970: 210) and Rennie (1978), who reported the introduction of many instruments which were aimed at undermining Africans, including the following:

The doubling of hut tax in 1904, which lifted the African contribution to state revenues to 41 per cent [*Arrighi*, 1970: 210], was followed by a spate of fresh levies and taxes between 1908 and 1914. All of them, including the Private Locations Ordinance of 1908 and the Kaffir Beer Ordinance of 1912 aimed at closing down peasant options outside of wage labour [*Rennie*, 1978], were designed to increase the flow of labour. In 1909, blacks living on the so-called unalienated land had to pay rent to the Chartered Company, and even higher rents, including grazing fees first imposed in 1912, were exacted from the tenants of private companies and white farmers. Dog tax was introduced in 1912, and two years later an Ordinance made cattle-dipping, at one to two shillings per head.

In other sectors such as mining, it is noteworthy that the discovery of abandoned shafts and pits did not only demonstrate that the ancient had 'picked the eyes' out of the country, but that the Shona people had engaged in mining activities in the pre-colonial period. In essence, therefore, it is the white settlers' agricultural policy that undermined Africans and stimulated peasantisation. Evidence seems to agree with some writers who noted that Africans were making economic progress with significant capital accumulation and differentiation before Europeans instituted mechanisms to derail such progress. However, despite efforts to undermine exertion by the natives, accumulation and differentiation among Africans remained evident in many provinces.

5.7 Conclusion

The arrival of Rhodes and his collaborators signalled the commencement of land alienation, subjugation of Africans and efforts to undermine upward mobility among the indegenous population. Access to credit, markets and introduction of taxes and levies were used as tools to advance European farmers and to undermine the Africans. Nothwithstanding these efforts, the Africans experienced an upward mobility, just as much as they did in the pre-colonial period. Tobacco farming was a major crop for the Africans in the pre-coloonial period, but the Europeans took over from 1907 onwards, leading to the crop becoming a major export crop and source of employment within the agrarian economy and in manufacturing.

Chapter Six

Changing Agrarian Relations, 1980-1999

6.1 Intoduction

The chapter outlines the development of the land and agrarian question from 1980 to1999 and examines agricultural developments from independence to the eve of the FTLRP. The first section of the chapter unpacks the state-capital complex relations and changing agrarian relations/structure from the time of independence to the time of the commencement of the FTLRP in 2000.

6.2 Evolving State-Capital Complex Interface, pre-2000

Whereas the post-independence Zimbabwean economic policies were propagated as a socialist rhetoric, Robert Mugabe's government recognised the existing reality that capitalism was a historical reality which could not be avoided and, as such, had 'to be purposefully harnessed, regulated and transformed as a partner in the overall national endeavour to achieve set national Plan goals' (Robert Mugabe, TNDP, 1983; see also Stoneman 1988: 43). As a result, the 'fairly sophisticated and diversified' economy had an industry that was 'heavily biased to the provision of luxury goods for a small minority and heavily dependent on the skills of the consumers of these goods' (Stoneman 1988: 44). As Moyo (2011) argues, the economy retained a disarticulated pattern of accumulation and as some scholars (Stoneman and Cliff 1989; Yeros 2002) observe, Zimbabwean agriculture remained pivotal and contributed 40% of GDP and exports, employing 70% of the total workforce. At the centre of delayed structural transformation that was aided by the 'willing buyer willing seller' clause in the Lancaster House negotiated constitution were geo-political interests of the United States of America (USA) and South Africans who needed to 'expand their commercial and financial relations' (Moyo 1991: 7). In this instance,

USA capitalist interests were to extend white dominance in the new independent state.

6.3 Post-independence Early Land Reform Programmes

At independence in 1980, the new nationalist government was met with an imperative to decide whether to inherit and perpetuate a situation of total economic dependence where between little or no trickle down and compensation for most of the masses was the order of the day or to confront international capital head-on (Stoneman 1981a), bearing in mind the consequences thereof. This situation was made worse by the incorporation of the 'willing seller, willing buyer' clause in the Lancaster House Constitution, because it reinforced the maintenance of the structural constraints as the Zimbabwe Government was compelled to comply with this provision and therefore retain the economic trade and investment links, including economic aid with the capitalist world (Stoneman 1988). Moyo (1991: 11) therefore opines that, 'The settlement in Zimbabwe resulted in the coming to power of a "socialist" government, which was restrained from major changes by the Lancaster House Agreement'. For Sachikonye (1989), the structures of ownership of the means of production, in the agrarian sector and the broader economy, was left intact.

The structural constraints also ensured that the minority white settlers maintained control of the means of production - most of the productive land, nearly all the mines, and almost all the manufacturing industry and other businesses, making it a point that blacks owned the service industry and its infrastructure, including the railways, roads, hospitals and schools (Stoneman 1988). Essentially, the post-colonial state was not fully restructured and in a sense, became an amalgam of colonial and post-colonial structures, processes and systems as well as that of the social forces which reflected the relative weight of the parties involved in the Lancaster House negotiations (Sachikonye 1989). In this regard, as Moyo (1991) elaborates, the British and Smith regime were quick to initiate a process whereby a radical agrarian reform process would not materialise, coupled with some cosmetic changes in the finance sector and piecemeal access to freehold farmland to some middle-class blacks (of a total of 4 million hectares was involved).

However, the ruling party and government took advantage of an absence of a hegemonic force from below demanding for land and structural transformation and allowed their own sectional interests to shape the agenda, assisted as it was by the notion of gradual transformation and the notion of slow movement towards socialism. This was aided by the strategic intent to avoid attracting opposition, avoid rural 'improvement' (see Cliff 1988), and was also constrained by the conditionalities that underpinned promises of money made at the Zimcord conference held in 1981 (Stoneman 1988; see also Masst 1996). Further constraints underpinning the retention of capitalism emanated from the South African government which leveraged on the possibility of application of direct force and control of trade and investment routes (Stoneman 1988) to secure less radical structural reform post 1980. Other constraining factors included the occurrence of drought in 1982-83, given its political and financial implications for the new government, lack of practical bureaucratic experience, which allowed markets to continue operations with minimum state intervention and shortage of foreign currency (Sachikonye 1989; Stoneman 1988).

However, the constraining conditions were ameliorated slightly in 1986 when the land acquisition modalities were modified, to allow the government the right of refusal to buy land on offer as well as to acquire land deemed to be underutilized. (Stoneman 1988). However, the first two years after independence witnessed spectacular growth in response to the arrival of peace and legitimacy, good rainfall in 1980 and 1981, stimulation of internal demand due to labour wage increases, access to economic aid and international borrowings, high agricultural productivity undergirded by the removal of restrictions and highly guaranteed crop prices (Stoneman 1988). This resulted in industrial growth and a GDP growth of 26% during this period. Nonetheless, by 1987, a capitalist economy and private international capital still drove production in agriculture, mining and industry.

According to Stoneman (ibid), there are two possible explanations to this; on one hand, a radical transformation could not be implemented because the government was in alliance with

113

capitalist elements or the government simply feared early confrontation with imperialism. On another hand, it could be that the government envisaged a two-staged process where it would complete the national democratic revolution (NDR) before pushing towards achieving a socialist stage. However, Sachikonye (1989) posits that in part, the government did not move forward on the land question because there was no systematic conceptualisation of both the nature of the envisaged transition and that of the transformation sought. Meanwhile, a combination of constitutional constraints and lack of clarity on the definitions of the land question resulted in lack of movement towards a comprehensive agrarian reform. Despite sporadic land occupations in many parts of the country, the need to balance local demands and international pressure ensured stagnation in policy implementation by the post-colonial government. As Sachikonye (1989) observes, local pressure of a diverse set of interest groups whose constellation was also changing, was worsened by escalating economic collapse begging from 1996, and with it, standards of living inevitably began to erode. Table 6-1 shows the different land reform models implemented from 1980, indicating the periodisation, the main charasterics of the land reform model and the type of beneficiaries. The Government of Zimbabwe initially 'purchased 3 million hectares of mostly marginal land from the LSCF, to settle about 52,000 households, constituting 30% of the initial targets' (Moyo 1991: 16) under what is now commonly known as the old resettlement, but this did not make a big mark on the overall conditions of the majority of Zimbabweans who remained outside the high potential areas.

Notwithstanding the expiry in 1990 of some provisions in the Lancaster House Constitution and the passing of the 1992 Land Acquisition Act which enabled compulsory land acquisitions by the government, the land reform policy was largely maintained under the market based approaches from 1980 to 1996. However, the 1992 Act was passed during ESAP, which encouraged renewed land concentration and foreign ownership. Nonetheless, increased pressure for land resulted in various efforts to resettle Zimbabweans, as shown in Table 6-2. These efforts culminated in the constitutional amendment of 2000 and the new Land Acqusition Act of 2000 (Moyo and Matondi 2000).

Table 6-1: Land Reform Models and Land Reform Beneficiaries

Resettlement Model	Period Implemented	Main Characteristics	Types of Beneficiaries
Model A	1980-early 1990s	Individual land allocation of 5ha arable land, 0.5ha for residential and communal grazing	War-displaced, refugees, poor households, war-veterans
Model B	1980-1990	Collective farming based on voluntary group membership Cooperative asset holding and production Collective grazing	War veterans, communal farmers
Model C	1980-1990	Central core estate run by the ARDA (a parastatal) Out-grower farmers, settled in villages as in Model A but also contributing labour to the core estate in return for supplies of essential services (e.g. draught power, transport, marketing, seedlings etc.)	Communal farmers with no clear evidence on their poverty status.
Model D	1984-1990	Availing land for rotational grazing to communal livestock in the drier parts of the country	Communal farmers, with no clear evidence on their poverty status
A1 Self-Contained	1992 to date	Self-contained plots for residential, arable and grazing land, with plot sizes of 25-50ha depending on natural region	Master Farmers Agricultural graduates and other skilled and experienced Farmers
A1 Villagised	1992 to current	Continuation of Model A, Villagized settlement with individual arable plots for residential and arable plots, with communal grazing	The poor, war veterans
Commercial Farm Settlement Scheme	1993-1997	Commercial farming units allocated to selected indigenous people with resources and farming experience	Trained and experienced farmers Resourced farmers
A2	1998 to Current	Commercial farming plots/farms with individual land for residential, cropping, grazing and woodlots Beneficiaries expected to utilize own resources	Trained and Experienced Farmers Well resourced Farmers

Source: Summarized from Gonese and Mukora 2003 and various Government documents

Ideological differences within government and the ruling party slowed down the process. Two broad tendencies advocated for different and competing approaches, with some seeing resettlement as a step towards broad social transformation and some seeking the maitenance of the status quo and increasing productivity. Following pressure from powerful War veterans, the government gazzetted 1471 farms in 1997 (Moyo 2000; Moyo 2006: Moyo and Matondi 2000). However, not much progresss was made due to limited consultations. The government then launched wider consultations, leading to the 1998 Donor Conference and the National Land Policy (NLP), and Phase 2 of the Land Redistribution and Resettlement

Programme (LRRP) launched in the same year and the Inception Phase Framework Plan (IPFP) (1999), as a proposed compromise for radical reform advocated by some moderates who preferred the capitalist status to be maintained, with government and the ruling party (Moyo 2000).

Table 6-2: Land Reform Process from 1990-2000

Year	Main Policy	Implications
1990:	• Constitutional Amendments • National Land Policy document	• State revokes the 'willing-seller-willing-buyer' provision • Sets its target of 5 million hectares
1992:	Land Acquisition Act	• New act is passed and allows for the designation of farms for compulsory acquisition, but the processes tended to be lengthy. It was revised 1996
1994:	Land Tenure Commission Report (Rukuni Commission)	Land tenure commission went country-wide soliciting the views of the people Recommendations made and some accepted by cabinet but there was little action in implementing them
1996:	Land Redistribution and Resettlement (Policy Paper)	
1997:	Government Gazette (on the designation of 1,471 farms)	Farms close to 3.2 million hectares gazetted as a way of achieving the 5 million hectares target
1998:	• Land Reform and Resettlement Programme, Phase II • National Land Policy – Framework Paper	• Government launches the Second Phase of Land Reform and Resettlement. Revises the land redistribution models • The National Land Policy document as a follow-up to the Land Tenure Commission is drawn
1999:	Inception Phase Framework Plan: 1999-2000	The plan is accepted by cabinet and government starts implementing it. Complementary approaches derailed by lack of funds
2000:	• Constitutional Amendment (2000) • New Land Acquisition Act (2000) • Accelerated Land Reform and Resettlement Implementation Plan – "Fast Track"	• Land occupations lead to constitutional amendments, done to beat the June elections that would • New act gazetted and farm listing under compulsory land acquisition starts

Source: Moyo and Matondi (2000)

In terms of beneficiaries of the land reform, scholars are generally agreed that the 'welfarist' programme whose objectives were to aid 'reconstruction and stability' (Cusworth 2000) and to meet popular expectations (Alexander 2006) was carried out in a technocratic and transparent manner (Herbst 1990: Zamchiya 2012). As a result, 'most of the beneficiaries of the the first phase of the land reform programme were the needy, landless, unemployed and refugees, mostly from adjacent communal areas (Alexander 2003; 2006; Cusworth 2000; Kinsey 2004; Palmer 1990; Zamchiya 2012). The 2000 Constitutional Referendum occassioned a conjectural moment that ushered in a new thrust of more radical occupations, acquisitions and resettlement, under what has become known as "Fast Track Land Reform Programme" or *jambanja*, albeit under huge domestic and international resistance.

6.4 Agricultural Financing, pre-2000

According to Moyo (1991: 15) the post-independence macro-economic framework was designed to encourage an 'export-led growth and forex-earning, correct and indiscriminate prices for all farmers to stimulate output as a major policy instrument'. This was to be assisted by the continuation of traditional market structures where access to state credit, private finance, service and infrastructure remain tilted in favour of the white settlers, while the African peasantry was only an extension of the supply side of the market. As a result, the financial markets were also tailored to serve the developed sector of the country while the 'less developed rural sector remained inadequately serviced by a poor formal financial system consisting of the Agricultural Finance Corporation credit systems and building societies' (Chimedza 1994: 321).

As Chimedza (1994, 323) observes, the 1979 scheme by the AFC resulted in the first group of 2,846 beneficiaries of credit securing a total of Z$478,000 with beneficiaries increasing to 18,000 in 1980/81 receiving Z$4.8 million under a government guarantee. At the same time, lending to the small-scale farmers increased from 1,545 loans in 1979/80 to 3,930 in 1981/82. According to this AFC (1982, 1984), beneficiaries of the land reform program also benefitted from concessionary lending by the AFC, as they received Z$0.5 million in 1981/82 and an increased amount of Z$10.6 million advanced through 19,874 loans in 1983/84. The bank also extended credit to married women farmers under the Resettlement Credit Scheme, which was however inadequate particularly for the Model B farmers. As a result, farmers created the Collective Self-Finance Scheme (CSFS) in 1988, to help provide bank guarantees for cooperative loans. According to Chimedza (1994), up to 1979 when the AFC began to lend to communal farmers and to SSCFs at a large scale, the group had relied on savings clubs, which were supported by church and Non-governmental organisations. These clubs resulted in an increase in purchase of fertilizers in the early 1980s, as the Agriculture Extension (AGRITEX) Rusape report 1980-1982 noted. However, in the post-independence period, the AFC has been the major source for rural development (communal and resettled) with its share of communal funding increasing to 40% in 1990 compared to the other five banks that accounted for 42%, this has been done at a loss (AFC 1990).

Whereas lending to communal farmers increased from 23,859 beneficiaries in 1980/81 to 95,269 beneficiaries in 1985/86, access to funding under the loan facility was biased towards the more productive provinces of Mashonaland West and Mashonaland Central and commercial type of agricultural production (AFC 1991 cited in Chimedza 1994; see also Table 6-3). However, the total number of beneficiaries declined to 36,742 CA farmers in 1990/91, with the decrease being firmer in communal and resettled areas, while arrears also dramatically increased to 80% of the communal farmers, 68% of the SSCFs and 77% of resettled farmers resulting in huge defaults and auctioning of property (Chimedza 1994).

Table 6-3: Number and Value of Agricultural Finance Corporation Loans by Type of Farmer, 1980/81-1990/91

Year end March	LSCFs		SSCFs		Resettlement		Communal		Grand Total	
	Number granted	Value Z$m	Number granted	Value Z$m	Number granted	Value Z$m	Number granted	Value Z$m	Number granted	Value Z$m
1980/81	2,526	86.9	3.333	3.7	-	-	18,000	4.2	23,859	94.8
1981/82	2,103	88.8	3.649	4.6	911	0.5	30.150	10.1	36.813	104.0
1982/83	1,645	88.7	,953	4.5	4,154	1.5	38,912	13.2	49,664	107.9
1983/84	1,400	110.2	3.052	8.1	19,874	10.6	50,036	23.4	74,362	152.3
1984/85	1,484	110.3	2,744	8.7	19,926	10.7	65,793	32.0	89,947	161.7
1985/86	1,308	114.0	2.569	11.5	13,866	8.5	77,526	38.9	95,269	171.9
1986/87	1,007	94.9	1,910	9.6	11,800	8.6	77,384	60.0	92,101	173.1
1987/88	990	111.2	1,542	6.8	11,217	9.0	69,885	49.4	83,634	176.4
1988/89	900	117.4	1,140	5.3	7,022	5.9	57,679	41.3	66,741	169.9
1989/90	969	136.3	844	4.5	5,193	5.9	43,846	33.3	50,852	180.1
1990/91	1,133	195.1	761	3.6	4,658	4.7	30,190	26.4	36,742	229.8

Source: AFC Annual Reports, compiled by Chimedza 1994

In turn, the AFC diversified lending to LSCFs and to cash crops such as tobacco, coffee, sugar, tea and livestock, resulting in a new surge in lending, including through group lending schemes. All in all, the state sought to advance and broaden participation by most of the masses by ensuring access to capital such as finance credit.

6.5   Agricultural Productivity, pre 2000

Zimbabwe inherited from the colony of Rhodesia a highly skewed production pattern in which 'cash crop production was heavily concentrated in the 6000 large capitalist farms owned by white settlers and transnational capital' (Masst 1996: 65). This is against a background of historical marginalisation of peasant agriculture, despite initial stimulation of production at the onset of colonisation (Weiner 1988: 67). Although maize and cotton were the most important crops for the approximately 800,000 African peasants during the 1970s, they accounted only for 5% of the marketed maize and 10-15% of the country's cotton crop even though an additional small contribution was coming from the SSCFs. In Weiner's (1988) view, in part, this is because, agricultural yields per acre had begun to decline in the last decades of the colonial period, due to shortage of land and slow start to the use of chemical fertilizers in their fields. A tiny minority of 5% used chemical fertilizers due to the high cost of fertilizers, poor access by peasant farmers (see Riddell and Chavhunduka Commissions Reports of 1981 and 1982 respectively) and reliance on crop rotation and application of cattle manure as soil fertility enhancement measures.

While in part this explains the low yield in African reserves, the productivity gap between Africans who averaged 256kg per acre and white commercial farms averaging 1,677kg per acre is also explained by the fact that peasants occupied natural region (NR) IV and V while white commercial farms occupied NR I and II, which are suitable for crop production and used hybrid seeds while only 30% of smallholder farmers used hybrid and other high-yielding types of seed (Masst 1996). Overall, this deterioration of peasant farming in the African reserves, during the colonial times resulted in peasants becoming mere 'labour reserves' under a process of 'semi-proletarianisation' (Weiner 1988: 67). The Mugabe government sought to change this situation for a number of reasons. Firstly, increased productivity and income would raise the standard of living for the peasants, secondly, to reduce the dependence on European farmers and thirdly to increase food security through improved production of maize and other grains (Masst 1996).

To achieve this, the government needed to address the agrarian question (Sachikonye 1989) by attending to the challenges identified in the Riddell Commission (GoZ 1981: 58), and ensure changes to the fortunes of the peasants. As Masst (1996: 91) shows, there was a huge increase in the marketed maize production, as sales to the GMB increased sixfold from 63,000 tonnes per annum in the later 1970s to 373,000 tonnes in the 1990s. The increase was in response to government's new agricultural policy that resulted in free handouts of seed and fertilizers. A substantial decline in maize was only witnessed from 1987/88. While acknowledging that the peasant production remained lower than that of LSCFs, Tattersfield (1982) and Weiner (1988) observe that maize yield stood at 695 kg/ha compared to 4726 kg/ha for the LSCF sector.

As Weiner (1988: 68) adds, research has revealed that peasant production is not inherently unproductive but is subjected to weaknesses in research methodologies adopted and inadequate access to productive resources. Weiner (1988, 69) observes that maize production rose ten-fold in the African reserves from 66,571 tonnes in 1979/80 to 772,000 tonnes in 1984/85. The trends in total production and sales of maize from CAs show that despite inter-seasonal flactuations related to climatic variations, total production is estimated to have more than doubled between the two three-year periods, 1977-80 and 1988-91 (Masst 1996). However, it must be observed that while sales figures to the GMB increased threefold; account must be taken of local sales which were predominant (between 50-75%) in the 1970s, and that production was generally low during the 1977-79 period due to war intensification (Weinrich 1975).

The production of cotton also went through an impressive expansion after independence, with sales growing threefold from 37,200 tonnes between the three-year period 1977-1980 and 1988-91, despite inter-seasonal flactuations linked to climatic variations, similar to those experienced in maize (Masst 1996). Weiner (1988) notes that cotton production also increased rapidly to between one-third and one-half of national production by 1984-5. Subsequently, from 1988, both cotton and maize began to fall. In any event, the initial boom in maize production from CAs was concentrated in 18 out of 170 CAs. The better performing districts are situated in NR I and II located mainly in the Mashonaland provinces (Zinyama 1988; Masst 1996), with most CAs areas situated in the drier regions of NR IV and V, receiving well below 600 mm of rainfall per annum. The scholars therefore noted that for the 1983-4 crop season, 63.1% of the marketed maize crop came from NR I and II where only 15% of the African peasants reside, while marketed surplus was limited in the NR IV and V where more than two thirds of the same population lived. According to some scholars, LSCF farmers abandoned the production of maize (Scoones 1987), cotton, cheaper vegetables (Moyo 2000) for more lucrative traditional exports and new exports such as ostrich and horticulture. As a result, CA farmers produced and supplied vegetables for the domestic market.

6.5.1 Agricultural Marketing

According to Weiner (1988: 69) the boom in production and sales of cash crops which has been hailed internationally as Zimbabwe's 'success story' in the early post-colonial period is accounted for by the transformation of the relationship between the government and the peasantry. The government facilitated farmers' access to marketing boards, research, extension services and credit in the first seven years after independence for the peasant farmers ensuring that farming became profitable for them. According to Moyo (2000), by 1995, market liberalisation had resulted in 'all major commodities markets being liberalised, opening the marketing to private buyers and contractors, while by 1996 three of the agricultural parastatals were ready for privatisation'. A full catalogue of policy changes and their intended benefits, are captured in Table 6-4.

Table 6-4: Agricultural Marketing and Pricing Policy Changes

Policy	Policy Features	Begun	Group affected
1. Pre-ESAP policies	Producer prices where announced before season's planting to boost producer incentives as it reduces risk and uncertainty.	1985	All
a) Pre-planting prices	Enables farmers to make decisions based on relative prices.		
b) Pre-harvest and post-harvest prices	Producer prices are set and announced around April-May. Enables government to gauge potential harvests and stocking levels before announcing prices.	1983	All
c) Pan-territorial pricing	Payment of uniform prices throughout the country Benefits farmers in remove surplus regions at the expense of those in deficit regions and those close to markets.	1985	
	Discouraged production of high value—low volume crops (export crops) as it infers an implicit transport subsidy to remote farmers.		All
d) Pan-seasonal pricing	Producer and consumer prices are set annually. No incentive for off season production. Encourages centralized as opposed to on farm storage.	1985	All
2. Post ESAP policies	Marketing of commodities was decontrolled as marketing boards were commercialized:	1992	CA
a) Decontrol of crops marketing	Maize (N.R. IV & V)		CA
	Sunflowers		All
	Cotton		CA
	Small grains		LSCF
	Beef		LSCF
	Milk		LSCF

Source: Adapted from Takavarasha, 1994 and Moyo, 1995a.

For instance, the introduction of producer prices in 1985 where prices were announced at the beginning of the year to enable producers to plan and reduce risk and uncertainty. In 1983, the government had also introduced pre- and post harvest commodity price announcement, which had the effect of ensuring predictability and stability of prices. As Moyo (2000: 55) observes, 'producer prices of all the agricultural commodities showed a steady rise in norminal terms, meaning that farmers could use last season's prices as guaranteed minimum prices for the current season in decision making'. However, in 1995, the government decontrolled most of the agricultural commodities, including; maize, sunflower, cotton, small gains, beef and milk. As Moyo (2000) elaborates, the commercialisation and eventual privatisation of the state marketing boards and state credit, the liberalisation of the commodity pricing, and the acceptance of middlemen agricultural commodity marketing impacted on the pricing and the land policy. Most, if not all, of the marketing boards created by the government to assist white commercial farmers in the pre-independence period were either dissolved or privatised in the 1990s, as Table 6-5 shows.

Table 6-5: Agricultural Marketing Boards Reforms

Board	Established	Functions	Current State
Agricultural Marketing Authority (AMA)	1967	Coordinates and arranges financing for the other marketing board.	Dissolved in 1994.
Grain Marketing Board (GMB)	1931	Purchase, grading, handling, transport, storage and disposal of maize, sorghum, groundnuts, soyabeans, wheat, coffee, rapoko, and sunflower.	Now residual trading board.
Cold Storage Commission (CSC)	1938	Purchase and distribution of cattle. Beef exporting.	Privatised in 1996.
Dairy Marketing Board (DMB)	1952	Trading board in the purchase, processing, distribution and external trade of all dairy products.	Privatised in 1994. Now Dairy Board Limited.
Cotton Marketing Board (CMB)	1969	Trading board in purchase, processing and export of cotton products.	Privatised in 1994. Now Cotton Company of Zimbabwe.
Tobacco Marketing Board (TMB)	1936	Determines where tobacco is sold.	Opened up in 1996, new players e.g. Boka.

Source: Muir (1994); Moyo (2000)

The transformation of the agricultural marketing infrastructure resulted in more 'middlemen' such as domestic agricbusiness firms, LSCF farmers, some indigenous businessmen, NGOs and some government officials pushing for new exports and demand participation in the agricultural inputs and output marketing, including the agro-processing value chains (Moyo 2000). The institutional changes and agrarian reforms included infrastructure such as roads and dams, credit and government services; research and extension, as well as pricing and marketing to the CA and SSCF sectors (Sachikonye 1989; Whitsund Foundation 1978; Riddell Report 1981; Chavhunduka Commission Report 1982).

The government also constructed roads and introduced trucks, constructed more GMB depots, introduced collection points and allowed the use of local trading stores to buy cash crops from the farmers. In Masst's (1996) view, improving marketing facilities was mainly responsible for post-independence boom in the communal areas. In the case of Kandeya Communal areas, improved transport infrastruture aided agricultural viability among the communal farmers. These changes were important in reconfiguring support towards the changed agrarian structure and base, where the peasants had begun to play a more meaningful role. The structural changes on production and marketing impacted positively on accumulation and class formation in rural Zimbabwe as the next section will illustrate.

6.6   Capital Accumulation and Farm Investment

The relaxation of the regulations barring SSCA farmers from engaging in diversified activities from 1992 (Gunning *et al.* 2000) opened opportunities for farmers to broaden their sources of income. As Kinsey (1999) observed, the major sources of income in the 1995-1996 farming season were agricultural produce sales (crop and livestock revenue), transfer income (remittance income and non-farm employment) and non-farm enterprise. However, crop income remains higher in both resettled areas and in CAs even though income from agricultural sales was higher in ORAs as compared to CAs.

Kinsey (2004) notes that farmers acquired farm equipment including scotch carts and bought household goods and other assets such as vehicles and bicycles. According to Gunning *et al.* (2000), the equipment was instrumental in improving farm productivity in the resettled areas. Difference in access to farm equipment, livestock and access to markets mainly accounted for differences in accumulation of assets among farmers, since households with access to livestock prepare land for crop production in time while large herds of livestock produce larger quantities of manure for soil enrichment

(Zamchiya 2012). Again, farmers in the ORAs owned more livestock than those in the CAs. However, studies by Kinsey (1999; 2004) reveal that increased income in the resettled areas did not translate into improved welfare for the resettled population due to increased population density in these areas.

Dekker and Kinsey (2011) observes a general trend of decline in agricultural production and accumulation in resettled areas in key crops such as maize, tobacco and cotton resulting in reduced agricultural produce sales in the post-2000 period. The decline followed increased economic-wide crises, as the study reveals, associated with a decline in access to inputs, delayed payment and shortage of money for sales made to state parastatals such as the GMB and Cottco, reversing gains made in the first two decades after resettlement in the ORAs. The economy-wide challenges resulted in a drop in companies involved in the agricultural inputs markets and a drop in industrial capacity utilisation. However, as Kinsey (1999) points out, the initial performance by the resettled farms in the ORAs was due to effective government support for the newly settled farmers and the donor friendly environment ensuing then, in pursuance to the growth with equity policy framework, in stark contrast to the post 2000 FTLRP, as shall be revealed in the sections to follow.

6.7   Class Formation, pre 2000

Colonialism, the subordination of the African peasants and the creation of the reserves initially intended for labour (see Arrighi, 1970) in less productive agro-ecological regions of Zimbabwe resulted in uneven development, since reserves in better regions (NR I to III) were better off than those located in poorer (NR IV to V). However, the emergence and proliferation of the rich peasant from these regions (NR I to III) remained curtailed by poor land legislation, production and marketing of the produce (Ranger 1978; Phimister 1977; Sachikonye 1989). However, in the pre-independence period, some regions in poorer areas also peformed better than others in both crop and livestock farming, mainly due to differentiated cattle ownership, farming equipment ownership as was the case in Matebeleland where some chiefs owned as much as 10,000 cattle (Phimister 1986; Sachikonye 1989). After 2000, some scholars (Cousins 2010; Dekker and Kinsey 2011; Scoones *et al.* 2010; Matondi *et al.* 2008; Zamchiya 2012) agree that differentiated access to land holdings, farming inputs, labour, tillage, extension services, assets, income and social networks resulted in differing levels of productivity.

6.8   Conclusion

The 'willing buyer willing seller' policy adopted by government on the eve of independence shaped accumualation and class formation among the Africans during the period immediately after independence. The policy was adopted out of the Lancaster House conference and was a result of power balances among the negotiating parties. However, the changes in the agriculture policy from 1980 resulted in increased opportunities for the improved production, marketing and capital accumulation among the peasantry and a reversal of the privileged positioning for the white settler farmers. However, the white settler farmers remained viable as they shifted production from food to cash crops , livestock, game and tourism venntures. Changes in policy under neo-liberalism also resulted in increased commodification of African peasantryinto the markets, at varying levels depending on the purpose of production and resourse endowment.

Chapter Seven

Changing Agrarian Dynamics, 2000-2015

7.1 Introduction

The chapter dwells on the changing agrarian dynamics in the 15 years since 2000 when the FTLRP commenced. The central thesis in this study is that beyond politics, state practice, corruption and power; the role of domestic and international capital has been pivotal to rural accumulation in the context of changing agrarian structure in post-2000 Zimbabwe, yet not enough research has been done, particularly at district level to reveal emerging accumulation and class formation trajectories (see Moyo and Chambati 2013).

7.2 Capital and State Policy Complex after 2000

The workings of capital have been reconfigured in the aftermath of the land redistribution programme from 2000 onwards. The changes were in response to the 'differentiated exposure of Zimbabwe's 15 main agricultural commodities to international and domestic commodity and financial markets' and the changing 'agrarian structure, changing state policy and increased speculation and volatility on global commodity markets, especially from 2005' (Moyo and Nyoni 2013: 197 citing Moyo 2011b). The Zimbabwean economy went through four distinct phases of agrarian reforms since 1980, namely; the promotion of the bi-modal agrarian structure revitalised by smallholder sector from 1980 to 1990; liberalisation and state withdrawal from 1990 to 2000; abandonment of the market and state re-introduction and radicalised land reform and broader agricultural reforms from 2000 to 2008 (Murisa and Chikweche 2015); and more recently, the re-insertion of capital, market liberalisation and dollarisation combined with state intervention from 2008 to 2016.

Some scholars who have studied the post-2000 agrarian relations have tended to focus on the 'chaos' and 'politicisation' associated with the land reform program thereby missing on 'the national and international reconfiguration of agricultural inputs, outputs and financial markets, not the shifting logic and orientation of state interventions in agriculture in response to capital' (Moyo and Nyoni 2013: 197). In this instance, on one hand, the state is narrowly defined on the basis of media-based reports highlighting corruption, patronage conceptualised under the neopatrimonialism with the ruling Zanu PF social agency being given prominence. As these authors reveal, under these perspectives, the emerging state-capital relations in agrarian markets and the new forms of surplus value creation and extraction are under studied. On the other hand, according to the Reserve Bank of Zimbabwe (RBZ) (2007a), the government has insisted that illegal external sanctions imposed on the country and three droughts experienced between 2001 and 2011 and sabotage by capital account for the decline in production, with allegations that commercial farmers destroyed farm infrastructure and commercial banks refused to fund the newly resettled farmers, due to inappropriate tenure of systems for collateral security and capital involved in input supply was 'more interested in profiteering and externalisation of earnings' (Moyo and Nyoni 2013, 197).

By 2010, white commercial farmers had been reduced to as few as 300 and operated alongside some agro-industrial estates and some 150,000 newly resettled families (Moyo and Nyoni 2013), restructuring agrarian relations post the FTLRP. According to these writers, despite the increased number of peasants on the land, middle-sized capitalist farmers also increased and held 40% of redistributed land on leasehold tenure, provided by the state, the main agro-industrial estates were retained but on reduced land area. The new tri-modal agrarian structure necessitated unorthodox economic agrarian policy reforms, and reversed the liberalization policy framework that had been adopted from 1990 to 2001, as the need for increased support became apparent amid increasing economy-wide challenges.

The new dirigiste framework adopted from 2001 to 2007 was implemented amidst efforts to normalise relations with capital, allowing it to operate in controlled markets with some agro-industrial estates and agri-businesses being subsidized, amidst the external-led sanctions, foreign currency and farming inputs shortages (Moyo 2011b). The government encouraged out grower schemes as part of efforts to broaden the production base, expanding food and agro-fuel production by the remaining agro-estates (Moyo and Nyoni 2013). Private estates were into eco-tourism, sugarcane production while state estates, mainly ARDA produced various seeds, maize and wheat (Moyo 2011b). Since 2009, Zimbabwe has witnessed a re-insertion of capital through the introduction of multi-currencies, commonly referred to as dollarization, liberalization of markets through eradication of monopolistic state institutions in the marketing of key crops such as the GMB for maize, wheat and other small grains, Cotton Marketing Board (CMB) for cotton and TIMB for Virginia and Burley tobacco.

Moyo, Chambati, Mazwi & Muchetu (2014) suggest that changes in production patterns and in the differentiated exposure of agricultural commodities to international, national and financial markets had coincided with the re-insertion of capital, now oriented towards extroverted agricultural production, and diversified integration into the global markets, has meant that production had to be shifted to align with the dictates and dominance of large-scale domestic and international capital. Such a strategy has meant that production shifted to cash crops produced mainly through out growers and contract farming for crops such as tobacco, sugar, soya beans, cotton and maize. The economic reforms included relaxation of restrictions on remittances on dividends and on import laws and the removal of local commodity marketing restrictions from the mid-2008.

7.3 Agricultural Financing after the FTRLP

According to Moyo and Nyoni (2013), the FTLRP alongside an agrarian reform ushered in a variety of changes on how capital is inserted on the agricultural sector and the interface of various agricultural commodities to international and domestic commodity and finance markets, given the emerging agrarian structure. While Moyo and Yeros (2007; 2009) acknowledge the prevalence of structural constraints, in their view, policy implementation was also 'riddled by inconsistencies and class contradictions', the dilemma was on how to finance agrarian reform in favour of increasing peasantry alongside political and class struggles during the radicalised land reform programme, underpinned by a highly polarised polity and international isolation. The RBZ introduced various schemes from 2000, as Table 7-1 shows. The agrarian reform strategy, particularly its specific policy instruments, did not begin as one holistic and coherent plan, but rather evolved in response to changing social and production conditions and struggles on the ground, especially as output fell and inputs shortages grew, in the face of increasing sanctions (Moyo and Nyoni 2013). Besides efforts to normalise relations with international capital at the back of imposition of sanctions by some countries in the West, the government through the RBZ also initiated a number of schemes aimed at attracting agricultural funding, as the table shows.

Table 7-1: Coverage of RBZ Agricultural Financing Schemes

Scheme/Years	Objectives of scheme	Support provided	Targeted beneficiaries	Comments on beneficiaries
Free Government Inputs 2002-2011	Support peasant production	Seed and fertiliser packs	Communal/A1 farmers	
Productive Sector Financing 2004	Provide agricultural credit when private finance declined	Subsidised loans at 25% interest vs. 300% private banks	A2 Farmers	
ASPEF 2005	Enhance food export production	Cheap credit	A2 farms, agro-industry, merchants, state farms	80% of funds targeted A2 farmers
Operation Maguta 2005	Boost food security through command agriculture	Inputs and ploughing support (maize/wheat)	A2 farms and A1 and CA in 2005/06	
Champion Farmer 2008-2009	Boost food security through capable farmers	Inputs subsidy	A2 farms	
Farm Mechanisation 2003-2008	Address labour shortages and expand cropped area	Machinery and equipment for free and on cheap credit	A2, A1 and state farms	Small proportion of large farmers benefitted
Seed supply recovery 2002-2008	Increase area and number of seed producers	Cheap credit; Subsidised forex; Output contracts	Seed producing firms to contract A2 farmers	Relied mostly on new larger-scale farms
Irrigation rehabilitation and development 2004-2011	To resuscitate and expand irrigation	Cheap credit for equipment; Subsidised water and electricity	A2 and state farms	Mostly benefited A2 farms
ARDA recovery 2003-2006	Increase ARDA cropped areas	Cheap credit; Seasonal land leases	ARDA farms Agribusiness	Agribusiness did not invest cash

Source: Adapted from AIAS research. World Bank; Scoones et al., (2010)

Post-2009, the government has increasingly liberalised the economy and has tended to be compelled and persuaded by capital through various policy measures, including the legalisation of contract farming in 2004. The 2000s were generally associated with extreme capital and credit scarcity amidst limited government budgetary capacity and funding options which resulted in limited governmet funding (Mkhize and Moyo 2012; Moyo *et al.* 2014). Sconnes *et al.* (2010) observed that lack of finance and credit was a frequent complaint in the new farms, especially in the A2 scheme. Long-term funding was virtually non-existent while short-term credit was available with a maximum of six months, due to limited financial deepening. In particular, Scoones *et al.* (2010) observe that the hyperinflationary environment meant that credit schemes could not work, resulting in reliance on own proceeds, remittances from formal employment and corrupt deals with financial institutions. To a large extent, financial institutions cited weak collateral security as a risk militating against lending to smallholder farmers.

Notwithstanding observations by some studies (Chimedza 2006; Zumbika 2006) that lending risk through defaults can be reduced by increased administration by the government, according to Moyo *et al.* (2014), agricultural credit provided by private banks since 2000 declined in a significant way. Agricultural credit fell from US$315 million in 1998 to US$6 million in 2008 (Maemi 2009), but the situation began to improve from 2009 as shown in Figure 7-1.

Figure 7-1: Commercial Bank Credit to Agriculture (US$)

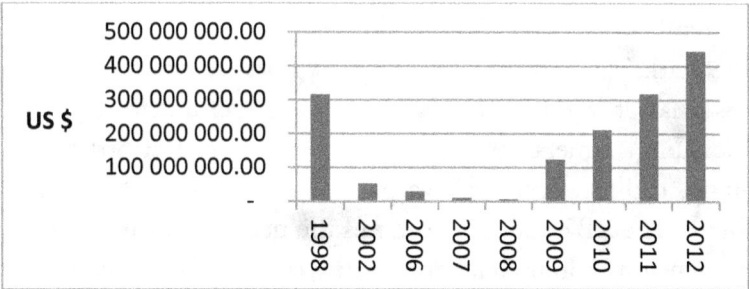

Source: RBZ monthly statistical bulletins

NB: Data shows closing credit balances owed to commercial banks as at 31st December of that year. Figures for 2012 are as at 31st March 2012 from World Bank Data

The introduction of multi-currency regime from 2009 has resulted in a rebound to US$805.2 million in 2009 and US$1.5 billion in 2010. Amidst 'powersharing' negotiations following economic collapse and a political stalemate, a variety of policy reforms took place, such that by end 2009, the economy had been liberalised, heralding the removal of controls on agricultural markets and the abandonment of capital and trade account and off-budget subsidies (Moyo and Nyoni 2013), and the dollarisation of the economy. By 2011, access to credit remained problematic and stood at 50% of the total requirement of US$2 billion (Ministry of Agriculture 2011, cited in Moyo and Nyoni 2013). Access to credit remained despite the normalisation and liberalisation of the economy from 2009 and the resuscitation of subsidised credit through the Agribank.

The main challenge was seen as 'unsecuritised' land tenure (Moyo and Nyoni 2013; Scoones *et al.* 2010) following the transformation of the tenure system, mainly from 2000. 'The financial position of most farmers has been eroded between 2000 and 2008, with wiped out savings and livestock assets, followed by a prolonged long period of limited access to inputs leading to low productivity, broken linkages with the manufacturing sector and low incomes' (Mkhize and Moyo 2012: 112), with only 2% of the land beneficiaries accessing credit during this period (see also AIAS 2006). Other forms of credit access to A2 farmers included salary based credit, cattle mortgaging, but these could not quench the appetite for credit due to overall illiquidity in the market (Mkhize and Moyo 2012). For instance, the RBZ (2016) notes that it remains critical for the government to focus on capacitating farmers through of the extension of affordable credit, training, technical expertise as part of efforts to return farming to viability. The RBZ (2016) also notes the need to move farmers from subsistence to commercial entities, expediting the evaluation of the remaining farms with a view to pay compensation for the improvements, enhance security of tenure by finalising the legal provisions for the 99 year leases so as to improve access to credit by the farmers and reduce land based conflicts.

The national budget for 2016 indicated that the total requirements for the 2016 agricultural season stood at US$1.7 billion, yet only US$944,558,297 had been secured through an RBZ and Bankers Association coordinated plan, representing only 56% of the total credit requirements for the seasonal year (RBZ 2016). This money was spread among five commodities with 63% going towards tobacco amounting to US$598.1 million, 8.5% to maize production, amounting to US$80.5 million, 2.6% to soya beans, amounting to US$25 million, 3.6% to cotton at US$34.5 million and 6.4% to livestock and poultry representing US$60.1 million. At least 38.4% of the credit was disbursed under contract farming arrangements and financed production for six crops under 483,850 hectares at a total cost of $362.9 million (MoF 2015) as per Table 7-2. As Mkhize and Moyo (2012) observed, constraints in private credit led to the rise of other forms of agricultural financing. For instance, in 2010, up to US$380 million (over 65%) of the private bank lending was advanced through private contractors through contract farming, reversing the past dominance of LSCFs funding, as the funded agro-industries and agricultural merchants who acted as intermediaries supported inputs supply for a broad base of producers (Moyo *et al.* 2014).

Table 7-2: Contract Farming Arrangement per Commodity for the 2015/16 Season

Crop Type	Hectarage Ha	Ave Cost/Ha US$	Total Cost US$
Maize	74 000	745	55 130 000
Soya beans	71 300	765	54 544 500
Sorghum	10 500	500	5 250 000
Sugar beans	1 050	530	556 500
Tobacco	72 000	1 400	100 800 000
Cotton	255 000	575	146 625 000
o/w Govt contribution	*60 870*	*575*	*35 000 000*
TOTAL	483 850		362 906 000

Source: Ministry of Agriculture, 2016

To achieve full productivity in the agricultural sector, the RBZ (2016) proposed to revolutionalise agriculture through measures such as; providing a risk sharing facility for banks involved in direct lending to farmers to reduce risk by introducing a government guarantee, training of bankers to enhance their understanding of smallholder farmer operations as part of an effort to tailor make products for the sector, establishing Credit Reference Bureau and Collateral Register for all farmers in the country so as to get rid of corruption during accessing of inputs under government funding and the development of diaspora bonds to securitise remittances.

In addition, the Central Bank proposed the operationalisation of the Warehouse Receipt System (WRS) and the Zimbabwe Agriculture Commodity Exchange (ZIMACE) to facilitate competitive and efficient trade of agricultural produce, finalise the contract farming legislative agenda to aid crop and livestock production, facilitatethe formation of producer organisations that facilitate the development and promotion of purchase agreements with farmers and receipt of financing from investors. In its plan, the RBZ also proposed the implementation of Value Chain Finance (VCF) through the commodification of contracts and relationships by linking segments of the commodity value chain, using guaranteed purchase agreements as collateral for cheap finance. However, the full implementation and full impact of the proposal is yet to be realised.

7.4 Capital Strike and State Support after the FTLRP

With regards to state support, some studies have revealed that the old resettlement of the 1950s was accompanied by significant government support and financial and technical support which was used to fund investments in production in inputs and infrastructure such as irrigation (Murisa and Chikweche 2015; Hanlon et al. 2013). To the contrary, beneficiaries of the FTLRP did not benefit from similar support and in the cases where such assistence was advanced, it targeted an elite few. This was made worse by an economy-wide crises on both the supply and demand sides. With regards to production, Scoones et al (2010) demonstrate how agricultural production was influenced by deliberate government economic policy framework and the deteriorating economic conditions in the country from 2000. Using the fertiliser industry, this study illustrated how a number of factors contributed to decline in production in the industry. Low production has been blamed on lack of foreign currency to import raw materials, frequent plant and machinery breakdowns and power cuts, and the reduced transportation capacity of the National Railways of Zimbabwe (NRZ), leading to increased costs of moving raw materials from mines and ports by road. Another factor was the introduction of price controls which, in the face of higher levels of inflation, forced fertilizer companies to run at a loss. As a result of these challenges, fertiliser use by farmers declined substantially.

However, various schemes aimed at improving production in many agrarian sectors were established by various state institutions. Government performance has remained weak and constrained due to increased economic crisis and limited fiscal resources, such that, between 2009 and 2012, the overall budget support amounted to US$1,252.2 million, an average of US$313.1 million per annum (See Figure 7-2).

Figure 7-2: Allocations to MAMID from National Budget (US$ million)

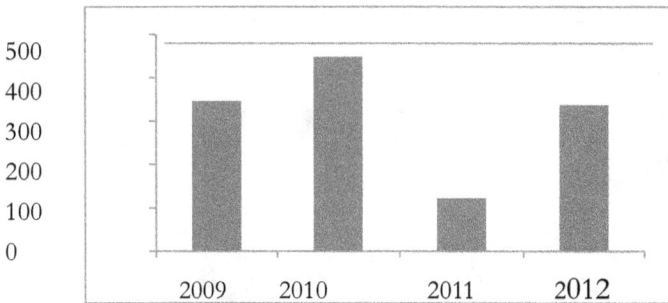

Source: MAMID (2012)

The decline in public funding for agriculture resulted in tremendous decline in rural infrastructural development with low investment in transport, water and electricity, irrigation and dams (Murisa and Chikweche 2015). The flight of capital particularly from 2004 to 2006 hiked as Zimbabwe was perceived to have the worst agricultural incentives in the World (Anderson 2010). The overall public agricultural funding has been well below 3% of the GDP dropping from a high of 9% in 1992 to a lowest 1% in 2000, as Figure 7-3 shows. In response to the mounting challenges, the government transferred key elements of the agricultural policy to the RBZ which involved the Joint Operation Command (JOC) in centralised command planning of the sector, and involved the security forces in policy implementation, including the distribution of inputs and enforcing the 'command agriculture' (see Murisa and Chikweche 2015). As such, the government introduced the Government Input Scheme from 2000, to assist farmers with inputs such as subsidised fuel, but the scheme faced funding challenges.

The RBZ also introduced the Productive Sector Facility (PSF) from 2005, which, in the face of declining bank credit, sought to provide low cost finance facilities to the productive sectors (IBID). Subsequent to this, in 2005, the RBZ set up the Agricultural Sector Productive Enhancement Facility (ASPEF) premised on the need for price stability and inflation reduction (Murisa *et al.* (2015) and cheap financing of farmers growing non-traditional commodities that did not access contract farming and targeted mainly A2 farmers (Scoones *et al* (2010).

Figure 7-3: Share of Agriculture in National Budget, 1980 – 2014 (%)

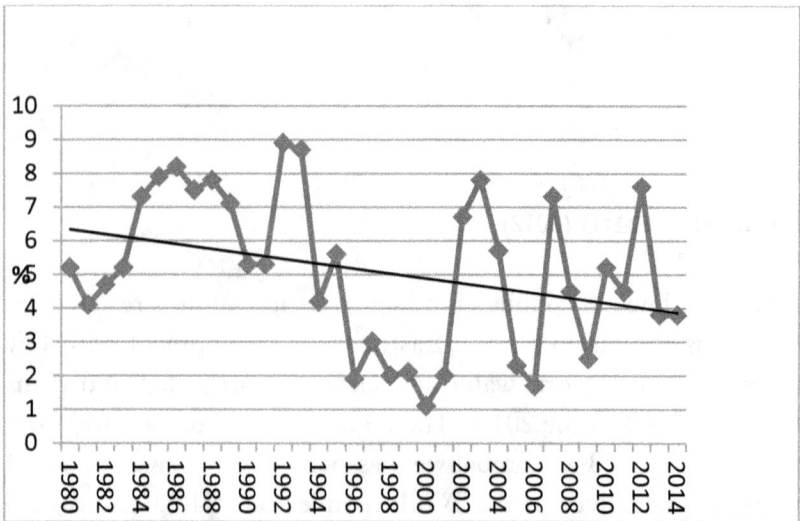

Source: Compiled from GoZ Budget Estimates various years

As Murisa *et al.* (2015) observe, the primary objective of the facility was to provide low-cost production finance to primary producers in the agricultural sector for enhancement of capacity utilisation, infrastructure development, food security and import substitution; and to generate foreign currency'. However, from mid-2008, Zimbabwe entered into a third agricultural policy regime centred on liberalisation of the economy including allowing permits to be given to firms to transact directly in a multicurrency regime, and remittance restrictions on dividends were relaxed (Murisa and Chikweche 2015). Imports were liberalized and local marketing and price controls removed, while the GMB monopoly on maize and wheat marketing was also ended (Murisa and Chikweche, 2015). At the same time, the level of foreign currency earnings surrendered by exporters was reduced (and later removed), while the partial removal of controls on the capital account, including the opening of foreign currency accounts, foreign payments and dividend remittances, enabled agriculture investors and merchants to improve their transactions and realizations. Similarly, dollarization was formalized in January 2009, but the use of multi-currency had already eased most domestic and foreign trade transactions in the six months before then, as Murisa and Chikweche (2015) reveal. According to the RBZ, by the end of February 2008, a total of ZW$114.2 trillion (approximately US$114.2 million) had been disbursed through commercial banks, as is detailed in Table 7-3

In September 2005, operation *Maguta* - a military led agricultual productivity enhancement program -which targeted the growing of maize and some small grains - was launched and had by February 2008, disbusred a total of ZW$3.038 trillion (approximately US$40.5 million) dollars for winter and summer crops (Murisa and Chikweche 2015). As Moyo *et al.* (2009: 52) observe, there was 'need for a more robust transformation of the economy to ensure that linkages among critical sectors are maintained or established, including improving input supply, credit support and access to markets, as well as the establishment of adequate physical infrastructure to support the new farming landscape.'

Table 7-3: Distribution of ASPEF Loans as at End of February 2008

Facility	Amount (US$)
Beef Cattle Support Facility	6 542 258.00
Horticulture Support Facility	13894 324.50
Irrigation Support Facility	5 252 900.80
Dairy Support Facility	1 796 651.30
Other crops and Livestock Facility	74 932 134.90
Piggery and Poultry Finance Facility	11 778 500.10
TOTAL	**114 196 769.60**

Source: Adopted from RBZ (2008) and Murisa and Chikweche (2015) calculations

The government also introduced a number of initiatives intended to assit farmers with inputs supply (See Table 7-4 below) . These included facilities run under the GMB, Agribank and TIMB, amongst others (Murisa and Chikweche 2015). To this end, subsidies became a key component of the agricultural production, as noted by Moyo *et al.* (2014).

Table 7-4: Overview of GoZ Input Support Programmes (ISPs) Between (2002 -2014)

Features of the ISPs	Targeted ISPs		Universal ISP
Period	2002/03 – 07/08	2009/10 – 12/13	2013/14
Maize			
Ave. No. of beneficiaries		1,065,000	1,617,2000
Ave. Value (US$)			
Targeted Area (Ha)			640,000
Ave. Area (Ha)		426,000	646,880
Targeted farmers	A1, A2, LSCF, Communal, Old Resettlement	A1, Communal, Old resettlement	A1, Communal, Old resettlement
% Subsidy	100%	100%	100%
Inputs	Seed, fertilizer	Seed, fertiliser	Seed, fertiliser, lime

Distribution mechanisms	Physical distribution – GMB, ARDA, Agritex	Physical distribution – GMB, Agritex	Physical distribution – GMB, Agritex
Participation of agro-dealers	No	No	No
Small grains			
Ave. No. of beneficiaries		118,667	21,490
Ave. Value (US$)			
Targeted Area (Ha)			
Ave Area (Ha)		59,333	10,745
Targeted farmers	A1, A2, LSCF, Communal, Old Resettlement	A1, Communal, Old resettlement	A1, Communal, Old resettlement
% Subsidy	100%	100%	100%
Inputs	Seed, fertilizer	Seed, fertiliser	Seed, fertiliser, lime
Distribution mechanisms	Physical distribution – GMB, ARDA, Agritex	Physical distribution – GMB, Agritex	Physical distribution – GMB, Agritex
Participation of agro-dealers	No	No	No
Total Ave. Value for all ISPs (US$)		58,366,667	161,000,000

Source: Moyo *et al.* (2014) Reserve Bank of Zimbabwe Annual Reports. US$ equivalent quoted at the official exchange rate. These amounts would have been much lower at prevailing parallel exchange rates.

The scale of ISP beneficiaries has been highly variable during the 2000s. State-subsidised input programmes were ratcheted up between 2002 until 2007, substantially downscaled in the 2008/9 season and then increased again from the 2009-10 season as indicated in Table 7-5.

Table 7-5: Zimbabwe Subsidy Policy Regime

Policy regimes	Period	Types of subsidies		
		Indirect	Direct	Distribution
I. Controlled regime	1965 – 1979	Extensive	Extensive	LSCFs
II. Heterodox policy Controlled capital accounts Interest rates regulation Mixed control of agricultural markets	1980 – 1990	Cheap foreign currency Subsidised credit Input price repression	Food relief Electricity Crop packs Extension	LSCFs Industry Small farmers
III. Liberalised environment	1990 – 2002	Grain market support	Crop inputs	Small scale farmers
IV. Post-Land Reform Structural change Controlled agricultural markets	2002 – 2008	Forex Credit Water Electricity	ISPs Mechanisation Fuel	All farms Industry A1/A2
V. Re-liberalisation Dollarisation; Trade; liberalization	2009 – 2016	Concessional credit Price offers	Crop inputs Livestock	Small farmers

Source: Moyo *et al.* (2014)

The beneficiaries of the development partners sponsored subsidy programmes (including agriculture inputs, extension services and market linkages) ranged between 421,764 and 541,824 households between 2005/06 and 2008/09 season, and they reached a peak in the 2009/10 season when over 944,048 households received support from the various components of the ISPs. Since then the number of beneficiaries has been on the decline following the switch to the highly targeted smart subsidies. Government's limited capacity led to scaling down on subsidy support since 2000. The scale and nature of distribution of subsidies was related to the economic and agricultural policy regimes. Prior to 1980, the subsidies were mainly targeted at white commercial farmers, while in the post-independence period, the programme shifted to both white commercial farmers and a broad range of black small-scale farmers, as aptly captured by Moyo *et al.* (2014).

7.5 Off-farm Income

The global financial crisis of 2008 resulted in a huge decline in remmitances by the Diaspora, while the urban-rural remittances also declined due to economy-wide crisises, epitomised by the hyper-inflationary environment experienced in 2007 and shrinking of the economy by 40% since 2000 (Moyo *et al.* 2014). According to the AIAS Survey Report (2005/6), farmers had also lost their Zimbabwe dollar (Z$) savings following dollarisation and the subsequent demonetisation caried out in February 2009. Over the same period, as the survey report revealed, commercial bank lending to commercial banks was targeted towards the A2 farmers (77.5%) compared to A1 farmers (37.5%). Micro finance institutions, to the contrary, targeted A1 farmers (37.5%) compared to A2 farmers (2.5%). In the face of such low opportunities for accessing bank credit, rural households relied on own savings, reinvestment of surplus from past seasons pensions, local and diaspora remittances (most common) and wages from formal employment. Whereas a survey conducted by AIAS in 2014 revealed that many farmers derive income from exploitation of natural resources, petty trading and pensions, empirical evidence from the survey also shows that the there is high level of income coming in to support agricultural activities from both the Diaspora and the local remittances (see Table 6-6).

For instance, the Diaspora is a source of funding to 16.4 % of 78 repondents/households in the A1 sector, 16.7% of 49 respondents/households in the A2 sector and 23.5% of 74 respondents/households in CAs in 2013/14, giving an overal support of 18.5% of the interviewed households in 2014. Local remittances also play a significant role in providing funding for agricultural activities post the FTLRP. For instance, local remittances contribute to an overall 24.3% of the households in funding. Pensions contributed an overal support of 16.9 % of A1 and 28.6% of A2 farmers. Similarly, formal employment contributes 17.9% of agricultural support with a high level of support in the A2 sector, which stands at 31.3%. In terms of income ranges received by the three sectors from both the Diaspora and local remittances, Table 7-7 shows that 32.1% of A1 farmers receive $500-$1000 from the Diaspora comapred to 30% of A2 and 39% for CA farmers.

Table 7-6: Source of Household Income by Settlement Type

Source of Income	A1		A2		Communal		Total	
	No.	%	No.	%	No.	%	No.	%
Remittances from Diaspora	78	16.4	49	16.7	74	23.5	201	18.5
Local Remittances	103	21.7	57	19.6	103	32.6	263	24.3
Pension	78	16.5	83	28.6	22	7.0	183	16.9
Formal Employment	61	12.9	91	31.3	41	13.0	193	17.9
Sale of Forest Products	22	4.6	2	0.7	9	2.9	33	3.1
Gold Panning	23	4.9	5	1.7	3	1.0	31	2.9
Hiring out Permanent Farm Labour	7	1.5	0	0.0	4	1.3	11	1.0
Hiring out Casual Labour	41	8.6	3	1.0	60	19.0	104	9.6
Petty Trading	47	9.9	23	7.9	29	9.2	99	9.2
Commercial Loan	6	1.3	8	2.8	2	0.6	16	1.5
Asset Selling	7	1.5	4	1.4	5	1.6	16	1.5
NGO Grant	9	1.9	0	0.0	13	4.1	22	2.0

Source: AIAS Household 2013/14 Survey, Household questionnaire

All in all 29.5% of small holder farmer receive over USD1000.00 in Diaspora remittances compared to 25.1% for local remittances. The AIAS 2013/14 Household Survey shows that local remittances are dominated by amounts that are above USD1000.00, with 24.3% for the A1 farmers, 57.9% for A2 farmers and 7.8% for CA farmers falling in this range.

Table 7-7: Income from Remittances by Settlement Type, 2013

Source of Income	Income Range	A1		A2		C/A		Total	
		No	%	No	%	No	%	No	%
Diaspora	$1-100	12	15.4	0	12	15	20.3	27	13.5
	$101-300	16	20.5	10	26	26	35.1	52	26
	$301-500	8	10.3	4	12	11	14.9	23	11.5
	$501-1000	25	32.1	5	30	9	12.2	39	19.5
	>$1000	17	21.8	29	46	13	17.6	59	29.5
Local	$1 – 100	19	18.4	3	5.3	35	34	57	21.7
	$101 – 300	24	23.3	4	7	34	33	62	23.6
	$301 -500	12	11.7	9	15.8	9	8.7	30	11.4
	$501 - 1000	23	22.3	8	14	17	16.5	48	18.3
	> $1000	25	24.3	33	57.9	8	7.8	66	25.1

Source: AIAS Household 2013/14 Survey, Household questionnaire

7.6 Land Redistribution since 2000

There has been a huge debate about the extensiveness and qualitative nature of distribution of Zimbabwe's land reform programme. Some scholars suggest that beneficiaries were selected in 'a partisan manner' with no 'technical considerations', but based on loyalty to the ruling Zanu PF party (Zamchiya 2012). On this basis, it is concluded that due to patronage, many potential beneficiaries lost out farm workers, women, white farmers and opposition supporters. Whereas Chambati *et al.* (2003) observes that the government established a land beneficiary process that involved submission of an application to be assessed through the provincial assessment committees comprised of technocrats from different Ministries, some scholars suggest that the process was heavily politicised, even though a diverse group of people benefited (Alexander 2006; Marongwe 2008; 2011; Zamchiya 2011).

For Alexander (2006), the government did not entirely trust the civil servants as these were suspected to be sympathetic to the opposition and as such formed parallel structures to manage the programme. As Marongwe (2011) concludes, politicians subverted the policy process and replaced the technocratic process with partisan political and social structures in the land allocation process. The parallel structures were made up of land identification committees comprising and dominated by Zanu PF members, members from the security forces, war veterans and traditional leaders (Marongwe 2011; Zamchiya 2011; 2012; Matondi 2011). Following this flawed process, Zamchiya (2012) concludes, in agreement with Marongwe (2008; 2011), that political elites and cronies got the land.

For Moyo (2011c), while cases of corruption by those elites involved in the distribution of acquired land can be noted, within the A2 sector and the estates, these do not warrant the conclusion that patronage and corruption were dominant, as suggested by others (Marongwe 2011; Zamchiya 2012) see also Scoones (2010 *et al.* 2010) for an elaboration of this argumentation. Highlights of corruption and patronage in favour of Zanu PF-linked elites have also been made by the media, but are based on a narrow perspective whereby all social agency and state action are perceived to be party-led, while the 'state is narrowly conceptualised as being intrinsically neo-patrimonial, allegedly driven by unproductive 'rent seeking' and consumptive distributional behaviour' (Moyo and Nyoni 2013: 197). Mukodzongi (2013) has also posited an alternative view that Zimbabweans tended to 'act Zanu PF' in order to gain access to land and other material benefits.

Moyo and Nyoni (2013: 197) assert that, ', the nuances of state agrarian intervention are clouded by perspectives which assume that 'chaos' and 'politicisation' pervaded the agrarian reform, missing the substantive class and regional dynamics in which state action is embedded'. Moyo (2011) adds that 13 million hectares of land had been transferred from 6,000 white commercial farmers to over 240,000 households, mainly with rural origin. By 2012, new small, medium and large-scale capitalists' farms on an average of 100 hectares, as the scholar points out, under the A2 scheme had reached 23,000 families (Murisa and Chikweche 2015). These authors also observe that approximately 60% of the beneficiaries (A1 and A2) were poor rural peasants while the second largest group came from their urban area counterparts, while Moyo *et al.* (2009) noted that

20.72% of the beneficiaries in the A1 sector were women compared to 14.7% in A2 plots. However, the sizes of the plots varied with agro-ecological regions (see Sukume and Moyo 2003; Moyo *et. al.* 2009). Table 7-8 illustrates the point.

Table 7-8: Land Reform Beneficiaries 1980 -2010: Acquisition and Allocation

Phase	Period	Acquired LSCF farms			Beneficiaries		
		No. of farmland properties	Area (ha)	% of total	No.	% of total	Avg. Area (ha)
Phase I	1980–1997	1,651	3,498,444	22.9	71,000	28.7	49.3
Inception phase	1998–1999		168,264	1.1	4,697	1.9	35.8
Fast track	*1999–2009*						
A1		2,564[1,2]	5,759,153[2]	37.7	145,775[2]	59.1	39.5
A2		2,295[1,2]	3,509,437[2]	23.0	22,896[2]	9.3	153.3
Unallocated gazetted land		*517*	*757,578*	*5.0*			
Sub-Total[2]		5,376	10,026,168		168,671		
Private transfers	1980–2009	1,069	676,325	4.4	1,069	0.4	632.7
Ungazetted total		1,409	912,147	6.0		0.6	647.4
Grand total			15,281,348	100.0	245,437	100.0	

Source: Ministry of Lands and Rural Resettlement (2009), Ministry of Lands and Rural Resettlement 2010 data. (1) includes some farms with multiple properties that have been counted as one; (2) GoZ data shows that there were 6,214 gazetted farms, of which over 501 farms (white, indigenous, churches, etc.), despite being gazetted, were recommended to stay (MLRR 2009).

Beyond the official figures, Moyo (2011) suggests that many people gained access to land through their relatives and colleagues. The AIAS Survey (2009) revealed that 27% of the respondents confirmed to having helped relatives, neighbours and friends to access land with over 35% of the people settled in both A1 and A2 sectors being former commercial farm workers who were not officially allocated land. After the resettlement programme, over 13% is now in the hands of middle-scale farmers (A2 and LSCFs) and small-scale capitalists (SSCFs) and 70% is now held by small scale producers, while 11% is held by large-scale farmers and estates (Moyo 2011). To be sure, capital did not rescind, as Moyo (2011, 510) confirms:

A broadly based agrarian capitalist class, built on former and new farming 'elites', has also emerged. The smaller segment of large-scale capitalist farmers now includes both black and white farmers, but their landholdings have been substantially downsized to an average of 700 hectares, compared to the average of 2,000 hectares held by large-scale landowners in the past. Over 75% of the new middle capitalist farmers have plots of less than 100 hectares, but these also vary across agro-ecological regions.

Prior to the FTLRP, the pattern of foreign ownership of land in Zimbabwe was differentiated in size with 267 farms owned by persons from 13 countries, 65% from European countries, 2% from United States of America; 70% being Germans, Dutch, Swiss and Italians (Moyo 2011). There were only three countries from the South holding land in Zimbabwe, namely South Africa, Mauritius and Indonesia but these controlled only 33% of the farms and 27% of the area. In terms of land size, 20% of the foreign owned farms ranged from 2,000 to 50,000 hectares. This situation has predominantly remained the same, especially in the LSCF plantation sub-sector because they were spared.

As Moyo (2011) notes, new large-scale investments seem to be underway (for example on the DTZ estates) by foreign capital amidst new debates about persisting insertion of extremely large and under-utilised foreign-owned estates, which perpetuates contradictions on the policy objective of redistributive land reform, and raising questions on the moral hazards of maintaining the status quo amidst rising local grievances over this inequity and land ownership. For Moyo and Nyoni (2013: 197), these perspectives reflect an 'under study of the emerging state-capital relations in the agrarian markets and the new forms of surplus value creation and extraction, as well as for the wider politics of agrarian reform'. To be sure, the government attracted foreign investment from the East and South into agriculture following the 2002/3 drought and focused on agro-industrial estates for critical export growth as part of the 'renewed Import Substitution Industrialisation strategy'.

7.7 Agricultural Productivity after 2000

Did the reconfigured agricultural sector result in changed agricultural productivity in Zimbabwe? Furthermore, as Moyo (2011) asks; has agriculture been destroyed or transformed post the FTLRP? Or as Scoones *et al.* (2010) query; has the land reform resulted in an explosion of productive activity, based on dynamic accumulation from below?' What explains the changes in production and productivity patterns across the settlement models? Moyo (2011) observes that in terms of productivity, yields for many agricultural commodities remained below historically realised averages and up to 2010-11, most expansion of output was based on expansion of the number of producers, and the cropped area. A similar trend was established for beef and and livestock products, even though the situation was varied for different crops and for different agro-ecological regions, as Figure 7-4 shows.

Figure 7-4: Agricultural Area Planted Trends (1990s ave vs 2000s)

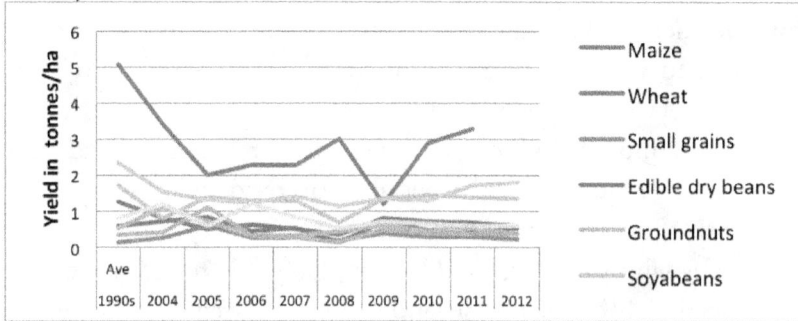

Source: MAMID (2010a, 2010b, 2011, 2012); World Bank 2006

Other studies (Zamchiya 2012; Cousins 2010; Moyo *et al.* 2008) agree that there has been a decline on almost all major agricultural commodities across the different settlement models, however, these scholars tend to differ in their interpretation of the folding dynamics post 2000. For instance, there was a boom in cotton production underpinned by contract farming, but beef production collapsed (Scoones *et al.* 2010). Moyo and Yeros (2007) suggest that the factors contributing to agricultural production levels and the evolution of agricultural inputs and outputs markets are complex, to the extent that they have operated under given economic frameworks. The World Bank (2006) suggests that the economy has been performing badly due to weak macro-economic management frameworks, frequent droughts, an unstable and unfavourable policy environment, and the negative effects of the FTLRP which triggered international isolation. Moyo *et al.* (2009) suggest that the droughts experienced from 2001 to 2005 and the state of the macro-economic situation contributed negatively to productivity as some agro-industrial

147

linkages developed over the years in the input and output markets were curtailed.

The A2 Land Audit of 2006, where 79 % of the allocated A2 farms were surveyed, shows that more than 50% of the farms were 'productive' and 4% was 'highly productive', despite the late uptake of farms and low finance availability (see Hanlon *et al.* (2013). A survey carried out by AIAS (Moyo *et al.* 2009: 50) concluded that some districts took as much as 3-5 years to allocate land, while 'among other factors, the level of farm establishment and commencement of farming activities tend to be affected by the year in which land was allocated'. In the same vein, 'In terms of farm establishment when a piece of land was allocated, beneficiaries had to prepare and mobilise resources for relocation and for infrastructural requirements, especially for residency and farming operations', (Just put the Source). For instance, 3.6% of the beneficiaries who were allocated land in 2000 only took up the land in 2003, while 1.1% took up the land in 2005. However, some people also took up the land before formal allocations, with 8% of the people who settled in 2000 getting land allocated to them in 2006, as shown in Table 7-9.

Table 7-9: Year when Piece of Land was Allocated vs. Year when Farming Commenced

Year allocated	Year when farming commenced															
	2000		2001		2002		2003		2004		2005		2006		Total	
	No	%	No	%	No	%	No	%	No	%	No	%	No	%	No	%
2000	127	46.2	111	40.4	21	7.6	10	3.6	3	1.1	3	1.1	0	0.0	275	14.4
2001	5	0.8	389	59.3	221	33.7	28	4.3	9	1.4	4	0.6	0	0.0	656	34.4
2002	2	0.4	7	1.5	332	71.6	112	24.1	7	1.5	4	0.9	0	0.0	464	24.3
2003	7	3.0	3	1.3	4	1.7	151	65.1	58	25.0	7	3.0	2	0.9	232	12.2
2004	2	1.3	5	3.3	6	3.9	3	2.0	97	63.8	34	22.4	5	3.3	152	8.0
2005	6	5.9	0	0.0	4	3.9	1	1.0	2	2.0	79	77.5	10	9.8	102	5.4
2006	2	8.0	1	4.0	2	8.0	1	4.0	0	0.0	0	0.0	19	76.0	25	1.3
Total	151	7.9	516	27.1	590	31.0	306	16.1	176	9.2	131	100.0	36	100.0	1906	100.0

Source: AIAS Household Baseline Survey, Household Questionnaire, 2009

However, the survey revealed that most beneficiaries settled in the same year that they were allocated land, as the case was in 2002 where 71.6% commenced operations in the same year of settlement.

The uptake in the same year of allocation was higher in 2005 and 2006, at 77.5% and 76% respectively. The AIAS Survey Report further highlights that various policy frameworks implemented since 2000, alongside the FTLRP have impacted on the productivity of almost all agricultural commodities as Table 7-10 reveals.

Table 7-10: Agricultural Production Trends (crops 000 tons): 1990s averages 2000s

Crop	1990s avg	2002/3	2003/4	2004/5	2005/6	2006/7	2007/8	2008/9	2009/10	2010/11	2011/12
Main foods											
Maize (%change compared to 1990s)	1,684	930 (-44.8)	1686.1 (0.0)	915.4 (-45.7)	1,485 (-11.8)	953 (43.4)	575.0 (-65.8)	1242.6 (-26.3)	1,327.6 (-21.2)	1,451.6 (-13.9)	968.0 (-42.5)
Wheat	248	122 (-50.8)	247.0 (-0.6)	229.1 (-7.8)	242 (-2.4)	147 (40.7)	(-75.0 (-69.8)	57.9 (-80.7)	41.5 (-83.3)	53.1 (-78.5)	
Small grains	167	373 (123.4)	196.1 (19.0)	65.8 (-60.1)	164 (1.8)	(-120 (28.1)	(-93.2 (44.2)	270.2 (64.0)	193.9 (16.1)	156.08 (-6.5)	108.7 (-34.9)
Edible dry Beans	5.3	7.1 (34.0)-	56.8 (971.7)	21.5 (305.7)	21.5 (305.7)	30 (471.7)	3.8 (-28.3)	37.3 (6.13)	17.2 (224.5)	13.1 (147.2)	10.8 (103.8)
Groundnuts (shelled)	86	86 (0)	64.2 (-24.5)	57.8 (-32.1)	83 (-3.5)	125 (45.3)	131.5 (53.5)	216.6 (154.8)	186.2 (116.5)	230.5 (168.0)	120.0 (39.5)
Oilseeds											
Soya beans	98	41 (-58.2)	85.8 (-12.4)	56.7 (-42.1)	71 (-27.5)	112 (14.3)	48.3 (-50.7)	115.8 (18.2)	70.3 (-28.3)	84.2 (-9.3)	70.5 (-28.1)
Sunflower	43	17 (-60.5)	20.2 (-50.9)	7.4 (-82.0)	17 (-60.5)	26 (-39.5)	5.5 (-87.2)	39.0 (-5.3)	14 (-67.4)	11.5 (-72.1)	6.9 (-84.0)
Key Export											
Tobacco	198	82 (-58.6)	78.3 (-60.5)	83.2 (-58.0)	55 (-72.2)	79 (-60.1)	69.8 (-64.7)	63.6 (-67.9)	103.9 (-47.5)	132.4 (-33.1)	120 (-39.3)
Cotton	201	132 (-34.3)	364.3 (81.2)	196.3 (-2.3)	153 (-23.9)	235 (16.9)	226.4 (12.6)	246.8 (22.8)	172.1 (-14.4)	249.9 (24.3)	254.9 (26.8)
Estate crops											
Sugar	138.9	502 (14.4)-	422 (-3.9)	429 (-2.3)	446 (1.6)	349 (-20.5)	259 (-41.0)	259 (-41.0)	350 (-20.3)	332 (-24.4)	372 (-15.2)
Tea	10.6	22.0 (107.5)	22.0 (107.5)	22.0 (107.5)	22.0 (107.5)	13.5 (27.4)	8.3 (-21.7)	11.5 (8.5)	14 (34.9)	20+ (88.6)	
Coffee	8.4	8 (-4.8)	5.8 (-31.0)	3.5 (-58.3)	1.3 (-84.5)	0.7 (-91.7)	0.8 (-90.5)	0.5 (-94.0)	0.3 (-96.4)	3+ (-64.3)	
Other crops											
Citrus	90	130 (44.4)	130 (44.4)	123 (36.7)	123 (36.7)	123 (36.7)	-				
Vegetables & Melons	149	180 (20.8)	181 (21.5)	161 (8.1)	161 (8.5)	162 (8.7)	-				

Source: Moyo (2011a) derived from Ministry of Agriculture, Mechanization and Irrigation Development (2010a, 2010b, 2011, 2012), FAO (2008, 2009), World Bank (2006), Gain Report (2010; 2012), Zimbabwe Tea Growers Association (2010), data. *RBZ (2011) projections, figure in brackets is percent change from 1990s averages.

149

Whereas tobacco production had declined by 50% with total area under production declining from 84,100 to 42,900 in 2006, a positive trend started developing from 2009 with production moving towards the 1990s levels of 220 million kilograms (Mkhize and Moyo 2012) and from commercial farmers to small-scale farmers. Increased total crop output for tobacco and maize is mainly due to increased cropping area while the introduction of contract farming also impacted positively for cotton and tobacco across all settlement sectors.7Evidently, access to land was not adequate for social reproduction and rural sector development. The issue of access to finance credit and that of input and output markets is critical for overall improvement in productivity. The period from 2000 to 2008 was characterised by an economy-wide collapse in credit.

While Zamchiya (2012), concurs that there has been a decline in most commodities, the author tends to tackle agricultural productivity from a political perspective. For instance, Zamchiya (2012) argues that Scoones *et al.* (2010), Moyo (2011c) and Cousins' (2010a) take a pro-small-scale farmers perspective whereupon they suggest that within the differentiated circumstances, some small-scale farmers have fared well. However, Scoones *et al.* (2010) rely on studies held in Masvingo and argue that some resettled small-scale farmers are accumulating from below, even though others are facing challenges and are therefore 'stepping out'. Zamchiya (2012) dismisses Cousins' (2010a) argument that it seemed hard for Mugabe's critics to admit that the fast-track land reform could have brought about positive change for rural Zimbabwe. For Cousins (2010a), it is possible to identify positive outcomes without endorsing violence and abuses that accompanied the seizure of farms, even if the argument of small-scale - higher production thesis was to be avoided.

Whereas Zamchiya (2012) accuses Moyo (2011) and Moyo *et al.* (2009) of political positioning with regards to the issues of production and productivity, and of eschewing violence and seeking to present positive aspects of production on the farms, the author fails to provide the specific examples to buttress the point. In any event, it seems most plausible that his own positioning is political. In turn, Moyo *et al.* (2009) agree that land utilisation has been low as at least 20.7% of the households had no land under crops, 13.1% had between 1-20% of their allocated land under crops in the 2004/5 season (see Figure 7-5), resulting in low productivity.

Figure 7-5: Arable Land Utilisation Levels

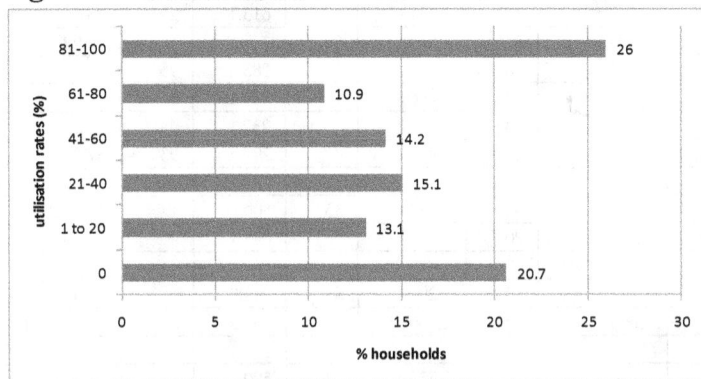

Source: AIAS Household Baseline Survey, Household Questionnaire, N=2089

Incidentally, the study by Moyo *et al.* (2009) which relies on an AIAS Household Baseline Survey of 2,089 participants reveals that the A1 sector had a higher proportion of households utilising land (25.4% utilising 1-40%) as compared to the A2 sector (38.7% utilising land). The AIAS Survey also showed that over 60% of farmers in both A1 and A2 sectors are engaged in maize production, including in the drier regions. Across the agro-ecological regions, more farmers are engaged in the production of main food crops (maize, wheat, small grains, edible dry beans and groundnuts), compared to oilseeds (soya beans, sunflower), key exports (tobacco and cotton) estate crops (sugar, tea and coffee) and horticultural crops (paprika, floriculture, citrus and vegetables). The 2014 survey by AIAS revealed that A2 farmers realised higher crop outputs in most of the crop commodities in the 2013/14 cropping season compared to A1 farmers who had higher production in rapoko and millet as per Table 7-11. The AIAS Survey of 2014 reveals that A2 farms had greater productivity as compared to A1 farms across most of the commodities. Maize production averaged 1,551.6 kg/ha in A2 and 975.8 kgs/ha in the A1 sectors.

151

Table 7-11: Crop Productivity by Sector, 2013/14 Season

Crop	Yield (Kg/Ha)							
	A1		A2		CA		Total	
	Mean	N	Mean	N	Mean	N	Mean	N
Main foods								
Maize	975.8	445	1,551.6	196	613.1	296	981.7	937
Wheat	2,020	3	1,200	2	-	-	1,692	5
Sorghum	451.3	86	472.2	3	285.4	75	375.8	164
Rapoko	628.1	12	555.6	1	813.1	8	695.1	21
Millet	483.8	24	-	-	232.1	44	321	68
Groundnuts	396.3	178	440.6	42	297.4	93	372.8	313
Oilseeds								
Soyabeans	1,323.7	31	1,553	35	500	1	1,431.2	67
Sunflower	321.1	20			647.1	4	333.8	24
Key exports								
Tobacco	1,107.6	54	1,290.6	55	2,000	1	1,207.2	110
Cotton	538.5	44	1,250	2	740.2	8	594.7	54
Plantation								
Sugar cane	4,150	2	9,533.5	38	500	1	9,050.6	41

Source: AIAS Household 2013/14 Survey, Household Questionnaire

By 2000, tobacco production continued to be dominated by 1800 LSCF farmers who included 300 black commercial farmers and produced 80% of the crop from the 1990s. Zimbabwe produced an average of 200 million kilograms on 85,000 hectares by 1999. The changed agrarian structure has seen an increase in production patterns where 105,000 mainly smallholders producing 214 million kilograms valued at US$677 million and earning over $1 billion dollars by 2014 up from 70,000 tonnes produced by 21,882 farmers in 2004 valued Z$593,5 million (TIMB, 2015).

By 2015, an upward trend had been consolidated with 198 million kilograms from 2004, following a re-insertion of capital post 2009, mainly under contract farming, as TIMB reports showed. The sector also benefited from the relaxation of exchange controls and deregulation of marketing of export crops, the surrendering of foreign currency earnings. As Mkhize and Moyo (2012) observes, changes in the macro-economic environment altered the orientation and processes of agricultural imports and exports, domestic output markets, agricultural investments and skyrocketing agricultural prices which combined to give a powerful set of incentives for the sector. 'This is (i) because of unified exchange rates, (ii) lower industrial protection and sharply reduced export taxation and (iii) removal of direct or indirect export controls' (Mkhize and Moyo 2012, 11). Overall, production remains constrained due to limited access to credit, among other factors (see Table 7-12).

Table 7-12: Production and Productivity Trends since about 2005/06

Crop	Area or animals	Yield	Production	Remarks	Dominant sector
Small grains, groundnuts, dry beans	Rapid growth during and post crisis, then decline	Growing	*Far above 1990s levels*	Because of drought and to enhance food security	Family farmers
Cotton	Never declined	Hardly declined	*Growing beyond 1990s levels*	Good global demand, contract farming	Family farmers
Maize Tobacco	Rapid recent growth	Reduced	*Close to recovery except in drought years*	Tobacco spread to small and communal farmers, contract farming	All farm classes, except estates
Poultry	Sharp decline, then almost full recovery	Animal productivity Reduced	*Close to recovery*	There remains an import substitution potential, contract farming	Commercial and family farmers
Sugarcane, sugar and ethanol	Sharp decline only during hyperinflation, then full recovery	Reduced productivity	*Recovering and new investments, including in Ethanol*	Benefits from high sugar and ethanol prices, and presence of foreign investors.	Plantations and estates, and outgrowers among commercial and family farmers
Beef	Fairly constant	Quality reduced	*Not yet recovered*	Large scale producers with shift to smaller units	All farm classes
Horticulture	Reduced	Reduced	*Slow recovery*	Limited medium term loans	All farm classes
Tea	Sharp decline	Reduced	*Stabilizing at low levels*	Some shifts to Macadamia	Estates and out grower family Farms
Wheat	Sharp decline	Very sharp decline	*Loss of irrigation, electricity problems, and relative decline in profitability*	Very little recovery, unwillingness to finance inputs, electricity problems	Commercial and market oriented family farms
Coffee, milk	Decline in area and livestock herd	Sharp declines	*Coffee collapsed, Milk sharply reduced*	Collapse of coffee prices. Unwillingness or inability of new farmers to continue production	Estates, Commercial, Market oriented family farms

Source: Mkhize and Moyo (2012)

Some scholars blame this on the creation of dead capital in resettled areas (De Soto 2000; Richardson 2005; Matondi *et al.* 2008). However, a study by Moyo and Chambati (2012), citing Haugerud (1989), and Okoth-Ogendo (1991) for Kenya, Pender *et al.* (2004) for Uganda, Place and Otsuka (2002) for Malawi and Gavin and Ehui

(1999) for Ethiopia, concluded that land titling has not been a major source of increased agricultural credit, investment productivity and therefore growth of employment and industrialisation, in much the same way that it has not been consequential in China and South East Asia in general. As already observed, Zamchiya (2012) argues from an agrarian politics perspective and positioning, belabouring to prove that the FTRLP caused a decline in agricultural productivity, because patronage and violence associated with land grabbing. However, beyond politics, the study also revealed that agro-ecological factors, economic environment and social networks and non-farm sources of income explained differential production levels. The role of agro-ecological regions was collaborated by an AIAS survey (Moyo *et al.* (2014), See Table 7-13 below.

Table 7-13: Major crops grown by agro-ecological region

Type of crop	I		II		III		IV		V		Total	
	No.	%	No.	%	No.	%	No.	%	No.	%	No.	%
Main foods												
Maize	247	93.2	829	87.8	429	91.5	129	84.3	149	57.8	1783	85.4
Wheat	3	1.1	44	4.7	28	6.0	-	-	10	3.9	85	4.1
Small grains	30	11.3	30	3.2	105	22.4	79	51.6	69	26.7	313	15.0
Edible dry beans	73	27.5	27	2.9	1	0.2	-	-	3	1.2	104	5.0
Groundnuts	23	8.7	124	13.1	194	41.4	36	23.5	56	21.7	433	20.7
Oilseeds												
Soya beans	9	3.4	57	6.0	50	10.7	-	-	21	8.1	137	6.6
Sunflower	5	1.9	4	0.4	25	5.3	5	3.3	7	2.7	46	2.2
Key exports												
Tobacco	1	0.4	91	9.6	4	0.9	-	-	1	0.4	97	4.6
Cotton	-	-	5	0.5	33	7.0	2	1.3	47	18.2	87	4.2
Estate crops												
Sugar	2	0.8	-	-	1	0.2	-	-	48	18.6	51	2.4
Tea	19	7.2	-	-	-	-	-	-	-	-	19	0.9
Coffee	6	2.3	-	-	-	-	-	-	-	-	6	0.3
Horticultural crops												
Paprika	3	1.1	6	0.6	1	0.2	-	-	2	0.8	12	0.6
Floriculture	-	-	1	0.1	-	-	-	-	-	-	1	-
Citrus	4	1.5	-	-	-	-	-	-	1	0.4	5	0.2
Vegetables	5	1.9	19	2.0	29	6.2	2	1.3	16	6.2	71	3.4

Source: AIAS Household Baseline Survey, Household Questionnaire, N=2089; 2014

Murisa (2011) agrees that social networks impact on access to assets and opportunities, as was revealed in his study of Goromonzi and Zvimba. The study revealed that local farmer groups gained access to inputs, enabled collective production of market crops, mobilisation of savings and credit and sharing of farm assets. However, many studies avoid the role of capital (credit, savings, government support and off-farm income in production patterns and in some cases, tend to view all government support from a patronage positioning (Zamchiya 2012; Alexander 2006). On this issue, Moyo (2011) notes that market-oriented small-holder famers and small commercial famers have the highest input intensities, while the medium and large scale commercial farmers are limited in terms of area utilised by various factors, including mechanisation, credit to purchase inputs and hired labour. Moyo (2011) discounts the possibility of limited farming skills, tenurial insecurity and collateral security leverage as impacting negatively on productivity. Beyond access to funding, markets play a crucial role in accumulation for farmers, across settlement sectors, as the next section will reveal.

7.8 Agricultural Marketing

Scholars have tended to concentrate on land allocation, production patterns and accumulation processes after 2000 (see Zamchiya 2012; Matondi 2012; Alexander 20006; Hanlon *et al.* (2013; Murisa and Chikweche 2015), and avoided the role of financing and marketing of the agricultural commodities, yet farmers are adversely inserted into international markets for their commodities, whereupon international and domestic capital pursue exploitative surplus extraction relationships with small-scale farmers in developing countries. According to Moyo (2000: 55), by 1995, market liberalisation had resulted in all major commodities markets being liberalised, opening the marketing to private buyers and contractors, while by 1996 three of the agricultural parastatals were ready for privatisation'. Mkhize and Moyo (2012: 49) argue that many studies have failed to frame the 'analyses of the nature of market developments, the complex output and productivity trends of the full range of Zimbabwe's agricultural commodities' which is critical in highlighting the 'differentiated drivers of and constraints to improved production' and how these impact on the potential of different sectors and classes of producers of agricultural commodities. Moreover, as the authors highlight, the efficacy of the agricultural markets for Zimbabwe are analysed through a binary framework of 'state controlled and uncontrolled commodities' as if these commodities are equally developed and equally linked to domestic and international markets.

What is obvious is that these commodities are differentially linked to both the domestic and international markets such that some are net imports (wheat) and others are net exports (tobacco), as some food crops are staple and therefore critical for food security, others are consumed by the middle class, but may all be vertically linked to the global food economy through processing, marketing and production, as the authors further observed. Going forward, as Mkhize and Moyo (2012, 49) suggest, thorough examination of the agricultural commodities must include a global contextual analysis, including 'the terms and of the reliability and volatility of international markets, including interventions by different country groups across the world' and how these are transmitted to the domestic market. As observed by these authors, the volume of agricultural export declined consideraby from 2003 to 2009 due to economic and political instability in the country (see Table 7-14).

Table 7-14: Trends in Agricultural Exports Relative to National Exports (Currency US$ Millions)

Year	Tobacco	Sugar	Horticulture	Cotton Lint	Other Agric Exports	Total Agric Exports	National Exports	Non-Agric Exports
2000	548.8	95.7	125.4	156	88.1	857.9	2191.7	1333.8
2001	594.1	70	119.1	81.9	49.8	832.9	2107.7	1274.8
2002	434.6	64.1	126.7	53.2	21.1	646.6	1794.3	1147.7
2003	321.3	54.8	118.7	67.2	21.1	516.0	1661.5	1145.6
2004	226.7	53.9	84.1	122.1	19.6	384.2	1671.4	1287.2
2005	203.8	43.1	75.9	96.3	13.1	335.9	1587.7	1251.2
2006	206.9	81	60.1	107.8	22.0	370.1	1721.4	1351.4
2007	234.0	51.8	65.1	103.4	45.9	396.8	1818.9	1422.2
2008	229.0	68.4	32.6	114	37.7	367.3	1657.3	1290.0
2009	300.8	48.3	23.7	65.3	40.7	413.3	1591.3	1178.0
2010	384.2	78.1	89.9	119.2	28.5	593.1	3317.5	2724
2011Est.	731.0	99.6	97.2	142.5	30.4	973.9	4496.4	3522.5
2012Proj.	756.3	119.3	102.4	144.5	31.9	1032.2	5089.7	4057.5
% decline 2000/12	37.8	24.7	-18.3	7.4	-63.8	20.3	132.2	204.2

Source: RBZ 2010 from World Bank Data

For instance, the main crops declined by between 45% and 58% and the value of exports declined by 52%, while horticulture alone declined by 81%, see Table 6-15. A resurgence was only witnessed from 2009 following the re-insertion of capital from mid-2008. As Mkhize and Moyo (2012) point out, the total contribution to exports of agricultural produce declined from 64.3% in 2000 to 25.4% in 2012. On a commodity by commodity basis, the crops responded differentially over this period. Even though total tobacco output increased by 37.8%, constituting the highest increase per crop, its total contribution to national exports declined from 41% to 18.6% over the same period. Whereas among the four top export crops (tobacco, sugar, horticulture and cotton), the highest drop in exports was experienced in horticulture, 18.3 %, the other agricultural exports dropped by 63.8% from US$88.1 million in 2000 to US$31.9 million in 2012. Overall, the liberalisation and dolarisation of the economy from 2008 resulted in improvement in exports from a low figure of US$367.3 million in 2008 to US$1032.2 million in 2012.

With regards to food grain crops, the marketing of wheat and maize was mainly dominated by the GMB, and state subsidy thereto, to buy the grain at controlled prices for onward sale to millers at subsidied prices (Mkhize and Moyo 2012). According to the World Bank (2006), such a process eroded the profitability of the grain food farmers such that the farmers ended up retaining most of their produce for family consumption, as assurance against frequent droughts or alternatively, it was sold through the parallel, informal and local markets. A Baseline Survey report by AIAS (2007) showed that A1 and A2 resettled farmers sold 53 and 58% of their maize to the GMB from 2002 to 2007 while 41 and 37% of these farmers, respectively, did not sell their produce at all. In the six districts surveyed by AIAS in 2007, the balance of 6 and 5% of the grain from A1 and A2 farmers respectively, was sold through local markets, mainly through barter trade mainly to gain access to (including other food) commodities.

The liberalisation of the economy from a commandist economy under *Maguta* introduced in 2005 resulted in the opening up of the agrarian economy by allowing the import of food grains from neighbouring countries. Increased imports (of foods, oilseed and meats) into Zimbabwe from countries such as Malawi, Zambia, Mozambique and South Africa from 2009 also sharpened competition to local production. According to Mkhize and Moyo (2012), such a situation was made worse by the fact that the government also began to impose a higher maize producer price that was pegged at a higher level than the regional price, where for instance, in 2012, the government, through the Minister of Agriculture set the maize producer price at US$295.00 against a regional price of US$285.00. However, as Scoones *et al.* (2010) note, local prices were higher than those offered by GMB such that in 2009 consequent to the removal of GMB monopoly in the purchase of maize in the same year, most farmers preferred to sell to local buyers. Moreover, the GMB had accumulated debts and therefore was unable to pay farmers for delivered maize since 2009, resulting in farmers either abandoning the crop or relying on private sellers. For Scoones *et al.* (2010), some farmers continued to sell through GMB because it was a requirement for farmers who would have secured inputs through the institution or to fulfill a condition for access to Agribank loans in the future.

Many crops have now developed complex marketing supply chains that involves input suppliers, small-scale producers, small traders and small millers dotted across the country, the GMB mainly limited to securing the strategic reserve of 290,000 tonnes, and four large formal-scale milling companies in urban centres, as the writers observed, assisted by limited contract farming. Their study reveals that by 2006, the maize market had ceased to exist in any significant manner and so was its input supply chain, which by and large had been replaced by dubious markets often with doubtful products. The supply chain inter-linkages generates an ex-farm value addition of US$137.00 and US$203.00 for milling and stock feeds respectively for maize (PWC 2010). The GMB has ceased to be the main buyer for small grains (soya beans, edible beans, groundnuts) following liberalisation of the agrarian economy and trade policy from 2008, resulting in the entrance of diverse private buyers including by contractors, agro-processing firms and agro-dealers (Mkhize and Moyo 2012). Overall, Zimbabwean producers face an uneven trading environment which impacts negatively on farmers' and agro-processors' viability. Efforts are underway to reverse these negative policies through the re-introduction of customs duty on processed food and food crops, although this is being applied differentially, as Mkhize and Moyo (2012) observe.

However, the introduction of contract farming for some crops, including cotton, sugar cane and tobacco have had a positive impact for some crops. With regards to tobacco, over 77% of the crop is now being produced and sold through contract farming (TIMB, 2014), however, over 98% of the crop is being exported in semi-processed form with the balance being used to manufacture cigarettes. With regards to the beef industry, the formal market collapse together with the grazing lands and Cold Storage Commission (CSC), and was replaced by an informal market, creating new value and supply chains as observed by Scoones et al. (2010). The issue of transport availability for the farmers in need of markets is a constraining factor for farmers, as cheap transport forms such as railway lines have ceased to operate in most areas. In areas where the train is available, marketing is a hive of activities during the period that the trains visit as is the case in some parts of Masvingo province as these writers elaborate. The study by Scoones et al. (2010) also observed that it is critical to review and find out if over time (15 years after the commencement of the FTLRP), 'can a reconfigured agriculture revitalise the sector, and indeed overcome the inequalities, inefficiencies and distortions that have affected the large-scale sector over the decades?' And can this be built on the back of successful local-level production and accumulation from below? Revealing the unfolding value chains that are linked locally, nationally and globally can potentially establish what multiplier effect (Delgado et al. 1998; Haggblade et al. 2007) on capital accumulation and class formation emerging in rural Zimbabwe.

7.9 Capital Accumulation and Investments

There has been intense debate on ongoing levels of capital accumulation and farm investments that are underpinned by political and ideological positioning by some scholars in Zimbabwe. For instance, Zamchiya (2012) observes that there is a general pattern of low investment on the new farms, citing Mangwe district where Matondi et al. (2008) earlier noted that farmers were only buying shovels, picks, mattocks, wheel barrows and axes. At the time of the study, only three of the farmers had bought tractors, with only two of these having bought tractor ploughs as well. Matondi *et al.* (2008) note disinvestment on resettled farms from 2000 with no meaningful investment by A1 farmers in Mazowe district. Besides axes, hoes and shovels, a few farmers had also bought cultivators, harrows and scotch carts in Mazowe. However, Matondi *et al.* (2008) and Matondi's (2011) studies neither explain the sources of income and the changes in ownership patterns before and after resettlement nor do they reveal the diverse ownership patterns in other settlement models. Marongwe's (2008) Goromonzi District study reveals cases of vandalisation of assets and infrastructure such as irrigation and reported disinvestment on the farms.

However, in Masvingo Province, a study by Scoones *et al.* (2008) revealed the new settlement schemes were doing well 'in many respects' given the overall political and economy-wide challenges in Zimbabwe since 2000, at aggregate level. This is evidenced by substantial economic returns in many sites of Masvingo studied by Scoones *et al.* (2010), notwithstanding that A1 were doing better than A2 farmers. In those sites, Scoones and others noted increased investment in rural infrastructure (housing, wells, fencing, and gardens) with A1 farmers getting surpluses from sale of agricultural commodities and proceeds being reinvested into agricultural production, demonstrating a pattern of 'accumulation from below' by an emerging group of new 'middle farmers' who accessed new land, as revealed by the study.

The Masvingo study observed that the patterns of accumulation are varied across settlement schemes, sites and social groups, while evidence shows that newly resettled farmers had an upward mobility, driven by agricultural production by smallholder farmers. The study noted better returns in an extensive ranch of production sites on an area basis compared to the pre-FTLRP of 2000. In addition, the study revealed that A2 farmers relying on dryland farming are performing badly due to limited commitment by owners, lack of infrastructure, limited connections to the commodity markets, and ongoing conflicts with neighbours among other issues and the predominance of patronage connections as means to gain access to land and farming inputs. The A2 farmers are still performing well below previous white commercial farmers' levels, mainly due to constrained state capacity to extend patronage support, resulting in low productivity (Scoones *et al.* 2010; Mkhize and Moyo 2012). However, Mkhize and Moyo (2012) suggest that while data on investments on farms after the FTLRP remain scant, the 2005/6 and 2009 surveys by AIAS (2009: 175) reveal that most beneficiaries of the programme are constructing new homesteads even though many are 'based on thatch, pole and dagga'. [See also Table 7-15 (a) and (b)].

Table 7-15: (a) Productive Investment (b) Masvingo Investment/Household in Resettled Areas

Type of investment	A1 model		A2 model		Total	
	No	%	No	%	No	%
Homestead	1089	66.0	206	47.0	1295	62.0
Irrigation equipment	168	10.2	48	11.0	216	10.3
Farm equipment & machinery	111	6.7	39	8.9	150	7.2
Storage Facilities	123	7.5	30	6.8	153	7.3
Livestock	200	12.1	79	18.0	279	13.4
Tobacco barns	22	1.3	6	1.4	28	1.3
Electricity	5	0.3	2	0.5	7	0.3
Worker housing	123	7.3	62	14.2	185	8.9
Plantations & orchards	12	0.7	2	0.5	14	0.7
Environmental works	18	1.1	5	1.1	23	1.1

Focus of investment	Average per household (US$)
Land clearance	385
Land/buildings	631
Cattle	612
Farm equipment	198
Transport	150
Toilets	77
Garden fencing	29
Wells	79
Total	2,161

Source: AIAS District Household Baseline Survey (2005/06); N 2089: Scoones et al. (2010)

The AIAS Survey of 2005/6 revealed that some households were doing well, investing in physical investments from their own savings, mainly in farm infrastructure (new irrigation infrastructure, barns, workers' houses and motorised machines) (25%). The 2005/6 AIAS survey also shows that most farmers used off-farm income such as wage income, remittances and little credit to finance investments, with A1 farmers investing more than A2 farmers on a per hectare basis. Public investment remained low in social service delivery, but this has a historical background where, according to AIAS Interdistrict survey (Moyo *at al.* 2014) which noted that the establishment of services has historically been ongoing through efforts by the state and the communities, but have generally been poorly developed in the former LSCFs compared to the CAs were

161

the post-colonial state rolled our extensive developmental initiatives in the economic and social service sector. To this end, access to social services tends to be differentiated between the newly redistributed farming areas and communal areas. The AIAS 2013/14 Survey showed that between 2011 and 2013, farmers were making agricultural investments on the farms as shown in Table 7-16. For instance, the survey noted that, of the households, investments increased significantly with housing at 20%, hand tools at 41.6% and livestock at 27.4%. There is greater investment in housing in the A1 sector at 27.9% than in A2 farms at 17.5%. In terms of irrigation infrastructure, there is greater investment in A2 farms at 3.7% compared to 0.2% in A1 households and none in the CAs. Other notable investments are in animal drawn implements, which totalled 10.4% for all the settlement sectors.

Table 7-16: Investments into Productive Assets by Settlement Type in 2012

Investment type	A1		A2		CA		Total	
	No.	%	No.	%	No.	%	No.	%
Hand tools	219	45.9	156	52.5	78	24.7	453	41.6
Infrastructure								
Housing	133	27.9	52	17.5	33	10.4	218	20
Deep wells	8	1.7	13	4.4	2	0.6	23	2.1
Boreholes	2	0.4	4	1.3	0	0	6	0.6
Storage facilities	5	1	7	2.4	1	0.3	13	1.2
Private tobacco barns	4	0.8	14	4.7	0	0	18	1.7
Irrigation	1	0.2	11	3.7	0	0	12	1.1
Animal drawn								
Livestock	166	34.8	88	29.6	45	14.2	299	27.4
Livestock facilities	25	5.2	30	10.1	14	4.4	69	6.3
Animal drawn implements	78	16.4	19	6.4	16	5.1	113	10.4
Power driven								
Farm implements	11	2.3	39	13.1	1	0.3	51	4.7
Generators	6	1.3	17	5.7	2	0.6	25	2.3
Grinding mills	2	0.4	5	1.7	0	0	7	0.6
Truck>1t	3	0.6	14	4.7	0	0	17	1.6
Cars	3	0.6	19	6.4	0	0	22	2
Single Cab trucks	4	0.8	7	2.4	0	0	11	1
Double Cab trucks	0	0	7	2.4	0	0	7	0.6

Source: AIAS Household 2013/14 Survey, Household Questionnaire

The survey therefore shows that there is greater investment in housing in A1 farms compared to the other sectors, while the A2 sector also had greater investment in cars, farm implements compared to the other sectors. These investments from across the settlement models were largely from re-investment of farm profits from sale of agricultural produce. However communal farmers mostly rely on savings for capital investments, as the survey report reveals.

7.10 Class Formation after 2000

The FTLRP transformed the agrarian structure in Zimbabwe by creating new categories of small producers, middle farmers, large farmers and estates in terms of landholding sizes, resulting in increased small-to medium-scale farmers, accounting for 80% of the land and significantly reduced large-scale farms and estates (Moyo 2011: 510), in a new trimodal agrarian structure and under an American path of agrarian reform. Agrarian change has also resulted in the emergence of a 'broadly based agrarian capitalist class, built around former and new farming 'elites' composed of a smaller segment of the large-scale capitalist farmers (white and blacks) with reduced landholding sizes of 700 hectares down from 2000 hectares formerly owned by white commercial farmers' (Moyo 2011, 510). For Moyo and Nyoni (2013), social differentiation is a result of agro-ecological variation, differences in land sizes, off-farm incomes and asset ownership.

According to Moyo (2011), 75% of the middle capitalist farmers own an average of 100 hectares, while small farm producers own between 1-30 hectares, and in some regions these peasants own between 0.2-5.0 hectares, numbering over 1.3million households, as Table 6-18 shows. In Moyo's view, the ongoing reconfiguration has resulted in the emergence of a middle capitalist farmers who have received government support in the means of production (inputs, credit and machinery) and better social networks. Moyo (2011, 513) observes the dominance of a 'merchant path' of agrarian social relations based on increased 'urban professionals, the petty-bourgeoisie, bureaucrats and private sector managers occupying

163

about 20% of the acquired land' who are differentiated by levels of capital intensification and use of hired compared to own family labour.

The labour relations that existed following land dispossession in the colonial era (Arrighi 1970), have been reversed as 'land-short, landless and poor peasants' who had been forced into an insecure subordinating and exploitative system of cheap farm wage labour have now been allocated land (Moyo 2011). The rural peasants who used to provide wage labour to a few rich farmers now apply their family labour in their own farming lands and account for their own social reproduction. Rural peasants now have a choice between selling their excess labour within a differentiated farming set-up as well as in non-farming activities, while those former LSCF farm workers who did not gain access to land are now 'freer to sell their labour to many new smaller-to medium sized farmers, in addition to their access to small plots to cultivate 'subsistence' crops, *albeit* under defined or 'squatting' tenures', as Moyo (2011: 513) further elaborates.

Whereas new plot holders in the A1 and A2 settlement employ the former LSCF farm workers, according to Chambati (2009), 68% of these workers still complain of lack of access to secure land for residency. Furthermore, according to Chambati and Moyo (2009) and Moyo *et al.* (2009), low wages under insecure living conditions provided by the new landholders remain problematic. The new landholders employ from among themselves (A1 and A2 farmers) unemployed and family members from contiguous rural areas (Chambati 2009), which constitute a new agrarian labour force and a new source of social differentiation. In this regard, the use of hired and family labour becomes critical as it reveals social differentiation in rural farming areas. Using disaggregated labour hiring patterns from Chambati and Moyo (2009), 26% of land beneficiaries use hired labour intensively, while on average most households command family pools of 3.5 persons as shown in Table 7-17.

Table 7-17: Structure of Rural Labour in new Resettlement Areas (A1 and A2).

Level of labour use	No. of households	% of HH	Average labour used (No. of persons)				
			Hired in				
			Full-time	Part-time	Family[4]	Family + full time	Hired out[4]
Low[1]	1351	64.67	0.0	5.52	3.61	3.61	0.13
Medium[2]	195	9.33	1.0	7.69	3.53	4.53	0.14
High[3]	543	25.99	7.55	12.87	3.77	11.31	0.10
Total	2089	100.00	2.05	7.64	3.64	5.70	0.12

Source: Moyo and Chambati (2009).
Notes: (1) Household utilises family labour in combination with part-time labour hired in; (2) Household hires in one full-time worker plus some part-time workers; (3) Household hires in at least two full-time workers plus some part-time workers; (4) Not statistically different across labour classes.

This analysis helps shade light on labour utilisation in the fast track areas (A1 and A2), but does not reveal social relations and social reproduction processes in other rural areas, such as the ORAs and CAs. Such an analysis will give a fuller picture about the differentiation in rural Zimbabwe. For Moyo (2011), the new land politics is a class struggle emerging from an ongoing differentiated class formation process driven by differential capacity among A2 and A1 beneficiaries to hire labour and in access finance from diverse sources that is more evidently expressed through differential land tenure dynamics and emerging land struggles. This study shades light on the dynamics in CAs in addition to resettled areas using Wheeze district as a study area.

Zamchiya (2012) uses the trimodal to categories farmers in terms of land access in Chipinge, Manicaland province, rather in a narrower descriptive sense, whereas Moyo (2011) applies it as a conceptual approach to discern agrarian transition and paths and class formation in rural Zimbabwe, post 2000, taking from Kausky (1988), Lenin (1964) and de Janvry (1981). Some scholars have also investigated social differentiation in the post 2000 period and tried to get a deeper understanding of the effects of changes on the agrarian structure on agrarian change (Bush and Cliff 1984; Cousins et al. 1992; Moyo 1995).

Scoones et al. (2010: 227) apply a livelihoods framework and conclude that farmers are differentiated in terms of how they have fared following the FTLRP and posit that social differentiation exist between sites, across and within rural households and including age, gender and ethic based dimensions of differentiation' For these writers, even though there is social differentiation, different sectors are distinct, with variations between A1 settlements, CAs, A2 settlements and LSCFs. The livelihood framework therefore applies success as a key factor to identify emerging class dynamics and farmers are categorised and correlated using indications of wealth, such as cattle ownership, land area, equipment owned and used, types of houses owned and engagement with the markets.

This process revealed that 10% is dropping out, 33.6% is hanging in, 21.4% is stepping out, while 35% is stepping up. For Moyo *et al.* (2014), the peasantry is a heterogeneous grouping of households where the poor predominate through semi-proletarianisation, mass super-exploitation exploitation and extraction of profits through self-employment and unremunerated labour, undertaken mainly by women. In turn, Moyo and Nyoni (2013) argue that this leads to a broadened home based on differentiated consumption and production of peasants, medium-scale and larger scale black capitalists and agrarian transformation, relying on cheap labour under functional dualism and extroverted patterns of accumulation. In all, re-peasantization appear to be the dominant process emerging in the rural areas, in particular following resettlement of both the rural poor and some urban former workers, with a new class of petty commodity producers accounting for 93.7 in resettled areas (see also Moyo and Yeros 2005).

7.11 Conclusion

The chapter traced the changing capital-state relations, economic and agrarian policies and the production patterns, marketing and capital accumulation and class formation over the years and through periodisation. Government policy has been evolving with varied impact on different agricultural sectors, while the capital fight in the early 2000s and its subsequent re-insertion from 2009 mainly through agricultural inputs funding arrangements by international and domestic capital, impacted variably on production marketing patterns, with differentiated impact on varied classes and sectors in different places within Zimbabwe's agro-ecological regions. The next chapter presents the research methodology, revealing what steps were taken to unravel agrarian development in Hwedza District, as the case study.

Chapter Eight

Hwedza's Socio-Economic History and Tobacco Production

8.1 Introduction

The purpose of this chapter is to assess and reveal the socio-economic history of, and the re-insertion of, capital in tobacco production in Hwedza District. Hwedza District fell under Marandellas District until 1954, as shown in Map 8.1. The name 'Hwedza', which the colonial authorities referred to as 'Wedza', literally translates to "The lightening of the sun". The area is connected to Rusape, Dorowa Mine, Marondera and Harare by tarred road. It is located between Save River on the west and Ruzawi River on the east. At a broader level, Hwedza District is climatically divided into two halves: Upper Hwedza which begins from St Barnabas Chisasike through Hwedza Centre to Watershed West, which is cooler and receives average to high rainfall, and Lower Hwedza which stretches from Mukamba through Goneso to Zviyambe and Makarara, which overly experience warmer to hot temperatures and lower rainfall. The cropping programmes for the two halves are in sync with the weather patterns; peasants in the Upper Hwedza grow tobacco, maize and paprika while those in Lower Hwedza grow cotton and sorghum/millet. Tobacco has recently emerged as a key crop in both Upper and Lower Hwedza.

Hwedza District straddles four agro-ecological regions; the part located in Watershed West, formerly the European area, falls under NR IIa and is mostly used for commercial farming. The area between the Watershed West, Goto and Dendenyore, is mostly NR IIb, occupied by the ORAs, A1, A2 farms and partly by the CAs, also formerly (partly) a European area suitable for mixed commercial farming. Currently tobacco and maize are the main crops grown in this area. The area between Gonese and Makwarimba is CA and is partly located under NR IIIa. The drier part of the district, Zviyambe is under NR IV under the SSCFs model (also see Map 8-1).

Map 8-1: Marandellas District in 1961

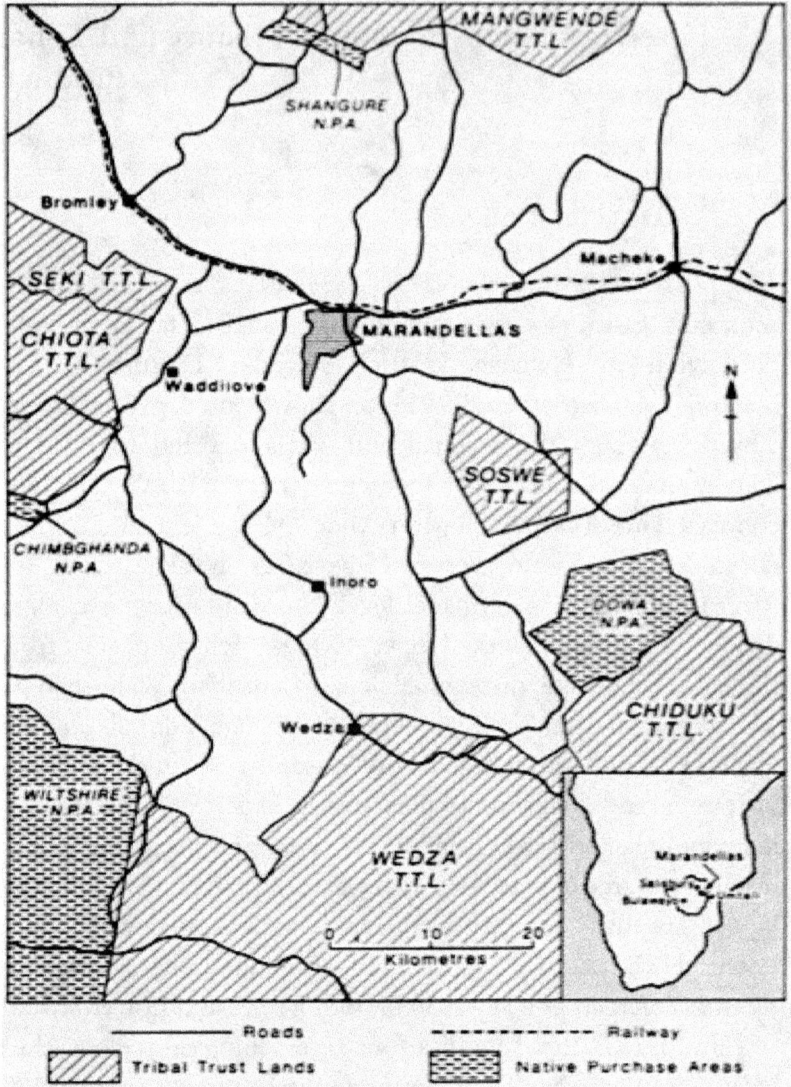

Source: Hodder-Williams, 1983.

The district is made up of basically granite stones with some intrusions of dolerite and greenstones which result in richer, redder soils compared to the predominantly sandy soils which are however responsive to manure and fertilizers and therefore suitable for growing a variety of crops (Hodder-Williams 1983). The national land resettlement program started in the 1950s under the native purchase areas where African yeoman farmers could gain limited ownership of farms (Ranger 1985, xi). This was created as a buffer between the blacks and the affluent white population. The second land resettlement program in Hwedza district commenced in 1982, whilst the third land resettlement program commenced in 2000. However, the Svosve people led land invasions in 1997 before leading the land occupation in 2000 (see Moyo 2000; Alexander 2006).

8.2 Origin of the Svosve People

Some writers (Beach 1994; Woodhouse and Chimhowu (2008) suggest that the Svosve people occupied this area in the eighteenth century. For instance, according to Woodhouse and Chimhowu (2008), the Svosve clan arrived in Hwedza in the mid-eighteenth century, coming from the north, and survived as an entity based in this area through the turbulent period of conquest fought between rival Ndebele, Ngoni and Rozvi groups in the nineteenth century. According to Beach (1980: 287), the Vambire settled under Nembire, whose son is called Dendenyore, after defeating the Masarirambi dynasty, which had come from Old Buhera to settle near the source of Sabi River on the main watershed, thereby taking over the Hwedza Mountain. The Hwedza area was thought to be ideal due to its location along the trade route, the prominent landmark of the Plateau and the base of the Njanja hoe industry, as Beach (1980) elaborates.

It is also thought that the Mbire people also referred to as the Svosve people came to this area during the same time with the whites, mainly some Portuguese coming through Mozambique and involved in barter trade. 'The whites eventually left, leaving behind one of them who was ill. He was later to recover and then to become Zinjanja tribe, later to settle in the Charter district', as revealed by the records at the National Archives (N3/33/8). The white man (Portuguese)/the district was central to the iron tools trade with the Svosve people and other far away areas such as Buhera, Bocha and Gutu. The Mbire people left for Marandellas and later Chief Svosve's son, Makanganise, settled in Svosve. Records at the National Archives (N3/33/8) reveal that:

171

The land apportionment act split the family while the 1896 rebellion further scattered the family. Three groupings later emerged, the vaZomba in Svosve TTL, Mbiranunge in Wedza and Marondera under Marondellas. There is acclaim by Madzimurema of another group under his leadership in Chihota TTL.

Woodhouse and Chimhowu (2008) agree with this view and note that some remained at Svosve, some resettled in Chihota to the west whilst some went to Hwedza, to the south. Those who settled in Hwedza were under Makwarimba, Goto, Chigondora and Musanhu Sub-chiefs, as Woodhouse and Chimhowu (2008) elaborate. Colonial dispossession was to later force Makanganise and his people to move back to Hwedza, as land alienation in favour of the whites intensified, triggering subsequent land occupations in the pre and post-independence era.

8.3 Precolonial Economic Activities in Hwedza District

The interconnectedness within Hwedza district and its linkages with other commercial centres, through time, has had immense influence on the well-being of Hwedza people since the pre-colonial period. In this section, it is argued that white national bourgeoisie capital and international capital interests shaped peasantry accumulation and class formation and have remained vested with these processes, initially through conquer, domination, land alienation and accumulation by dispossession from the 1890s to today, amidst Africans' resistance. This trajectory is supported by Bond (1998) who argues that '[t]he financial penetration of space has, it seems, enormous implications for the nature of territorial divisions of production and reproduction, as well as for the operation of financial power across different scales'.

There are accounts of indigenous Africans being involved in agriculture prior to the arrival of Europeans, with evidence of capacity beyond subsistence farming to produce in excess of needs, managing to supply local and distant markets in Zimbabwe (Bhila 1982; Beach 1977; Palmer 1977a; Phimister 1977). At the same time, white settlers are known to have been primarily transport riders,

172

storekeepers or traders, who relied on buying and stealing food from Africans (Palmer 1977a). Among Africans, increased demands for their produce resulted in increased income and caused some changes in labour processes, including the emergence of wage-labour amongst them. The people of Hwedza district are known to have thrived in both mining and farming as their main economic activities from the pre-colonial period. Participation in mining was confirmed by the Native Commissioner, Marandellas, Mr Morris, while responding to C. D. Wise, the Director of Land Settlement, on his request to alienate more land located around Hwedza Mountain, which was endowed with iron ore when he responded on 18 September 1906 that the Chief and his people strongly objected, a position he agreed with. In Morris' view, '[t] here are a large number of natives around Hwedza who also work the iron mines on the Western slope of the mountain' to the effect that land further alienation would have deprived them of their livelihoods.

In terms of social and economic linkages, the Hwedza people were heavily connected to the Njanja people in Charter district through trade in hoes for goats and cattle (Beach 1977, 49). The increasing demand for new hoes, was a direct response to increasing land utilisation as the Shona population grew, resulting in accumulation through cattle, goats and chicken. It is, however, noteworthy that hoes were also used for marriage ceremonies in many parts of the Reserves. Agriculture, therefore, rose to become one of the main economic activities that sustained the people of Hwedza district, with high production of maize and raring of cattle. Ranger (1981) notes that, with regards to other crops, by 1932, the people of Hwedza were producing some of the best crops grown in Rhodesia at the time and as such they were able to sell their maize to the Control Board classified under the best grade as much as it was targeted for direct export. According to Harrison (1964), tobacco farming, which was being carried out on 25 farms in this district, was established to be the major crop under production by the 1962/3 farming season. Indeed, the history of tobacco farming in Zimbabwe is tied to Marandellas district, incorporating Hwedza area. One of the experimenting and training farms was established at the Marandellas

Central farm under the management of Scorror by 1907 (Hodder-Williams 1983).

8.4 Land Alienation and Peasants Struggles in Hwedza District

The Svosve people faced land alienation challenges following the passing of Ordinance 51 of 1898. The alienation of areas with heavy red and black loams, which had been favoured by Africans prior to 1890, to Europeans by the Native Commissioners, was a key ingredient of the creation of Reserves. The Reserves, which were fully established by 1902 (CNC 1902), were created in areas far away from the railway lines and on the plateau (Moyana 1984). During this period, the Hwedza Reserves together with Svosve and Chihota fell under Native Commissioner of Marandellas district that was in charge of drawing demarcations for Native Reserves and land alienation for European settlement post the 1896 uprisings. However, the BSAC sought to push the Africans further from these good soils. In one incident, the white administration offered an inferior piece of land (the Marandellas block of farms) in exchange for better off land. Mr. C. D. Wise, the Director of Land Settlement captured the administration views in a memorandum dated 4 March 1910, when stating that 'the reserves should be reduced where they were situated on the route of the projected branch railway lines, and pressed for the exchange of all ready 'red and black soil which the natives never work, for a lighter class of soil' (see also Palmer 1977: 84).

Indeed, Mr. Morris, the NC for Marandellas sarcastically reported that Africans were willing to exchange rich red soils under NR IIb, for sandy soils adjoining the Hwedza Reserves, for part of an area that falls under NR III. This was captured in a memorandum dated 20 November 1906 addressed to Chief Secretary Castens, written in reference to six farms as shown in Map 8-2. These farms were successfully exchanged with land adjoining alienated land in a more favourable farming environment, with the settlers taking over the red and black soil and exchanging it for sandy soils that are less productive, thereby undermining the accumulation trajectory for Africans. As it turned out, and contrary to the NC Marandellas (Mr.

Morris) views, the Native Affairs Commission which was set from 1910 to 1911 was later to be informed that some Reserves had poor soils in a large portion of the soil, while water is deficient and in some cases, completely unsuitable for human occupation.

Map 8-2: Map of the farms proposed for exchange by the BSAC, 1910

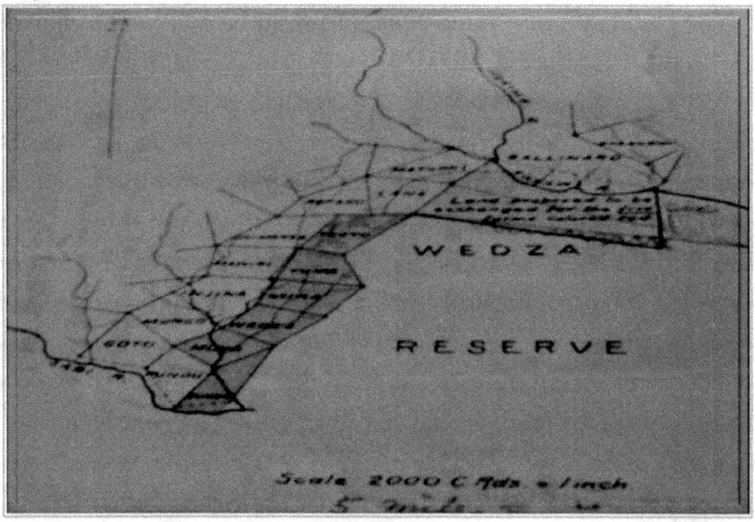

Source: National Archives of Zimbabwe,
Notes: Extracted on 23 September 2014, permission to use this map was granted.

8.5 Marketing, Labour Relations and Accumulation Patterns

The 'white agricultural policy' instituted from 1908 to 1914 was designed to expand white farmers participation in agriculture and to exclude the Africans. As Phimister (1988: 4) reports, by 1895 Hwedza District was already exporting 'large quantities of grain to mines in Matabeleland province', and these was produced by Black Africans in the district.

8.5.1 Marketing and labour relations
It was in the marketing of the produce that Europeans curbed African effort the most. Having replaced Africans as the major producers of tobacco and maize, post 1907 (Palmer 1977: 91-93), the

175

settlers using both political and capital power went on to impose levies and to undermine access to produce markets and the pricing of the produce, using Trade stores. As Moyana (1984: 15) observes, the GMB bought produce from Africans at lower prices than that of European commodities. The net effect of the levies was to reduce the purchase price and income accruing to the African farmers even though the quality of produce would have been as good.

The challenge of limited access to market was further illustrated well in the case of Hwedza Reserves, in the Marondellas district where the Svosve people were affected by 'pacification' during the clearing process for the railway line between Salisbury to Umtali and they ended up being driven into nearby hills and mountains where they were eventually settled by the Native Commissioner who mistook the new areas to be their original homes, as Moyana (year) elaborates. The 'pacification' process ensured that Africans had no access to railway roads and therefore curbed their access to markets. Indeed, one white farmer in Hwedza told the Morris Carter Commission, that land should 'be nearer to centres where they can dispose of their produce' (Moyana 1984). As Hodder-Williams (1983) notes, citing Seeger's Memorandum to the Secretary of Mines and Roads, dated 3 February 1919:

[T]here were also economic factors, which were bound to loom large to these essentially poor farmers. One farmer, for instance, complained that his neighbour refused blacks from the Wedza Reserve permission to pass through his land so that he could corner the whole trade in grain and cattle: 'I believe the whole matter is that of bad feeling towards me, as he does not like to see natives go past his store and go on elsewhere to trade'. Since so many farmers depended upon trading in the Reserves to meet their own maize requirements or to provide their basic income, these squabbles were serious.

With regards to the provision of labour, in the case of Marandellas District, an agreement was reached where the Mashona remained on their kraals rent free. They were, therefore, an immediate source of labour for the European farms. To this end, by 1961, 40,000 Africans still lived in farm villages (Hodder-Williams

1983) supplying labour to the white farmers in this area. The N/C for Marandellas district admitted together with others, at some point, that 'force was needed to make the Shona comply with their instruction' of working on their lands, due to labour shortages as Hodder-Williams (1983) elaborate.

8.5.2 Hwedza accumulation patterns

In spite of the shenanigans to undermine Africans, 'A combination of those pockets of pre-colonial accumulation which had survived the violence of the 1890s, and the productive reinvestment of income earned in wage labour, gave rise to a distinctive pattern of rural differentiation' (Phimister 1986: 254). As the CNC for Southern Rhodesia acknowledged in a 1920 report, 'an active class of small farmers ... [was] being evolved' despite domination efforts by the white settlers. The people of Hwedza who remained on the Highveld producing grain on the European farms, mostly migrant labour, continued to excel in the accumulation processes.

8.6 Tobacco Farming in Hwedza District

The study of the origin, role and contribution of tobacco in the social, economic and political dynamics of Hwedza District is crucial in the context of its contribution to both the Marandellas District (then incorporating Chihota, Marondera and Hwedza until 1954) and subsequently Hwedza District, among other crops. The study of tobacco production positions this study at a vintage point for unpacking the role of capital and the state in accumulation in Zimbabwe's countryside, as it has evolved and transformed for over a century, from 1890. For Hodder-Williams (1983: 2-3), the expansion of tobacco as the country's major foreign currency and revenue earner is tied to Marandellas district. At the same time Marandellas development 'has been intimately bound up with the fluctuations of the tobacco industry'.

The history of tobacco farming indicates that primitive types of tobacco *(Nicotiana rustica)* was already being grown in Rhodesia by the Shongwe people of Gokwe (Phimister 1977) before the arrival of the

Pioneer Column in 1888 (Clements and Harben 1962). Clements and Harben (1962) also note that the cultivation of the crop was widespread in many parts of the country, but Wankie and Sebungwe and some Eastern district were the main centres. Limited trading of crude tobacco such as the 'Nyoka' tobacco is known to have occurred in Gokwe and was sold in the form of balls reaching as far as the Bankota lands and the Kariba markets among the African underground workers in the Copperbelt in the now Zambia.

At the turn of the century, upon the realisation of the poor returns from gold explorations, the BSAC turned from mining to tobacco farming as a way of recouping on losses incurred since the BSAC in Rhodesia. Clements and Harben (1962) observe that the settlers were 'restless and discontented', with returns from mining, while shareholders of the company in England became unsettled when half investment to the tune of a million was spent without any prospect of a return. As a result, tobacco was soon identified as the new crop to propel the Colony's economic and social development (Clements and Herben 1962).

8.6.1 The boom and bust in tobacco production

The first auction floor for the crop was carried out on 20th January 1910, following the adoption of an improved variety. The BSAC entered into tobacco farming in 1907 and opened a block of farms between Hwedza and Marondellas district with H. K. Scorror as the farmer at the Marandellas Central farm (Clements and Harben 1962; Hodder-Williams 1983). A subsidiary of the BSAC, the Tobacco Company of Rhodesia, was created and tasked with the responsibility to provide growers with loans for the development of their farms, and to pay advances on crops, while accepting tobacco as security for the loans (Clements and Harben 1962). However, the monopoly of the UTC from the Cape Colony resulted in unfavourable prices for the crop in subsequent years, such that the Minister of Agriculture of the first government post in 1923 posited that '[t]he growers must be able to get out of the hands of that monopoly, the United Tobacco Company, which [these past] few years has been considered by the tobacco farmers as a very grievous burden' (Clements and Harben 1962).

According to Hodder-Williams (1983), a market was established in 1924 to supply the crop to Britain, which in turn changed the fortunes of tobacco producers and resulted in an increase in the number of farmers. The visit to Britain in search of new markets was said to have proved the availability of good prices for the farmers and the existence of adequate markets for all the tobacco crop produced by the Colony. (Government printers, 1924, cited in Hodder-Williams 1983). As Clements and Harben (1962) observe, production of tobacco increased as the number of farmers growing the crop increased from 189 in 1925 to 336 in 1926 and 763 in 1928. A combination of this increase, which was followed by an increase in settlers, mainly from Britain where the word about the viability of the Rhodesian crop had spread and the high prices secured after a negotiation with South African buyers as well as encouragement from the government, resulted in a surge of production as Table 8-1 shows.

Table 8-1: Production of Tobacco in Southern Rhodesia, 1918 -19 to 1927-28

	Acres grown	Total yield	Average yield per acre	Average price per pound
1918–19	3,198	1,179,932	369	n.a.
1919–20	5,546	2,435,994	435	n.a.
1920–1	7,888	3,192,662	404	n.a.
1921–2	9,007	2,880,104	318	n.a.
1922–3	7,758	2,540,942	327	8.75
1923–4	7,001	3,426,390	489	11.75
1924–5	7,550	1,987,382	263	13.73
1925–6	13,160	5,313,186	404	16.61
1926–7	29,172	18,631,069	638	9.72
1927–8	45,711	24,491,464	536	7.04

SOURCE Report of Secretary, Department of Agriculture, for years 1925 to 1929.

However, tobacco production experienced a decline from 1928 to 1936, due to a collapse in markets, as was the case in 1914, but this time the government and farmers responded by diversifying into livestock and other crops (Hodder-Williams 1983). Nevertheless, the fortunes changed from 1946 to 1957 due to the arrival of new entrants into tobacco farming, mainly ex-servicemen who received support in the form of loans on favourable terms, post market resilience, good prices offered in Britain and the construction of necessary infrastructure in the farming communities (Hodder-Williams 1983; Clements and Harben 1962). (See Figure 8-1 below).

'The London Agreement' signed between Rhodesian tobacco growers and the cigarette manufacturers on 12th December 1947, heralded new fortunes for the industry in Southern Rhodesia. The agreement ensured a market for 46 million pounds, in mass of Rhodesian tobacco renewable every five years, before a review in 1950 to 130 million pounds. Further markets were secured in Australia and other traditional merchants who had sustained the crop before the 'London Agreement'. According to Hodder-Williams (1983), problems beset the farming community from the late 1950s mainly due to increases in fertiliser and fuel prices and erratic weather patterns. At the same time, agriculture ceased to be the engine for growth in Rhodesia with increased industrialisation, especially after the Unilateral Declaration of Independence (UDI) in 1965 and throughout the period leading to independence in 1980. However, in the post-independence period, the crop has continued to contribute significantly to the economic development of the country.

Figure 8-1: Tobacco Growers Numbers and Output around the 1928 Crash

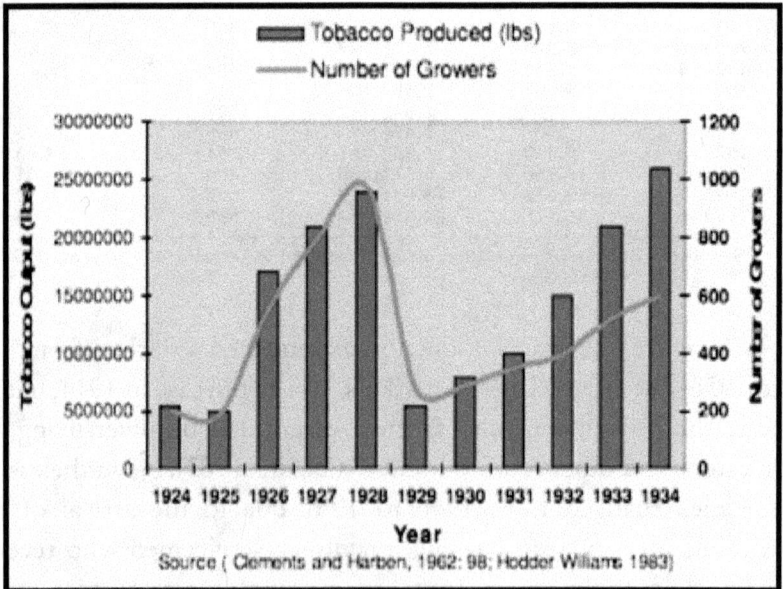

Source (Clements and Harben, 1962: 98; Hodder Williams 1983)

As a result of the upward trend in production which continued throughout the post-independence years, the country grew to be the 5th largest producer of the crop in the world, although production remained dominated by 1 800 large scale commercial farmers who included 300 black commercial farmers producing over 80% of the total output during the 1990's (averaging 200 million kilograms produced on about 85 000 hectares per year), with over 6 000 smallholders producing the balance of 20% (Moyo, 2001). A changed agrarian structure resulted in an increase in production patterns with 107,000 hectares put under tobacco by 105 000 mainly smallholder farmers producing 214 million kilograms and fetching US$677 million and earning over US$1 billion dollars (inclusive of exports) by 2014, up from 70,000 tonnes produced by 21,882 farmers in 2004 valued at Z$593 537 303 (TIMB 2014). There were slight reductions in production that are related to erratic weather patterns and volatile prices experienced in 2015 and 2016, but these are only seen as temporary.

8.6.2 Re-insertion of capital from 2009

The upward surge in production is mainly as a result of the re-insertion of capital after 2009, which has generally seen an increase in tobacco contract farming, and broadened to include smallholders. A total of 16 companies are currently involved in contract farming at various levels of participation. Similarly, international capital has re-entered the fray and is now involved in the financing, buying, processing and manufacturing of cigarettes for domestic and export markets (see Figure 8-2).

However, Zimbabwe has remained the fifth largest producer of tobacco after China, Brazil, India and the United States of America. China has risen to become the largest producer and destination of processed tobacco, accounting for 44.6% in 2013 among the 55-country export destinations of Zimbabwean tobacco (FAO, 2015). In terms of contribution to the employment creation, tobacco industry contributed to an increase in employment from 254,000 in 1936, 377,000 in 1946 to 600,000 in 1956 (Arrighi 1966). However, by 2015, the tobacco industry employed 350,000 wage workers (TIMB, 2015).

Figure 8-2: Contract Tobacco Purchases

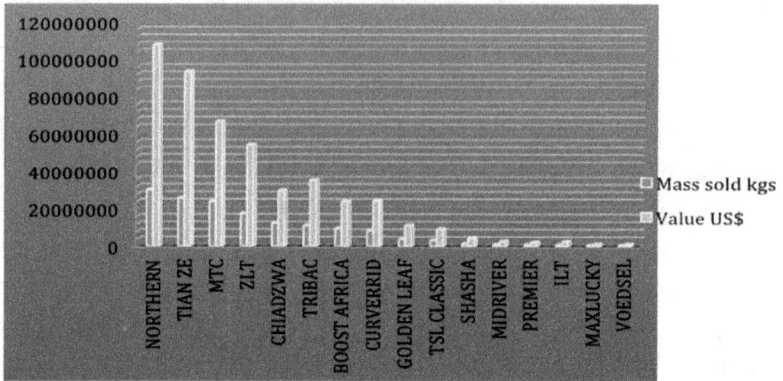

Source: Chidziva Tobacco Company, 2015 Source: TIMB, 2014

8.6.3 Production of tobacco in Hwedza District, 2000-2015

The production patterns for tobacco in Hwedza has also responded to the changing agrarian structure. Initially, in response to land dispossessions from the LSCA, Hwedza district experienced a deep slide in total production by white commercial farmers. For instance, tobacco production by commercial farmers fell from over 12,900 tonnes, contributing 99% in 2000 to well below 472.9 tonnes, contributing 17% in the 2014/2015 season, as shown in Figure 8-3. Even though there has been a slight improvement in total production by this sector, the yield levels have remained below 500 tonnes per annum

Figure 8-3: Tobacco Production by Sector, 2000 – 2015

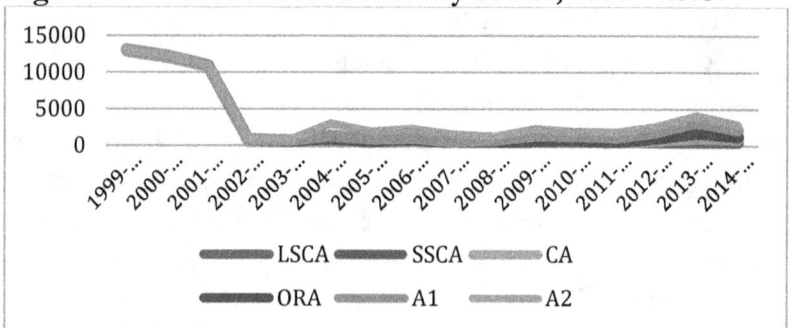

Source: Author using data from Ministry of Agriculture, Agritex Department, 2016

Overall, tobacco production and foreign currency earnings have been on the increase over the period from 2004 to 2015. The trend in production has witnessed changes across the settlement models, as fully illustrated in Tables 8.2.

Table 8-2: Tobacco Production from 1975 to 2015

| Year | Growers | Area (ha) | Mass sold (kg) | Average price and yield | | | Gross value | |
				ZW$/kg	US$/kg	Yield kg/ha	US$	ZW$
2015	97616	107546	198,954,849		2.95	1850	586,544,231	
2014	87166	107371	216,196,683		3.17	2,014	685,244,013	
2013	78 756	88,627	166,572,097		3.67	1,852	612,135,672	
2012	60 047	76 359	144 565 253		3.65	1 893	527 805 943	
2011	56,656	78 415	132,431,905		2.73	1 689	361,448,679	
2010	51 685	67 054	123 503 681		2.88	1 842	355 572 326	
2009	29 018	62 737	58 570 652		2.98	934	174 457 761	
2008	35 094	61 622	48 775 178		3.21	792	156 663 816	
2007	26 412	54 551	73 039 015		2.32	1 339	169 159 675	
2006	20 565	58 808	55 466 689	0.35	2	943		19 527108 198
2005	31 761	57 511	73 376 990	22.71	1.61	1 300		1 666 410 523
2004	21 882	44 025	68 901 129	861.43	2	1 565		593 537 303
2003	20 513	49 571	81 806 414	180.31	2.25	1 673		147 508 194
2002	14 353	74 295	165 835 001	35.93	2.27	2 213		59 576 224
2001	7 937	76 017	202 535 209	17.46	1.75	2 664		35 371 686
2000	8 537	84 857	236 946 295	8.13	1.69	2 792		19 266 709
1999	7 194	84 762	192 145 383	6.62	1.74	2 267		12 726 314
1998	8 334	91 905	215 913 864	3.47	1.72	2 349		75 501 393
1997	5 101	90 630	171 542 696	2.9	2.33	1 893		4 976 043
1996	2 921	81 231	201 550 527	2.9	2.94	2 481		5 848 818
1995	2 525	74 550	198 751 924	1.8	2.12	2 666		3 584 710
1994	2 338	67 416	169 218 196	1.38	1.73	2 510		2 335 875
1993	2 999	82 900	218 370 345	0.8	1.24	2 634		1 752 685
1992	2 604	80 070	201 161 921	0.81	1.62	2 512		1 630 161
1991	1 746	66 927	170 149 851	1.16		2 542		1 969 134
1990	1 493	59 425	133 866 041	0.65		2 253		868 180
1989	1 448	57 660	129 960 308	0.43		2 254		558 459
1988	1 486	59 178	119 912 584	0.39		2 026		471 837
1987	1 519	63 536	127 996 176	0.22		2 015		278 938
1986	1 426	57 349	114 304 117	0.31		1 993		358 206
1985	1 296	52 464	105 555 569	0.27		2 012		283 394
1984	1 186	50 486	119 636 157	0.21		2 370		247 119
1983	1 155	46 622	94 295 739	0.12		2 023		177 798
1982	1 257	46 427	89 387 652	0.17		1 925		149 563
1981	1 145	38 099	67 356 019	0.18		1 768		123 774
1980	1 547	64 310	122 571 366	0.08		1 906		97 437
1979	1 556	59 631	111 686 415	0.08		1 873		92 023
1978	1 612	54 939	82 968 508	0.1		1 510		81 994
1977	1 638	56 993	83 373 667	0.07		1 463		61 085
1976	1 696	66 290	110 533 041	0.07		1 667		76 046
1975	1 731	65 834	83 919 914	0.07		1 275		57 736

Source: TIMB Annual Report, 2015

While there have been increases in yield across sectors, the resettled farmers have experienced the greatest improvement in yield and are led by the A1 farmers who increased from 23.8 tonnes in the

2003/2004 season to 1504.7 tonnes in 2013/2014, contributing 32% of total production, compared to A2 farmers who contributed 23%. However, erratic rains and poor prices resulted in a decrease to 926.6 tonnes in 2015 for the A1 sector. The A2 farmers had an improvement in yield from 76.8 tonnes in 2003/2004 to 1642.5 tonnes in 2004/2005, but the sector has been experiencing swings in total tobacco production on a yearly basis and generally remains below 1,000 tonnes per annum. Tobacco production by the ORAs improved from 175 tonnes in 1999/2000 to 356.09 tonnes in 2014/2015 while the sector's total contribution increased from 1 percent in 2000 to 12 percent in 2015. The total tobacco production by the SSCFs increased from 12 tonnes in 2004/2005 to 79.4 tonnes, with a contribution of 3 percent in 2015. CA farmers also improved in tobacco production from 16 tonnes in 1999/2000 to 369.2 tonnes in 2014/2015, contributing 13% of the total requirements.

All in all, small-scale farmers (A1, 32%; ORA, 12%; CA, 13%) currently contribute 57%t while middle farmers (A2 and SSCA) contribute 26% in total tobacco production in Hwedza District (see Figure 8-4).

Figure 8-4: Percentage Changes in Sector Contribution, 2000-2015

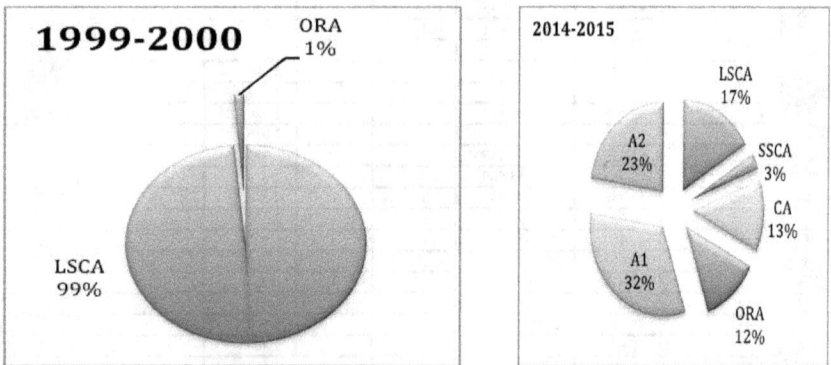

Source: Source: Ministry of Agriculture, Agritex department, Hwedza District Offices, 2016

All the sectors experienced a decline in tobacco production in 2008-9 due to the economy-wide challenges in the country. The liberalisation of the economy from 2009 and the consolidation of the multiple currencies benefited the tobacco industry as farmers were paid in hard currency upon delivery and successful auctioning of tobacco. Similarly, the re-financialisation of agricultural production through the introduction of contract farming for cash and export crops benefitted this sector as more smallholder farmers accessed inputs for tobacco production.

8.6.4 Grain crops

The Svosve people of Hwedza also grew grain crops for household food supply and for trading with the white settlers during the early colonial period. An in-depth discussion of maize production is carried out as the crop was both a food and cash crop. For instance, records show that the people of Hwedza District were generally left in alienated land because they were producing maize, which the white farmers needed for their labour force (Phimister 1988). The study by Phimister also noted that some African farmers from Hwedza District were trading in grain with areas as far as Matabeleland. With regards to the maize supply to Hwedza Mine, Hodder-Williams (1983) observes that 'An increasing number of Mashona went in for growing maize as a cash crop at this time in order to meet the growing demand by miners at Hwedza Mine and for commercial farmers' labour. As illustrated by Hodder-Williams (1983), maize sales exceeded 3,000 bags per annum from 1918. See Table 8-3 below.

Table 8-3: Maize and Tobacco Production in Marandellas, 1918-19 to 1921-26 to 1927 to 28

	Total acreage under cultivation	Bags of maize for sale	Bags of maize consumed	Tobacco acreage	Tobacco production
1918–19	5,670	3,309	4,131	1,098 (1)	424,854 (1)
1919–20	5,912	3,368	4,587	1,866 (1)	778,795 (1)
1920–21	6,128	3,479	4,825	2,734 (1)	1,078,248 (1)
1921–22	6,062	3,270	2,616	2,689 (1)	765,463 (1)
1925–6	8,673	3,464	9,263	2,662 (1)	1,178,838 (1)
1926–7	8,025	— 11,791 —		4,061 (3)	2,529,181 (4)
1927–8	9,683	17,285		4,576 (6)	2,650,162 (6)

SOURCES (i) Summer crop returns, published in *Rhodesian Agricultural Journal*, 1919–1922
(ii) *Report on Summer Crop Returns* for 1927 and 1928 (Salisbury, Government Printer, 1928 and 1929).
NOTE The numbers in parentheses indicate the order among all Mashonaland tobacco growing districts held by Marandellas.

Source: Hodder-Williams (1983)

Overall, maize production increased from 7,440 tonnes in 1919 to 17,285 in 1928.However, maize experienced the greatest decline, from 40,000 tonnes in 2001 to below 5,000 tonnes in 2015, as Figure 8.5a shows. With regards to other crops, oils; inclusive of groundnuts, sunflower and soya beans have consistently remained below 10,000 tonnes per year, but the improvement experienced from 2011/2012 has started to dissipate, particularly from 2014. While all the crops experienced a major decline in the 2007/2008 season, maize had the largest drop, from over 45,000 tonnes in 2007 to below 10,000 in 2008. This drop in production across all sectors is reflective of the economy-wide challenges that the country was facing during this period.

Dekker and Kinsey's (2011) study which included Sengezi ORA in Hwedza District revealed that the resettled farmers in the ORA were doing better than farmers in communal areas. However, maize production figures for Hwedza show that the CAs have sustained pole position in maize production in the post FTLRP period, producing 21,641 tonnes in 2001 and 1,954 tonnes in 2015, while the LSCFs production went down from 12,900 tonnes in 2001 to 81 tonnes in 2014. The ORA declined from 3,240 tonnes in 2001 to 357 tonnes in 2015, as shown in Figure 8.5b.

Figure 8.5a: Tobacco, Maize and Oils 8.5b Maize Production across Sectors, 2000-2015 Production, 1999-2015

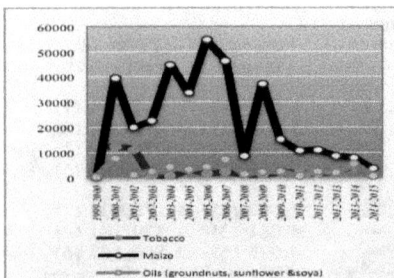

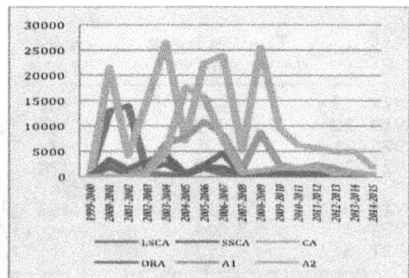

Source: compiled by Author; using various sources; Ministry of Agriculture, Zimstats and TIMB, 2015
Source: Author using data from Ministry of Agriculture, Agritex Department, 2016

There is a decline in production figures across the settlement sectors other than in the CA, such that by 2014, production dropped to less than 1,000 tonnes, with LSCF production decreasing to as low as 108 tonnes, SSCFs to 210 tonnes and A2 farms to 421 tonnes in 2015.

8.7 Changing land ownership in Hwedza district

The growth of the Svosve people resulted in land pressure in the Svosve Reserve by 1925. For Hodder-Williams (1983: 139), the Native Department officials knew about this pressure which was building up, yet they preferred to call for better farming practices, which was only a temporary palliative – the demand for land was set to grow. Whilst there was continued demand for land alienation for European settlers, the availability of land outside the Native Reserves was now doubtful. To the contrary, some natives now occupied alienated land reserved for future white settlement. Some writers (Sadomba 2008; Moyo 1995) suggest that land pressure in the Svosve area was due to poor soils and increased population. For instance, Sadomba (2008) argues that high 'population density, poor soils and poor infrastructure in Svosve and other areas such as Chikwaka in Mashonaland East led to the land occupations.

Besides, these areas 'lie adjacent to prime agricultural lands with fertile soils, abundant rainfall, highly developed infrastructure with a good network of roads, a railway line, telecommunications and wide distribution of electricity' (Sadomba 2008: 97). In the case of Svosve, some war veterans mobilised for the occupation of farms beginning in 1997 (Mamdani 2008; Sadomba 2008), but these were met with interchanging support and brutal rebuttal by the government (Alexander 2006: 184). Marandellas District also epitomised the preeminent role of speculative capital in land ownership with companies rather than individuals securing land ownership particularly in the Highveld area (see Map 8-3). The Svosve people are not known to have been involved in the normal low intensity occupations from 1985 to 1996.

They are, however, known to have led the 'high intensity high profile' occupations/invasions from September 1997 as part of self-provisioning – popular struggles for land. Moyo (2001) argues that these occupations were generally instigated by some government officials or by ruling Zanu PF supporters, even though in areas such as Hwedza, Mazowe and Marondera, war veterans took a leading role. Map 8-3 shows the companies which were holding land in Marandellas by 1900. For example, the BSAC held land under Marandellas Estates for speculative and productive purposes. However private white people held most of the land.

Map 8-3: Companies Holding Land in Marandellas by 1900

Source: Hodder-Williams (1983)

Table 8-4: Hwedza – Sizes of Farm Sectors in 2000

Sector	1980	%	2000 (ha)	%
LSCF	102,329	40	76,332	29.9
Old Resettlement	0	0	16,127	6.3
Communal	108,252	42.3	108,252	42.3
SSCFC	38,524	15.1	38,524	15.1
A1	0	0	0	0
A2	0	0	0	0
Conservancies	6586	2.6	6586	2.6
Institutional			9,870	3.9
Total			**255,691**	**100**

Source: Compiled by Author; Data from various sources; Ministry of Lands; Hwedza District Agritex office

The non-conforming war veterans' involvement in land occupations in Hwedza District is reflected in land beneficiaries as shall be detailed in later sections. By 2000, the land ownership structure for Hwedza District remained skewed in favour of the minority white farmers who held 29.9% of the total land. The ORAs had taken up 6.3%, while communal areas occupied 42.3% and the SSCF had taken up 15.1% of the drier part of the district (see Table 8-4).

An elaborate illustration of land ownership in 2000 is shown on Map 8-4. A few indigenous LSCF occupied 0.1% of the land in NR IIb of the district, but these accessed their land through private purchases. The resettled people in the ORA mainly came from the CA, from areas such as Makanda and Gonese as well as from the SSCFs in Zviyambe, looking for better farming conditions in better agro-ecological regions. They accessed land through a technical process through the District Administrator (DA), which involved submission of applications by interested households and some government assistance in agricultural production (Robert Mwade, Interview).

Map 8-4: Hwedza changing agrarian structure

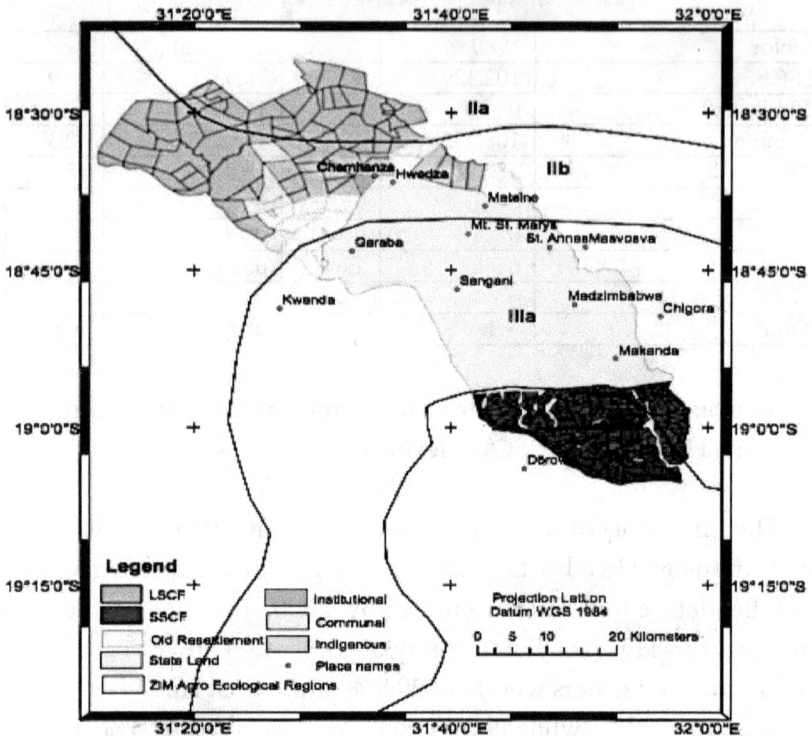

Source: Ministry of Lands, 2016

By 2012, Hwedza District, which remains occupied by the Svosve people, had a total population of 70,698, (48.8% of whom are male and 51.2% being female) with 31,854 (77.6%) being economically active, as captured in Table 8-5.

Table 8-5: Hwedza District Economically Active Population

	Total Population	15 years and above	Active population	Paid employees	Employer	Own account worker	Unpaid family worker	Looking for work
Population per sector	70698	41033	31854	5257	87	22279	3054	1177
Percentage per category	100	58	77.6	16.5	0.3	69.9	9.6	3.7

Source: Author, compiled data collected Zimstats, 2012

Among the economically active population, 5,257 (16.5%) are paid employees, 22,279 (69.9%) are own account workers, 3,054 (9.6%) are unpaid labour workers while 1,177 (3.7%) people are actively looking for employment.

8.8   Accumulation and Class Formation in Hwedza

As earlier observed, capital has been at the centre of class formation in Hwedza District. As Palmer (1977: 72) observed, in reference to Hwedza District, '[i]ndeed, some Shona near Salisbury were at this time employing other Africans as wage labourers for 10/- per month' illustrating upward mobility of African Shona peasants in the district. Similarly, Hodder-Williams (1983: 138-139), relying on evidence by Edward Webb, Margret Keithley and Harry Meade, the ANC Hwedza to the Morris Carter Commission (ZAH 1/1/4), noted the regression in black farming from the 1925 maize production levels:

The most distinguished farmer of his day was Solomon Ndawa, a Shangaan at the northern extremities of the Wedza Reserve, who cultivated 500 acres in 1925, irrigated some of his land on which he grew winter wheat, and sold over 300 bags of maize which he transported on his own wagons to Salisbury. He also had twenty-five acres down to cotton, possessed a scotch cart as well as his wagon and three spans of oxen, and oversaw a blacksmith and a forge... The steady expulsion of blacks from the white areas, increased population, and the return of white miners to the Wedza Mountain forced Ndawa, and others, to retreat more and more into subsistence farming. By 1939, there were no such farming enterprises left.

Indeed, these farmers regressed more as they were pushed further away from the railway line, limiting their access to markets and subjected to discriminatory prices imposed on their maize by the Maize Marketing Board, while the national economy was generally depressed (Hodder-Williams 1983). Consequent to this regression, farmers ended up looking for work as they sought to augment their earnings for payment of taxes and to buy manufactured goods that they required. If the lost income from sale of their produce was not enough to induce impoverishment, the drop in wages following improvements in labour supply for the white commercial farmers inevitably resulted in a drop in wages, and increased suffering among the blacks, (ibid). A combination of manipulated commodity prices and dropping wages resulted in reversal of early colonial settlement upward mobility for the Africans. In the post-independence period, class formation was differentiated along the settlement models. Dekker and Kinsey (2011) highlight these differences for ORAs and CA for the period up to 1999, as shown in Table 8.6.

Table 8-6: Livelihood Portfolios of Resettled and Communal Households, 1999

	Resettled households	Similar communal households
Household income (Z$ 1995)	9,255	5,625
	(percent)	
Of which:		
Crop income	65	35
Off-farm business revenues	11	20
Livestock produce	1	1
Livestock growth	10	9
Remittances	5	16
Female income	6	4
Off-farm income	2	15

Source: Based on ZRHDS data and adjusted from Deininger et al. (2004).

The study by Dekker and Kinsey (2011), which relied on a panel of data collected partly from Sengezi in Hwedza ORAs and some surrounding CAs, resettled farmers earned more income from agricultural production as compared to CAs farmers. In the same vein, CA farmers earned more income from off-farm income, remittances and off-farm business revenues.

8.9 Emerging Agrarian Structure

Scholars are generally agreed that there has been a change in the agrarian relations following the FTLRP initiated in February 2000, despite its violent and patronage characterisation. The agrarian relations in Hwedza District resulted in a total of 3,264 households being resettled; 2,861 of which are under A1 farms and 303 households under the A2 farms. At least 6586.2 ha on four farms were retained under Imire Game Park and three farms were retained under indigenous LSCF. Most of the people settled in Hwedza District are 'ordinary' poor peasants who came from the ORA, former farm workers or are from the contiguous Hwedza Communal Area. For instance, Simba, who is settled under the old resettlement scheme in 1986, on Plot Number 5128 on Zana Farm, originally came from Mukamba in Hwedza Communal Area, and had two sons, Tinashe and Tapfumaneyi, who settled on Mtokwe Farm under the FTLRP (Simba Manungira, Interview).

Whereas at least 38% of the 2,861 people settled on A1 plots on 47 farms are from Hwedza District, the figure drops to only 46 people or 15% of the 303 beneficiaries allocated A2 plots on 27 farms, with 40% being constituted of people originally from Harare. This evidence tends to collaborate with observations made by Scoones *et al.* (2010, 47), that 'some of the invaders got plots, but most went to outsiders, including senior officials in Masvingo Province. As Table 8-7 shows, Hwedza District had a total of 27 farms measuring 31,417ha were allocated to 303 beneficiaries under A2, while 49 farms with a total size of 44,514 ha were allocated to 2,861 plot holders under the A1 plots. The scale is tilted in favour of the few A2 farms because the FTLRP process was 'intended for aspirant black medium scale commercial producers' who were expected to have access to capital for farm investment among other requirements (GoZ 2001).

The tilted allocation where more land was earmarked for commercial farming illustrates how the government allowed capital to retain superior positioning in post-FTLRP Zimbabwe. The social relations have also shifted resulting in the development of new linkages; with some CAs farmers, A1 farmers and ORA farmers supplying short-term/casual labour to some small-scale farmers across and within the new structure, including themselves, the A2 farmers and the remaining estates. This collaborates Moyo and Nyoni's (2013: 203) findings which suggest that at national level, 75% of the farming land is now under an enlarged peasantry relying on 'self- employment of family labour towards producing foods for auto-consumption and selling some surpluses, as well as various non-farm work and short-term wage labour'. The peasants have 'differentiated capacities to hire limited labour, and some provide labour services to others' while land is held on customary rights for the communal areas and state permits A1 in the resettled area.

Table 8-7: Hwedza District Emerging Agrarian Structure.

Farm categories	Farms/households						Area held (ha)						Average Farm size (ha)		
	1980		2000		2015		1980		2000*		2015		1980	2000	2015
	No	%	No	%	No	%	ha	%	ha	%	ha	%	1980	2000	2015
Communal	13647	93.0	14866	88.9	12491	71.2	108252	42.3	108252	42.3	108252	42.3	7.28	7.28	8.67
Old Resettlement	0	0.0	830	5.0	943	5.4	0	0.0	16127	6.3	16127	6.3	0.00	19.43	17.10
A1	0	0.0	0	0.0	2861	16.3	0	0.0	0	0.0	44514	17.4	0.00	0.00	15.56
Peasantry	13647	93.0	15696	93.9	16295	92.9	108252	42.3	124379	48.6	168893	66.1	7.92	7.92	10.36
Old SSCF/CFSS	930	6.3	930	5.6	930	5.3	38524	15.1	38524	15.1	38524	15.1	41.42	41.42	41.42
Small A2	0	0.0	0	0.0	303	1.7	0	0.0	0	0.0	31417	12.3	0.00	0.00	103.68
Medium	930	6.3	930	5.6	1233	7.0	38524	15.1	38524	15.1	69941	27.4	41.42	41.42	56.72
LSCF	101	0.7	90	0.5	3	0.0	102329	40.0	76332	29.9	400	0.2	1013.16	848.13	133.33
Large scale	101	0.7	90	0.5	3	0.0	102329	40.0	76332	29.9	400	0.2	1013.16	848.13	133.33
Corporate		0.00		0.00		0.00		0.0		0.0		0.0	0.00	0.00	0.00
Conservancies	1	0.01	1	0.01	1	0.01	6586	2.6	6586	2.6	6586	2.6	6586.24	6586.24	6586.24
Parastatal	0	0.00	0	0.00	0	0.00	0	0.0	0	0.0	0	0.0	0.00	0.00	0.00
Institutions	0	0.00	2	0.01	2	0.01	0	0.0	9870	3.9	9871	3.9		4935.21	4935.50
Agro-estates	1	0.01	3	0.02	3	0.02	6586	2.6	16457	6.4	16457	6.4	6586.00	5485.55	5485.75
Total	14679	100.0	16719	100.0	17534	100.0	255691	100.0	255691	100.0	255691	100.0	17.42	15.29	14.58

Source: Author, data collected from MAMID and Zimstat (2014), 2016

Notes: *The farm categories have been adopted from Moyo (2011a)*

195

They produce for domestic and export markets through independent and/or contract farming are therefore linked to international and domestic capital and world markets. At the same time, the production of labour intensive crops such as tobacco has resulted in most peasants hiring other peasants across the variegated settlement models, for some critical labour intensive field and tobacco grading processes.

8.10 Conclusion

The controlling and speculative tendencies of capital, which at the turn of the century invaded Southern Rhodesia and won against the First Chimurenga uprising of 1896, alienated farms for the settlers before instituting various taxation mechanisms in order to curb the prosperity Africans achieved before the advent of colonialism, is traceable in Hwedza District. Primitive accumulation has remained potent despite the resistance of Africans, and has managed to change its shape, mode and approach in line with the changing agrarian relations in Zimbabwe. The emerging agrarian structure in Hwedza District has enabled capital to pursue its interests in various ways. In the main, post-2009 Hwedza District has seen the re-insertion of capital turning peasants into proletariats on their own farms Under this emerging situation, a new class of worker peasants who either provide self-employment on their farms or work on other small scale farmers' plots under the supervision of a contracting company has emerged.

Chapter Nine

Sectoral Commodity Production in Hwedza, 2000-15

9.1 Introduction

This chapter presents empirical data on production patterns on food, cash and export crops and livestock to reveal how the production trends are both influenced and influencing capital, social reproduction and labour relations after 2000 in Hwedza District. It gives a detailed comparative review of crop production patterns (food and cash crops) and livestock in the five settlement models, across the three agro-ecological regions. The chapter therefore begins with a comparative analysis of land-use in the differentiated settings and before carrying out a comparative analysis of crop and livestock production patterns within and across the settlement sectors and agro-ecological regions in Hwedza district. The factors influencing production trends are then discussed. Although this Book focuses on tobacco production, this chapter presents an analysis of production covering other crops to situate the study. Furthermore, whereas five sites were selected for in depth study, this chapter begins with a district-wide crop production analysis to situate trends revealed from the study sites.

9.2 Production Patterns for Food, Cash Crops and Livestock

9.2.1 Land utilisation

Land utilisation in Hwedza district is central in revealing rural agricultural production, 15 years after the FTLRP initiation. This study begins with an in-depth analysis of land utilisation at district level and within the studied wards, farms and villages studied. Figure 9-1 shows that although the LSCF sector own a total arable land of 6,586ha constituting 2.68% of the total arable land in Hwedza district, the total cropped area stood at 142ha (0.01% of arable land). The average cropped area of 35.5ha per household is higher than the other sectors. For instance, the SSCF has 930 households and an

197

arable land of 38,524ha, cropped area of 2,389ha and an averaged cropped area of 2.6% of available arable land. The ORA has 943 households, 16,127ha of arable land, a cropped land of 1,856.1ha and an average of 17.1ha per household, and an average of 2ha of cropped land per household, as shown in Figure 9.1(a) and (b).

Figures 9-1 (a): Total Cropped Area by Sectors (b) Irrigated Area per Crop in 1999-2015

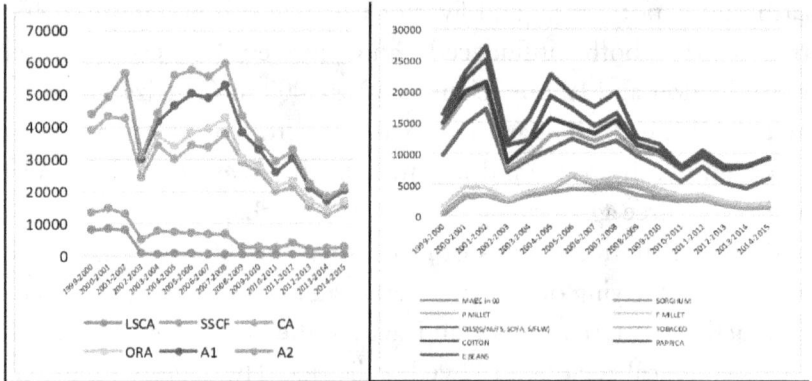

Source: Author, compiled from data collected from the Department of Agritex, Ministry of Agriculture, Hwedza district, 2015

Notes: Cropped area in hectares

The ORA constitute 6.57% of the total arable land, 8.77% of the cropped area, while the cropped area is 11.51% of the arable land in the sector. While, the CA has 108,252ha, constituting 44.11% of the total arable land in Hwedza District, only 12,535ha was under crop in 2015. Again, even though the land under crop stood at 59.22% of the all cropped land in Hwedza District, this represented only 5.77% of the land within the CA sector. On average, each household in the CA sector owns 8.77ha while an average of 1ha was under crop in 2015. The A1 sector has 2,861 households and own a total of 44,514ha at an average of 15.6ha per household. The sector had an average of 1.1ha under crop in 2015 with a total of 3,198.6ha under crop in this sector.

There are 303 households in the A2 sector. The total arable land is 31,417ha (103,7ha per household) of which 1,019.5ha were under crop in 2015, at an average of 3.4ha per household. All the sectors have experienced a decline in the area under crops and the area under irrigation from 2008 despite an increase in cropped area experienced from 2003 -2007. The decline from 2008 onwards and the resurgence from 2014 are in line with the national production patterns where some commodities (tobacco groundnuts and maize) have begun to resurge, although in a differentiated fashion. The continued decline in some commodities in spite of the re-introduction of neo-liberalism is indicative that some factors of production in the agricultural input/output markets remained unresolved beyond 2009.

Turning on to the study sites, the respondents (Table 9-1) revealed an average arable land of 5.7ha and average cropped area of 1.8ha as compared to 15.6ha and 1ha recorded by the Agritex department respectively, for the A1 sector. The difference in landholding figures is accounted for by the fact that some respondents did not include grazing land during data collection. The SSCF sector has an average arable land size of 93.1ha and an average cropped area of 3.5ha up compared 1.1ha cited in the district wide Agritex figures. The land sizes in the SSCF are therefore below government stipulated land sizes where minimum land sizes for the NRIV had been set 120ha per household.

Table 9-1: Arable Lands, Cropped Area and Irrigated Area, Interviewed, 2015

Model	No	Total area per sector	Average area available	Arable lands	Average arable land	Cropped area	Average cropped area	Irrigated area	Average Irrigated area
A1	46	348.2	7.6	263.5	5.7	84.7	1.8	0	0
%		4.70%		75.67%		24%		0.00%	
SSCF	51	4924	96.5	4747	93.1	177	3.5	0	0
%		67.17%		96.41%		3.59%		-	
A2	26	1462.5	56.3	1264	48.6	198.5	7.6	4.5	0.173077
%		19.90%		86.40%		13.57%		2.30%	
ORA	45	428.2	9.5	371.4	8.3	56.8	1.3	0	0
%		5.80%		86.70%		13.26%		0.0%	
CA	46	168.25	3.7	85.85	1.9	80.3	1.7	6.5	0.141304
%		2.30%		51.03%		47.73%		8.56%	
Total		7331.15	34.26	7077.0	33	686.38	3.2	13.31	
%		100%		96.53%		9.36%		1.94%	

Source: Author, compiled from own survey data, 2016

The A2 have an average arable area of 48.6ha and average cropped area of 7.6ha while the ORA has an average arable area of 8.3ha and average cropped area of 1.3ha. The highly reduced average cropped area is due to the exclusion of three LSCF in Hwedza district from the study area. The CA has an average arable area of 1.9ha and an average cropped area of 1.7ha. Overall, the CA utilises a larger proportion of land available at 47.7% compared to 24 % for the A1, 13.6% for the A2, 13.3% for the ORA, and 3.6% for the SSCF, translating to an overall land utilisation of 9.36% in 2015. Informal land sales in response to the expansion of Hwedza Growth Point has resulted in land shortages among the CA sector respondents compared to land generally available in Hwedza. Mr Obert Mataruse (all names cited are not actual names) observed that:

> *We generally have small pieces of land here in Wagoneka because many people have sold their land to people working at Hwedza Growth Point. These people want to build houses in anticipation of the expansion of the growth point. Most of us here provide service and material to these people, either in the form of brick moulding, building of houses or some other manual labour. We also work for farmers here in the communal areas or in the resettled area.* (Interview)

Land shortages experienced in the ORA sector are due to limited land available for the landholders' growing families resulting in limitless subdivision of available land. (Personal observation, Sengezi, 10 July 2016). This is corroborated by Tapiwa Mapinga who said:

> *I have two wives and 17 sons who need land but the government allocated me 6ha in 1982. Now all these sons have had to build their houses on the 2acre plot once they got married. In addition, I have been forced to share with them the 6ha plat allocated to me by the government. With the industries closing, even those who had migrated to the towns are coming back resulting in pressure for land in my family* (Interview).

With regards to cropped areas for grain crops, in the variegated settlement settings, the A2 sector utilised in excess of 142ha per annum from 2013 to 2015, followed by the SSCF, with a minimum of 123.4ha achieved in 2015, as shown in Figure 9-2.

Figure 9-2: Maize Cropped Area, 2012/13-2014/15

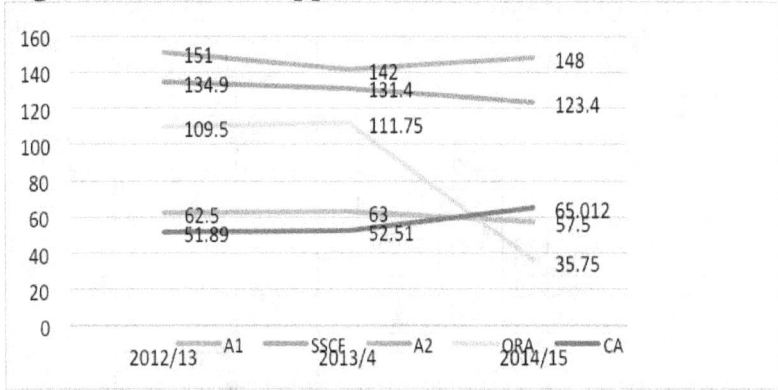

Source: Author, compiled from own survey data, 2016

There was a drastic reduction in the cropped land for maize from 109.5ha in 2012/12 and 111.75ha in 2013/14 to 35.75ha in 2014/15, as producers declined from 41 to 27 over the same period. Many people ended up not tilling their land because of uncertainties caused by changes in rainfall patterns as the delayed commencement of the rainfall season resulted in farmers being unsure of possibilities of attaining viable yields in 2014/15 season. Table 9-2 shows the number of household growing the key commodities, total hectarage and mean per crop from 2012/13 to 2014/13 for the five settlement models. Over the period under review, maize and tobacco were the main commodities under production, maize had higher sizes of land over the period from 2012/13 to 2013/14. Generally the SSCF grow more groundnuts than the other sectors, with a cropped area of 19.4ha compared to the second highest of 2.4ha in the CA in 2012/3.

Table: 9-2: Cropped area, 2012/13-2014/15

Statistics year		2012/13			2013/14			2014/15		
Model	Crop	N	Sum	Mean	N	Sum	Mean	N	Sum	Mean
A1	Maize	37	62.5	1.68919	36	63	1.75	37	57.5	1.55405
	Tobacco	26	29.5	1.13462	25	27	1.08	20	24	1.2
	Groundnuts	2	0.9	0.45	2	1.4	0.7	3	1.9	0.63333
	Soya beans	0			0			0		
	Potatoes	2	1.2	0.6	1	0	0	1	0.2	0.2
	Sugar beans	1	0.4	0.4	2	1.2	0.6	1	0.4	0.4
	Cowpeas	1	1	1	0			0		
	Round nuts	3	1.7	0.56667	0			2	0.7	0.35
SSCF	Maize	52	134.9	2.59423	34	131.400	1.45294	45	123.4	2.74222
	Tobacco	30	57.3	1.91	23	49.400	0.84348	29	32.4	1.11724
	Groundnuts	23	21.25	0.92391	0	19.400		18	15.55	0.86389
	Soya beans	0			1		0.25	0		
	Sweet potatoes	4	0.9	0.225	9	3	0.33333	3	0.95	0.31667
	Sugar beans	1	0.25	0.25	4	0.25	0.3125	1	0.75	0.75
	Cowpeas	4	1.052	0.263	0			5	1.3	0.26
	Round nuts	9	2.75	0.30556	26		5.46154	8	2.35	0.29375
A2	Maize	26	151	5.80769	8	142	2.20625	30	148	4.93333
	Tobacco	10	15.6	1.56	1	17.65	1	10	21.3	2.13
	Groundnuts	7	6.75	0.96429	0	1		9	13.25	1.47222
	Soya beans	3	2	0.66667	1		1	2	1.4	0.7
	Sweet potatoes	3	2	0.66667	0	1		2	1.5	0.75
	Sugar beans	0			0			3	10	3.33333
	Cowpeas	0			41		2.72561	0		
	Round nuts	2	1.2	0.6	26		0.91346	2	3	1.5
ORA	Maize	41	109.5	2.67073	0	111.75		27	35.75	1.32407
	Tobacco	19	16.5	0.86842	0	23.75		14	13.5	0.96429
	Groundnuts	9	8	0.88889	9		0.33333	5	3.5	0.7
	Soya beans	0			0			0		
	Sweet potatoes	4	1.75	0.4375	0	3		4	1.75	0.4375
	Sugar beans	0			48		1.094	0		
	Cowpeas	1	0.25	0.25	3		0.66667	1	0.25	0.25
	Round nuts	6	1.75	0.29167	5		0.48	4	2	0.5
CA	Maize	47	51.89	1.10404	0	52.512		44	65.012	1.47755
	Tobacco	2	2	1	7	2	0.37143	4	2.5	0.625
	Groundnuts	5	2.75	0.55	4	2.4	0.8125	4	3.2	0.8
	Soya beans	0			0			0		
	Sweet potatoes	4	3.35	0.8375		2.6		4	2.2	0.55
	Sugar beans	0				3.25		0		
	Cowpeas	4	3.25	0.8125				2	0.5	0.25
	Round nuts	6	52.25	8.70833				7	252.35	36.05

NOTES: N - number of farmers.

Source: Author, compiled from own survey data, 2016

However, as Figure 9-4 shows, tobacco and groundnuts cropped areas are generally on the decrease, save for the CA. The increase in the area under tobacco from 2012/3 to 2013/4 in the A2 and the ORA was reversed in 2014/15.

Other scholars such as Cousins (2010a) also observed an upward trend in agricultural production in maize and tobacco crops. The participation of the CA sector in tobacco production is low compared to the other sectors, including the ORA, even though the ORA is situated in NRII which received high rainfall. The conclusion made on land utilisation is that some households got excessively big sizes of land as observed by Moyo *et al.* (2009), landlessness and land shortages remain in the CA sector, while most land remains unutilised, particularly in the A2 and SSCF sectors.

Figure 9-3: Tobacco Cropped Area, 2002/13-2014/15

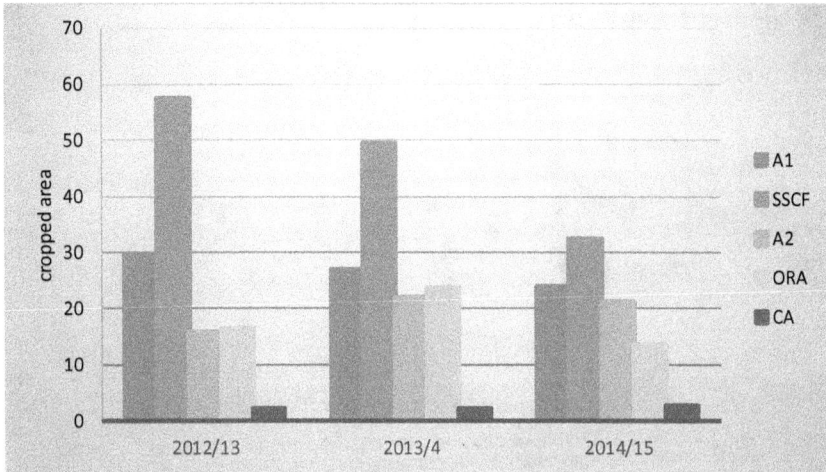

Source: Author, compiled from own survey data, 2016

9.2.2 Crop production trends per sector

The commodity production patterns in Hwedza district show a general decline from 1999 and particularly from 2004 due to the collapsed agrarian economy as evidenced by the drop in the input/outputs markets. Some scholars who looked at these production trends tended to treat the small-scale farmers as homogeneous and as such failed to reveal the underlying differences in production patterns among the settlement sectors as Figure 9-4 shows. Secondary data collected from the Agritex Department at Hwedza District show that the recovery of commodities post- 2008 has not been homogeneous as well.

Figure 9-4: Percentage of Households Producing Crops by Settlement Type, 2015

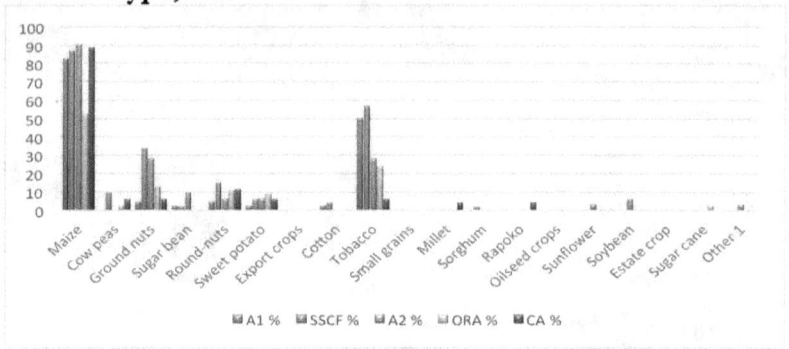

However, across the settlement sectors, some commodities such as tobacco and oils (groundnuts, soya beans and sunflowers) started to recover from 2009 while maize recovered from 2014 onwards as illustrated in Figure 9-5. The crop production recovery trends are indicative of the changing macro-economic conditions in the country as opposed to state practice (Alexander 2006) and politics linked to patronage (Zamchiya 2012). The data from Hwedza District shows that the major crops produced from 2000 to 2015 are maize, oils and tobacco.

Figure 9-5: Commodity Production Patterns

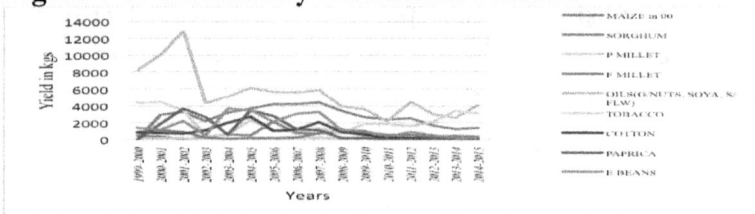

With regards to production of different crops within the five settlement sectors, as Agritex (2015) revealed, the respondents revealed that maize is generally grown by 85.7% of the farmers, while 65.7% grow tobacco. The third most popular crop is groundnuts.

9.2.3 Tobacco production

Tobacco experienced the greatest increase in production figures particularly from 2008/9 season, in response to the liberalisation of the marketing of crop as farmers were allowed to retain proceeds from crop sales in hard currency, thereby increasing confidence in the marketing of the crop and increasing the revenue for the farmers as well as improving the scope for agricultural re-investment. The increase in total production was against a background of decreased area under tobacco production as Figure 9-3 shows.

Table 9-3: Tobacco Production, 2013-2015

Year	Sector		Quantity of tobacco sold (kg) <250KGS	250-500KGS	500-750KG	750-1000KGS	1000-2500KGS	2500-5000KGS	>5000	Total
2013	A1	No	1	2	2	5	7	0	0	17
		%	6%	12%	12%	29%	41%	0%	0%	100%
	SSCF	No	2	4	1	3	7	3	1	21
		% e	10%	19%	5%	14%	33%	14%	5%	100%
	A2	No	1	0	0	0	2	2	2	7
		%	14%	0%	0%	0%	29%	29%	29%	100%
	ORA	No	1	1	3	4	5	1	0	15
		%	7%	7%	20%	27%	33%	7%	0%	100%
	CA	No	0	1	0	0	0	0	0	1
		%	0%	100%	0%	0%	0%	0%	0%	100%
	Total	No	5	8	6	12	21	6	3	61
		% o	8%	13%	10%	20%	34%	10%	5%	100%
2014	A1	No	1	0	0	5	10	0	0	16
		%	6%	0%	0%	31%	63%	0%	0%	100%
	SSCF	No	2	25	4	6	5	2	2	26
		% e	8%	19%	15%	23%	19%	8%	8%	100%
	A2	No	1	0	1	1	3	2	2	10
		%	10%	0%	10%	10%	30%	20%	20%	100%
	ORA	No	1	1	3	8	3	0	0	16
		%	6%	6%	19%	50%	19%	0%	0%	100%
	CA	No	0	0	1	0	0	0	0	1
		%	0%	0%	100%	0%	0%	0%	0%	100%
	Total	No	5	6	9	20	21	4	4	69
		% o	7%	9%	13%	29%	30%	6%	6%	100%
2015	A1	No	0	1	0	4	8	1	0	14
		%	0%	7%	0%	29%	57%	7%	0%	100%
	SSCF	No	2	5	5	4	8	2	1	27
		% e	7%	19%	19%	15%	30%	7%	4%	100%
	A2	No	0	0	0	1	4	1	2	8
		%	0%	0%	0%	13%	50%	13%	25%	100%
	ORA	No	0	7	5	5	5	0	0	22
		%	0%	32%	23%	23%	23%	0%	0%	100%
	CA	No	0	0	0	1	0	0	0	1
		%	0%	0%	0%	100%	0%	0%	0%	100%
	Total	No	2	13	10	115	25	4	3	72
		% o	3%	18%	14%	21%	35%	6%	4%	100%

Source: Author, compiled from own survey data, 2016

However, during the period from 2002-2009, the SSCF sector performed better, while the A1 sector overtook the SSCF in 2012/13, as Figure 9-6 shows. This study shows that the number of households involved in tobacco production increased from 61 in 2013 to 72 in 2015. Similarly, the number of households producing more than

1000kgs/ha increased from 30 in 2013 to 32 in 2015 with no definitive production pattern across the sectors. The A1 and the A2 sectors have experienced the biggest hike in tobacco production as Figure 9.6 reveals.

Figure 9-6: District Tobacco Production, 1999-2015 (b) Maize Production, 1999-2015

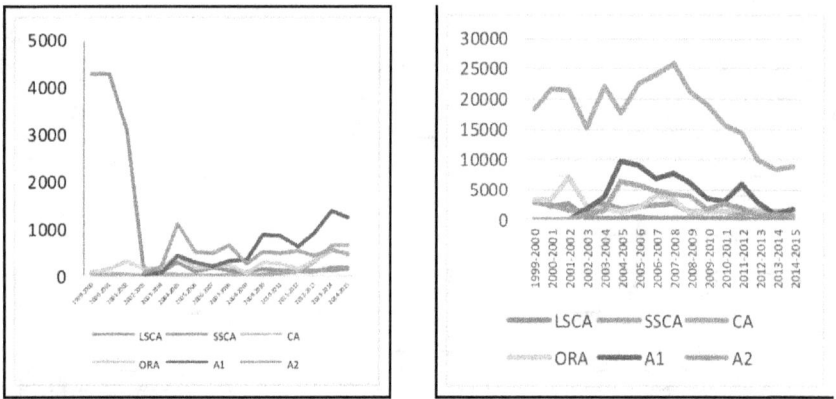

Source: Author, Data collected from the Ministry of Agriculture, Hwedza offices, 2016

Tobacco yield is differentiated among the settlement models as shown in Table 9-4. In 2014/5, the A1 achieved 931.2kg/ha compared to 547.1kg/ha for the SSCF, 1294.4kg/ha for A2, 950kg/ha for both the ORA and the CA sectors, in yield. The mean yield for all the crops is higher among the A2 farmers and generally low among the CA, although the sector has experienced an improvement during the period under review. On a sector-to-sector basis, tobacco production differed as 28.1% of the A2, 50% in A1, 56.6% in SSCF grew the crop, with an overall 33% participation by respondents in 2015.

The increase in overall output in tobacco reflect changes in productivity as empirical data from the respondents show. Some farmers have dropped tobacco due to the reduced income earnings linked to low yields, high inputs costs and low commodity prices. For instance, one farmer noted:

> *I have grown tobacco for four seasons from 2011. But in 2015, I dropped the crop due to unfavourable marketing conditions. In the first three years, the crop was rewarding but prices started falling and we as farmers were getting the wrong end of the stick. I have destroyed my barns and used the bricks to build a house because I didn't want to ever get tempted to go back to the crop. I now grow tomatoes and employ five casual workers. From these tomatoes sales, I am able to support my husband who works for the government in Marondera and I can also send my two children to boarding schools.* (Simbisai Manungira, Interview)

9.2.4 Maize production

On a sector-by-sector basis, 88.7% of the CA, 90.6% in the A2 sector, 82.6% in the A1 sector, 86.8% in the SSCF and 52.2% in the ORA, grow maize, as Figure 9-6 shows. While tobacco is grown for cash sales, maize is a staple food for Zimbabwe, as such 77.4% of the households in Hwedza district grow the crop for own consumption, while 13.9% grow the crop for sale. Maize production generally had a deep in production from 2004 serve for the CA sector where production increased from 2004 and only started declining from 2008. Across the five settlement sectors, maize production levels began to recover from 2014 despite the drought situation experienced in 2015. However, some crops such as maize and groundnuts, sweet potatoes that were grown for own consumption are also used as payment for wage labour employed either as permanent or as casual workers, in particular in the resettled areas. However the purpose of growing crops by the farmers differ per sector. For instance, whereas 97.9% of the households in the CA grow the maize for own consumption, only 31% do so for the same purpose in the A2 sector. As shown in Table 9-5, in the A2 sector, 55.2% grow maize for profitability purposes. Although over 6.2% of the households in Hwedza district do not grow the crop, the highest proportion of farmers not growing this crop in the A1 sector is 14.6%. Whereas the government in the past had relied on directives under *Maguta/ Sithuthi* 'Operation we are full' (Murisa and Chikweche 2015; Scoones *et al.* 2010), from 2005, evidence in Hwedza District shows minimal government directives, with.5% of the respondents having confirmed growing crops in order to comply with policy in 2015, as the study reveals.

Table 9-4: Average Yields Achieved, 2012/13-2014/15

Model	Crop	2012/13			2013/14			2014/15		
		N	Sum	Mean	N	Sum	Mean	N	Sum	Mean
A1	Maize	30	25771.1	859,0	35	26.453,3	755,8	35	16.378,7	468,0
	Tobacco	25	28.236,7	1.129,5	24	29.866,7	1.244,4	20	18.623,3	931,2
	Groundnuts	2	600,0	300,0	2	50,0	25,0	3	720,0	240,0
	Soybean	0	.	.	0	.	.	0	.	.
	S/potato	1	,0	,0	1	,0	,0	1	,0	,0
	Sugar bean	1	,0	,0	0	.	.	1	,0	,0
	Cowpeas	0	.	.	0	.	.	0	.	.
	Roundnuts	2	200,0	100,0	1	,0	,0	2	40,0	20,0
SSCF	Maize	48	39308.7	818,9	51	42.811,1	839,4	45	24.619	547,1
	Tobacco	29	29.784,3	1.027,0	33	32.865,0	995,9	28	22.079,7	788,6
	Groundnuts	22	9.115,0	414,3	22	13.590,0	617,7	18	9.250,0	513,9
	Soybean	0	.	.	0	.	.	0	.	.
	S/potato	4	13.020,0	3.255,0	3	500,0	166,7	3	200,0	66,7
	Sugar bean	1	6.000,0	6.000,0	1	2.000,0	2.000,0	1	333,3	333,3
	Cow peas	4	11.565,3	2.891,3	4	4.350,0	1.087,5	5	1.500,0	300,0
	Round-nuts	8	7.730,0	966,3	8	,0	,0	8	3.560,0	445,0
A2	Maize	24	80916.9	3371.5	24	50.813,8	2.117,2	29	56.167,9	1.936,8
	Tobacco	9	15.216,7	1.690,7	12	15.233,3	1.269,4	9	11.650,0	1.294,4
	Groundnuts	6	8.450,0	1.408,3	6	7.283,3	1.213,9	9	7.583,3	842,6
	Soybean	2	2.000,0	1.000,0	1	1.000,0	1.000,0	2	1.625,0	812,5
	S/ potato	2	2.000,0	1.000,0	1	1.000,0	1.000,0	2	7.000,0	3.500,0
	Sugar bean	0	.	.	0	.	.	3	1.200,0	400,0
	Cow peas	0	.	.	0	.	.	0	.	.
	Round-nuts	2	1.001,0	500,5	1	,0	,0	2	1.300,0	650,0
ORA	Maize	38	18408.87	484.4	38	35.164,0	925,4	22	15.780,0	717,3
	Tobacco	18	22.321,0	1.240,1	24	33.792,0	1.408,0	10	9.500,0	950,0
	Groundnuts	9	4.248,0	472,0	9	2.250,0	250,0	5	1.340,0	268,0
	Soybean	0	.	.	0	.	.	0	.	.
	S/potato	4	124,0	31,0	5	170,0	34,0	2	40,0	20,0
	Sugar bean	0	.	.	0	.	.	0	.	.
	Cow peas	0	.	.	0	.	.	0	.	.
	Round-nuts	6	920,0	153,3	0	.	.	3	320,0	106,7
CA	Maize	42	20423.7	486.3	47	26272.74	558.9945	42	7445.196	177.2666
	Tobacco	2	1.000,0	500,0	2	1.000,0	500,0	2	1.900,0	950,0
	Groundnuts	5	520,0	104,0	5	1.150,0	230,0	3	325,0	108,3
	Soybean	0	.	.	0	.	.	0	.	.
	Sweet potato	4	300,0	75,0	5	340,0	68,0	1	50,0	50,0
	Sugar bean	0	.	.	0	.	.	0	.	.
	Cow peas	4	141,0	35,3	4	500,0	125,0	1	80,0	80,0
	Round-nuts	6	591,0	98,5	7	,0	,0	6	440,0	73,3
TOTAL	Maize	182	272218,7	1495.707	195	231.649,6	1.187,9	173	146.119	844,6
	Tobacco	83	96.558,7	1.163,4	95	112.757	1.186,9	69	63.753	924
	Groundnuts	44	22.933,0	521,2	44	24.323,3	552,8	38	19.218,3	505,7
	Soybean	2	2.000,0	1.000,0	1	1.000,0	1.000,0	2	1.625,0	812,5
	S/potato	15	15.444,0	1.029,6	15	2.010,0	134,0	9	7.290,0	810,0
	Sugar bean	2	6.000,0	3.000,0	1	2.000,0	2.000,0	5	1.533,3	306,7
	Cow peas	8	11.706,3	1.463,3	8	4.850,0	606,3	6	1.580,0	263,3
	Round-nuts	24	10.442,0	435,1	17	,0	,0	21	5.660,0	269,5

Source: Author, compiled from own survey data, 2016

Table 9-5: Reason for Growing Maize, 2015

Model		Reason for growing crop						Total
		Crop not grown	GoZ directive	own consumption	profitability of venture	compatibility with available equipment	other	
A1	No	6	0	34	1	0	0	41
	%	14.6%	.0%	82.9%	2.4%	.0%	.0%	100.0%
SSCF	No	1	0	44	6	1	0	52
	%	1.9%	.0%	84.6%	11.5%	1.9%	.0%	100.0%
A2	No	3	0	9	16	0	1	29
	%	10.3%	.0%	31.0%	55.2%	.0%	3.4%	100.0%
ORA	No	3	1	28	5	0	2	39
	%	7.7%	2.6%	71.8%	12.8%	.0%	5.1%	100.0%
CA	No	0	0	46	1	0	0	47
	%	.0%	.0%	97.9%	2.1%	.0%	.0%	100.0%
Total	No	13	1	161	29	1	3	208
	%	6.2%	.5%	77.4%	13.9%	.5%	1.4%	100.0%

Source: Author, compiled from own survey data, 2016

The major maize producing sectors are the CA and A1. All sectors other than the SSCF had a hike in 2014/5 as shown in Table 9-6.

Within the same sector, farmers producing between 500-1 000kgs stood at 20% in 2013, 50% in 2014 and 33% in 2015, while those above this yield stood at 16.7% only in 2015. The SSCF had all the farmers producing between 750-2500kgs in 2013, which dropped to 37.5 in 2014 and increased to 75% in 2015. The sector had 25% of the farmers achieving yields above 2500kgs in 2014. In the case of the A2 sector, 22% of the households produced above 5000kgs of maize, before hiking to 36.4% in 2014 and 55.6% in 2015. Even though there was an increase in the number of households achieving above 1 000kgs per annum in 2014, the ORA sector suffered a decline in 2015 with the number of households declining from 50% to 37.5% in 2015. All the CA farmers achieved total production above 2 500kgs in 2014 yet in 2015, 75% of the farmers achieved less than 1 001kgs of maize in yield. All in all, while there are more CAs involved in maize production, total yield levels are lower than those in the A2 and SSCF sectors.

Table 9-6: Maize Production, 2013-2015

Year	Model	narrative	<250KGS	250-500KGS	500-750KG	750-1000KGS	1000-2500KGS	2500-5000KGS	>5000	Total
2013	A1	No	2	2	0	1	0	0	0	5
		%	40%	40%	0%	20%	0%	0%	0%	100%
	SSCF	No	0	0	0	1	3	0	0	4
		%e	0.00%	0.00%	0.00%	25.00%	75.00%	0.00%	0.00%	100.00%
	A2	No	1	0	0	1	4	1	2	9
		%	11%	0%	0%	11%	44%	11%	22%	100%
	ORA	No	1	2	0	0	1	1	0	5
		%	20%	40%	0%	0%	20%	20%	0%	100%
	CA	No	1	1	1	0	0	0	0	3
		%	33%	33%	33%	0%	0%	0%	0%	100%
	Total	No	5	5	1	3	8	2	2	26
		%o	19%	19%	4%	12%	31%	8%	8%	100%
2014	A1	No	2	0	0%	2	0	0	0	4
		%	50.00%	0.00%	0%	50.00%	0.00%	0.00%	0.00%	100.00%
	SSCF	No	1	2		2	1	2	0	8
		%e	12.50%	25.00%	0%	25.00%	12.50%	25.00%	0.00%	100.00%
	A2	No	1	0	0	0	4	2	4	11
		%	9.10%	0.00%	0%	0.00%	36.40%	18.20%	36.40%	100.00%
	ORA	No	0	3	0	1	0	4	0	8
		%	0.00%	37.50%	0%	12.50%	0.00%	50.00%	0.00%	100.00%
	CA	No	0	0	0	0	0	1	0	1
		%	0.00%	0.00%	0%	0.00%	0.00%	100.00%	0.00%	100.00%
	Total	No	4	5	0	5	5	9	4	32
		%o	12.50%	15.60%	0%	15.60%	15.60%	28.10%	12.50%	100.00%
2015	A1	No	1	2	0	2	1	0	0	6
		%	16.70%	33.30%	0.00%	33.30%	16.70%	0.00%	0.00%	100.00%
	SSCF	No	0	0	0	0	3	0	1	4
		%e	0.00%	0.00%	0.00%	0.00%	75.00%	0.00%	25.00%	100.00%
	A2	No	0	0	0	0	2	2	5	9
		%	0.00%	0.00%	0.00%	0.00%	22.20%	22.20%	55.60%	100.00%
	ORA	No	1	1	0	3	0	3	0	8
		%	12.50%	12.50%	0.00%	37.50%	0.00%	37.50%	0.00%	100.00%
	CA	No	1	0	1	1	0	1	0	4
		%	25.00%	0.00%	25.00%	25.00%	0.00%	25.00%	0.00%	100.00%
	Total	No	3	3	1	6	6	6	6	31
		%o	3%	3%	19%	19%	19%	19%	19%	100%

Source: Author, compiled from own survey data, 2016

The agricultural productions for eight key crops in Hwedza District show that total production went up in the 2013/14 season before dropping in the 2014/5 season. However, the mean for A1 farmers producing maize dropped from 859kg/ha in 2012/13 to 755.8kg/ha in 2013/14 to 468kg/ha. Maize yield for SSCF farmers increased from 818.9kg/ha in 2012/13 to 839.4kg/ha in 2013/14 before dropping to 547kg/ha in 2014/15. However maize yield for the A2 households dropped from 3371.5kg/ha to 2117.2kg/ha in 2013/14 and 1936.8kgs/ha in 2014/15. The ORA and the CA also experienced a hike in yield from 2012/13 to 2013/14 before a drop in 2014/15. The differences in agro-ecological regions have no definitive impact on yield given that households in the SSCF situated in NRIV have better yields compared to the CA situated in NRIII in maize, despite all the farmers accessing fertilizers and green revolutions improved seeds and chemicals. This evidence refutes the argument by Matondi *et al.* (2008, 44) that low production is due to low rainfall and other factors such as 'poor agronomic practices especially late planting, poor soils, and …lack of fertilizers both compound D and ammonium nitrate'.

However, the survey by Matondi *et al.* (2008) does not differentiate crop production from the different settlement sectors, serve for the fast track areas (A2 and A1). The survey by Moyo *et al.* (2009) however shows differentiated production patterns aligned to climatic conditions as shown by figures from high rainfall areas in Goromonzi and Zvimba Districts compared to the dry Lowveld areas of Mangwe and Chiredzi Districts. Overall, maize producers declined from 182 in 2012/13 to 173 in 2014/15; tobacco producers declined from 83 to 69 over the same period, while groundnuts producers declined from 44 in 2012/13 and 2013/14 to 38 in 2014/15.

Groundnuts is mostly grown in the A2 at 28.1% with an overall participation of 16.5% of the households. Sweet potatoes were grown by 15 producers in 2012/13 and 2013/14 and dropped to 9 in 2014/15. All in all, as Moyo *at el.* (2009: 52) observe, there is need to achieve 'robust transformation of the economy', the development of linkages among critical sectors such as that of input supply, credit support and access to markets and physical infrastructure in support of the new agrarian structure as this study sought to establish.

9.2.5 Horticultural crops

Most households participate in the horticultural crop production as Table 9-7 shows. Overall, the most popular crops are tomatoes and *Rugare/Covo* at 12.2% for both.

Table 9-7: Horticultural Crops Grown by Settlement Types, 2015

	A1		SSSC		A2		ORA		CA		Total	
Sample size	46		53		32		46		53		230	
	No.	%	No.	%	No.	%	No.	%	No.	%	No.	%
Baby corn	0	0.0	0	0.0	0	0.0	0	0.0	0	0.0	0	0.0
Pumpkins	0	0.0	1	1.9	0	0.0	0	0.0	1	1.9	2	0.9
Watermelons	0	0.0	1	1.9	0	0.0	0	0.0	0	0.0	1	0.4
Okra	0	0.0	1	1.9	0	0.0	0	0.0	0	0.0	1	0.4
Tomatoes	2	4.3	6	11.3	9	28.1	5	10.9	6	11.3	28	12.2
Rape	0	0.0	3	5.7	3	9.4	3	6.5	3	5.7	12	5.2
Onions	0	0.0	3	5.7	4	12.5	4	8.7	2	3.8	13	5.7
Peas	0	0.0	1	1.9	1	3.1	1	2.2	0	0.0	3	1.3
Green beans	0	0.0	1	1.9	0	0.0	2	4.3	1	1.9	4	1.7
Gen squash	0	0.0	0	0.0	0	0.0	0	0.0	1	1.9	1	0.4
Cabbage	0	0.0	1	1.9	1	3.1	1	2.2	1	1.9	4	1.7
Rugare/covo	4	8.7	7	13.2	1	3.1	8	17.4	8	15.1	28	12.2
Cut flowers	0	0.0	0	0.0	0	0.0	0	0.0	0	0.0	0	0.0
Butternut	0	0.0	1	1.9	2	6.3	0	0.0	0	0.0	3	1.3
Potatoes	1	2.2	1	1.9	4	12.5	0	0.0	1	1.9	7	3.0
Paprika	0	0.0	1	1.9	0	0.0	0	0.0	0	0.0	1	0.4
Other	0	0.0	0	0.0	0	0.0	1	2.2	0	0.0	1	0.4

Source: Author, compiled from own survey data, 2016

While most of the crops are grown for consumption purposes, tomatoes, onions, *Rugare/Covo* and Rape are grown for cash sales. Generally, more A1 households produce horticultural crops than other sectors.

9.2.6 Livestock production patterns

Whereas, 68.7% of the households in Hwedza district own cattle, only 13 (24.5%) of the CA possess a herd of cattle, as shown on Figure 9-7. The SSCF sector householder have a greater number of cattle owners at 50 (94.3%), which is in tandem with the agro-ecological regions, where Zviyambe area receives less rainfall compared to other areas as it is situated in NRIV. The study shows that 82 of the respondents rear goats while 133 rear free runner chickens. The differentiated cattle ownership also impacts on crop production as cattle provides draught power for land preparation, weeding and other farming operations.

Figure 9-7: Livestock Ownership, 2015

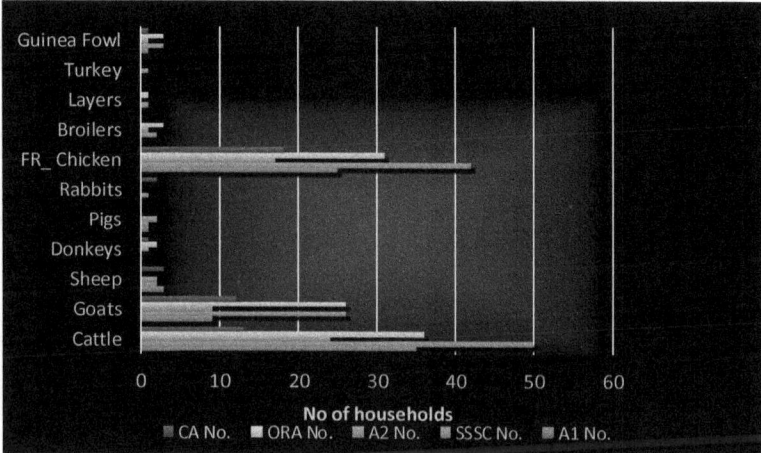

Source: Author, compiled from own survey data, 2016

Animal husbandry also provides a source of income for crop production requirements, food and play important roles in the social relations of the communities, including for payment of *Lobola* and stowage of wealth and exchange transactions (Gabriel Musiiwa, Interview).

9.3   The Inputs Markets

9.3.1 Source to inputs
Access to inputs is a critical factor in agricultural production. To fully reveal the agricultural production trends in post-2000 rural Zimbabwe, it is important that data on access, source, utilisation and pricing of inputs be investigated. Table 9-8 shows a high level of local linkages with 68.1% being secured from local traders and 6.9 % from traders within the district.

213

Table 9-8: Common Source of Inputs, 2015

Model	Narrative	Common source of input											Total
		Not applicable	Purchased from local agro-dealer	Purchased from CA agro-dealer	Purchased from other farmers	Received from government	Received from NGOs	Nearest urban area	Received from relatives/friends	Own source	Contractor	Other	
A1	No	2	31	5	0	5	0	0	0	0	0	0	43
	%	4.7%	72.1%	11.6%	.0%	11.6%	.0%	.0%	.0%	.0%	.0%	.0%	100.0%
SSCF	No	2	36	1	0	2	0	10	0	0	1	1	53
	% c	3.8%	67.9%	1.9%	.0%	3.8%	.0%	18.9%	.0%	.0%	1.9%	1.9%	100.0%
A2	No	0	21	0	0	0	0	7	1	0	0	0	29
	%	.0%	72.4%	.0%	.0%	.0%	.0%	24.1%	3.4%	.0%	.0%	.0%	100.0%
ORA	No	0	33	8	0	3	0	0	0	0	1	0	45
	%	.0%	73.3%	17.8%	.0%	6.7%	.0%	.0%	.0%	.0%	2.2%	.0%	100.0%
CA	No	1	26	1	1	14	1	0	1	1	0	0	46
	%	2.2%	56.5%	2.2%	2.2%	30.4%	2.2%	.0%	2.2%	2.2%	.0%	.0%	100.0%
Total	No	5	147	15	1	24	1	17	2	1	2	1	216
	% o	2.3%	68.1%	6.9%	.5%	11.1%	.5%	7.9%	.9%	.5%	.9%	.5%	100.0%

Source: Author, compiled from own survey data, 2016

The government offers inputs support to 11.1% of the households but this is more concentrated in the CA sector, at 30.4% at the total exclusion of A2 farmers. Among the 216 households who grew maize in 2015, 7.9% bought their produce from the nearest urban areas, being Marondera Town, located 50 kilometres from Hwedza district. Empirical evidence shows that contrary to Scoones *et al.* (2010) who observed that 2.7% had purchased fertilisers, in Hwedza district, a total 96.8% had purchased fertilisers and .05% secured support from Non-Governmental Organisations (NGOs). The limited government support (11.1%) curtailed possible cases of corruption and partisan distribution in Hwedza district.

9.3.2 Access to farming inputs

Access to fertilizers, chemicals, seeds and livestock manure was differentiated along settlement models. For instance, while 215 of the 222 who responded on the issue of access to fertilizers were affirmative, 7 households were not using fertilizers, 4 of whom were from the CA sector as shown in Table 9-9. All the households in the SSCF used fertilizers. The use of herbicides chemicals (herbicides, pesticides and livestock drugs) was also differentiated. The use of herbicides stood at 7.8% compared to pesticides which stood at 22% and livestock drugs at 28.5% in 2015. The use of animal manure was overall high and stood at 55.3%, with the greatest reliance on it being in the CA sector, at 87.5% in 2015.

Table 9-9: Access to Farming Inputs, 2015

Model		Use of fertilizers		Total	Use of herbicides		Total	Use of pesticides		Total	Use of animal manure		Total	Use of certified seed		Total	Use of livestock drugs		Total
		yes	no		yes	no		yes	no		yes	no		yes	no		yes	no	
A1	No	43	1	44	3	41	44	4	40	44	18	26	44	40	4	44	5	39	44
	%	97.7	2.3	100	6.8	93.2	100	9.1	90.9	100	40.9	59.1	100	90.9	9.1	100	11.4	88.6	100
SSCF	No	53	0	53	5	48	53	14	39	53	42	11	53	52	1	53	18	35	53
	%	100	0.0	100	9.4	90.6	100	26.4	73.6	100	79.2	20.8	100	98.1	1.9	100	34.0	66.0	100
A2	No	29	1	30	4	14	18	5	12	17	9	10	19	26	4	30	9	11	20
	%	96.7	3.3	100	22	77.8	100	29.4	70.6	100	47.4	52.6	100	86.7	13.3	100	45.0	55.0	100
ORA	No	45	1	46	0	46	46	12	34	46	18	28	46	35	11	46	14	32	46
	%	97.8	2.2	100	0.0	100.	100	26.1	73.9	100	39.1	60.9	100	76.1	23.9	100	30.4	69.6	100
CA	No	45	4	49	1	4	5	1	3	4	7	1	8	32	1	33	1	1	2
	%	91.8	8.2	100	20.	80.0	100	25.0	75.0	100	87.5	12.5	100	97.0	3.0	100	50.0	50.0	100
Total	No	215	7	222	13	153	166	36	128	164	94	76	170	185	21	206	47	118	165
	%	96.8	3.2	100	7.8	92.2	100	22	78.	100	55.3	44.7	100	89.8	10.2	100	28.5	71.5	100

Source: Author, compiled from own survey data, 2015

On the same note, the use of certified seed was high and overall stood at 89.8%, 98.1% for the SSCF, 97% for the CA, and the lowest was recorded in the A2 sector at 86.7%. Whereas Murisa (2011) identified social networks as contributing to access to crop inputs, Hwedza district households barely have such networks, as such this has not affected access to inputs by farmers across the settlement sectors.

9.3.3 Households access to draught power

The interviewed households relied on varied draught power for tillage as Table 9-10 shows. In 2012, for instance, across the settlement models, the use of animals for draught power was very high, with 27.9% of the land tilled being over 3.1ha, 20.9% being 2.1-3ha, 13.4 being 1.1-2ha and 37.8% being less than 1ha. A total of 160 ha was tilled using hired animals for tillage, of which 13ha are in the A2 sector, 48ha in the SSCF, 45ha in A1, 46ha in ORA and 8ha are situated in the CA sector.

Table 9-10: Access to Draught Power, 2012

Model		Area tilled (ha) own animals				Area tilled (ha) hired animals		Area tilled (ha) own tractor			Area tilled (ha) DDF	Area tilled (ha) ARDA	Area tilled (ha) hired private tractor			
		Less than 1 ha	1.1-2ha	2.1-3ha	>3.1	Less than 1 ha	1.1-2ha	Less than 1 ha	1.1-2ha	>3.1	Less than 1 ha	Less than 1 ha	Less than 1 ha	1.1-2ha	2.1-3ha	>3.1
A1	No	14	8	18	5	42	3	45	0	0	45	45	45	0	0	0
	%	31.1%	17.8%	40.0%	11.1%	93.3%	6.7%	100.0%	0.0%	0.0%	100.%	100.%	100.0%	0.0%	0.0%	0.0%
SSCF	No	6	5	12	27	48	0	46	0	2	47	47	47	0	0	0
	%	12.%	10.0%	24.0%	54.0%	100.0%	0.0%	95.8%	0.0%	4.2%	100.%	100.%	100.0%	0.0%	0.0%	0.0%
A2	No	6	0	2	15	13	0	11	0	6	14	14	14	0	2	2
	%	26.1%	0.0%	8.7%	65.2%	100.0%	0.0%	64.7%	0.0%	35.3%	100.%	100.%	77.8%	0.0%	11.1%	11.1%
ORA	No	23	10	6	7	45	1	45	1	0	46	46	45	1	0	0
	%	50%	21.7%	13.0%	15.2%	97.8%	2.2%	97.8%	2.2%	0.0%	100.%	100.%	97.8%	2.2%	0.0%	0.0%
CA	No	27	4	4	2	6	2	1	0	0	0	0	0	0	0	0
	%	73%	10.8%	10.8%	5.4%	75.0%	25.0%	100.0%	0.0%	0.0%	0	0	0	0	0	0
Total	No	76	27	42	56	154	6	148	1	8	152	152	151	1	2	2
	% of Total	37.8%	13.4%	20.9%	27.9%	96.2%	3.8%	94.3%	0.6%	5.1%	100%	100%	96.8%	0.6%	1.3%	1.3%

Source: Author, compiled from own survey data, 2016

A total of 1 57ha were also tilled using hired tractors and 94.3% of the tilled was less than 1ha per household. The District Development Fund and the Agricultural and Rural Development Authority tractors were hired and tilled 152ha apiece. Reduced access to land in the CA sector presents a limitation on cattle and other animal holdings thereby causing land tillage challenges, despite limited land access. The use of hired private tractors was also high, with a total of 156ha tilled across the five settlement sectors of Hwedza district. Of the 617ha tilled by the interviewed households, 361ha, constituting 58.5%, were tilled using animal power.

9.3.4 Residency and security of tenure

The nature of residence by the farmers and their security of tenure impacts on farm productivity. An investigation into these factors revealed that an overall 45.7% reside on the farms as Figure 9-8 again shows. However, residency on the farm is differentiated among the settlement models, with the A2 farmers being the least at 18.75% and the CAs being the highest at 69.8%. The low residency of plot owners in Hwedza district confirms Moyo and Yeros (2005) observation on the existence of the political motivated functional dualism and semi-proletarianisation where petty commodity production by mostly female unwaged labour subsidise male waged labour in the modern and peasantry sectors.

Figure 9-8: Residency of Plot Owners by Settlement Type

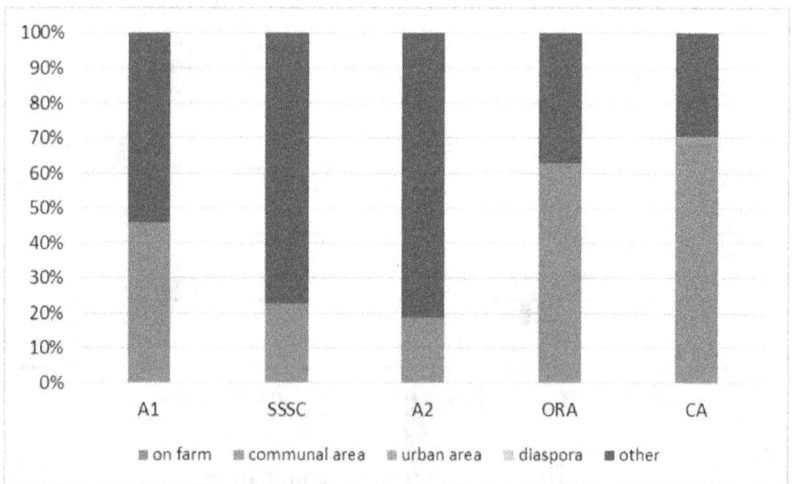

Source: Author, compiled from own survey data, 2016

With regards to security of tenure, Figure 9.9 shows that 93% of the respondents indicated that they are not under any threat of eviction. Within the newly resettled areas, 97.8% of the household in the A1 advised that they had not received any threat of eviction. This is a huge improvement from the levels of threats recorded by Moyo *at al.* (2009), of 16.5% for the A1 sector and 13.6% for the A2 sectors.

Figure 9-9: Eviction Threats Received Households by Settlement Type, 2013-2015

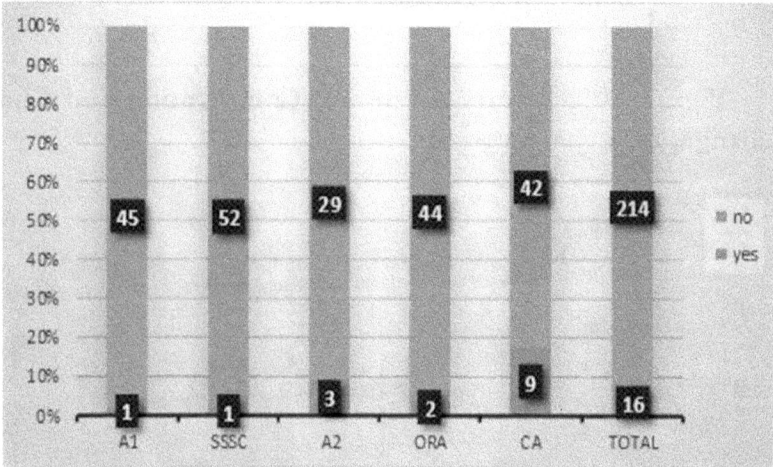

Source: Author, compiled from own survey data, 2016

The differences in land tenure types have no impact on security of tenure and did not result in differentiated access to loans as all the households across the settlement models have not accessed credit in the last three seasons, as will be fully revealed in the next sections. In the SSCF sector, 98.1 did not receive and threats, while in other sectors it was 90.6% in the A2, 95.7 in the ORA. Quite to the contrary, households in the 17% of the CA sector household have been threatened with eviction in the past, compared to 9.4% in the A2 and 2.2% in the A1 settlement sector. This revelation is fundamental in that analysts have argued that tenure insecurity on the land has impacted negatively on agricultural production within the resettled areas. The findings also challenge the argument put forward by some writers (Zamchiya 2012; Alexzander 2006) that state practise and patronage has impacted negatively on agricultural production, given that there are no significant politically motivated threats to tenure security for the 'newly' resettled households.

9.4   Conservation, Climate Change and Production Patterns

The impact of natural resource conservations and climate change on agricultural production was also investigated in this study. The study revealed that overall, 78.4% and 97.85% of the respondents knew about soil conservation and climate change respectively as shown in Figure 9-10.

Figure 9-10: Awareness to Soil Conservation and Climate change, 2016

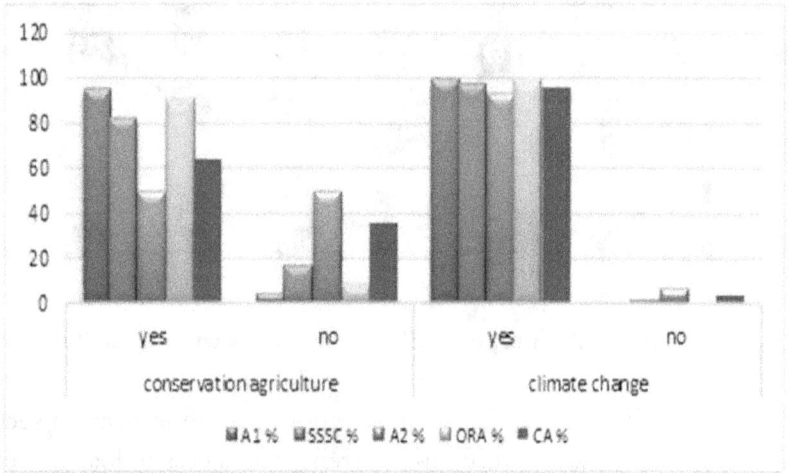

Source: Author, compiled from own survey data, 2016

Soil conservation awareness was highest in the A1 sector at 95.6%, while all the farmers in the A1, A2 and ORA sectors confirmed awareness to climate change. Most the farmers have adapted to new farming methods in response to changing climate conditions as shown in Figure 9-11.

Overall, 92.7% of the respondents have adopted new farming methods, but the least compliance was observed in the SSCF at 87.8% while the highest compliance is in the ORA at 97.6%. However, climate change remains a serious threat to agricultural productivity. The consistent recurrence of drought due to climate change has caused alterations in the cropping programmes and a drop in production levels (crops and livestock) across the settlement models (Masimba, Interview). To this end, the quality of mechanism for adaptation to climate change remains unresolved, particularly in the absence of a coherent government programme towards clarifying government policy and empowering the Agritex officers and communities to deal with the climate change and conservation methods.

Figure 9-11: Changed Cropping Programme, 2016

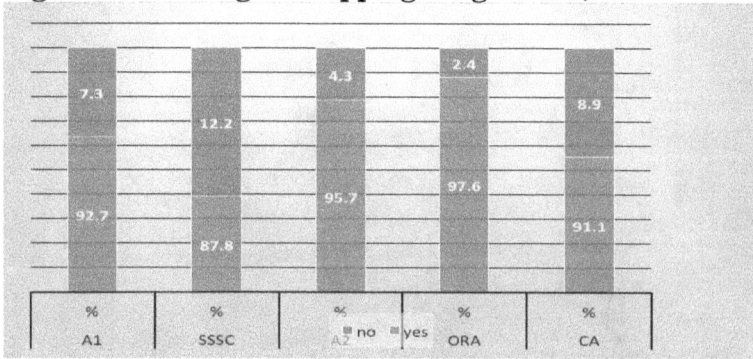

Source: Author, compiled from own survey data, 2016

9.5   Access to Farming Assets

Resource endowment gives leverage on agricultural productivity and also reflects capital accumulation either from below and/or from above. This study made a comparative study of asset ownership across the five settlement sectors in the studied area of Hwedza district. Assessing access to the seven key farming assets (irrigation, water pump, borehole, scotch cart, tractor, plough and grinding mill) as shown in Table 9-11, help shade light on the differentiated capacities to till the land and how asset accumulation is panning out within the settlement sectors of Hwedza District. As low as 4.8% of the respondents has access to irrigation infrastructure at their farms, of which 6 of the 11 farmers who accessed were situated in the A2 settlement model, constituting 18.8% of the respondents within this model.

Table 9-11: Access to Farming Assets, by Settlement Models, 2015

Model		Access to irrigation		No. owned water pump		No. owned borehole		No. owned scotch cart		No. owned tractor		No. owned plough		No. owned grinding mill	
		yes	no	yes	no	yes	no	yes	no	yes	no	yes	no	yes	no
A1	No	0	46	11	35	5	41	31	15	0	46	33	13	3	43
	%	0.0%	100.0%	23.9%	76.1%	10.9%	89.1%	67.4%	32.6%	0.0%	100.0%	71.7%	28.3%	6.5%	93.5%
SSCF	No	2	51	7	46	8	45	45	8	4	49	46	7	0	53
	%	3.8%	96.2%	13.2%	86.8%	15.1%	84.9%	84.9%	15.1%	7.5%	92.5%	86.8%	13.2%	0.0%	100%
A2	No	6	26	17	15	6	26	23	9	7	25	27	5	4	28
	%	18.8%	81.2%	53.1%	46.9%	18.8%	81.2%	71.9%	28.1%	21.9%	78.1%	84.4%	15.6%	12.5%	87.5%
ORA	No	2	44	9	37	2	44	36	10	2	44	39	7	2	44
	%	4.3%	95.7%	19.6%	80.4%	4.3%	95.7%	78.3%	21.7%	4.3%	95.7%	84.8%	15.2%	4.3%	95.7%
CA	No	1	52	1	52	0	53	13	40	1	52	17	36	1	52
	%	1.9%	98.1%	1.9%	98.1%	0.0%	100.0%	24.5%	75.5%	1.9%	98.1%	32.1%	67.9%	1.9%	98.1%
Total	No	11	219	45	185	21	209	148	82	14	216	162	68	10	220
	%	4.8%	95.2%	19.6%	80.4%	9.1%	90.9%	64.3%	35.7%	6.1%	93.9%	70.4%	29.6%	4.3%	95.7%

Source: Author, compiled from own survey data, 2016

Whereas none of the A1 farmers had irrigation equipment in 2015, 23.9% had water pumps, compared 53.1% revealed for the A2, 19.6% in the ORA, and 13.2% in the SSCF sectors. The CA remained with low access of 1.9% for both irrigation and water pumps, revealing their total dependence on rain-fed agricultural activities and therefore increased vulnerability to climate change and drought. While access to boreholes was varied among the farming sectors, the CA sector recorded that none of the farmers had boreholes installed on their plots. Even though the CA sector had the lowest assess to scotch carts at 24.5%, access to this asset was generally high among the households across the other sectors. The SSCF had greater access at 84.9%, compared to ORA at 78.1%, A2 at 71.9% and A1 at 67. 4%. The ownership of tractors revealed tilted distribution in favour of the A2 sector where 21.9% households within the sector had at least one tractor, even though the overall level of tractor ownership was low at 6.1% of the 230 interviewed households. All in all, 14 out of 230 respondents had tractors, with none in the A1 and one in the CA sectors. The ownership of ploughs was generally high and above 70% among the sectors serve for the CA where it stood at 32.1%. Grinding mills reflect diversification into non-farm income earning activities. A total of 10 households had grinding mills, of which 40% were owned by households in the A2 sector, 20% in the ORA and 30% in the A1 sector and 10% was in the CA sector. This shows that engagement in non-farm activities is prevalent across the settlement sector.

9.5.1 Cattle ownership by settlement model

Cattle ownership is high with 78.7% of the respondents owning a herd of cattle across the different settlement models as Figure 9-12 shows. The A1 households are dominated by farmers who own cattle, ranging between 1 and 2 herd, with 10 of the 22 households falling in this category. However this category has fewer households owning more than 51 herd of cattle compared to other sectors. The A1 sector also dominated households owning 6-10 herd of cattle, with 13 out of a total 41 households The SSCF dominate the category of farmers who own a herd of cattle numbering from 11 cattle upwards, with 33 households, followed by the A2 sector with 15 households.

Figure 9-12: Cattle Ownership by Settlement Models, 2015

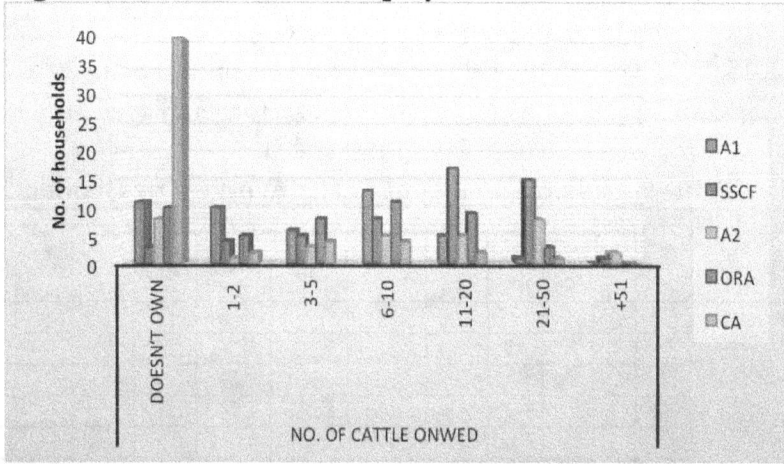

Source: Author, compiled from own survey data, 2016

Even though the category of farmers who own 6-10 has a high number of households at 41, overall there are more households owing in excess of 6 herd of cattle as compared to those owning less. Since 58.35% of the land was tilled using animal power in 2015, and 55.3% of the households who grow maize rely on animal manure, households with higher number of cattle are set to produce more than those with less or who depend on hiring for tillage purposes.

9.6   Labour Relations and Agricultural Production

Access and use of hired and family labour is a critical factor in class analysis. This study sought to reveal how wage labour employment is differentiated across the settlement sectors. The interviewed households show in Table 9-12 that the 42 (18.3%) out of 230 households employed permanent workers in 2015. Of these, only 4.3% employed two male workers, while 86.1% of the respondents did not employ male permanent workers, a total of 11 (4.8%) households employed one permanent worker, 12 (5.2%) employed two, 14 (6.1%) employed 3-4 workers. In the SSCF sector, 45.5% of the households employed single workers permanently, compared to 27.2% in the A2 sector while the balance is shared equally among the A1, ORA and the CA sectors. A total of 58 (25.2%) households employed female workers compared to 32 (13.9% of 230) households who employed male workers on a causal basis. Of the 10 (4.3%) households who employed a single worker in 2015, 50% were employed as casual workers in the SSCF, 20% were employed in the A2 sector, while other sectors employed 10% each.

Table 9-12: Permanent and Casual Workers by Gender, 2015

Type of worker	Model		No. of males 2015					No. of females 2015				Total
			No worker	Single	2 workers	3-4 workers	Total males	No worker	2 workers	3-4 workers	Total female	
Permanent	A1	No	45	1	0	0	1	45	0	0	1	2
		%	97.80	2.20	0.00	0.00	3.10	97.80	0.00	0.00	10.00	5.00
	SSCF	No	44	5	3	1	9	51	0	1	2	11
		%	83.00	9.40	5.70	1.90	28.10	96.20	0.00	1.90	20.00	27.50
	A2	No	14	3	6	9	18	26	2	2	4	22
		%	43.80	9.40	18.80	28.10	56.30	81.20	6.20	6.20	60.00	55.00
	ORA	No	44	1	1	0	2	46	0	0	0	2
		%	95.70	2.20	2.20	0.0	6.30	100.00	0.00	0.00	0.00	5.00
	CA	No	51	1	0	1	2	52	0	0	1	3
		%	96.20	1.90	0.00	1.90	6.30	98.10	0.00	0.00	10.00	7.50
	Total	No	198	11	10	11	32	220	2	3	10	40
		%	86.10	4.80	4.30	4.80	100	95.70	0.90	1.30	100.0	100.0
Casual	A1	No	45	1	0	0	1	32	4	6	10	11
		%	97.80	2.20	0.00	0.00	3.10	69.60	8.70	13.00	17.20	100.0
	SSCF	No	42	5	4	2	11	34	6	10	16	27
		%	79.20	9.40	7.50	3.80	34.40	64.20	11.30	18.90	27.60	100.0
	A2	No	16	2	6	8	16	9	2	21	23	49
		%	50.00	6.20	18.80	25.00	50.00	28.10	6.20	65.60	39.70	100.0
	ORA	No	44	1	1	0	2	36	2	4	6	8
		%	95.70	2.20	2.20	0.00	6.30	78.30	4.30	8.70	10.30	100.0
	CA	No	51	1	1	0	2	50	3	0	3	5
		%	96.20	1.90	1.90	0.00	6.30	94.30	5.70	0.00	5.20	100.0
	Total	No	198	10	12	10	32	161	17	41	58	90
		%	86.10	4.30	5.20	4.30	100	70.00	7.40	17.80	100	100

Source: Author, compiled from own survey data, 2016

The 2 and 3-4 category are dominated by the A2 farmers for both male and female workers, constituting 33.3% and 50% for the male workers and 50% apiece for the female workers. Similarly, a total of 90 households employed wage workers on a casual basis with more women than man employed in this category. A total of 14 households, the A2 sector dominated the category who employed 2 and 3-4 male casual workers, compared to 6 in the SSCF, none in the A1, 1 in the ORA and 1 in the CA sectors. A total of 58 households, have between 2 and 3-4 casual female workers, compared to 22 male casual workers. All in all the A2 and the SSCF sector employed more permanent and causal workers compared to the other sectors.

9.6.1 Labour provision, gender and age by plot holders

At least 70 (30.4%) respondents provide wage labour to other plot holders in the different settlement models. Tables 9-12 shows a gender and age wage labour distribution across the settlement sectors, where 34 (14.8%) households provide male workers, while 26 (11.3%) are a source of female workers separately and 21 (9.1%) families engage children under the age of 10 years as wage workers. There is one household providing a male worker from A2, while 14 (5.2%) households from ORA and the CA equally and 1 household from the A1 sectors. Similarly, the A2, A1 and the SSCF have 1 household employing 1 female worker each, while two households from the A1, 6 from the ORA and 15 are from the CA sectors. Of the 10 households employing children under the age of 16, seven households are from the CA and 3 households are from the ORA sector. Empirical data collected in Hwedza District show that 188 (82.1%) respondents indicate that they provide labour for agricultural activities on their farms as shown on Figure 9-13(a) and (b). Within the CA sector, 94.3% of the farmers confirmed that they provide labour on agricultural activities compared to 67.7% in the A2, 91.3% in the A1, 75.5% in the SSCF, and 76.1% in the ORA sector.

Even though the CA has some high percentage households (38%) who hire out wage labour, all the other sectors investigated also hire out labour albeit at lower levels. For instance, the ORA sector has 30% of the households hiring out labour, A2 has 9.7%, SSCF has 5.7% and A1 has 4.4% of the households providing wage labour to other farmers within Hwedza District. This evidence shows that the sectors are heterogeneous in that some sectors considered to be capital intensive have some households within the sector hiring out rather than hiring in wage labour. A more nuanced analysis beyond labour employment patterns is therefore required to reveal the production and social differentiation patterns in rural Zimbabwe. The presence of wage workers/peasants in the A2 sector is in sync with observations made by Scoones *et al.* (2010) that many migrant workers remained in the Highveld areas, either settled, employed or unemployed. As Scoones *et al.* (2010) observe, many of the workers employed by the respondents were from across the varied settlement areas.

Figure 9-13: (a) Family Members/relatives (b) Households who Hire Out Providing Manual Labour Wage Labour

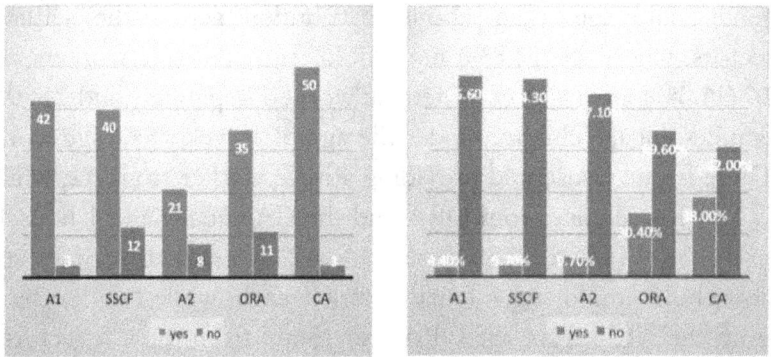

Source: Author, compiled from own survey data, 2016

The mode of payment for hired labour is generally through cash, in kind and in some cases as a combination of the two methods as Table 9-13 shows. With regards to permanent workers, the CA and the A2 sectors favour the use cash payments, while the A1 and the SSCF use this mode of payment for casual wage workers. The use of cash and kind for payment of casual wage workers is common in the A2, the ORA, and the CA sectors at 30.8%, 53.3% and 66.7% respectively. As Scoones *et al.* (2010) observe, payment in kind gain currency during the period of economy-wide crisis where the Zimbabwean dollar became worthless and as such became valueless as a mode of payment.

Table 9-13: Mode of Payment for Permanent and Casual Workers, 2015

Model		Mode of payment for permanent workers				Mode of payment for casual workers				
		Not applicable	Cash	Cash and kind	Total	Not applicable	Cash	Kind	Cash and kind	Total
A1	No	12	3	0	15	3	10	0	2	15
	%	80.0%	20.0%	0.0%	100.0%	20.0%	66.7%	0.0%	13.3%	100.0%
SSCF	No	21	9	0	30	2	20	2	6	30
	%	70%	30.0%	0.0%	100.0%	6.7%	66.7%	6.7%	20.0%	100.0%
A2	No	8	17	2	27	3	12	3	8	26
	%	29.6%	63.0%	7.4%	100.0%	11.5%	46.2%	11.5%	30.8%	100.0%
ORA	No	14	1	0	15	2	5	0	8	15
	%	93.3%	6.7%	0.0%	100.0%	13.3%	33.3%	0.0%	53.3%	100.0%
CA	No	1	2	0	3	1	0	0	2	3
	%	33.3%	66.7%	0.0%	100.0%	33.3%	0.0%	0.0%	66.7%	100.0%
Total	No	56	32	2	90	11	47	5	26	89
	%	61.1%	35.6%	2.2%	100.0%	12.4%	52.8%	5.6%	29.2%	100.0%

Source: Author, compiled from own survey data, 2016

The reliance on cash and kind (mainly maize and groundnuts and sweet potatoes) as a differentiating factor for wage labour hiring impact on agricultural productivity and is therefore a driving factor for social differentiation.

9. 7   Food Security

Food is a critical measurement of agricultural productivity. The study reveals in Table 9-14 that 14.9% of the respondents faced food shortage in 2015, of which, 32.7% were in the CA sector, 15% were in the SSCF, 10.9% were in the ORA, 6.3% were in the A2 and 2.6% were in the A1 sectors.

Table 9-14: Household Food Shortage and Meals Received per day, 2016

		Households food shortage				Households meals per day			
		not applicable	Yes	No.	Total	1	2	3	Total
A1	No	1	1	36	38	0	17	19	36
	%	2.6%	2.6%	94.7%	100.0%	0.0%	47.2%	52.8%	100.0%
SSCF	No	0	8	45	53	0	11	41	52
	%	0%	15%	85%	100%	0%	21%	79%	100%
A2	No	3	2	27	32	0	8	22	30
	%	9.4%	6.3%	84.4%	100.0%	0.0%	26.7%	73.3%	100.0%
ORA	No	4	5	37	46	0	21	23	44
	%	8.7%	10.9%	80.4%	100.0%	0.0%	47.7%	52.3%	100.0%
CA	No	1	17	34	52	4	36	12	52
	%	1.9%	32.7%	65.4%	100.0%	7.7%	69.2%	23.1%	100.0%
Total	No	5.2	33	179	221	4	93	117	214
	%	2.7%	14.9%	81.0%	100.0%	1.9%	43.5%	54.7%	100.0%

Source: Author, compiled from own survey data, 2016

In the CA sector, 7.7% of the respondents indicated that they have access to one meal per day, 69.2% take 2 meals and 23.1% percent get 3 meals per day. In all the other sectors, all the respondents get at least 2 meals per day. However the A2 sector has the highest proportion (73.3%) of respondents who get three meals per day at 73.3%, followed by the SSCF at 79%. Overall 54.7% of the respondents have access to three meals a day, 43.5% have access to 2 meals a day. The study therefore reveals that the CA sector is more vulnerable than the resettled households, as already been observed, due to low agricultural productivity. As Table 9-15 shows, there are 12 households in the A1 (2), SSCF (5) and ORA (5) whose food security situation cannot be ensured only for month.

Table 9-15: Months' Supply of Maize, 2015

| Sector | Months that maize harvest last | | | | | | | | | | | | | | | Total |
	Not applicable	0	1	2	3	4	5	6	7	8	9	10	11	12	
A1	8	2	0	1	0	0	0	0	1	11	5	9	5	1	43
SSCF	2	5	2	0	0	1	1	2	1	6	2	19	2	10	53
A2	3	5	0	1	0	0	0	0	0	1	0	4	4	14	32
ORA	10	0	3	1	0	1	0	1	0	16	3	6	1	3	45
CA	11	0	4	5	3	2	3	1	6	2	5	8	2	1	53
Total	34	12	9	8	3	4	4	4	8	36	15	46	14	29	226

Source: Author, compiled from own survey data, 2016

There are five households whose food security situation provides a month's supply, with five of the households being in the CA sector. Overall, whereas there are 29 households whose food supply will last 12 months, only one each is situated in the CA and A1 sectors, three are in the ORA, 10 are in the SSCF and 14 are in the A2 sector.

9.8   Production Grievances by Land Holders, 2015

Under the harsh economy-wide crises currently bedevilling the agrarian sector, the establishment of challenges affecting agricultural production is critical for knowledge and policy development. Households were asked to rank the three major challenges affecting production. The biggest challenge faced by farmers is HIV/AIDS as cited by 60 (26.1%) of the interviewed households, followed by poor road networks, experienced by 57 (24.8%) of the interviewed households, access to credit faced by 56 (24.3%) of the interviewed households and drought which was experienced by (41 (17.8%) of the interviewed households (see Figure 9.14).

Figure 9-14: Challenges Faced by the Farmers, 2015

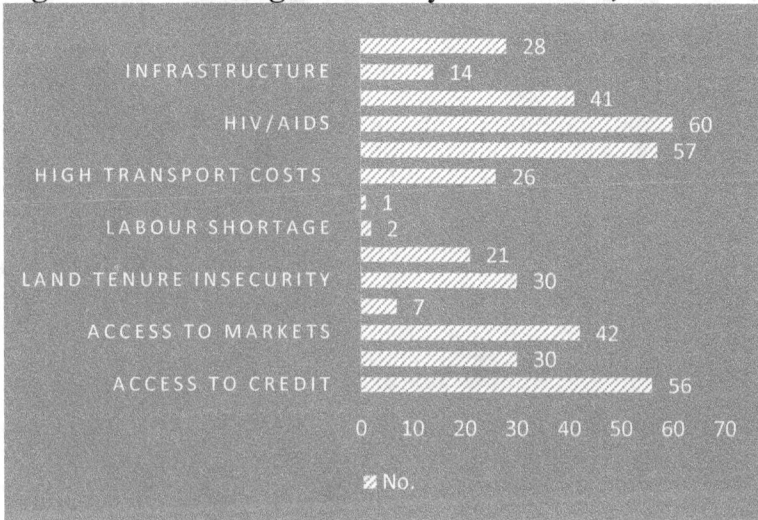

There are 30 (13%) of the interviewed households who mentioned access to inputs and land tenure insecurity separately. Other cited problems relate to lack of working capital high transport costs, and shortage of draught power. Whereas HIV/AIDS, poor road network and droughts are community based challenges, differentiated access to credit, access to markets, land insecurity and lack of working capital result in varied production capacities of the individual farmers.

9.9   Conclusions

This chapter has revealed that agricultural smallholder farmers from variegated settlement models have differentiated access to farming assets and as such are differentially capacitated for agricultural production in cash crops, food crops and livestock. The chapter revealed that crop production is linked to assess to capital. In particular, tobacco contract farming linked to export finance has gained momentum across the settlement sectors. Access to labour, both family labour and hired labour is crucial in driving social differentiation across the settlement models. However tobacco farming has altered tobacco utilisation patterns across the settlement sectors and agro-ecological regions. The next chapter reveals how access to varying types of capital has impacted on production and class formation.

Chapter Ten

Capital and Commodity Markets

10.1 Introduction

The chapter presents data on the different circuits of capital and markets relations and how these mediate accumulation for small holder farmers. It focuses on contract farming, credit, remittances, off- and on-farm income, government support programmes and state practice and how these impact on agricultural production. Local, national and international commodity circuits and linkages will be revealed and analysed. Even though the study focuses on contract farming, the chapter analyses a wider range of funding sources to situate the study. However a detailed analysis of contract farming is done as part of the wider analysis. The analysis is based on data collected from the five study sub-sites in Hwedza District.

10.2 Agricultural Financing

In order to reveal the changing role of capital in agrarian relations in rural Zimbabwe, this study focuses on the changing nature of agricultural finance sector and the related inputs/outputs markets, relying on empirical data gathered in Hwedza district for the period. This analysis is done on a comparative basis in order to establish the effect of agricultural finance and commodity markets on the variegated agro-ecological and tenural settings presented by Hwedza district. To begin with, the macro-economic policies prevailing in the country have gone through transformation and policy shifts over the years, and more recently, the introduction of a multi-currency regime from 2009, commonly known as dollarisation, has impacted posivitively on the operational environment for rural farmers.

Across the settlement sectors, 94.2% of the farmers perceive that dollarisation had a positive effect on the agricultural economy, as Figure 10-1 shows. With regards to inflation control, 88.6% of the respondents observed that the new regime of controlled inflation had a postive effect on farming operations. Similarly, 85.1% of the studied households noted that the stabilisation of the regime had a positive impact while 84.8% regarded the opening of the commodity markets through the liberalisation of the economy under the government of national unity (GNU) to have resulted in positive impact on marketing options for the households.

Figure 10-1: Effect of Economic Liberalisation from 2009

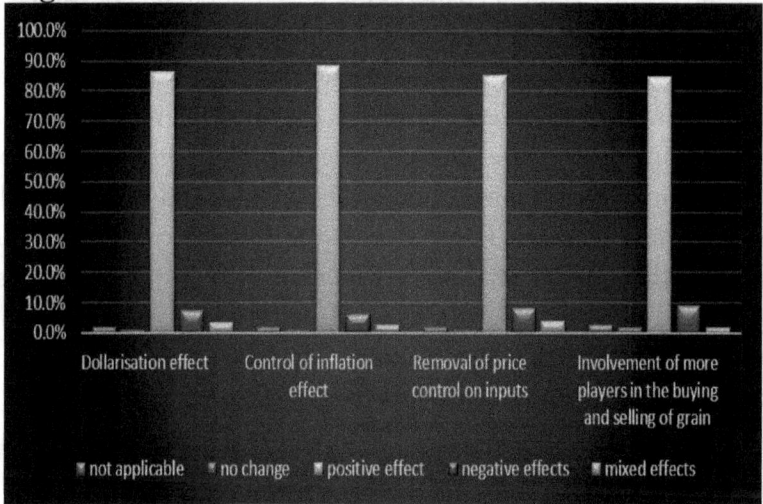

Source: Author, compiled from own survey data, 2016

These macro-economic changes were expected to result in improved agricultural finance conditions which would have spurred agricultural development as was the case in the newly independent Zimbabwe in the early 80s (see also Sachikonye 1989).

10.2.1 Domestic capital and bank credit

Evidence from Hwedza District shows that 13.2% of the respodnenst faced challenges in accessing credit (see Figure 10-2a). However, of the 83.7% who did not face challenges, 43.3% of the studied households never tried to borrow, 11.6% of those who tried to borrow were requested to present security of tenure. In the A1 sector 71.1% of respodnenst d that never tried to borrow from the bank compared to 17.4% for the ORA sector, 35.8% for the CA sector, 44.8% for the A2 sector and 49% for the SSCF sector (see Figure 10-2b). Partly due to percieved reluctance by the banks to lend money to farmers due to poor of tenural arrangements, households in Hwedza District end up not approaching banks for credit facilities.

Resultantly, the households indicate that they have not faced problems in accessing bank credit. For instance, 94.3% of the households in the CA sector never faced any challenges in accessing agricultural finance, compared to 90.4% for the SSCF, 80% for the A1, 76.1% for the ORA and 71% for the A2 sectors.

Figure 10-2: (a) Challenges in Accessing Credit (b) Requests for Collateral Security, 2015

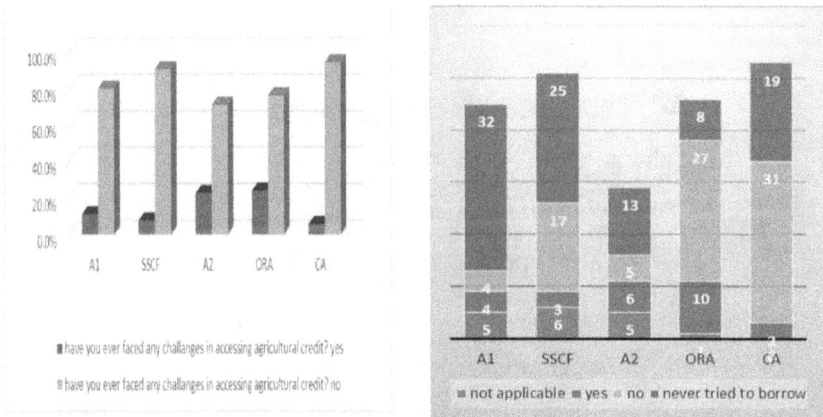

Source: Author, compiled from own survey data, 2016

Regarding the nature of challenges faced by the farmers in accessing credit, Figure 10-3 shows that 34.4% had no security and 35.1% could not meet other bank requirements (excluding collateral).

The issue of collateral security presented the biggest threat to SSCF where 60% were affected, while 55.6% of A1 farmers and 44.4% from the A2 sector were similarly affected. In addition, 11.1% of the A2 farmers noted that they were not able to write business proposals for purposes of accessing bank credit, while 20% of the SSCF farmers felt that bank credit attracted high interest rates. On the same note, 90.9% and 100% of the farmers who responded to this question from the ORA and the CA sectors respectively noted that they failed to meet the bank requirements outside the issue of collateral security. In spite of the challenges in accessing bank credit, 11.1% of the respondents who accessed credit from the SSCF sector

235

used title deeds for urban property and the 99 year lease equally. At the same time, 22.2% of the respondents in the A2 sector used title deeds for urban properties compared to 11.1% who relied on the 99 year lease. In this regard, access to credit is differentiated along the tenure systems of the settlement models in Hwedza District, in which case, the SSCF and the A2 households relying on properties owned under the 99 year lease and title deeds stand better chances of accessing bank credit.

Figure 10-3: Challenges in Accessing Credit by Settlement Model, 2015

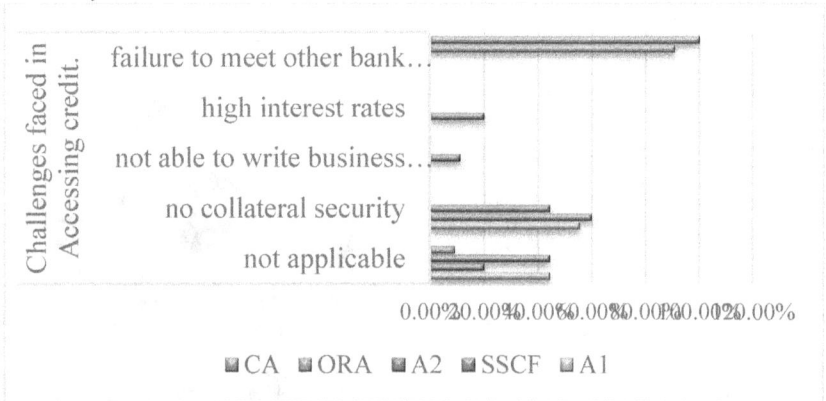

Source: Author, compiled from own survey data, 2016

The study also revealed that households in the A2 sector who faced challenges in repayment of loans advanced by the banks were affected by poor commodity prices while those in the CA sector faced social problems. Based on the reviewed empirical evidence, a conclusion can be reached to the effect that households from across the settlement models and from varied agro-ecological circumstances interviewed in Hwedza District are facing challenges in accessing credit from local banks. On the main, inability to meet credit conditionalities around collateral security specified by the banks is drawing back on access to credit as cited by Scoones *et al* (2010) in their studies in Masvingo province. Studies carried out since 2000 (see Murisa and Chikweche 2015) have observed that limited agricultural funding results in reduced investment in transport, water and electricity, irrigation and dam infrastructures. Whereas Moyo *et al.* (2009) suggested that capital flight experienced from 2000 had the effect of reducing access to credit, the re-insertion of financialised capital from 2009 changed the funding options and opportunities for the farmers.

10.2.2 International capital and contract farming merchants

Tobacco contract farming provides a unique opportunity for farmers to secure credit, agricultural extension services, inputs, transport services and markets for the commodity. There are are at least 22 merchants involved in contract farming covering different settlement sectors of Zimbabwe. Emperical evidence in Table 10-1 gathered in Hwedza district show that 27 farmers involved in tobacco production are involved in contract farming, representing 33.3% of tobacco growers in 2015. The contract farming households secured agricultural assistance from the Mashonaland Tobacco Company (MTC) – a subsidiary of the Allinace One Tobacco Company.

Table 10-1: Access to Tobacco Contract Farming, 2015

Model	Crop contract Farming		Tobacco growers			Total
		Yes	no		Tobacco growers	
A1	No.	9	37	26		46
	%	19.6%	80.4%	56.5%		100.0%
SSCF	No.	7	46	27		53
	%	13.2%	86.8%	50.9%		100.0%
A2	No.	3	29	5		32
	%	9.4%	90.6%	15.6%		100.0%
ORA	No.	7	39	21		46
	%	15.2%	84.8%	45.7%		100.0%
CA	No.	1	52	2		53
	%	1.9%	98.1%	3.8%		100.0%
Total	No.	27	203	81		230
	%	33.30%	88.3%	35.20%		100.0%
	%	11.70%	88.30%	100.00%		100.00%

Source: Author, compiled from own survey data, 2016

The Alliance One is an international company engaged in tobacco contract farming, buying through both contract and auction floors, processing and export to varions destinations but mainly to

the USA (Farai Vheru, Interview). According to Chengetai, the five
major funders of tobacco farming in Zimbabwe are MTC, Northern
Tobacco, Zimbabwe Leaf Tobacco (ZLT), Tian Ze and Boost Africa
(Interview; See also Figure 10-4). The shareholding stuctures of these
companies show that MTC is wholy owned by Alliance One tobacco
merchant company which is registred in the USA. The Northern
Tobacco Company is involved in contract farming and is wholly
owned by the British American Tobacco (BAT) Company which also
operates the Tobacco Processing Company of Zimbabwe (TPZ) that
is involved in the processing of tobacco for export and domestic
cigarrete manufacturing. The ZLT is involved in contract farming,
auction and contract buying, tobacco processing and export.

Figure 10-4: Tobacco Contract and Auction Floors, 2016

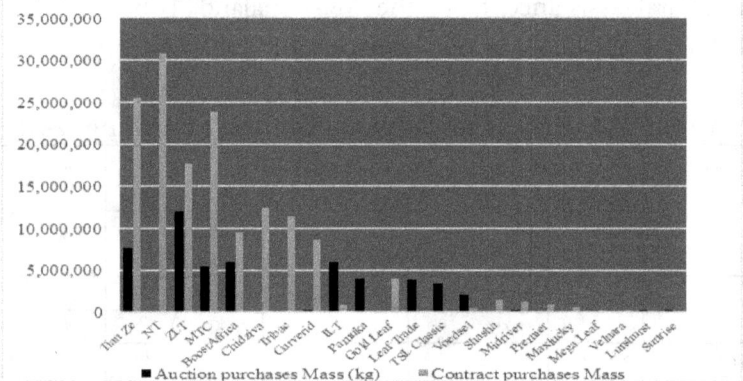

Source: Author, compiled from own survey data, 2016

Tian Ze is owned by China Tobacco Company (CTC) based in
China. The company is involved in contract farming, and thus
finances tobacco farming, acquires tobacco through buying from its
contract farmers, the auction floors and from other tobacco
merchants and from other African countries. The tobacco is
processed through a jointly owned processing unit with MTC. Tian
Ze exports to CTC in China. Boost Africa is is involved in contract
farming, buying (through the auction floors and under contract) and
exporting of processed tobacco. As Figure 10-4 reveals, secondary
data gathered show that MTC had contracted the highest number of
farmers, mainly from the CA sector, followed by Chidziva who

238

contracted mainly from the A1 and CA sectors, ZLT mainly concentrated on the A1 sector while Boost Africa contrated farmers from the CA and A1 sectors. Hwedza District had a total of 2,572 tobacco growers who produced 6,207,757 kgs of tobacco from 2952ha at an average yield of 2,103kg/ha, earning a total of US$19,058,897 in 2015 as Table 10-2 shows. However, the farmers noted that they were facing challenges as 50% of the respondents highlighted limited support resulting in limited hectarage under crop; 30% highlighted poor output prices and 10% highlighted high input costs and challenges related to interpretation of the contract agreement.

Table 10-2: Mashonaland East Tobacco Production per District, 2015

PROVINCE &	MASS	USD	USD/	GROWE	Ha (Harvest	Yield Kg/
MASHONALA	52.514.0	171.415.	3.26	14.766	26.894	1.948
Marondera	15,890,9	54,233,7	3.41	3,370	5,947	2,672
Murehwa	7,897,45	23,470,0	2.97	3,408	4,833	1,634
Seke	7,637,72	27,172,5	3.56	1,038	4,896	1,560
Chikomba	6,631,54	22,318,6	3.37	1,793	2,429	2,730
Hwedza	6,207,75	19,058,8	3.07	2,572	2,952	2,103
Goromonzi	5,396,85	17,404,1	3.22	991	3,641	1,482
Mutoko	2,538,47	6,846,13	2.70	1,420	1,935	1,312
Uzumba	313,305	910,778	2.91	174	261	1,200

Source: TIMB, 2016

The reviewed data show that contract farming is emerging as the main funding for tobacco farming, even though funding remains inadequate. The main funding merchants are international corporations linked to the USA, China and Britain and the European Union. However, funding arrangements are tied to domestic capital in that some banks prefer to lend though reputable international merchants who contract tobacco to farmers across the settlement models (Chipochashe, Interview), mainly under a management contract arrangement. Whereas country-wide, contract farming also involves cotton and sugar (Mkhize and Moyo 2012) in the case of

Hwedza District, contract farming is confined to tobacco farming, as empirical evidence shows.

However some farmers compliant that they are being exploited under arrangements where the companies have total control of decision making from production to the marketing of the crop. Some farmer felt that 'they have been converted into labourers on their farmers' in a bid to secure funding and earn some income (Simbisai Manungira, Interview).

10.2.3 Non-farm income

Households in Hwedza have also relied on some on-farm income sources of income for cropping and livestock production, even though differently per sector, as Figure 10-5 shows.

For instance, a total of 6 farmers hired out tractors and earned between US$140 and US$1 500 in 2015. Similarly, 23 farmers also hired out animals for draught purposes and earned between US$40.00 and US$400.00 in the 2014/15 agricultural season. In all, farmers in the ORA received more income from animal tillage compared to other settlement sectors, some A1 farmers hardly earned some income from tillage services.

Figure 10-5: Income from Tillage Services by Settlement Types, 2015

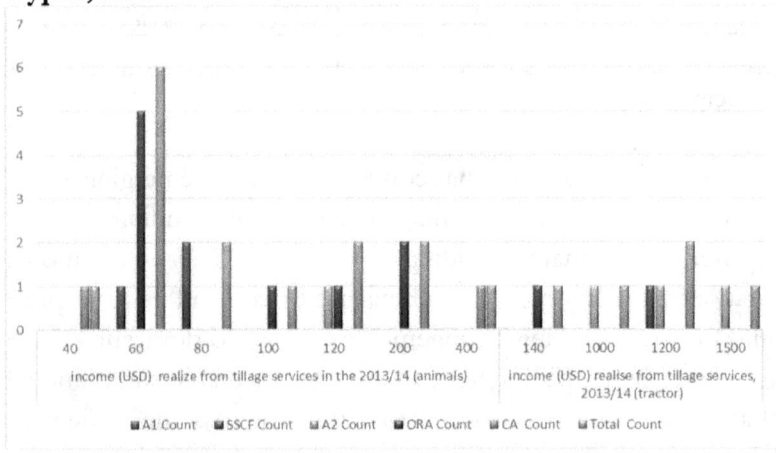

Source: Author, compiled from own survey data, 2016

Another source of income relied upon for agricultural production was hired out labour. However, the level of labour hired out was differentiated across the settlement sectors. In 2015, 38% of the CA sector farmers were engaged in labour hired out compared to 30.4% in the ORA sector, 9.7% in the A2 sector, 5.7% in the SSCF sector and 4.4% in the A1 sector, as shown in Figure 10-6.

Figure 10-6: Labour Hired Out by Settlement Type, 2015

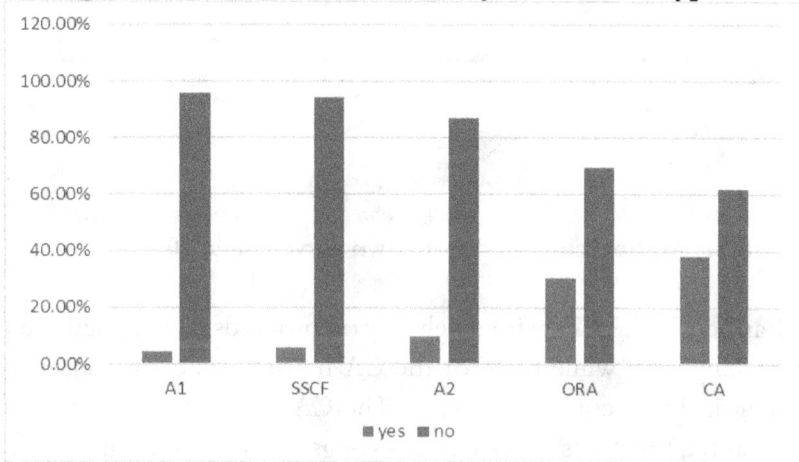

Source: Author, compiled from own survey data, 2016

Whereas, on-farm income is an established source of income for farmers across the settlement sectors, on-farm activities such as provision of hired out labour to other farmers within rural Hwedza was not a critical source of income in all the sectors, save for the ORA sector. Similarly, provision of tillage services was important for the A1 sector, SSCF and A2 sectors, even though it has proved to be a real source of income for production enhancement.

10.2.4 Off-farm income and personal savings

Low levels of access to credit and limited availability of contract finance that stood at 1.3% and 11.7% respectively as well as low income from labour hired out and tillage services across the the settlement sectors has meant that farmers have had to rely on off-farm income to finance crop production and for social reproduction. Figure 10-7 shows that 52.6% of the farmers across the settlement sectors relied on proceeds from agricultural commodities sales,

241

26.3% on personal savings outside agriculture and 10.5% on diaspora remittances.

Figure 10-7: Sources of Funding by Settlement Models, 2015

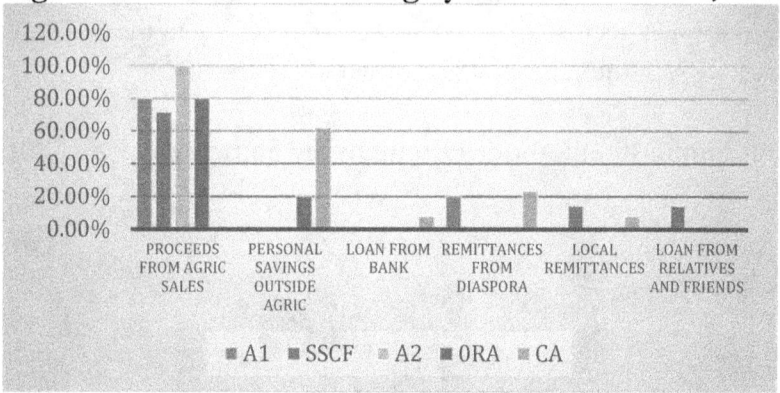

Source: Author, compiled from own survey data, 2016

Farmers in the A2 sector solely rely on proceeds from agricultural commodity sales while none of the CA households earned income from agricultural commodity sales. The CA relied on 60% of their financial requirements on personal savings earned from outside the agricultural sector (see also Moyo *et al.* 2014), compared to 20% of the ORA. The two sectors also receive funding through remittances from the diaspora (23.1% and 20% respectively). The study therefore reveals that, to the extent that the CA households did not receive income from sale of agricultural proceeds, despite some sections of the CA households studied falling under NRII which recieves above normal rainfall ideal for rainfed cropping program, other factors beyond climatic variations are at play. The low agricultural production and low agricultural commodity sales in the CA in Hwedza District leadsto limited commoditisation and exclusion from local, national and internation commodity circuits, compared to other sectors.

Given that the CA sector has an average arable land of 1.9ha, the lowest arable land available per sector, limited land access is impacting negatively on crop and livestock production. In terms of sources of off-farm income, Figure 10-8 shows that there were 19 households involved in bricklaying, 18 in building, 9 in thatching and 7 in vending of clothes and motor mechanics, among other activities.

Figure 10-8: No. of Households Involved and Income Earned per Activity, 2015.

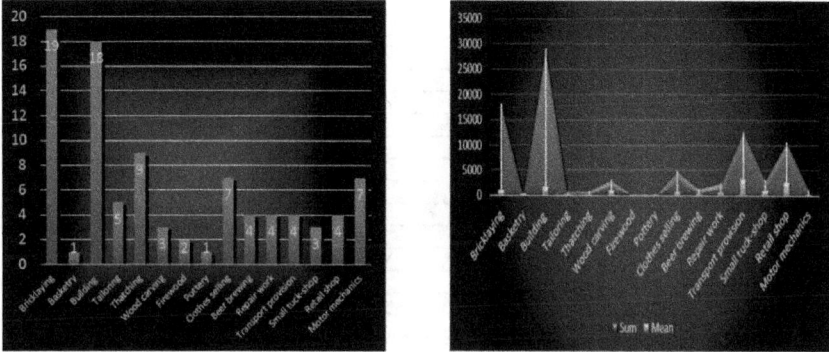

Source: Author, compiled from own survey data, 2016

On average, households who are involved in bricklaying earn an US$950.79 compared to those in building who earned an average of US$1 616.11, woodcarving earned an average of US$1 026.67, transport earned USD3 180.00, small tuckshops earned an average of USD1050.00 and those operating retail shops earned an average of US$ 2675, per annum. The off-farm activities link households across settlement models and urban areas and beyond as Table 10-3 shows. For instances, 22.2% of the people involved in building from the ORA sector, operate in urban areas, and 55.6% in the FTLRP area.

The CA households involved in building activities operate in the FTLRP area while those from this CA involved in bricklaying operate in urban areas. Some households from the A2 sector involved in the bricklaying business also operate in the CA sector while18.2% of the households from the ORA involved in bricklaying operate in the FTLRP area, 9.1% of the households operate CA and63.6% operate in the urban areas.

Table 10-3: Linkages in Off-farm Activities by Settlement Types, 2015

Source	Model		Place of the non-farm activity					Total
			FTLRP area	Communal area	urban area	other	99	
Building	A1	No	1	1	0	0	0	2
		%	50.0%	50.0%	0.0%	0.0%	0.0%	100.0%
	SSCF	No	2	1	0	0	0	3
		%	66.7%	33.3%	0.0%	0.0%	0.0%	100.0%
	A2	No	1	0	1	1	0	3
		%	33.3%	0.0%	33.3%	33.3%	0.0%	100.0%
	ORA	No	5	0	2	1	1	9
		%	55.6%	0.0%	22.2%	11.1%	11.1%	100.0%
	CA	No	1	0	0	0	0	1
		%	100.0%	0.0%	0.0%	0.0%	0.0%	100.0%
	Total	No	10	2	3	2	1	18
		%	55.6%	11.1%	16.7%	11.1%	5.6%	100.0%
Bricklaying	A1	No	0	0	0	0	1	1
		%	0.0%	0.0%	0.0%	0.0%	100.0%	100.0%
	A2	No	0	1	0	0	0	1
		%	0.0%	100.0%	0.0%	0.0%	0.0%	100.0%
	ORA	No	2	1	7	0	1	11
		%	18.2%	9.1%	63.6%	0.0%	9.1%	100.0%
	CA	No	0	0	5	1	0	6
		%	0.0%	0.0%	83.3%	16.7%	0.0%	100.0%
	Total	No	2	2	12	1	2	19
		%	10.5%	10.5%	63.2%	5.3%	10.5%	100.0%

Source: Author, compiled from own survey data, 2016

10.2.5 Diaspora and local remittances

Using empirical data on hoes and brick houses built under thatch, the study revealed the main sources of finance for capital accumulation across the settlement models. The level of reliance on diaspora remittances for the purchase of capital assets stood at 23.1% for hoes and 22.2% for brick under thatch houses as Figure 10-9 shows. The A1 and ORA farmers depended fully on diaspora remittances for the purchase of hoes while the ORA farmers depended on local remittances wholly. The purchase of hoes by the CA was financed to the tune of 22.2% from local remmitances. The reliance on diaspora and local remittances for productive assets and fixed assets was therefore observed to be higher than what Moyo *et al.* (2014) observed in the AIAS survey carried out in 6 district in 2013/4.

Figure: 10-9 (a): Sources of Income for Hoes 10.9 (b) Brick Under Thatch Houses, 2015

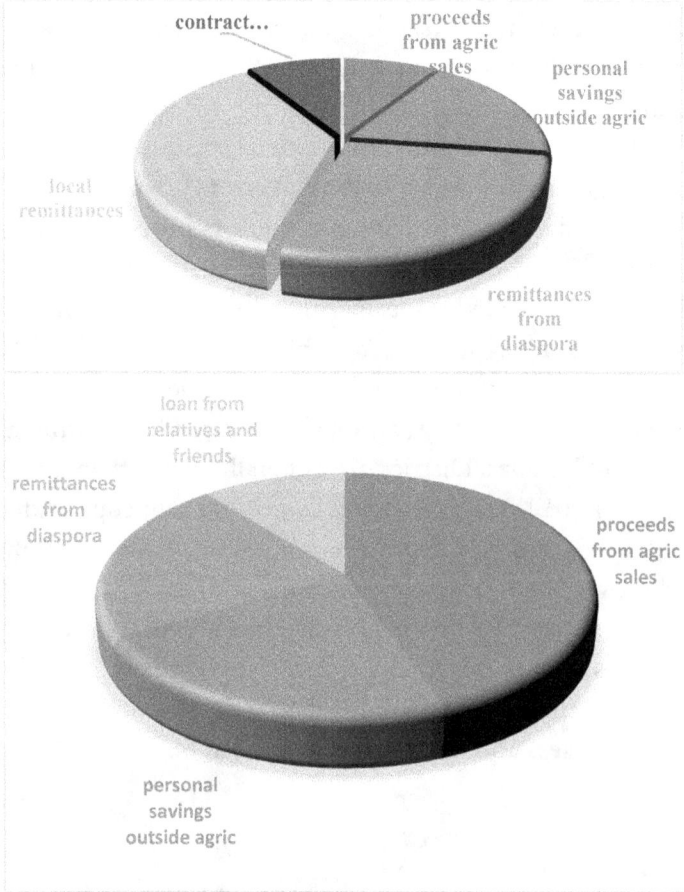

Source: Author, compiled from own survey data, 2016

For instance, the study observed that the A2 farmers made an investment productive assets from diaspora income, 2.7% from diaspora and 1.8% from local remittaces for investment in productive assets (AIAS Survey, 2014). Increased dependance on diapora after 2013 is a consequent of the deepening economic crisis in Zimbabwe, in the post-GNU period. The study therefore reveals that local and diaspora remmitances contribute significantly in rural development. To this end, Zimbabwe's different sectors are singularly linked to global and domestic finance through familial ties and the global capital system through contract farming in both commodity markets and capital development processes.

10.2.6 Personal savings from within and outside agriculture

Unlike other sectors, the CA utilised all the sources of income (proceeds from agricultural sales, personal savings outside agriculture, remittances from the diaspora, local remittances and contract farming) for productive assets. With regards to fixed assets development, the CA households interviewed mainly relied on proceeds from agriculture and personal savings from outside agriculture. The study reveals that the use of proceeds from agriculture was low at 7.7% for productive assets such as hand tools but was high at 44.4% for fixed assets in 2015. The SSCF households relied on proceeds from agriculture for the construction of brick under thatch houses. Some farmers in the CA also relied on contract farming for agricultural financing, although the overall investment figures observed in Hwedza District are generally lower than what the AIAS Survey of 2014 observed. Overall, government support to the agricultural sector declined from 9% in 1980 to 4% in 2000 in response to the overall GDP decline of 50% and unavoidable re-alignment of expenditure in an economy faced with numerous shortages of goods and rising inputs costs (Moyo, Chambati and Siziba 2014). The reliance on personal savings by the respondents for the purchase of fertilisers and certified seed stood at 68.1% and 75% respectively.

10.2.7 Government support

The study uses common sources of finance for purchasing inputs to establish the level of government support. In the case of fertiliser purchased in 2015, farmers secured 11.1% support from the government, as Figure 10-10 shows. The CA sector located in NRII and NRIII received the highest level of government support at 30.4%, followed by the A1 farmers, of whom 11.6% of the interviewed households got support from the government. The A2 farmers did not receive any support from the government, either for fertiliser or certified seed purchases. The A1 sector got 15% support and the CA sector got 12.5%. A total of 24 (11.1%) farmers received government support for fertiliser supply compared to 15 (8.1%) farmers who accessed government assistance for certified seed (see

Figure 10-10). Overall, 185 (80.4%) out of a total of 230 households accessed certified seed in 2015.

Figure 10-10: Common Sources of Fertilisers and Certified Seeds, 2014/15

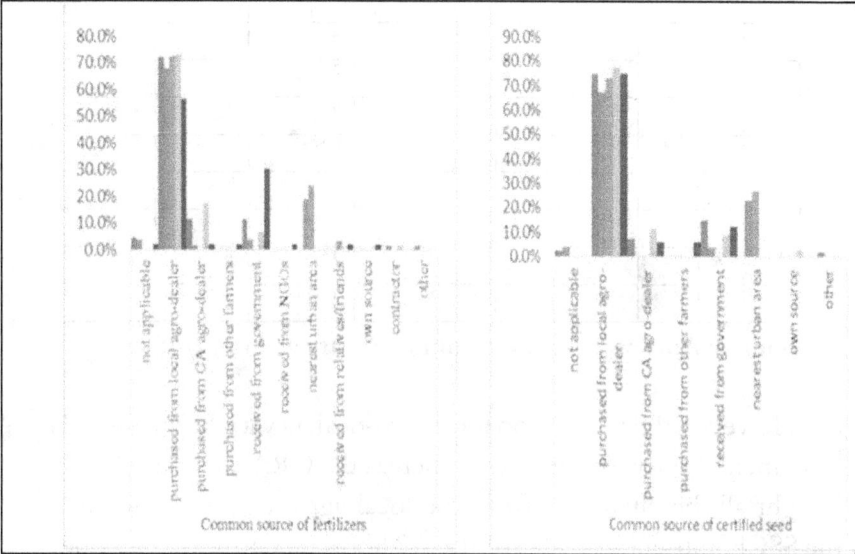

Source: Author, compiled from own survey data, 2016

The limited government support is consequent of its limited capacity in the face of economy-wide crises bedevilling the country (see Moyo, Chambati and Siziba 2014). Smallholder farmers have had to rely on their own ingenuity to fund agricultural activities. In terms of linkages with the local economy, the next section will reveal in detail how the input sector has developed in the FTLRP.

10.3 Commodity Markets

10.3.1 Farming inputs (seed, fertilisers and chemicals)

The input markets illustrated workings of the political economy of Hwedza District. The study reveals in Table 10-4 that 65.8% of the agricultural chemicals applied during the period from 2011-2015 were secured from local agro-dealers within the vicinity of the different sites studied in Hwedza District.

Table 10-4: Common Source of Chemicals, 2011-2015

Model		Common source of input					Total
		n/a	purchased from local agro-dealer	purchased from CA agro-dealer	nearest urban area	contractor	
A1	No	0	3	1	0	0	4
	%	0.00%	75.00%	25.00%	0.00%	0.00%	100.00%
SSCF	No	1	6	0	7	1	15
	%	6.70%	40.00%	0.00%	46.70%	6.70%	100.00%
A2	No	0	3	1	2	0	6
	%	0.00%	50.00%	16.70%	33.30%	0.00%	100.00%
ORA	No	0	12	0	0	0	12
	%	0.00%	100.00%	0.00%	0.00%	0.00%	100.00%
CA	No	0	1	0	0	0	1
	%	0.00%	100.00%	0.00%	0.00%	0.00%	100.00%
Total	No	1	25	2	9	1	38
	%	2.60%	65.80%	5.30%	23.70%	2.60%	100.00%

Source: Author, compiled from own survey data, 2016

However, the reliance on local agro-dealers was differentiated per settlement model. For instance, whereas the ORA and the CA sectors bought all the chemicals from the local agro-dealers, while 40% of the SSCF households, 50% of the A2 households and 75% of the A1 farmers depended on the agro-dealers for the purchase of chemicals. The balance of 25% of the A1 farmers secure agro-chemicals from local agro-dealers with Hwedza district compared 16.7% of the A2 households. The SSCF and the A2 sectors also relied on the nearest urban area, Marondera for the purchase of chemicals for crop and livestock production, while 6.7% of the SSCF also depended on contracting companies for agro-chemicals. However, a different pattern is observable for tobacco growers, as they secure 81.5% of the chemicals from local agro-dealers, with 88.5% of the A1 farmers relying on this source, compared to 77.8% for the SSCF farmers and 85.7% ORA farmers. With regards to tobacco, more farmers rely on contract farming, with 11.5% of the A1 households relying on this source compared to 7.4% in the SSCF sector and 4.8% in the ORA sector. Table 10-5 shows that tobacco farmers also secure chemicals from Marondera and Harare at 40% and 20% respectively. There are households from the SSCF sector who rely on Marondera and Harare, but the level of reliance is lower at both 7.4%.

Table 10-5: Income Sources for the Tobacco Agro-Chemicals, 2015

Model		Tobacco source of chemicals					Total
		not applicable	local agro-dealer/retailer	nearest town	Harare agro-dealer	contract scheme	
A1	No	0	23	0	0	3	26
	%	0.0%	88.5%	0.0%	0.0%	11.5%	100.0%
SSCF	No	0	21	2	2	2	27
	%	0.0%	77.8%	7.4%	7.4%	7.4%	100.0%
A2	No	0	2	2	1	0	5
	%	0.0%	40.0%	40.0%	20.0%	0.0%	100.0%
ORA	No	2	18	0	0	1	21
	%	9.5%	85.7%	0.0%	0.0%	4.8%	100.0%
CA	No	0	2	0	0	0	2
	%	0.0%	100.0%	0.0%	0.0%	0.0%	100.0%
Total	No	2	66	4	3	6	81
	%	2.5%	81.5%	4.9%	3.7%	7.4%	100.0%

Source: Author, compiled from own survey data, 2016

A disaggregation of the data for maize seed (Table 10.6) shows that 82.4% and 84.6% of A1 and SSCF sectors respectively, compared to 76.3% of households in the ORA sector, 71.4% of the households in the A2 and 57.1% of households in the CA sector rely on local agro-dealers/retailers for supply. Some households in the SSCF, A2 and CA sectors buy their inputs from Harare and in some cases from Marondera town.

Table 10-6: Sources of Seed Maize for 2015

Model	T	not applicable	Sources of maize seed local agro-dealer/retailer	govt inputs scheme	nearest town	Harare agro-dealer	given by relative/friend	own source	other	Total
A1	No	0	28	5	0	0	0	1	0	34
	%	0.0%	82.4%	14.7%	0.0%	0.0%	0.0%	2.9%	0.0%	100.0%
SSCF	No	0	44	2	5	1	0	0	0	52
	%	0.0%	84.6%	3.8%	9.6%	1.9%	0.0%	0.0%	0.0%	100.0%
A2	No	0	20	1	4	3	0	0	0	28
	%	0.0%	71.4%	3.6%	14.3%	10.7%	0.0%	0.0%	0.0%	100.0%
ORA	No	1	29	3	0	0	1	1	4	38
	%	2.6%	76.3%	7.9%	0.0%	0.0%	2.6%	2.6%	8.5%	100.0%
CA	No	0	24	10	0	1	0	6	0	42
	%	0.0%	57.1%	23.8%	0.0%	2.4%	0.0%	14.3%	0.0%	100.0%
Total	No	1	145	21	9	5	1	8	4	194
	%	0.5%	74.7%	10.8%	4.6%	2.6%	0.5%	4.1%	2.0%	100.0%

Source: Author, compiled from own survey data, 2016

This evidence contradicts the view presented by agro-dealers who felt that the tobacco farmers generally buy their inputs from Harare after selling tobacco at the auction and contract merchants floors.

Agro-inputs demand is generally low in Hwedza. Farmers tend to take advantage of hired vehicles for tobacco deliveries to the auction floors and buy and transport their farming inputs from Harare. As a result, our connections with the tobacco farmers are very limited since they also buy their groceries from Harare upon selling their tobacco crop at the auction floors there. It is only the balances of their farming requirements that they end up buyig from our shops, during the course of the farming season. (Agritex Officer, Interview).

Certified seed maize presents a different picture with 74,7% securig seed from the local markets compared to 4.6% who bought from Marondera, and 10.7% who bought from Harare as shown in Table 10-6. In part, purchases of seed maize from Harare confirm that some farmers are funded thorough diaspora and local remittances in which case the farmers end up buying from urban areas. The purchase of farm machinery and livestock feed is mainly carried out from Harare where supply is readily available. However, small farming hand tools and farming equipment such as hoes and animal drawn ploughs are secured from Hwedza Growth Point.

10.3.2 Labour supply
While Figure 10-11 highlights that households in the A2, ORA and CA sectors gain significant revenue from hiring out wage labour in agricultural activities and being hired by households across the five settlement sectors under study, further analysis shows that the source of workers employed was differentiated, as shown in Figure 10-11.

Figure 10-11: Number of Workers from Specified Areas by Settlement Type, 2015

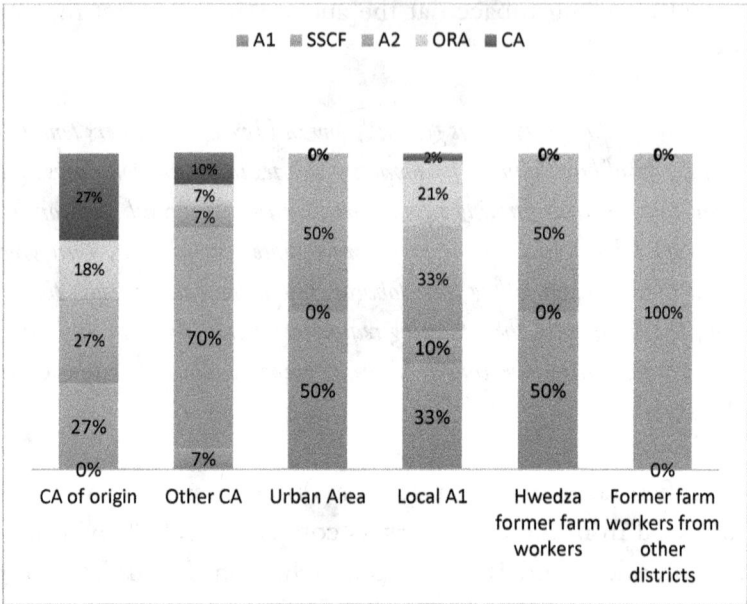

■ A1 ▨ SSCF ■ A2 ▨ ORA ■ CA

Source: Author, compiled from own survey data, 2016

Some CA households employed from CA, ORA and A1 households within Hwedza District, and CA houeholds in other districts. The A2 farmers employed three workers from CA households in Hwedza District, two from CA in other districts, one from an urban area, I former farm workers and another former farm worker from another district. Among other areas, the SSCF households employed 21 from CA in other districts (Buhera and Chikomba mainly). Former farms workers are employed in the A2 and A1 sectors while all the sector employ workers from CA households in other districts. Wage workers therefore provide an important source of income for the farming households and source of economic link between and among farming sectors in Hwedza district. All former farm workers employed in Hwedza are employed by A2 farmers.

10.3.3 The outputs markets

The agricultural commodity outputs markets play an important role in the overall performance of the agrarian economy and contributes to re-investment in agricultural production and capital formation in Zimbabwe's rural economy. The study established that there are five commodities that households in Hwedza rely on for income; namely maize, tobacco, groundnuts, tomatoes and livestock. Tobacco has emerged as the most marketed crop in both quantity produced and revenue earned between 2013 and 2015 as shown in Figure 10-12. The study revealed that, the increase in revenue experienced from 2013 to 2014 from US$202,382 to US$267,067 for the studied households was reversed to US$197,187 in 2015. A similar trends was observed in groundnuts sales where an increase in total sales from US$4,495 to US$4,601 fell to US$2,740 over the same period.

Figure 10-12: Key Commodities Marketed, 2013-15

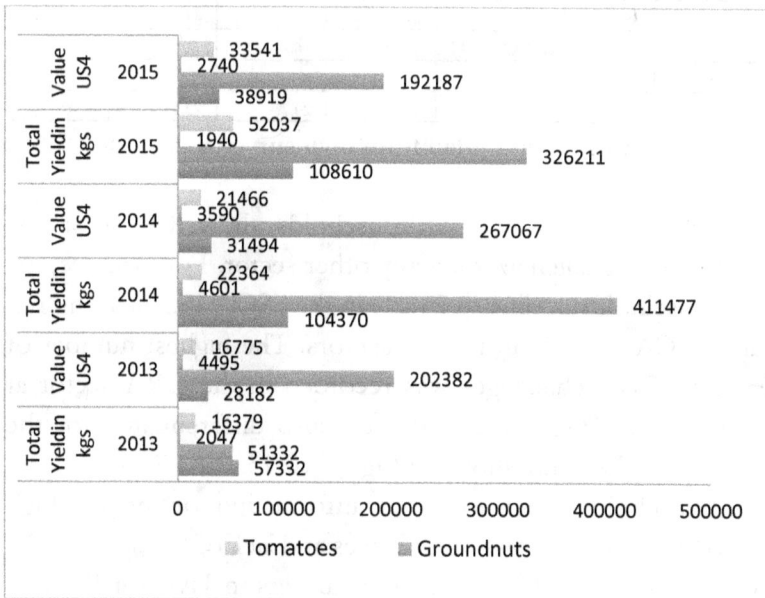

The study shows that the total sales in maize increased from US$28,182 in 2013 to US$31,494 in 2014 and US$38,919 for the studied households, in 2015. Total tomatoes sales for the studied households also firmed from US$16,775 to US$21,466 and US$33,541 in 2013, 2014 and 2015 respectively.

10.3.4 Marketing constraints

Repondents in the five settlement sectors indicated that they faced challenges in the marketing of commodities, but these were differentiated per commodity and sector as shown in Table 10-7. In total, 15% of the farmers confirmed having faced challenges in the last three seasons (2013-2015), while 83.33% indicated that they did not face any challenges.

Table 10-7: Constraints in Marketing Crops by Settlement Model, 2013-2015

Response		Constraints in marketing crops					Total
		A1	SSCF	A2	ORA	CA	
n/a	No	1	0	2	1	0	4
	%	25.0%	0.0%	50.0%	25.0%	0.0%	1.80%
Yes	No	1	8	6	15	3	33
	%	3.0%	24.2%	18.2%	45.5%	9.1%	15%
No	No	39	45	24	30	47	185
	%	21.1%	24.3%	13.0%	16.2%	25.4%	83.33%
Total	No	41	53	32	46	50	222
	%	18.5%	23.9%	14.4%	20.7%	22.5%	100.0%

Source: Author, compiled from own survey data, 2016

At 45.5% of the interviewed households, the ORA sector was affected by more challenges than any other sector. For instance, the affected houselholds decline to 24.2% in the SSCF, 18.2% in the A2, 9.1% in the CA and 3% in the A1 sectors. The highest number of farmers who faced challenges was recorded in the ORA sector at 45.5%. The marketing constraints were also differentiated for the commodities as the study shows in Figure 10-13.

The households identified poor information on prices, high handing costs, limited buyers, poor prices and lack of transport as the main constraints faced by smallholder farmers in Hwedza District. All the settlement sectors complained of poor prices and as a major constraining factor in commodity production, while all the other sectors except for the A1 also identified few/limited buyers as constraining. Partly, resulting from these challenges, 12.6% of the respondents are involved in barter trading, although differentially. Farmers across the settlement sectors therefore engaged in barter trading using free range chickens, maize, groundnuts, sorghums and millet for labour, groceries and clothes. The practise in more common among the SSCF (20.8%), A2 (15.6%), ORA (15.2%) and far less in the CA (7.7%).

Figure 10-13: Commodity Marketing Constraints by Settlement Types, 2013-2015

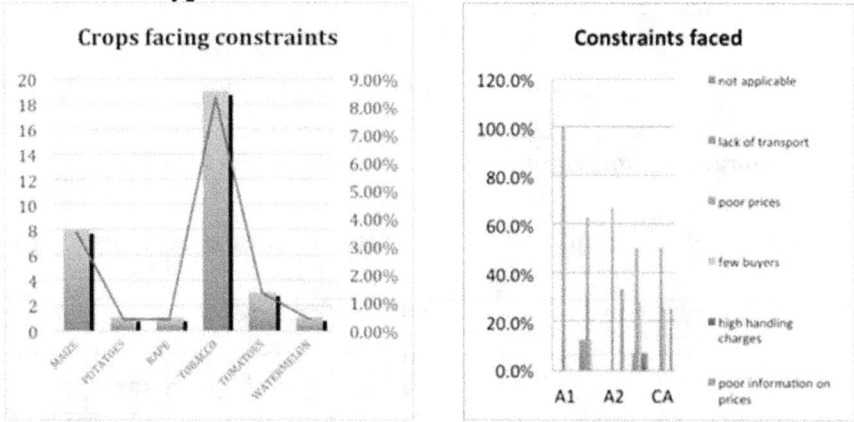

Source: Author, compiled from own survey data, 2016

10.4 Marketing Information

Availability and use of commodity pricing and marketing information is critical in revealing commodity markets trends on a sectoral and commodity basis. Respondents in this study revealed different ways of accessing and using information. Farming households in Hwedza District faced challenges in accessing information on prices. Overall, as Table 10-8 shows, 35.58% of the farmers across the settlement sectors confirmed that they receive marketing information on commodities. For instance, 39.2% of the farmers in the ORA indicated that they receive the information compared to 24.3% in the SSCF, 18.9% in the A2 sectors. Less than 10% of other farming sectors (A1 and CA) receive marketing information on commodity prices.

Table 10-8: Access to Commodty Prices Information by Settlement Models, 2013-2015

		Receiving marketing information					Total
		A1	SSCF	A2	ORA	CA	
yes	No	7	18	14	29	6	74
	%	9.5%	24.3%	18.9%	39.2%	8.1%	35.58%
No	No	31	34	11	17	32	125
	%	24.8%	27.2%	8.8%	13.6%	25.6%	60.10%
Total	No	38	53	25	46	38	208

Source: Author, compiled from own survey data, 2016

Table 10-9: Commodity Demand Information Sources, 2013-2015

Sources of information		Sources of information					Total
		A1	SSCF	A2	ORA	CA	
other farmers	No	1	1	3	5	1	11
	%	9.1%	9.1%	27.3%	45.5%	9.1%	100.0%
family and friends	No	0	0	1	2	3	6
	%	0.0%	0.0%	16.7%	33.3%	50.0%	100.0%
Radio/TV	No	0	4	0	0	1	5
	%	0.0%	80.0%	0.0%	0.0%	20.0%	100.0%
market place posters/posted bulletin	No	0	0	0	0	1	1
	%	0.0%	0.0%	0.0%	0.0%	100.0%	100.0%
Agricultural traders	No	0	0	0	1	0	1
	%	0.0%	0.0%	0.0%	100.0%	0.0%	100.0%
SMS messages	No	1	10	2	0	0	13
	%	7.7%	76.9%	15.4%	0.0%	0.0%	100.0%
Newspapers	No	0	0	2	0	0	2
	%	0.0%	0.0%	100.0%	0.0%	0.0%	100.0%
extension officers	No	0	0	2	0	0	2
	%	0.0%	0.0%	100.0%	0.0%	0.0%	100.0%
Other	No	0	0	2	3	0	5
	%	0.0%	0.0%	40.0%	60.0%	0.0%	100.0%
Total	No	5	17	19	16	7	64

Source: Author, compiled from own survey data, 2016

The most common sources of information are Radio/TV and SMS messages for the SSCF sector as 80% and 76.9% of the farmers relied on this source, as Table 10-9 shows. Reliance on family farmers and friends for information on commodity prices was limited to A2 farmers, ORA and the CA sectors, while reliance on other farmers was common in all the settlement sectors. The study revealed that only the A2 farmers got marketing information from newspapers and government extension officers. In terms of marketing information utilisation, farmers across the settlement models used the information to resolve varied marketing challenges.

Figure 10-14 shows that farmers in A1 sector used the information to make farming decisions on finputs purchases, with 31.6% of the interviewed households applying the information for the purpose. At the same time, farmers in the SSCF sector use the information mostly for stocking and investment decisions, contributing 50% of the households.

Figure 10-14: Pricing Information Affecting Decisions by Settlement Types, 2015

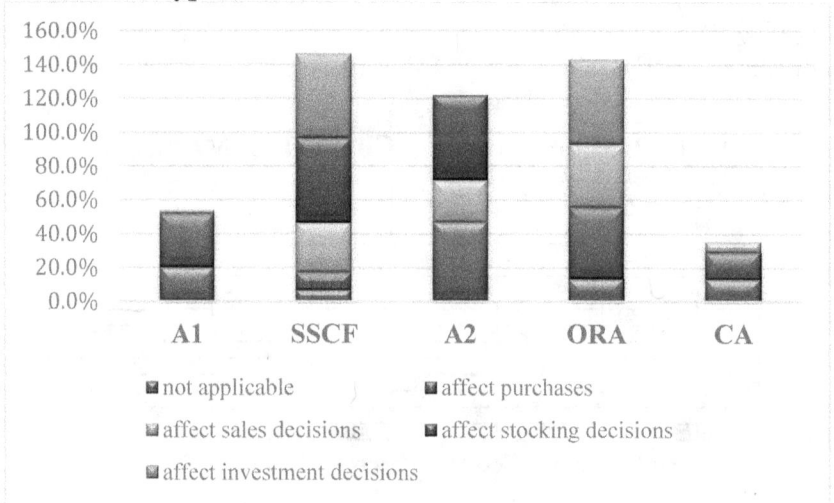

Source: Author, compiled from own survey data, 2016

The A2 farmers apply pricing information for sales decisions (25%) and stocking decisions (50%) while in the ORA sector, the information was used for investment decisions (10%), sales decisions (9%) and purchasing (23%) decisions. The CA sector contribute only 9.3% and the A1 sector 11.6% of the households who rely on pricing and marketmg information, demonstrating how the households' incorpration into commodity circuits remains limited. All in all, the SSCF sector contribute more households (33.7%) who rely on pricing information. The other sectors where farmers rely on the information are the A2 (23.3%) and the ORA (22.1) sectors. The study therefore reveals that there is a connection between the level of access to marketing information and level of participation in local, national and global markets by the farming households. In this regard, the study observed that the A1 and CA sectors are less incorporated into the commodity markets both in terms of reciepts of proceeds from sales and access to information.

10.4.1 Food crops

Among other food crops (roundnuts, small grains – millet, sorghum and rapoko), maize is a key crop as it provides staple food for Zimbabweans. Most farmers (33.4%) sold their maize produce through the state marketing board (GMB) and local/village market (27.6%), while the balance was sold through the on-farm middlemen (13.8%) and the nearest urban area market (13.8%) and on farm consumers (6.9%), as shown in Table 10.10.

Table 10-10: Main Marketing Channel for Maize 2015

Model		Total not applicable	Maize marketing channels					Total
			local/village market	on farm to middlemen	nearest urban area market	on farm to consumers	state marketing board	
A1	No	1	1	1	1	1	1	6
	%	16.7%	16.7%	16.7%	16.7%	16.7%	16.7%	100.0%
SSCF	No	0	3	0	0	1	0	4
	%	0.0%	75.0%	0.0%	0.0%	25.0%	0.0%	100.0%
A2	No	0	3	3	1	0	2	9
	%	0.0%	33.3%	33.3%	11.1%	0.0%	22.2%	100.0%
ORA	No	0	1	0	2	0	5	8
	%	0.0%	12.5%	0.0%	25.0%	0.0%	62.5%	100.0%
CA	No	0	0	0	0	0	2	2
	%	0.0%	0.0%	0.0%	0.0%	0.0%	100.0%	100.0%
Total	No	1	8	4	4	2	10	29
	%	3.4%	27.6%	13.8%	13.8%	6.9%	33.4%	100.0%

Source: Author, compiled from own survey data, 2016

The choice for the marketing channels was selected mainly because farmers had no alternatives (32.1%), ease accessibility to the market (21.4%) and better price offers (21.4%), as Table 10-11 shows.

A few other farmers chose the markets because of statutory requirements (7.1%) and proximity to the market (10.7%). Reliance on the GMB despite the liberalised marketing environment is consequent of low industrial capacity utilisation after the GNU period. Maize markets are hugely localised and state driven with as little as 10.7% being sold through the nearest town of Marondera located 40km away from Hwedza District.

Table 10-11: Reasons for Choosing the Marketing Channel by Settlement Type, 2015

		Reason for choosing marketing channel for maize						Total
		Not applicable	Statutory requirement	Offer higher prices	Proximity to market	Accessibility to market	No alternative	
A1	No	2	0	2	1	1	0	6
	%	33.3%	0.0%	33.3%	16.7%	16.7%	0.0%	100.0%
SSCF	No	0	0	0	2	1	1	4
	%	0.0%	0.0%	0.0%	50.0%	25.0%	25.0%	100.0%
A2	No	0	1	1	0	2	5	9
	%	0.0%	11.1%	11.1%	0.0%	22.2%	55.6%	100.0%
ORA	No	0	1	3	0	2	2	8
	%	0.0%	12.5%	37.5%	0.0%	25.0%	25.0%	100.0%
CA	No	0	0	0	0	0	1	1
	%	0.0%	0.0%	0.0%	0.0%	0.0%	100.0%	100.0%
Total	No	2		6	3	6	9	28
	%	%	7.1%	21.4%	10.7%	21.4%	32.1%	100.0%

Source: Author, compiled from own survey data, 2016

10.4.2 Cash crops

The main cash crops produced in Hwedza are groundnuts, sweet potatoes, tomatoes and soya beans. To illustrate the marketing channels for cash crops, the study uses groundnuts and tomatoes (field and horticultural) crops respectively. The marketing of groundnuts by SSCF and A2 farmers was solely through the local/village markets while the ORA sold through the GMB, demonstrating the level to which the markets remain de-linked from the formal and urban markets, serve through the state, whose purcahses constitute only 20% of total sales. The decisons for choosing the markets are not price driven, nor are they viability related, farmers chose the markets after considering proximity and accessibilty to the markets and due to limited options for the farmers. On the contrary, most tomato farmers through the nearest urban area, including Harare- Mbare *Musika*, Chitungwiza – Chikwana markets, Marondera town and Murambinda Growth Point. As Chipo, a vendor at Chimbwa turnoff, in Zviyambe, Hwedza, confirmed:

> *The biggest challenge that we face in our work is to do with getting adequate constant sources of produce to sell. Most of the farmers from across Hwedza sell their produce in Harare and Chitungwiza. In turn we also have to go to Harare and Chitungwiza to buy the same products in bulk for resell to travellers and local consumers here in Hwedza* (Interview).

On-farm sales, destined to Mbare and Chitungwiza markets, stood at 14.3% of the marketed crop, (see Figures 10-15). Tomatoes emerge as a crop whose market is a highly consolidated verticaly and horizontally, across the settlement sectors. The crop is sold through differential markets: on-farm consumers, nearest urban area – Marondera, on-farm middle-men and local/village sales. Farmers also indicate that the choice of the commodity market is driven by accessibility to the market and proximity to the market and higher prices.

Figure 10-15: Tomatoes Markets and Reason for Choosing the Markets by Settlement Types, 2015

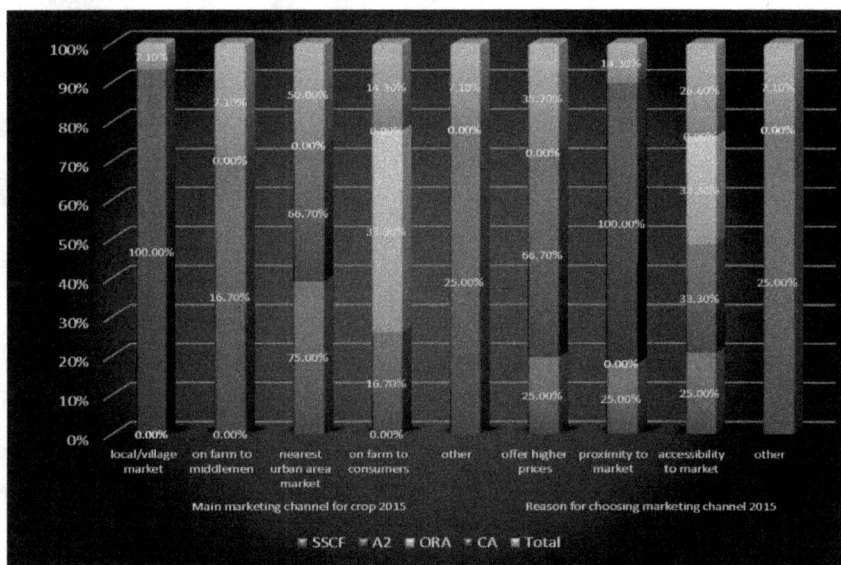

Source: Author, compiled from own survey data, 2016

However, the choices are differentiated in terms of settlement patterns, CA farmers preferring local/village market and citing proximity to the market as the driving factor. The A2 farmers sell 16.7% of their produce through some middle-men who deliver mainly to Mbare in Harare and Chikwanha in Chitungwiza markets, while 66.75% of their produce is delivered to Marondera, Hwedza growth point and Murambinda growth point in Buhera. The A2 farmer cite higher prices (66.7%) and accessibility to the markets

(33.3%) as the driving factors for their choices. On-farm sales constitute 16.7% of the produce. The SSCF farmers deliver 75% of their tomato produce to Marondera, Hwedza and Murambinda growth points, citing the offer of higher prices, proximity to the market and accessibility as the driving factors (25% each). Farmers from the ORA (33.3%) market tomatoes through on-farm sales to consumers and cite accessibility to the markets as the main driving factor. All in all, none of the interviewed A1 farmers produced tomatoes in the 2013/14 farming season, while 50% of the producers deliver tomatoes to the nearest urban area citing offer of better prices (35.7%), accessibility to the market (28.6%) and proximity to the markets (14.3%). The marketing patterns show that A2 farmers are more commercialised and integrated into the commodity markets at national level, while communal farmers are only linked to the local markets.10.4.3 Export crops.

Tobacco is the main export crop grown in Hwedza District across the settlement models. The crop became more common in the post FTLRP phase following the liberalisation of the economy and changed marketing structure since 2008. Farmers were, from 2008 allowed to retain their proceeds in United States dollars. The marketing channels for tobacco have been driven by limited options available to the farmers as Table 10-12 shows.

Table 10-12: Reason for Choosing Marketing Channels for Tobacco by Settlement Type, 2013-2015

Model		Reason for choosing marketing channel							Total
		Not applicable	Statutory requirement	Offer higher prices	Proximity to market	Accessibility to market	No alternative	Contract agreement	
A1	No	2	2	2	0	1	4	4	15
	%	13.3%	13.3%	13.3%	0.0%	6.7%	26.7%	26.7%	100.0%
SSCF	No	0	6	4	0	0	15	2	27
	%	0.0%	22.2%	14.8%	0.0%	0.0%	55.6%	7.4%	100.0%
A2	No	2	2	0	0	1	3	0	8
	%	25.0%	25.0%	0.0%	0.0%	12.5%	37.5%	0.0%	100.0%
ORA	No	3	8	0	1	0	8	3	23
	%	13.0%	34.8%	0.0%	4.3%	0.0%	34.8%	13.0%	100.0%
CA	No	0	0	0	1	0	0	0	1
	%	0.0%	0.0%	0.0%	100.0%	0.0%	0.0%	0.0%	100.0%
Total	No	7	18	6	2	2	30	9	74
	%	9.5%	24.3%	8.1%	2.7%	2.7%	40.5%	12.2%	100.0%

Source: Author, compiled from own survey data, 2016

For instance, the study reveals that 40.5% of the respondents had no alternative marketing options while 24.3% chose the marketing channel in compliance with the statutory requirements. Some 11.2% of the farmers also relied on the signed agreements which were based production management contract farming arrangements while 8.1% preferred the chosen markets in response to better prices offered. In all, there were 22 companies involved in contract farming in 2016, as Figure 10-16 shows. With regards to purchases, Nothern Tobacco had the highest purchases on contract farming, followed by Tian Ze, MTC, ZLT, Chidziva and Tribac. The ZLT leads in auction floor purchases, followed by Tian Ze, Internatioonal Leaf Tobacco (ILT) Boost Africa and MTC. At a national level, ontract farming has increeased from 16 million kgsfarmers in 2004 to 165 million kgs in 2014. Whereas this study reveals that contract farming contribues 33.5% towards tobacco farming in Hwedza District, other studies such as the AIAS Survey of 2014 observed that the contract farming also financed sugarcane (86%), and cotton (45.1%), contributing significantly to crop productivity, food security and accumulation processes among rural households.

Figure 10-16: Tobacco contract and auction floors, 2016

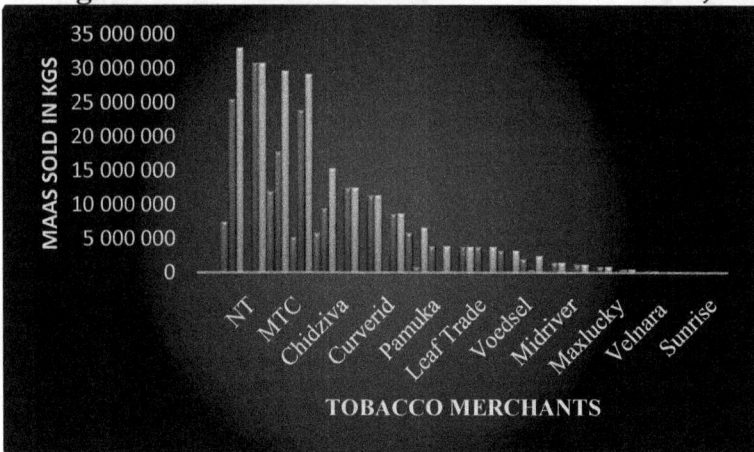

Source: TIMB, 2016

Secondary data collected from the Tobacco Industry Marketing Board (TIMB, 2016) show that 61.7 million kgs of tobacco representing is exported to China, constituting 52% of total sales (see

Figure 10-17) and earning US$512.95 million for 2015. Africa and the European Union took 17% of tobacco exports each, in 2015. South Africa imported 8.9% of total exports in 2015. Tobacco sales have increased its contributed to both exports and the national gross domestic propduct (GDP) from USD300.75 million, being 18% of total exports in 2009 to USD853.97 million being 24% of total exports in 2015. During the same period, tobacco sales contribution to the nominal GDP increased from 2.1% in 2009 to 4.8% in 2014 before slowing down to 4.1% in 2015.

Figure 10-17: Tobacco Export Destinations for 2014 and 2015

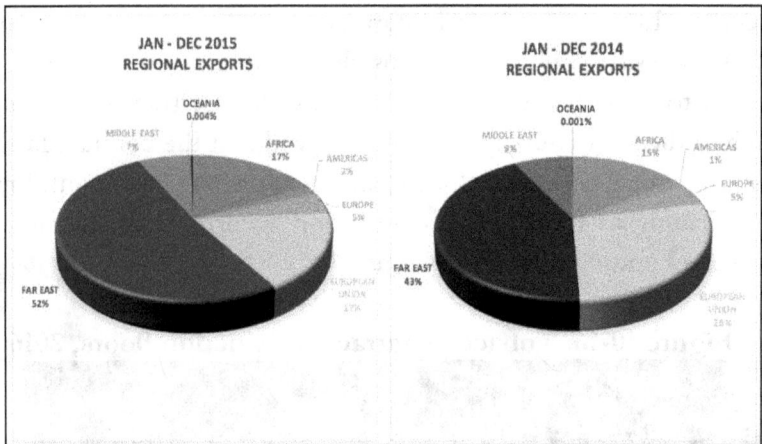

Source: TIMB, 2016

The tobacco merchants involved in contract farming offer differentiated options under the management contract arrangements. In the case of Hwedza District, data from the surveyed households show that 11.8% of the household farmers engaged in contract farming were supplied with fertilizers, 64.3% received seed, fertilizers, chemicals, technical advice and transport support to the market, while 21.6% were receiving other support other than those cited above. In terms of value of support, contracted farmers received varied levels, with 29% receiving up to US$100.00, 7% receiving US$200.00, 36% receiving US$1, 100.00 and 7% receiving US$1, 700.00 in 2015 as shown in Table 10-13.

Table 10-13: Tobacco Contribution to exports and GDP, 2009-2015

US$M	2009	2010	2011	2012	2013	2014	2015
Total Exports	1644.93	3289.83	4576.01	4003.97	3861.78	3717.18	3614.21
Tobacco Exports	300.75	384.24	731.04	773.04	877.34	772.61	854.97
Contribution	18%	12%	16%	19%	23%	21%	24%
US$M							
Nominal GDP	8157.077	9456.808	10956.23	12472.42	13490.23	14196.91	14395.19
Sales	174.46	355.57	361.45	527.81	612.13	685.244	586.44
Contribution	2.1%	3.8%	3.3%	4.2%	4.5%	4.8%	4.1%

Source: TIMB, 2016

The tobacco commodity circuits are extensive and connect local, national and global inputs and outputs markets. At a local level, the purchase of inputs through local trade stores and the nearest towns as well as the links provided by labour employment patterns across the settlement sectors link across CA, resettled and urban areas. The tobacco merchants and exporting companies provide global linkages through both global finance through contract farming and through markets for semi-processed tobacco, as Figure 10-18 shows. It shows that tobacco growers from across the settlement models are linked to international capital though contracting companies and banks, to seed processing companies and fertiliser and chemical manufacturing companies as part of the input markets for the crop.

The study revealed that most farmers buy their input from local trading shops which tends to benefit the local economy in employment creation, transport cost reduction, among others. In the output markets, farmers are linked to local auction floors and contracting companies for the sale of their crop. The crop is subsequently processed and exported as semi-processed or used tom produce cigarettes in the country. However, tobacco growers are disconnected from international markets as tobacco merchants are involved in the export of the crop and farmers remain confined to primary production.

Figure 10-18: Tobacco Local, National and Global Commodity Circuits, 2016

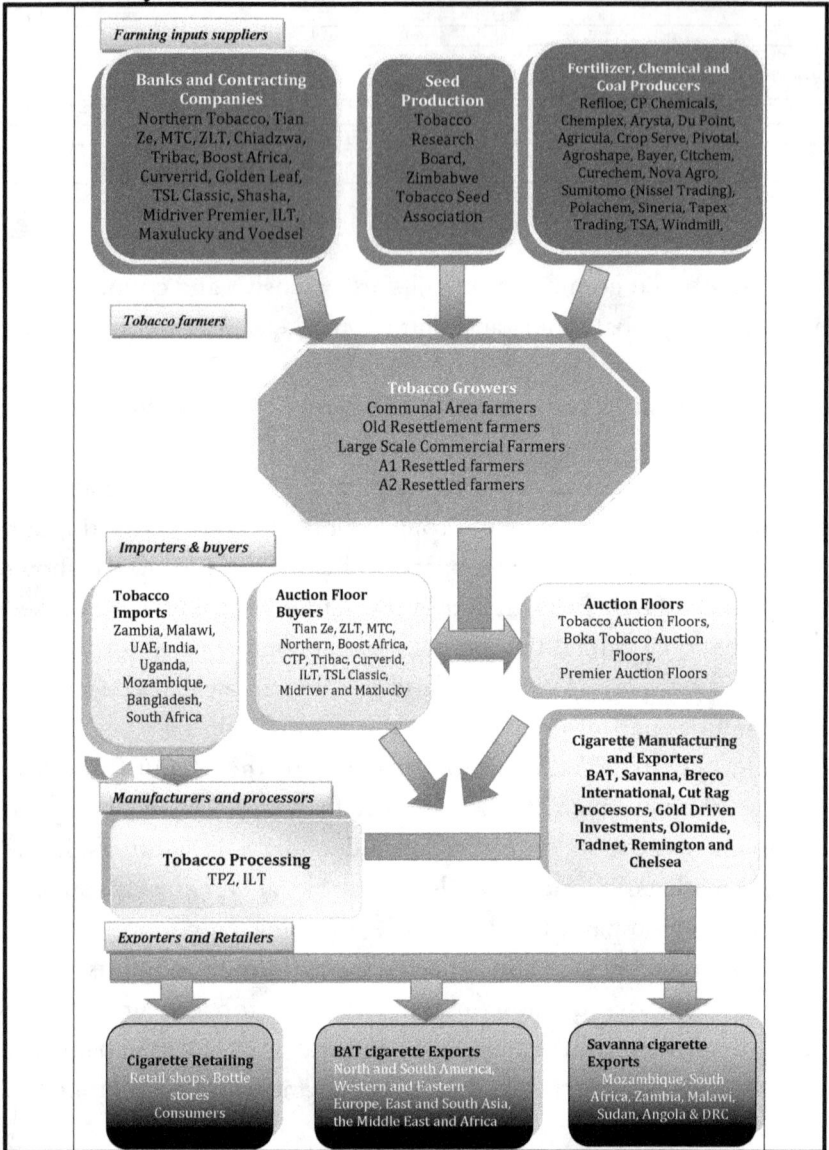

Source: Author, 2016

10.4.4 Livestock markets

Livestock production is an important source of income for the SSCF and the A2 sectors in Hwedza District. The main animals reared for marketing purposes are pigs and cattle. Cattle are mostly bought through the local buyers for onward sell to local buyers and to arbattors in Marondera and Harare as was noted by one household member in Zviyambe;

> We have local buyers to whom we sell our cattle whenever we need to raise funds for our children's school fees, farming inputs and any other household needs. The buyers either resell to local butcheries, schools and to urban abattoirs. (Masimba, Interview).

Households who rear pigs and cattle for sale use proceeds for crop inputs and social reproduction purposes. Livestock is also a key in eco-tourism at Imire Estates in Hwedza. The estate is connected to global finance through tourism, tobacco and flower exports.

10.5 Associational Groups

Marketing opportunities are generaaly affected by the low availability of farmers groups in Hwedza District. The study shows that there are a few households (4.1%) that participated in farming groups, illustrating the low farmers collective efforts towards resolving challenges associated with securing of farming inputs and outputs markets for agricutural produce across the setllement sectors, as Table 10-14 shows.

Table 10-14: Farmer Groups in Hwedza District by Settlement Types, 2015

		Farmer groups in Hwedza district					Total
		A1	SSCF	A2	ORA	CA	
Not applicable	No	2	3	2	0	0	7
	%	28.6%	42.9%	28.6%	0.0%	0.0%	100.0%
Yes	No	0	2	3	2	2	9
	%	0.0%	22.2%	33.3%	22.2%	22.2%	100.0%
No	No	39	48	27	44	47	205
	%	19.0%	23.4%	13.2%	21.5%	22.9%	100.0%
Total	No	41	53	32	46	49	221
	%	18.6%	24.0%	14.5%	20.8%	22.2%	100.0%

Source: Author, compiled from own survey data, 2016

In all, there are more households participating in associational groups in the A2 sector (33.3%) compared to other groups. The low associational group's participation by households across the settlement sector impact negatively on the development of economic linkages across sectors, and urban centres.

10.6 Conclusion

This chapter identified the various financial and commercial circuits of capital access by peasants in Hwedza District and how these are linked to the inputs and outputs markets through funding, input purchases, remittances and contract farming surpluses, locally, nationally and globally. Some crops are more national integrated (tomatoes) than others (groundnuts and maize), while others are more nationally and globally connected (tobacco). Households' re-investments in agriculture has emerged as a major funding option for farmers in all sectors other than the CA sector. The next chapter gives an overview of capital accumulation in Hwedza, with particular focus on the domestic and international capital involved in the tobacco contract farming system, in marketing of local produce and, to some extent, in game farming.

Chapter Eleven

Hwedza's Agrarian Capital Accumulation Model

11.1 Introduction

This chapter develops the capital accumulation model emerging in Hwedza District with particular focus on the role of domestic and international capital involved in the tobacco contract farming system, in marketing of local produce and to some extent in game farming. The chapter revisits agrarian change and peasant classification formulation in rural Zimbabwe. It also develops a model/framework of Zimbabwe's agricultural productivity, capital accumulation and class formation as a consequent of emerging farming practices in post FTLRP Zimbabwe, based on presented empirical data. To reveal the emerging classes in rural Zimbabwe, the chapter applies the developed model in Hwedza to identify and characterise rural peasants in Hwedza District. A conclusion is then reached on the nature of agrarian development path emerging in the District.

11.2 Revisiting the Peasantry Classification Model

Revisting the capital accumulation model emerging in Zimbabwe's transforming rural agrarian sector is central to understanding the changing nature of Zimbabwe's rural agrarian economy post the FTLRP. The agrarian economy is swayed by domestic and global production and distribution subtleties that are subject to broad political, economic and social under-currencies centred on geo-political, national and global macro-economic policy frameworks and emerging agrarian path of Zimbabwe's country-side. To the extent that capital, besides established and in some cases contested assertions of politicisation of production and distribution patterns through patronage and politics (Zamchiya 2012; Alexzander 2006), has remained central to the accumulation and classification in rural Zimbabwe, a revisit of the literature on the world systems analysis and the analytic framework of agrarian capitalist transition is

269

opportune. The objective is to review what literature on capital's movement from capitalist to pre-capitalist societies reveal on, and how this is shaping production and distribution patterns in, Zimbabwe's rural economy.

Critique on Marx's deterministic formulation regarding the transition to capitalism in agriculture by Kautsky (1988) and Lenin (1964) has shaped our understanding of the agrarian question in Southern Africa today. In the main, these theorists observed that primitive accumulation did not render petty commodity production obsolete;, instead it co-exists alongside large capitalist farming serving the interests of capital by subsidizing social reproduction of labour through peasant plots 'production sites for new labour-power under persistent semi-proletarianisation (Moyo and Yeros 2005, 19). Some underdevelopment theorists have since advanced the argument that such semi-proletarianisation promotes labour super-exploitation and has the effect of sustaining disarticulated economies in the periphery and configuring economies in the developing countries to resolve crises in the centre (de Janvry 1981) as capital to non-capitalist zones in search of cheap labour and cheap raw materials.

Emperical evidence collected under this study show that petty commodity production co-exists alongside largescale agricultural production financed by domestic and international capital under contract farming. The evidence also shows the existence of semi-proletarianisation where peasants support capital exigencies by way of providing for the social reproduction of underpaid labour in the formal sector. The high dependency by respondents on personal savings outside agriculture, remittances from the diaspora and local remmitances demonstrates investments of earning from outside the rural agricutural economy in peasant production. Agricultural investments based on varied sources of finance, including contract farming, proceeds from agricultural finance, government support, diaspora and local remittances and bank credit loans have combined in ways that created differentiated growth trajectories for rural peasants in Hwedza District. Patnaik (1968) therefore suggests that ascertaining the class status of peasant households is a crucial basis for establishing the economic characteristics of peasant farms.

11.3 Siginicance Testing

Initially, using maize output and relying on scales determined by the researcher, four clusters were formed as Table 11.2 shows. With regards to the average maize output cluster in Table 11-2, maize output was seen as an appropriate variable as a continuous indicator and as a staple food crop – maize.

Table 11-1: Average Maize Output - based Clusters

Maize Output Clusters Model type Cross tabulation								
Maize Output Clusters			Settlement Model type					Total
			A1	SSCF	A2	ORA	CA	
1	0	No	13	4	3	5	10	35
		%	37.1%	11.4%	8.6%	14.3%	28.6%	100.0%
2	0.1-1000	No	6	6	4	9	20	45
		%	13.3%	13.3%	8.9%	20.0%	44.4%	100.0%
3	1001-2500	No	10	5	2	16	17	50
		%	20.0%	10.0%	4.0%	32.0%	34.0%	100.0%
4	2500+	No	17	38	23	16	6	100
		%	17.0%	38.0%	23.0%	16.0%	6.0%	100.0%
Total		No	46	53	32	46	53	230
		%	20.0%	23.0%	13.9%	20.0%	23.0%	100.0%

Source: Author, compiled from own survey data, 2016

Overall, the 'average maize output' clusters categorised 35% producing zero output, 45% producing 0.1-1 000, 50% producing 1001-2500 and 100 households producing above 2 500kgs per annum. Using category reference 1 for the maize clusters (see Table 11-2), the significance testing carried out revealed that, of the twenty two factors ('average income', 'average total tobacco output', 'average total maize sold value', 'average labour hired out', 'average family labour involved', 'average cattle owned', 'average tobacco sold value', 'year settled', 'respondent's age', 'household size', 'arable lands', 'food security', 'gender' and 'contract farming involvement', 'access to electricity', 'access to credit', 'access to irrigation', 'gender', 'involvement in non-farm activities', 'access to property documentation') identified from the collected data (see Table 11-2) only five were relevant for classification of the households in Hwedza District, as the discussion below reveals. The likelihod ratio tests showed that 17 of these factors had high significance of zero as shown in Table 11-2.

Table 11-2: Second Average Maize Output Custer Likelihood Ratio Testing

Effect	Model Fitting Criteria			Likelihood Ratio Tests		
	AIC of Reduced Model	BIC of Reduced Model	-2 Log Likelihood of Reduced Model	Chi-Square	df	Sig.
Intercept	401.461	698.274	2.275E2[a]	.000	0	.
Respondent's age	564.436	851.015	3.964E2[b]	168.976	3	.000
House hold size 2015	560.403	846.981	3.924E2[b]	164.943	3	.000
Arable	447.212	733.790	2.792E2[c]	51.751	3	.000
Scotch carts owned 2014	539.274	825.852	3.713E2[c]	143.813	3	.000
Income average	557.998	844.576	3.900E2[b]	162.537	3	.000
Average family labour	558.128	844.707	3.901E2[b]	162.668	3	.000
Average Labour Hired Out	566.567	853.146	3.986E2[b]	171.107	3	.000
Average Male Permanent workers	557.703	844.281	3.897E2[b]	162.242	3	.000
Maize average value	567.881	854.459	3.999E2[b]	172.421	3	.000
Year settled	535.237	821.815	3.672E2[c]	139.776	3	.000
Number of months maize to last	504.766	791.345	3.368E2[c]	109.306	3	.000
Average Tobacco Output	527.032	813.610	3.590E2[c]	131.572	3	.000
Average Maize Output	527.853	814.431	3.599E2[c]	132.393	3	.000
Average Cattle Owned	417.652	704.230	2.497E2[c]	22.191	3	.000
Involvement in non-farm activities	191.178	477.757	23.178[c]	.	3	
Access to credit	208.905	495.483	40.905[c]	.	3	
Access to contract farming	557.153	843.731	3.892E2[b]	161.692	3	.000
Access to irrigation	168.451	455.029	.451[c]	.	3	.
Gender	138.115	373.519	.115[c]	.	18	
Availability of electricity	556.684	833.027	3.947E2[b]	167.224	6	.000
Availability of documentation	450.498	737.076	2.825E2[c]	55.038	3	.000

The chi-square statistic is the difference in -2 log-likelihoods between the final model and a reduced model. The reduced model is formed by omitting an effect from the final model. The null hypothesis is that all parameters of that effect are 0.

a. This reduced model is equivalent to the final model because omitting the effect does not increase the degrees of freedom.

b. The log-likelihood value cannot be further increased after maximum number of step-halving.

c. Unexpected singularities in the Hessian matrix are encountered. This indicates that either some predictor variables should be excluded or some categories should be merged.

Source: Author, compiled from own survey data, 2016

As Table 11-3 shows, the average cattle owned had a significance level of 0.020 for the period 2013-2015, was a significant 5% and positive coefficient (meaning that possession of cattle [draft power] increases the likelihood of a household being in cluster 2). The 'average family labour hired out' for the same period, was significant 10% and had a negative coefficient which implies that those households which high out labour less labour were likely to be in cluster 2, using category 1 as the reference point. Using the same variables and relying on the category 1 as reference, the mutlinomial regression analysis for the third maize cluster showed a significance relationship 0.055 (10%) for 'food security (the number of months that maize harvested will last)' and a positive coefficient (meaning that households with greater food security are likely to be placed in cluster of the maize based classes) zero for the average maize output and was significant 1% with a positive coefficinet (which increases the chances to place the households with higher maize output in cluster of the maize classes and 0.089 (10% significant) for average cattle owned.

Table 11-3: Variable Regression Significance Testing

Parameter Estimates									
Average maize cluster		B	Std. Error	Wald	Df	Sig.	Exp(B)	95% Confidence Interval for Exp(B)	
								Lower Bound	Upper Bound
2	Intercept	-2.591	24.121	.012	1	.914			
	Respondent's age	.009	.018	.270	1	.603	1.009	.974	1.045
	House hold size 2015	.138	.114	1.474	1	.225	1.148	.919	1.435
	Arable	-.060	.214	.080	1	.778	.941	.618	1.433
	Scotch carts owned 2014	-.255	.536	.226	1	.634	.775	.271	2.216
	Income average	.000	.000	2.044	1	.153	1.000	.999	1.000
	Average family labour involved in agriculture	-.232	.273	.723	1	.395	.793	.465	1.353
	Average family Labour Hired Out	-.607	.357	2.895	1	.089	.545	.271	1.097
	Average Male Permanent workers	-.631	.386	2.673	1	.102	.532	.250	1.134
	Maize average value	.489	.520	.886	1	.346	1.631	.589	4.515
	Year settled	.000	.000	.046	1	.831	1.000	.999	1.001
	Number of months maize to last	.064	.064	.992	1	.319	1.066	.940	1.208
	Average Tobacco Output	.000	.001	.315	1	.574	1.000	.998	1.001
	Average Maize Output	.000	.001	.472	1	.492	1.000	.999	1.002
	Average Cattle Owned	.162	.069	5.449	1	.020	1.176	1.026	1.347
	Average Dryland Tobacco Sold	-.142	.295	.232	1	.630	.868	.487	1.545
	Involvement in non-farm activities	.099	.525	.036	1	.850	1.104	.394	3.091
	Access to credit	-3.746	8.851	.179	1	.672	.024	6.908E-10	806640.642
	Access to contract farming	.479	1.056	.205	1	.650	1.614	.204	12.798
	Access to irrigation	2.891	4.461	.420	1	.517	18.009	.003	112968.480
	Gender	2.298	24.087	.009	1	.924	9.958	3.128E-20	3.170E21
	Availability of electricity	1.634	7.194	.052	1	.820	5.124	3.852E-6	6816780.745
	Availability of documentation	-.792	.631	1.577	1	.209	.453	.131	1.560

a. The reference category is: 1.00.
b. This parameter is set to zero because it is redundant.
c. Floating point overflow occurred while computing this statistic. Its value is therefore set to system missing.

Source: Author, compiled from own survey data, 2016

The use of category 4 shows avergage tobacco output and average maize out significance level of 0.013 and 0.018 respectively.The relationship between the first, second and third maize cluster showed that 'cattle ownership' was a common variable impacting on classification. Similarly, average 'maize output' was common in the relationship between cluster 1 and clusters 3 and 4. The Two-Step cluster analysis therefore relied on five variables namely average 'maize output', average 'tobacco output', average 'cattle holdings', 'number of months maize harvest will last' and 'family labour hired out'. However, the family labour hired out has a negative (0.607) co-efficient factor such that the factor is inversely reflected.

This is contrary to Moyo (2011c: 944) who suggests a reliance on 'differences on land size, forms of land tenure, social status of landholders and capacity to hire labour'. The reliance of farm size was rejected by Patnaik (1976) on the basis that it avoids factoring in other important aspects such as distribution of productive assets, method and purpose of production. In line with Lenin (1964) and Kautsky's (1987) postulations, Harron Akram-Lodhi (1993, 563) proposes a consideration of the 'cropped area', 'amount of rented land', 'number of animals', 'water availability', 'quality of soils', 'quality of seed' and 'fertilisers', 'degree of mechanisation' and 'availability and use labour'. These factors speak to the notion that resource endowment is a critical fact:r in differentiating production and accumulation patterns and as such class formation among the farmers.

Whereas the study relied on statistical regression analysis based on SPSS multinomial logistic processes, Patnaik's (1976) variables were largely observed as relevant, to the exclusion of amount of rented land, which is not a common practise in Zimbabwe. Crop output on maize and tobacco help capture the effect of 'cropped area', 'water availability', 'quality of soil', 'quality of seed' and 'fertilizers' and 'degree of mechanisation'. 'Cattle holdings', 'food security' and 'labour utilisation' are captured separately. The AIAS 2005/6Ssurvey Report also captured 'livestock holdings', 'food security' and 'access to capital' as important factors, among others. By emphasising food and cash crop output, this study also places importance on access to capital, as chapter 10 revealed. Overall, as the nominal regression analysis showed, zero significance which implies that the hypothesis should be rejected and that there is a relation among the factors being considered, as shown in Table 11-4.

Table 11-4: Model Fitting Likelihood Ratio Testing

Model Fitting Information						
	Model Fitting Criteria			Likelihood Ratio Tests		
Model	AIC	BIC	-2 Log Likelihood	Chi-Square	df	Sig.
Intercept Only	541.823	552.058	535.823			
Final	401.461	698.274	227.461	308.362	84	.000

Source: Author, compiled from own survey data, 2016

Access to irrigation was eliminated as a factor on its own as Table 11-3 shows. Whereas such factors as arable land available identified by Moyo (2011c) were seen as relevant for class formation, the regression analysis of the relations among categories identifed for maize failed to reach the same conclusion. As such, the factors identified for the Two-Step Cluster Analysis (namely, average 'maize output', average 'tobacco output', average 'cattle holdings', 'number of months maize harvest will last' and 'family labour hired out') are ideal for the process, singularly, as per Table 11-3, and collectively as shown in Table 11-4.

11.4 Quadi –PMMR-Cluster Model Agrarian Structure

As indicated in section 11.4, the Two-Step clustering technique uses both am auto-selection of the number of clusters, using the log likelihood which relies on chi-square with degrees of freedom and the Akaike's Information Criterion (AIC), on complete data. The clustering process established that there are four classes in Hwedza, based on collected data from five sites in the district. Based on SPSS auto-selection and clustering, the Two-Step Cluster Analysis placed the households in four classes using factors identified from the multinomial logistic regression analysis which was based on the average maize output clusters, set by the researcher, as Table 11-5 shows.

Table 11-5: Quadi-PMMR-Cluster Model Agrarian Structure

Cluster		N	%	A1	%	SSCF	%	A2	%	ORA	%	CA	
3	Poor peasants	73	31.70%	13	28.26%	10	18.87%	9	28.13%	15	33%	26	49%
1	Middle Peasants	119	51.70%	32	69.57%	32	60.38%	13	40.625%	20	43%	22	42%
4	Middle to rich peasants	34	14.80%	1	2%	8	15.09%	9	28.13%	11	24%	5	9%
2	Rich peasants	4	1.70%	0	0%	3	5.66%	1	3.13%	0	0%	0	0%
	Combined	230	100%	46	100%	53	100%	32	100%	46	100%	53	100%

Source: Author, compiled from own survey data, 2016

The study identifies the emerging model as the Quadi-PMMR Cluster Model for Agrarian Change. Quadi refers to the four classes identified while PMMR denotes the poor, middle, middle-to-rich and rich small scale farmers. The cluster analysis involved a series of actions which were intended to achieving effective classification based on agrarian change over the last 15 years. Following the regression analysis carried out using variables drawn from literature and collected data, an automatic clustering analysis for five factors (average 'maize output', average 'tobacco output', average 'cattle holdings', 'number of months maize harvest will last' and 'family labour hired out') produced 2 clusters where 226 out of 230 are placed in one cluster and the balance of 4 households constitute the second cluster. A repeat of the process using the same factors, with the exclusion of the average 'family labour hired out', produced four clusters. The process was therefore repeated with a pre-set number of clusters of four using all the factors (including family labour hired out) and this produced four clusters, as Figure 11-1 (a) and (b) shows.

The classification revealed the existence of 73 poor peasants representing 31.7% of the respondents, 119 middle peasants representing 51.7%, 34 middle-to-rich peasants representing 14.8% and four rich capitalists representing 1.7% of the respondent households. The characterisation of these clusters is aided by the factors identified and profiled in Table 11-6.

Figure 11-1: (a) Quadi-PMMR- Cluster Model Agrarian Structure (b) Class by Model Type

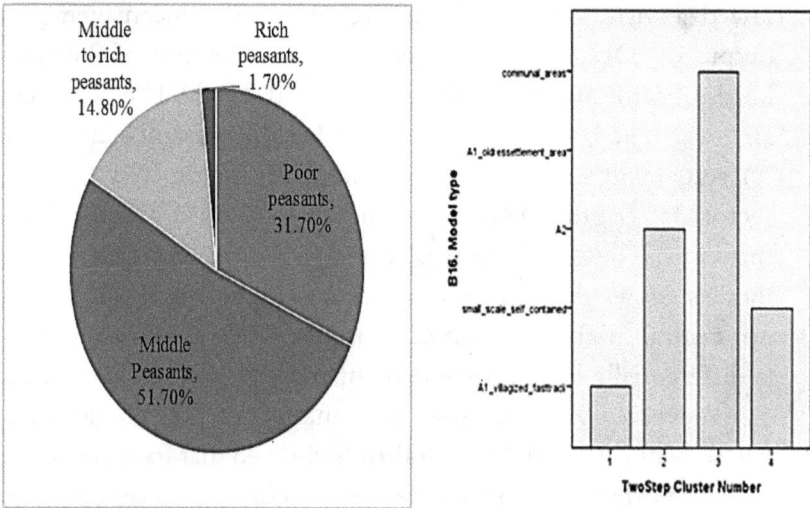

Source: Author, compiled from own survey data, 2016

Table 11-6: Quadi-PMMR Clustering Profiles

Centroids										
Cluster	Average maize Output		Average tobacco Output		Average Cattle Owned		How many months did maize harvest last		Average Labour Hired out	
	Mean	Std. Deviation	Mean	Std. Deviation	Mean	Std. Deviation	Mean	Std. Deviation	Mean	Std. Deviation
3 Poor peasants	821.429 2	1863.0104 5	267.986	675.79441	4.3105	5.97638	.68	1.165	.2785	.56112
1 *Middle Peasants*	1.4865E 3	2600.2995 7	448.435 6	944.08658	4.5686	4.34231	9.24	1.784	.1148	.55986
4 Middle to rich peasants	2.6795E 3	3026.9035 1	767.529 4	829.44753	24.715 7	7.36729	10.0 6	2.228	.3235	.87803
2 Rich capitalists	6.9167E 4	93381.547 67	1.9433E 4	38866.666 67	25.416 7	30.8189 2	11.0 0	2.000	8.666 7	16.6733 3
Combined	2.6288E 3	14113.3217 7	768.505 1	5168.17370	7.8275	9.92078	6.67	4.439	.3464	2.29175

Source: Author, compiled from own survey data, 2016

The study identifies the Quadi-PMMR-Cluster Model following Moyo's (2011c) Tri-modal structure which reveals rural transformation tied to global capital insertion and increasing reliance on proceeds from agricultural sales as well as off-farm income by households across the settlement models. In addition, the model reveals broadened participation combined with a robust shift from poor to middle peasants with a total of 66.5% of the respondents across the settlement models, now belonging to this class. The following section carries out a deeper analysis of the emerging classes.

11.4.1 Poor peasants

The poor peasants constitute 31.7% of the respondents in Hwedza District. Poor peasants are those with a mean average maize output of 821kgs, a mean average tobacco output of 268kgs, four heads of cattle and hardly a month of food supply. The poor peasants are located across the settlement models. For instance, 28.3% of the A1 settlement sector, 18.9% of the SSCF sector, 28.1% of the A2 sector, 33% of the ORA sector and 49% of the CA sector fall under this class. The distribution of poor peasants across the settlement models shows that agro-ecological regions and tenurial systems are not central to classification of peasants, while resource endowment is differentially linked to settlement models, as the Hwedza district case reveals. With regards to ranking of key indicators, the Bonferroni Adjusted Ranking Profile showed that food security is the most important variable for the households in this class, as shown in Figure 11-2.

Figure 11-2: Poor Peasants Classification Indicator Ranking Profile

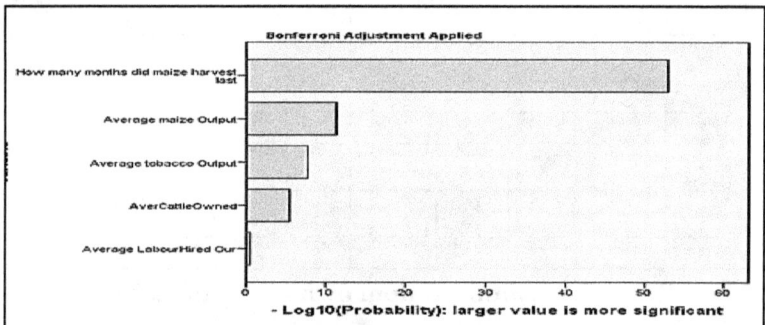

Source: Author, compiled from own survey data, 2016

Maize output is important to lesser extent, followed by tobacco output and cattle owned. The CA provides 35.6% of the poor peasants due to their limited remittances from local, urban and diaspora sources (see Figure 10.7) as well as reliance on rain-fed farming in the context of increased frequency of droughts due to the effects of climate change. These poor-peasants, contrary to Moyo and Yeros (2005), are not involved in family labour hiring out and therefore there is limited proletarianisation and semi-proletarianisation, at the same time, the farmers have limited access to remittances and proceeds from sale of agricultural proceeds. In addition, this class of farmers is on the decrease consequence to accumulation from below tendencies in Hwedza. As Figure 11-3 shows, the poor category (3), has the least male population employed on a permanent basis, and the least family members involved in agriculture production.

Figure 11-3: (a) Males Employed on Permanent Basis (b) Family Labour Involved

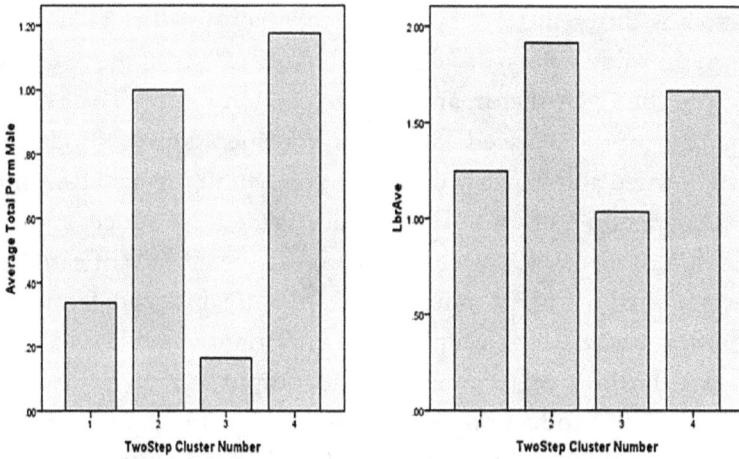

Source: Author, compiled from own survey data, 2016

The limited family involvement is a consequent of the limited access to resource endowment in the form of cattle, land and capital for agricultural production which inevitably result in low participation in agricultural production leading to food insecurity and increased poverty among the households. The poor-peasants have limited integration into the global commodity markets due to the limited production of cash crops, limited purchase of farming inputs and access to diaspora and other global funds, either through credit or contract farming. The prevalence of poor peasants is not confined to some and not all agro-ecological regions and as such the accumulation and class formation is not completely defined by location of households along geographical differentiated places in Zimbabwe. Similarly, through upward mobility due to accumulation from agriculture and other diversified activities, the peasantry has generally escaped poverty and moved towards middle peasant status, as the following section reveals. This is contrary to the position adopted by Moyo (2011c), revealing the sustenance of peasantisation in rural Zimbabwe.

11.4.2 Middle peasants

The Quadi-PMMR-Model Agrarian Structure shows a middle peasantry constituted of 51.3% of the respondents in Hwedza District. The distribution of the middle farmers across the settlement sectors is differentiated. For instance, 69.6% of the A1 households are in the middle peasants' class, and so are 60.4% of the SSCF sector, 43% of the ORA sector, and 42% of the CA sector. The peasants in this category are placed therein in consideration of food security, cattle owned and maize produced, as shown in Figure 11-4. In terms of production patterns, the middle farmers produce a mean of 1500kgs of maize, 450kgs of tobacco, keep five heads of cattle, maize harvest that last up to nine months do not hire out family in any significant way. Maize output is an important variable and indicator in classification on account of the output which is driven by a derivative of production factors such as labour, capital, arable land and access to technology and green revolution farming inputs.

Most importnatly, maize is a staple food and as such, a source of food security for the middle peasants producing higher output compared to cash crops such as tobacco. The middle farmers are also involved in labour hiring out as Figure 11-5 shows. The middle peasants were identified by Moyo (2015) as semi-subsistence producers focussed mainly on producing food crops. As Figure 11-4 (a) and (b) shows, only a few of the male population of the middle peasants are employed on a permanent basis, while family labour involvement in agricultural activities is higher than that for the poor peasants but lower than the level found within the middle-to-rich peasants and rich capitalist farmers. As Akram-Lodhi (1993) observes, whereas the middle peasants employ wage labour, they employ more family labour in their agricultural activities, see also Figure 11-4(b).

Figure 11-4: Middle Peasants Classification Ranking Profile

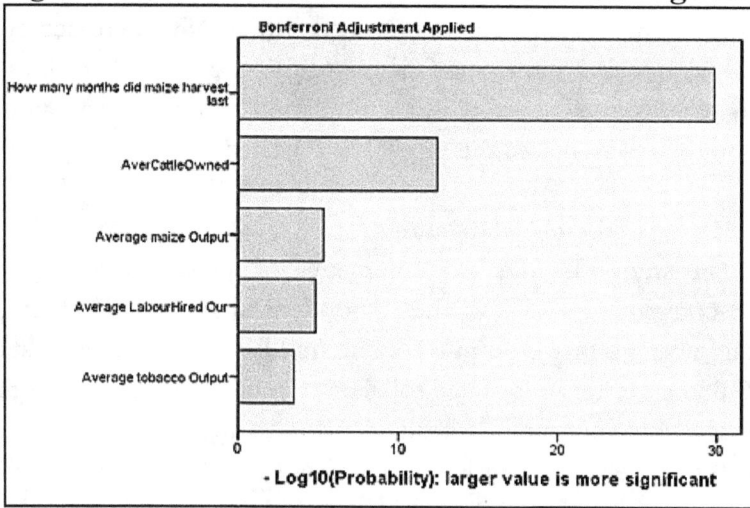

Source: Author, compiled from own survey data, 2016

Even though maize is an important variable for classification for the middle peasants, this category produces very low maize output compared the middle-to-rich and the rich capitalist farmers, as shown in Figure 11-5 (a).

Figure 11-5: (a) Maize Output per Class (b) Average Income by Class

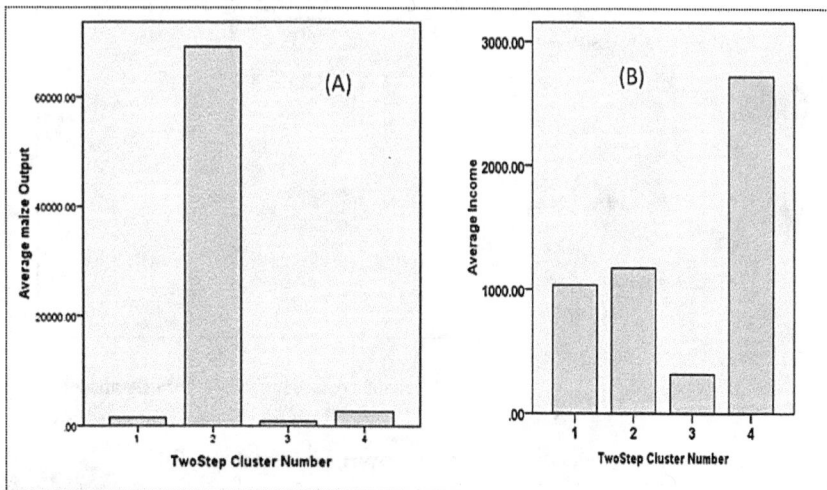

Source: Author, compiled from own survey data, 2016

281

Moyo's (2011c) categorisation on the basis of land size which identified the existence of middle-sized farmers who increased on the basis of new A2 farm beneficiaries (estimated at 31,000) does not fully capture the dynamics in accumulation and class formation for the middle peasants, as this study has revealed.

11.4.3 Middle-to-rich peasants

The study identifies the emergence of middle-to-rich peasants who constituted 14.8% of the respondent in Hwedza District. The mean 'average maize output' for the middle-to-rich peasants stands at 2 680kgs, a mean 'average tobacco output' of 770kgs while mean average 'cattle output is 25 head of cattle, 10 'months of food supply' and they barely 'hire out labour'. These were placed differentially in some of the settlement models, being 15.1% SSCF households, 28.1% of the A2 farmers, 24% of the ORA households and 9% of the CA households and 2% of the A1 households. In terms of the differentiating varibales, Figure 11-6 shows that 'cattle owned' and 'food security' were critical in the cluster analysis.

Figure 11-6: Middle-to-Rich Class Indicators Profiles

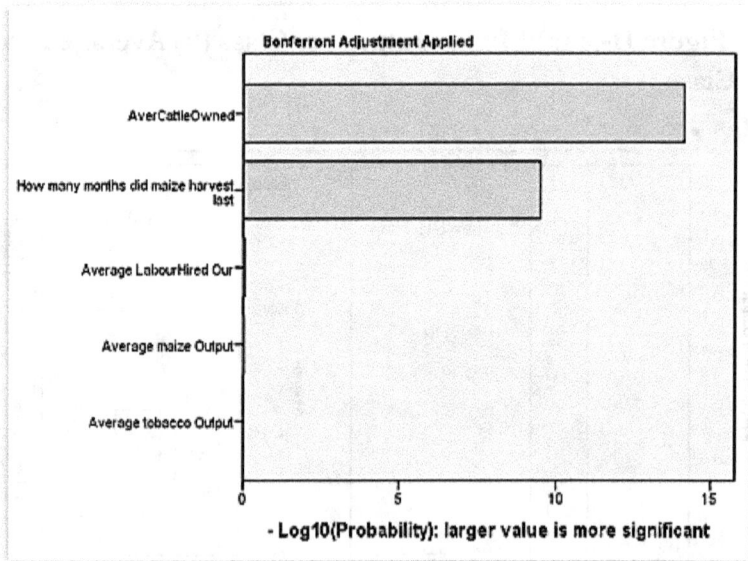

Source: Author, compiled from own survey data, 2016

'Cattle holdings' are an important variables for the middle-to-rich peasants as it provides a source storage of wealth, draught power, sales proceeds and an important for the social standing for the households. However, the middle-to-rich pesants from the A2 and the SSCF sectors do not rely on cattle for tillage income as compared to middle farmers mostly located in the ORA and SSCF sectors (Figure 7b). Since 85.3% of the farmers are located in the SSCF and the A2 sectors, they hold rights in the form tittle deeds and 99 years leases over their land and are therefore better placed to access credit. However, access to credit has been mainly in the form of contract farming that is linked to international and domestic capital, financing tobacco crops. International capital is mainly from China, Britain and the United States of America while domestic capital is mobilised through local banks seeking to avoid the risk of direct credit to the 'new' farmers. This class employ family to a slightly less proportion to hired labour (both casual and permanent, men and women).

Figure 11-7: (a) scotch carts owned per class (b) Cattle owned per class

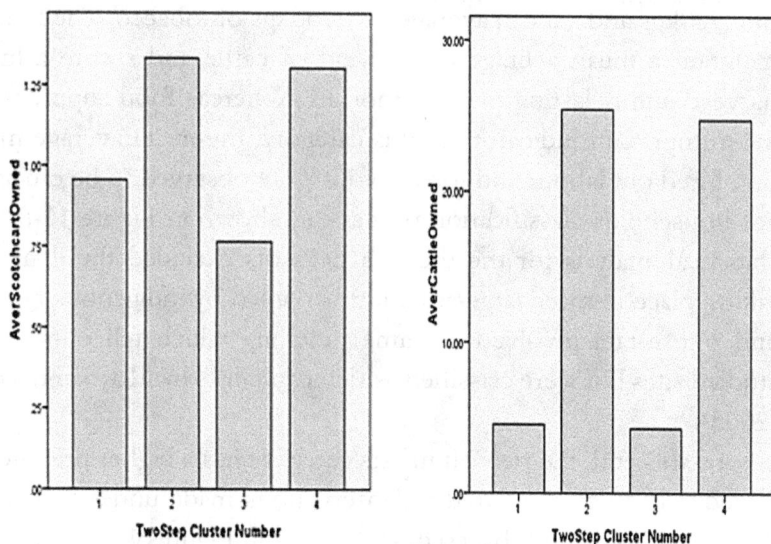

Source: Author, compiled from own survey data, 2016

The prevalence of the middle-to-rich farmers in the SSCF and A2 sectors is connsistent with what Moyo (2011c) under the Trimodal agrarian structure. The household participation in the global commodity circuits is pronounced. The observation by this study to the effect that the combined set of middle farmers constituting 66.1% of rural farmers agrees with Scoones (2015) study where he concluded that middle farmers now predominate. Given low government support for agriculture across the settlement models, the emerging middle farmers have become dettached from the state and state-linked patronage system and are linked to global commodity markets through contract farming and global commodity markets batressed through the tobacco marketing process. However, a more nuanced analysis reveals that a few elites benefit from the contract farming systems as gatekeepers for the contracting companies who aid in ensuring complince by contracted peasants in the rural areas, across the settlement sectors.

11.4.4 The rich capitalist farmers

The rich capitalist farmers constitute 1.7% of the respondents and these were situated in the SSCF and the A2 sectors in equal proportions. The rich farmers produce a mean average maize output of 6,920kgs and a mean average of 1,950kgs of tobacco. The farmers maintain a mean average of 25 head of cattle and secure a maize harvest supply lasting over 11 months. Whereas food supply is the most important indicator for this category, the mean average maize out, hired out labour and tobacco out were observed to be crucial in the households classification process, as shown in Figure 11-8. The statistical analysis for the the rich peasants excluded the dynamics taking place in three large-scale farms owned by indigenous farmers and one estate involved in game ranching which fell outside the studied sites but were classified as rich capitalists by Moyo and Yeros (2005).

To this end, the rich capitalists category has a higher presence in Hwedza District compared to observations made under this study. The maize sold and tobacco output tables in Figures 11-9 (a) and (b) show that the rich capitalist farmers secured the highest sales figures and output levels for the period, 2013-2015. This is linked to differentiated resource endowment in the form of access to capital, productive assets, quality of seed and fertilizers and sound agronomic standards used by the resettled farmers. In terms of productive assets ownership, the rich capitalist farmers had the highest number of households in possession of scotch carts and the biggest arrable lands available for the crop and livestock production.

Figure 11-8: Variance Importance for Class Analysis

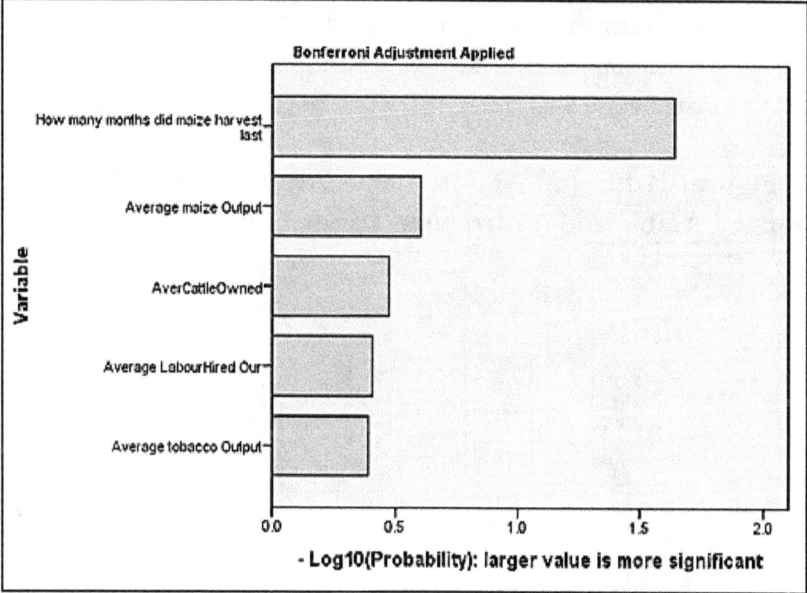

Source: Author, compiled from own survey data, 2016

Figure 11-9: Maize Sold and Tobbaco Output, 2013-2015

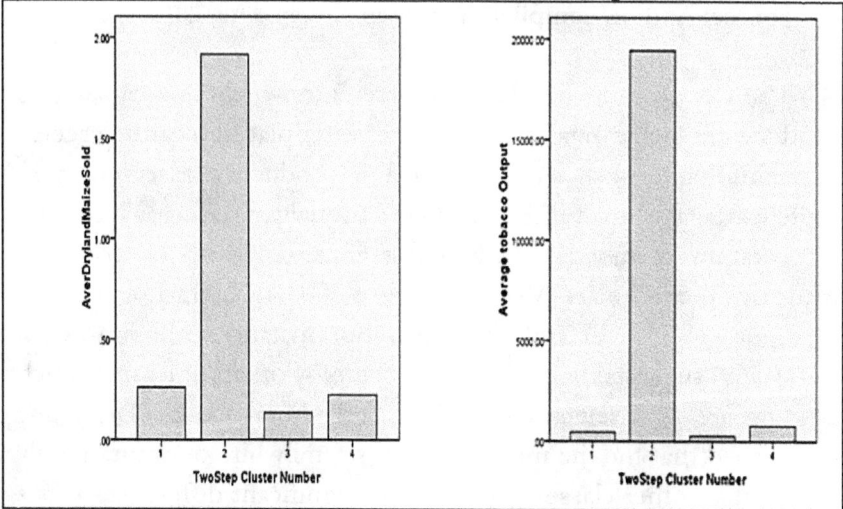

Source: Author, compiled from own survey data, 2016

The middle-to-rich peasants and rich capitalist farmers have an average of between 30.1-120 hectares of land and onescotch cart each, on average. This gives them greater scope in livestock and crop production. However, land utilisation is generally lower than the available land. For instance, as shown in Figure 11-10 (a) and (b) middle-to-rich capitalist farmers and rich capitalist farmers in possession of farms to the extent of 30.1-120ha till a a maximum of 4ha, which eliminates land size as an important indicator in rural Hwedza distrit class analysis.

Figure 11-10: (a) Arable Land Available (b) Clustered Cropped Arable and (c) Irrigated Lands Class

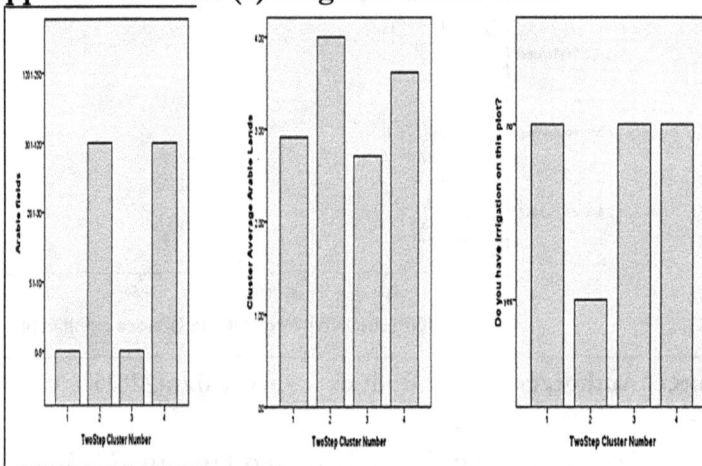

Source: Author, compiled from own survey data, 2016

The CA peasants had low resource endowment and capacity to produce, the rich capitalist farmers are better placed regarding access to technologies such as irrigation and productive assets such as scotchcarts, as shown in Figure 11-12. Equally, the sector hired out more family members, which is not consistent with observations made by other scholars (Moyo and Yeros 2005; Akhram-Loghi 1993), as Figures 11-13 (a) and (b) show. For instance, Akhram-Lodhi (1993:569) suggests that rich farmers 'employ others at least as much as they are themselves engaged in agricultural work'. The study established that the the middle peasants family hire out more family labour than other classes. Similarly, no significant differences exists among all classes other than the middle peasants regarding household sizes, as shown in Figure 11-12 (b). Figure 11-2 (b) also shows that the rich capitalists employ more family labour in their operations than other classes. In addition, the middle-to-rich peasants and the rich capitalist employ employ male permanent employs than other classes, in line with Chambati's (2011) observations.

Figure 11-11: (a) Family Labour Hired Out and (b) Household Size per Class

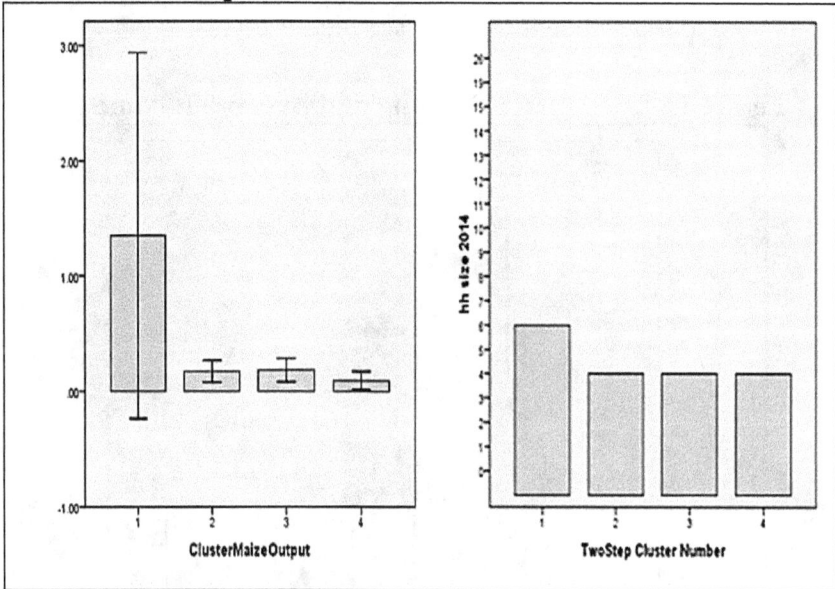

Source: Author, compiled from own survey data, 2016

However, contrary to Moyo (2011c) who observes that the middle-to-rich peasants are the once who rely more on family labour to produce for auto-consumption and to sell the surplus, the rich peasants were observed to employ more family labour for agricultural production. The rich capitalist farmers are located in the SSCF sector and A2 settlement sectors and produce more commodities for sale and as such are connected the global commodity markets, throught exports and contract farming.

11.5 Tobacco Production under Contract Farming

This section seeks to reveal how contract tobacco farming has impacted on class formation and accumulations patterns in rural Hwedza District. The average tobacco output was found to be relevant in the classification process on the basis of the importance of factors of production. For instance, the interactive bar graphs plotted showed that farmers on contract farming had higher income compared to independent farmers (see Figure 11-12).

Figure 11-12: Contract Farming and Average Income

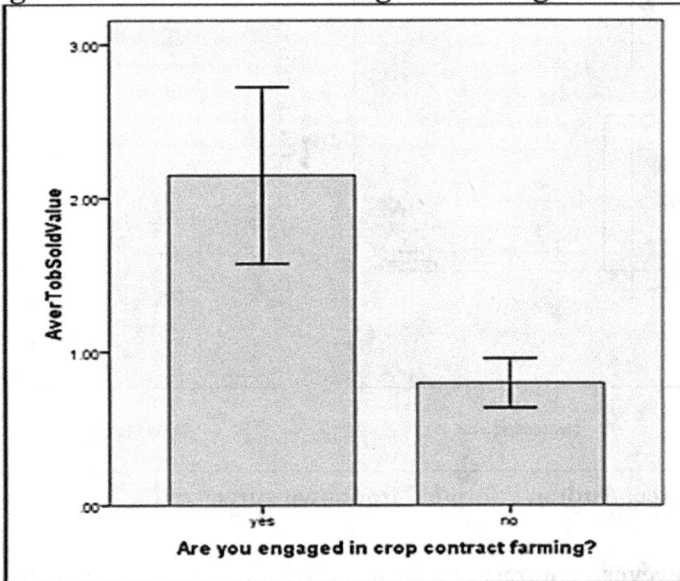

Source: Author, compiled from own survey data, 2016

Similarly, tobacco sales income was higher for farmers on contract farming compared to independent farmers (see Figure 11-13). As a result, these households do well in accumulation of productive assets, send their children to better schools and have access to inputs for a broader and diversified cropping programme.

Figure 11-13: Contract Farming and Tobacco Sales

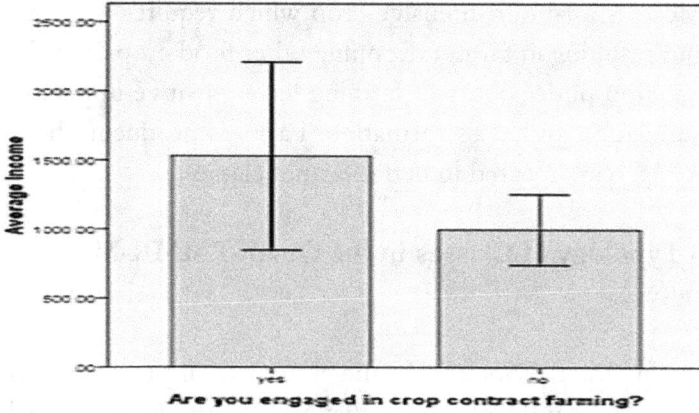

Source: Author, compiled from own survey data, 2016

Most of these households are able to move to the middle to rich classes, depending on scale of production. On the contrary, the maize farmers who are not in tobacco contracts produce more maize than those on contract farming. To this end, it is plausible to conclude that farmers engaged in tobacco contract farming are less likely to engage in maize crops. For instance, the interactive bar graphs (Figure 11-14) show that farmers engaged in tobacco contract farming are unlikely to produce maize.

Figure 11-14: Contract farming and Maize sales

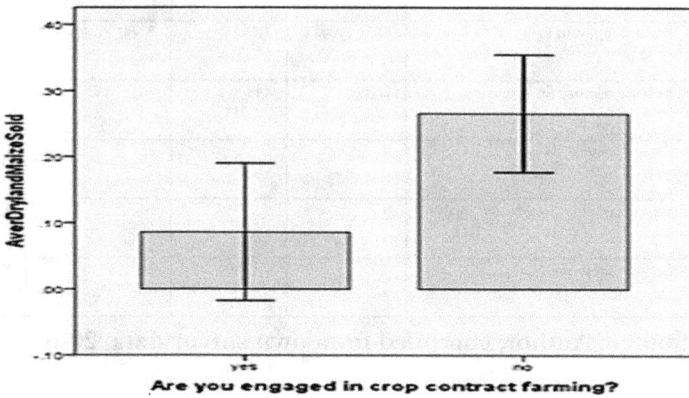

Source: Author, compiled from own survey data, 2016

As Getrude Mhande, a respondent in the Sengezi ORA observed, 'tobacco is a labour intensive crop which requires huge amount of labour resulting in farmer dropping other food crops'. In all, tobacco production under contract farming has a positive impact on capital accumulation and class formation. Farmers producing higher levels of tobacco are located in better farmer classes.

11.6 Typology of Classes in the Quadi-PMMR-Model Agrarian Structure

Using the factors used in the classification process as criteria for analysis, the study observed that poor farmers produce less that 1,000kgs of maise, below 300kgs of tobacco and keep an average of four heard of cattle and face severe food shortage as stocks do not last a month supply. The poor family relies on labour hiring out. The middle peasants produce less between 1,000 -1,500kgs of maize, below 500kgs of tobacco and maintain an average heard of five cattle, with at least nine months food supply as Table 11.7 shows. The middles peasants also access local and diaspora remmitances, in turn used to fund agricultural activities.

Table 11.7: Characteristics of Peasants in the Quadi-PMMR-Model Agrarian Structure

Criteria		Poor peasants	Middle peasants	Middle to Rich Peasants	Rich capitalists
1.	Maize output (in kgs)	821	1,487	2,680	6,917
2.	Tobacco output (in kgs)	268	448	768	19,433
3.	Cattle Owned	4	5	25	25
4.	Months of harvested maize supply	0.7	9	10	11
5.	Labour hired out	0.3	0.1	0.3	8.7

Source: Author, compiled from own survey data, 2016

The middle to rich peasants produce in excess of 2700kgs of maize, 800 kgs of tobacco and keep 25 heard of cattle, with ten month food supply. These households are highly commoditised and secure a large among of money from agricultural produce sales, as shown in Table 11.8.

Table 11.8: Typology of their Sources of accumulation

Criteria	Poor peasants	Middle peasants	Middle to Rich Peasants	Rich capitalists
1. Proceeds from own production and sales	Low access	Moderate access	Highly accessible	Highly dependent and accessible
2. Remittances (Diaspora and local)	No access	Highly accessible	Moderate access	Low reliance and access
3. Non-farm income	Engaged in labour hired out	Highly engaged	Low to moderate access	Access through diversification into trade stores, grinding meals and so forth
4. Personal savings and off farm income	Low to moderate access	Highly access on pensions funds	Moderates access	Low to moderate
5. Government support	Access is moderate	Low access	No access	Limited access
6. Credit and contract farming	No access	Low	Moderate access	High access

Source: Author, compiled from own survey data, 2016

In turn, the rich peasant produces 7000kgs of tobacco, earning resources used to pay wages and buy inputs in an expanded agricultural production system. The rich peasants therefore have greater access to global markets for cash crops, hire more labour and are less reliant of family labour.

11.7 Extended Theoretical Framework Considerations

A re-visit of the theoretical framework shows a direct link between global capital and accumulation processes in rural Zimbabwe, where 35.2% of the farmers are engaged in the growing of tobacco with 33.3 accessing contract farming (see diagram 11.1). However 52. 6% of the households rely on sales proceeds to fund agriculture and 26.3% rely on personal savings and 10.5% on diaspora remittances, while government support benefits 11.1% of the poor to middle peasant classes.

Diagram 11.1: Schematic Extended Theoretical framework

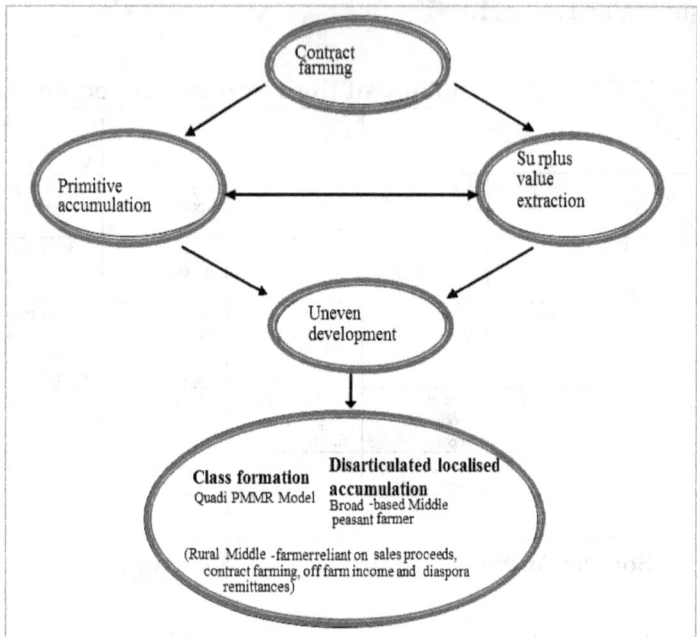

Source: Author, compiled from own survey data, 2016

As has already been highlighted, there is no direct evidence to the effect that contract farming is negatively impacting on other crops. A connection is conceivable through the linkage between farmers' reliance on sales proceeds and tobacco sales proceeds. Given that some farmers are opting out of contract farming citing unfair prices, this study concludes that farmers could do far better had their insertion into the global markets been fairer. Unfair pricing and non-participation in the value chain by the peasants maintains a disarticulated relationship between Zimbabwe and the centre. A combination of these agricultural funding arrangements results in the growth of the middle farmers now representing 66.5% of the respondents in Hwedza district, showing a large movement of farmers from poor to middle class, reminiscent of the American path. However, to the extent that the farmers' produce (tobacco, tomatoes, onions and cabbages) are mostly sold to buyers in urban areas in their raw form means that the financial returns in Hwedza are limited and that surplus value is being exported to those sectors and centres where the commodities are being processed and sold at higher prices.

The local economy therefore remains heavily dependent on urban areas for the supply of processed and manufactured goods consumed by rural households.

Similarly, to the extent that agricultural commodities produced in Hwedza are sold to urban centres in raw form means that the goods go on to create employment opportunities in those areas where they are eventually processed (locally and global centres), leading to uneven development and furthering the deepening of a disarticulated economy at a micro-level and at the macro-level. However, the co-existence of a disarticulated economy and growing middle class needs further investigation. Similarly, the growth of the middle class in rural Hwedza against an economy in crisis at national level also needs further research to reveal the underlying dynamics for agrarian change.

11.9 Conclusion

The Two-Step Cluster Analysis produced a Quadi-PMMR-Cluster Model which explains the ongoing agrarian change in Zimbabwe. The model is constituted of four classes; namely, the poor peasants, the middle peasants, the middle-to-rich peasants and the rich capitalist farmers. The classification was based on five variables; maize output, tobacco output, cattle holdings, food security and labour hired out. Crop output helps take into account cropped area, input applied access to capital and labour hiring levels. The accumulation trajectory shows an upward mobility of rural peasants from poor to middle class across settlement models, agro-ecological regions and gender. The movement is fuelled by agricultural sales proceeds which is related to access to finance - credit, contract farming and government support, non-farm income and off-farm income earned differentially across the emerging agrarian classes.

Chapter Twelve

Conclusion

12.1 Introduction

The changing agrarian relations have been shaped by the changing role of capital from the pre-colonial period, heralded by the arrival of Rhodes and his collaborators in 1888 (Tshuma 1997) and the invasion of Mashonaland in September of 1890, through to the FTLPR beginning in 2000. The BSAC bought the Lippert Concession in 1891, providing itself with scope for colonisation, domination, alienations and suppression of the African peasants. This was aided by reversal gains made by the indigenous agricultural production, marketing and sales income over the period through to the independence period 1980. In the post-independence period, capital has remained inserted in the agrarian change dynamics, beginning with the compromises made during the Lancaster House negotiations and the subsequent pronouncement of the reconciliation policy which stalled structural reforms and maintain international capital hold and the perpetuation of a white minority economy. As such, by 1978, white commercial produced 75% of the marketed crops, up from 30% in 1960 (Riddell 1978a). Despite some intermittent changes in ideological and policy thrust; from liberal and neo-liberal to socialist and redistributive, capital and the state have maintained a grip in shaping the development trajectory in agriculture and agrarian change. However the agrarian question has remained unresolved. The main findings of this study are outlined below and the theoretical reflections and policy implications drawn from these findings are also outlined below. From the outset, it is critical to highlight the findings of this study mainly apply to Hwedza district. Generalisation for Zimbabwe should be treated with caution as the Hwedza settings may not be replicated in some districts. However the agro-ecological patterns, settlement sectors and agricultural production patterns represent a larger section of the country.

12.2 Main Research Findings

12.2.1 How have land reform and contract farming changed the financing of the agrarian economy, and affected production patterns, accumulation and class formation for communal and resettled smallholder farmers in Hwedza District?

Agricultural production, capital accumulation and class formation are undergirded by state policy and the level of intensification of capital insertion in the different settlement sectors and agricultural production purposes and the performance of the broader economy. State support in the establishment of support infrastructure and credit facilities for white settler agriculture promoted capital accumulation processes that left out the African peasantry or ended up squeezing them through credit (Bond 1998; Sachikonye 1989) in the colonial state. The post-independence period was met with positive changes regarding access to government support in funding, markets and extension services following changes to the agricultural policy from 1980 onwards. The same policy resulted in either the dissolution of or privatisation of marketing boards that supported LSCFs run by white capital during the pre-independence period as Moyo (2000) and Kinsey (1999) earlier observed. However, the liberalisation of the economy in the early 1990s resulted in shrinking of government support to the peasantry and subsequently, for many commodities the collapse of the production and markets for same following the introduction of redistributive policies from 2000. The *re-financialisation* which led to reinsertion of capital from 2000 revitalised commodity production from 2008 onwards, however this was differentiated per crop and settlement model.

One of the key drivers to productivity has been the differentiated access to land across the settlement models. The CA and ORA face land shortages for different reasons. The expansion of Hwedza Growth Point resulted in vernacular land sales by the peasants residing in areas surrounding the growth point, thereby impacting on the land access, but this may not be common in areas far removed from the growth point. Population growth has generated pressure for land for the ORA peasants, thereby resulted in informal allocations

296

and access to grazing lands for cropping programs, or simply reducing land available for the cropping programs. However, in the other settlement models such as the A2 and the SSCF, households leave excessive land lying idle with average cropped areas of 1.8ha (24%) for the A1, 3.5ha (3.59%), for SSCF, 7.6ha (13.6%) for the A2, 1.3ha (13.2%) for the ORA and 1.7ha (47.7%) for the CA and an average of 3.2ha (9.36%) across the settlement sectors. In some cases, the SSCF and A2 households use smaller or equal land sizes to that of the other sectors despite that these other sectors have far less sizes of arable land available for the cropping programmes. Generally, farmers have face no threats of evictions and as such security of tenure is assured across the settlement models. However, the nature of the tenure system does not assure access to funding through the banking system.

Across the settlement models in Hwedza, maize and tobacco are the main crops (food and cash respectively). However, groundnuts and tomatoes are also major crops for the A2 farmers and in some cases tomatoes are emerging as replacement to tobacco, where farmers are dropping the crop in response to falling and fluctuating commodity prices and unfavourable contract arrangement with contractors, high inputs costs. The other common crops grown by farmers across the sectors are round nuts and sweet potatoes. Some farmers have increased the production of tomatoes and Rugare/Covo as cash crops across the sectors, as replacement for the tobacco and maize crops. The CA is generally facing a decline in tobacco and ground nuts productions. The study revealed that despite frequent drought, the differences in agro-ecological locations of the farmers has had no significant bearing on productivity. However, government response to climate change has been slow, with government workers barely knowledgeable about the government policy on same as well as on adaptation mechanisms that farmers must adopt. Similarly, access to farming inputs is generally high across the settlement sectors even tough government support is tilted in favour of the CA sector. The production of livestock is higher among the SSCF, A2 and ORA sectors, while most CA do not maintain a head of cattle due to limited agricultural activities and limited land access. However, animal drought provides tillage power

297

to 58.4% of the cropped land, 55.3% of the households rely on cattle manure for fertilizer and cattle draught power hiring for tillage services is a source of income for farmers who maintain a head of cattle.

12.2.2 Which financial and commercial circuits of capital accumulation have emerged to extract surpluses from transnational corporate tobacco merchants and commercial banks to small vegetable vendors?

As Palmer (1977) observes, it was through the marketing of agricultural produce that Africans were undermined the most. This was achieved through the pricing policy, limiting access to markets and introduction of levies and taxes. These processes led to reduced income and food for the African peasants and as such many Africans were turned into proletarians, working for white settler capital. Notwithstanding these machinations, some Africans were seen to experience upward mobility on the back of crop and livestock production, to the extent that some were employing other Africans for wage labour during the colonial period (Mining Commissioner, Bulawayo, 1907). Modern day Zimbabwe therefore inherited a disarticulated economy where the few luxury goods produced were for the minority white community and the rest of the population remained dependent on low wage income and subsistence farming (Stoneman 1988), while primary goods were exported as cheap raw material.

Households in Hwedza acknowledge that the liberalisation and dollarisation of the economy had a positive impact on the agrarian economy in Zimbabwe. However, rural farmers continue to face challenges in accessing bank credit, to the extent that most farmers end up not approaching the banks for credit at all. The failure to meet bank conditionalities is drawing back on the farmers' capabilities access bank credit, notwithstanding the re-insertion of capital from 2008. In the face of these challenges, merchant companies who seek to maintain a supply of agricultural produce have resorted to contract farming targeted at peasants across the settlement models. In the case of Hwedza, 35.2% of the farmers grow tobacco and 33.3% of these are engaged in contract farming. However, some of the merchants are funded locally by the banks for onward lending to the farmers. Contracting companies engage farmers under management contract arrangements which define the quality of produce, production systems and pricing of the product and as such limit the scope for decision making for the farmers. The farmers engaged in contract farming for tobacco also indicate that they suffer from exorbitant prices for inputs and unfavourable interest rates charges for inputs and cash advanced. Independent tobacco producers also complain of high auction floor charges which (combined with profits on inputs and interest rates) are seen as aiding the extraction of surplus by domestic and international capital, leaving the farmers with little scope for upward mobility.

12.2.3 How has agrarian change impacted on emerging local-national-global linkages within the agrarian economy (capital, social and labour relations, land use, commodity markets, climate change)?

The comparative study revealed that agricultural financing has shifted from bank credit to contract farming, local and Diaspora remmittances agricultural proceeds and personal savings from non-farm income post the FTLRP. Collateral security tied to land tenure has therefore ceased to be central to access to credit given that contract farming arrangement are not supported by land security but management contract arrangements and as such, is accessible to farmers across the settlement models. Similarly, contract farmers have a direct lsnk with the peasants under contract farming which has tended to limit patronge, state control and as such increased the independence of the farmers who are now more inserted into the global commodity chains through the inputs and outputs markets. Tobacco is a major income source for the peasantry in Hwedza. For instance, in 2015, the crop farmers earned a total of US$19, 06 million in hard currency from the crop, thereby injecting significant capital into the local economy and triggering various economic activities and capital accumulation processes.

Most farmers buy their inputs from local trading stores, even though a few buys from Harare either using remittances from urban areas or tobacco sales proceeds. There are barely any social networks involved in sourcing of inputs for the farmers. Horticultural production by poor peasants and rich capitalist farmers had a local and national characterisation. Some vegetable and tomato producers sell to local and urban vendors, however the linkages between producers and vendors remains very weak. For instance, some producers sell their produce to buyers from Mbare and Chikwanha markets, yet local vendors at Hwedza Growth Point and Chibgwa near Makarara purchase the same commodities from Mbare and Chikwanha for resell to local and travelling masses respectively. This is mainly as a result of limited dissemination of marketing information across the commodity chains. However, most farmers confirm that they buy their farming tools such as hoes and ploughs from within Hwedza District.

Whereas re-peasantisation has taken place, given the increased smallholder farmers under an American developmental trajectory, following the FTLRP, most farmers do not reside at their plots, confirming semi-proletarinisation thesis, especially among the A2 households were tenant's occupation was low at 18.75% of the respondents. As a result, remittances from the Diaspora and local sources remains a key source of funding for agricultural production in rural Zimbabwe, as the case of Hwedza reveals. Rural agricultural production therefore continues to be linked to urban employment in such a way that urban dwellers are supported by rural production in similar fashion to what Arrighi (1967) established. Peasant farming supports capitalism, however remittances by the employed also support rural production.

Even though farmers have generally adapted to climate change, its effects remain significant across the settlement areas. Irrigation facilities and other farming assets are more prevalent in the A2 sectors compared to other sectors. Similarly, the A2 and SSCF farmers employ more permanent and casual workers than the other sectors. Female workers are generally employed as casual workers while male workers are generally employed on a permanent basis across the settlement sectors. The A1, ORA and CA sector employ more single permanent and casual workers. The sources of workers and non-farm activities provide another source of linkages between CAs (Buhera and Hwedza, Chikomba and Hwedza) and sectors with Hwedza District as well as urban areas, much as hoes were a source of linkages in the pre-colonial era. The employment of wage labour has shifted following the introduction of tobacco production across the settlement models due to the demand for labour for certain agricultural activities; such as planting, weeding, harvesting and grading, such that poor peasants also hire in labour. Similarly, CA farmers are more vulnerable to food insecurity due to limited land access and low agricultural production levels. On the same note, farmers producing maize, groundnuts and sweet potatoes stand a good chance of accessing labour as these crops are used as means for payment for labour, generally secured from across the settlement models.

12.2.4 What are the agrarian classes emerging in Hwedza District in Zimbabwe since 2000, and how do these relate to land reform opportunities as well as the new contract-farming regime?

The average tobacco output was found to be relevant in the classification process on the basis of the importance of factors of production. For instance, the interactive bar graphs plotted showed that farmers on contract farming had higher income compared to independent farmers. Similarly, tobacco farmers produce more maize even though the maize producers do not access contract funding. Farmers tend to apply proceeds from tobacco towards purchasing of inputs for the maize and other crops. However, maize production has declined in all the sectors from 2005 and is mostly grown for own consumption, save for the A2 sector where the crop was grown for both consumption and profitability purposes. The completion for family labour has resulted in some households dropping maize production to concentrate on the labour intensive tobacco crop. Agricultural proceeds have emerged to be a major source of funding for the agricultural production, in addition to local and diaspora remittances, non-farm income, personal savings and government support. To the extent that access to government (11.1%) is limited, the scope for corruption and patronage is therefore low and is hardly a driving factor for productivity, accumulation and class formation. Instead tobacco production under contract farming has a positive impact on capital accumulation and class formation. Farmers producing higher levels of tobacco are located in better farmer classes.

12.3 Theoretical Reflections

12.3.1 What explains accumulation and class formation for smallholder farmers in Hwedza in post-2000 Zimbabwe, particularly in terms of land reform and contract farming?

The critical variable for classification were identified as maize production, tobacco production, labour hired out, food security and cattle holding. These variables impact and are related to the cropped area for the households involved in rural agriculture. Additionally, the variables are linked to resource endowment, contract farming and as such to domestic and international capital insertion into peasant agricultural production. In the case of middle farmers located in the CA areas, remittances and personal savings are key drivers of accumulation and class formation as agricultural production is limited due to land shortage and low resource endowment. A large quantity of the cropped area is tilled using animal drawn ploughs across the settlement models. As such, farmers with high ownership of cattle are better positioned to produce agricultural crops. However, the SSCF sector owns more cattle than other sectors and are therefore better capacitated to till the land. The biggest challenge cited by the farmers across the settlement models is the prevalence of HIV/AIDS, access to credit and poor road networks and these can more or less be generalised. Other challenges being faced are droughts, access to markets and inputs, land tenure insecurity and lack of working capital.

12.3.2 What model/framework of Zimbabwe's agricultural productivity, capital accumulation and class formation can be developed as a consequence of emerging farming practices in post-FTLRP Zimbabwe?

Relying on statistical regression analysis, the study revealed that four clusters have emerged in Hwedza following the FTLRP of 2000. This study named; the Quadi-PMMR-model agrarian structure to reveal the 4 clusters; P (poor), M (Middle peasants), M (middle-to-rich peasants) and R (rich). The poor peasants constitute 31.7% of

302

the respondents and are located across the settlement models. They produce a mean average of 821kg of maize, 368kgs of tobacco, maintain a head of four cattle and often times have a month supply of food. They are a source of labour for the other classes of farmers. As a result, these peasants have limited integration into the global commodity chains. The Middle peasants constitute 51.3% of the respondents. However, the middle peasants come from the A1, SSCF, ORA and the CA. They maintain 9 months of harvest maize supply, five head of cattle and rely on family labour for agricultural production.

The middle-to-rich peasants constitute 14.8% of the respondents and mostly located in the A2, SSCF and ORA sectors. However, 9 % of the CA and 2% of the A1 are located in this class as well. The middle-to-rich peasants produce a mean average of 2680kgs of maize, 770kgs of tobacco, and own 25 head of cattle and maintain 10 month of maize harvest supply. These farmers generally tend to higher levels of resource endowment that is linked to global finance capital through increased access to contract farming. This class employs family labour and also hired labour (both casual and permanent, men and women). The rich capitalist farmers constitute a mere 1.7% of the interviewed households in Hwedza District and are equally constituted of households from the A2 and SSCF sectors, only. The rich capitalists maintain 11 months of food supply, 25 head of cattle and produce 6920kgs of maize, 1950kgs of tobacco. They are particularly differentiated on the basis of higher resource endowment than other sectors. With regards to the A2 farmers, this is tied to the land reform beneficiary selection criterion where those who had better chances of accessing credit and financing were allocated land. To this end, these farmers have better access to productive farming assets.

12.3.3 How have the accumulation and class formation affected broader social relations in Hwedza District, and are these patterns likely to prevail more generally in Zimbabwe?

The model developed and revealed by this study indicates a general increase in the middle farmers (middle and middle-to-rich) who constitute 66.5% of the Hwedza's rural peasantry. Hwedza's middle peasants are spread across the settlement models, including the CA. This dispels the myth that land reform is the key driver of accumulation and class formation in post FTLRP Zimbabwe. To this end, re-peasantisation and rural decongestion have taken place, demonstrating the pre-dominance of the American path. The movement of peasants towards the middle farmer is driven by merchant capital and other local sources of funding, mainly proceeds from agricultural production, non-farm income and remittances. In the case of Hwedza, in some areas, vernacular land sales are reversing de-congestion efforts in the CA, and natural population growth in the ORA has resulted in increased land shortage and demand. Hwedza District provides a unique learning opportunity because as is located in four agro-ecological regions and five settlement models which increases the chances for generalisation.

12.4   Realisation of Objectives

12.4.1   To assess the role of capital in rural accumulation and class formation in the variegated farming sectors in Hwedza District.

This comparative study revealed that capital (contract farming, local and diaspora remittances, off farm and personal savings, proceeds from agricultural commodity sales, non-farm income and government support) impact differentially on accumulation across the settlement models in rural Hwedza District. To this end, the role of internal capital is limited to tobacco farmers who constitute 35.2% of the respondents in this study, with only 33.3% participating in contract farming. At least 52.6% rely on proceeds from agricultural commodity sales, 26.3% rely on personal savings, 10.5% on diaspora remittances and 11.1% of the respondents get government support. The various capital sources are used for investment securing productive assets, household assets, children's education requirements and for family reproduction.

12.4.2 To analyse emerging local-national-global linkages within the agrarian economy (capital, social and labour relations, land use, commodity markets, climate change).

The main driver of local-national and international linkages is agrarian capital. The study analysed the input and output markets for the agrarian economy to establish how linkages have developed since the FTLRP. As already noted, global capital finance associated with contract farming and tobacco export through international merchants is driven the rural economy through tobacco farming in Hwedza, even though some farmers are now quitting the crop in favour of tomatoes and vegetables. The output (horticultural and other food) commodity markets, labour relations and the input (fertilisers, seed and chemical) markets link farmers to local traders, villagers and urban centres in a fashion that has seen the deepening of the commodification of the rural peasants. Climate change has changed differentiation in the scope of farmers' vulnerability and success due to frequent droughts that tend to affect farming in equally devastating measure. To this end, agricultural productivity, capital accumulation and class formation have barely been impacted upon by differences in agro-ecological regions.

However, the production and circulation patterns revealed by this study shows that the economy remains disarticulated at local and global levels. The farmers in Hwedza sell unprocessed agricultural commodities to the urban centres who in turn export semi-processed goods to the developed world. To this end, surplus value is extracted and exported from less developed sectors to the developed sectors and centres through the operations of capital finance. However, the persistence of a disarticulated agrarian economy coincides with a growing middle class base, which calls for deeper and more nuanced investigation into the underlying emerging dynamics.

12.4.3 To develop a model/framework of Zimbabwe's agricultural productivity, capital accumulation and class formation as a consequent of emerging farming practices in post-FTLRP Zimbabwe.

The study developed a Quadi-PMMR-Cluster Model Agrarian Structure consisting of four classes [P (poor), M (Middle peasants),

M (middle-to-rich) and R (rich)] to explain the development trajectory in post-2000 rural Zimbabwe. The model is reliant on five factors, namely; 'maize output', 'tobacco output' and 'food security', 'cattle holding's and 'labour hired out', which denote the importance of capital and resource endowment as critical in agricultural productivity, capital accumulation and class formation. The model revealed a growing middle-scale farmer base constituted of 66.5% whose sources of accumulation differ within and across settlement sectors.

12.5 Contributions to Knowledge

The findings show an emerging Quadi-PMMR-Model Agrarian Structure composed of the poor, middle, middle-to-rich peasants and some rich capitalists with a growing middle farmer base constituting two thirds of the rural population. The sources of accumulation are differentiated within and across the variegated settlement sectors and agro-ecological regions. With regards to state practise, limited government capacity has resulted in low support for the agricultural sector, curtailing chances and significance of politics, patronage and corruption in the agricultural sector.

Secondly, the study reveals the drivers (variables) of rural accumulation and agrarian change are connected to how *re-financialisation* through domestic and international capital has restructured resource endowment and impacted on the cropped area and crop productivity, over-time. However, personal savings, remittances and non-farm income have also emerged as major sources of funding while 'maize output', 'tobacco output' and 'food security', 'cattle holdings and 'labour hired out' emerged as key indicators driving classification of the peasants. Contract tobacco production is an independent driver of capital accumulation and class formation.

Thirdly, the study contributes to debate on changing labour relations linked changing production patterns where peasant (including poor) farmers combine hired casual labour and family labour during critical stages of tobacco farming have changed sources of labour, providing linkages across rural sectors and urban areas.

Fourthly, the findings show that climate change and increased prevalence of droughts have curtailed variations in agrarian change across the agro-ecological regions.

Fifth, maize production has declined giving way to tobacco, now declining as farmers have begun shifting to horticultural crops (tomatoes and onions), due to unfavourable markets. However, farmers producing tobacco use their proceeds to grow maize and therefore increase the scope for food security.

Sixth, variations in landholding across the settlement models have a narrow impact on agricultural productivity across the settlement models while there are emerging land shortages associated to vernacular land sales in the CA and population growth in the ORA, reversing decongestion gains achieved through resettlement programs.

Seventh, at a theoretical level, the Hwedza economy is disarticulated in favour of urban centres and ultimately the developed world where the agricultural produce from Hwedza are exported in semi-processed form. Since the agricultural produce from Hwedza is exported in its raw form, this means that jobs created during processing benefit those located where value addition takes place. In any event, the farmers are excluded from ownership of the companies involved in the commodity chain, ensuring a complete detachment from value creation and capital accumulation opportunities.

12.6 Policy Implications and Recommendations

The developed model deepens our understanding of ongoing structural transformation in the rural economy aiding theorisation, policy designing and implementation. Tobacco contract farming-led rural capital accumulation requires legislative framework on how capital insertion into peasant agriculture impacts on agrarian change, to protect the farmers. Beyond on-farm production dynamics revealed by this study, commodity circulation linked to contract farming purchases, further than the auction floors, through the global commodity circuits, remain understudied despite the historical significance of tobacco farming to the Zimbabwean economy.

Further research is required.

The agrarian economy remains disarticulated, exporting raw produce to the developed (articulated) sectors and centres locally and globally. The exportation of unprocessed agricultural commodities deepens the disconnectedness of the local economy, its reliance on, and consumption of, imported goods from urban centres and the developed world. To this extent, the production and circulation patterns revealed at the micro-level show that surplus extraction and exportation through export capital finance mechanics is undermining capital accumulation and class formation in Hwedza District. However, there is a movement towards a broadening of the middle class in the disarticulated economy, who are connected to agricultural production financed by proceeds from agricultural commodity sales, local and domestic, personal savings, contract and credit finances (linked to international finance capital) and government input support. Access to capital finance remain a constraint on the rural agrarian economy, even though the economy has gone through cycles of policy changes from command to neo-liberal and vice-versa, and therefore requires policy and state intervention.

12.7 Conclusion

The comparative study across the settlement models and agro-ecological settings revealed productivity, accumulation and class formation in Hwedza. Overall, the study contributes to the ongoing debate on agrarian change in Zimbabwe and Southern Africa. To this end, the study contributes to debate on emerging and changing aspects of agricultural production and marketing in rural Zimbabwe. Previous comparative studies focussed on CA and fast track areas, whereas this study took a holistic view and investigated ongoing change in resettled areas (pre-and post-colonial), across Zimbabwe's agro-ecological regions and therefore the study gives a complete picture of how the land reform, changing state policy and capital finance have impacted on agricultural productivity, capital accumulation and class formation in rural Zimbabwe.

This study has contributed to knowledge on how capital–tobacco contract farming is inserted into rural agricultural production, accumulation and class formation. The study also reviewed the emerging rural classes in Hwedza District and developed a model to explain the emerging agrarian structure. The American path involving re-peasantisation and semi-proletarianisation, and a growing middle class driven by merchant capital, contract farming, remittances and agricultural proceeds/resources, is emerging in Hwedza district.

However, the rural economy is heavily disarticulated in favour of the developed urban areas and centres, which limit the scope for capital accumulation and class formation in rural areas. The exclusion of the rural households from the commodity circuits where surplus is extracted to, on its way to the centre also undermine rural development, given the limited capacity of the state in post 2000 Zimbabwe.

References

Aglietta, M. 1979. *A Theory of Capitalist Regulation: The U.S. Experience*. London: New Left Books.

Agricultural Finance Corporation. 1990. Annual Report, Harare; Agricultural Finance Corporation.

AGRITEX Rusape Report 1980-1982.

African Institute for Agrarian Studies 2006. *Inter-district Household Baseline and Farm worker Survey*, 2005/06. Harare: AIAS.

African Institute for Agrarian Studies 2006. The Monopoly Role of the GMB in Food Security. Paper Prepared for the Zimbabwe Project Trust Dialogue on Land and Resource Rights.

African Institute for Agrarian Studies Baseline Survey, 2007. Inter-district household and whole farm survey database. African Institute for Agrarian Studies (AIAS), Harare.

Alexander, J. 2003. 'Squatters', Veterans and the State in Zimbabwe.' In: Hammar, A. et al., Eds. *Zimbabwe's Unfinished Business: Rethinking Land, State and Nation in the Context of Crisis*. Harare: Weaver Press.

Alexander, J. 2006: *The Unsettled Land: State Making and the Politics of Land in Zimbabwe 1893- 2003*. Oxford, Harare and Athens: James Curry, Weaver Press, Ohio University Press.

Amin, S. 1976. *Unequal Development*, trans. B. Pearce. New York, NY & London: Monthly Review Press.

Amin, S. 1990. *Maldevelopment, Anatomy of a Global Failure*. The United Nations University, Third World Forum, Studies in African Political Economy, Zed Books Limited, London and New Jersey.

Amin, S. 2015. Contemporary Imperialism, Monthly Review Press.

Amin, S., 1974. *Accumulation on a World Scale: A Critique of the Theory of Underdevelopment*. 2 Vols. Monthly Review Press, New York.

Anderson, K., ed. 2010. *The Political Economy of Agricultural Price Distortions*. Cambridge University Press. Cambridge.

Arendt, H., 1968. *Imperialism: Part Two of the Origins of Totalitarianism*. Houghton Mifflin Harcourt.

Arrighi, G. and Saul, JS 1973b. Essays on the political economy of Africa, London and New York: Monthly Review Press

Arrighi, G. 1970. Labour Supplies in Historical Perspective: A study of the Proletarianisation of the African Peasantry in Rhodesia. *Journal of Development Studies*, 6(3): 197–234.

Arrighi, G. 1973. The Political Economy of Rhodesia. In: G. Arrighi and J. Saul, eds. *Essays in the Political Economy of Africa*. New York: Monthly Review Press.

Arrighi, G., 1966. The Political Economy of Rhodesia. *New Left Review*, (39):.35.

Arrighi, G., 1967. The Political Economy of Rhodesia, The Hague. Mouton & Co., Printers, Arrighi, G., 2010. *The World Economy and the Cold War. MP Leffler and OA Westad, The Cambridge History of the Cold War*, pp.23-45.

Babbie, E. 1995. *The Practice of Social Research*, 7th edition. Bowker, J. M. Belmont, CA: Wadsworth Publishing Co.

Baran, P.A., Sweezy, P.M. and Torrents, R., 1969. *El Capitalismo Monopolista*. Anagrama.

Bardhan, P., 1982. Agrarian Class Formation in India. *The Journal of Peasant Studies*, 10(1), pp.73-94.

Barkin, J.S., 1998. The Evolution of the Constitution of Sovereignty and the Emergence of Human Rights Norms. *Millennium-Journal of International Studies*, 27(2), pp.229-252.

Barret, C.B. and Reardon, T., 2000. Asset, Activity, and Income Diversification among African Agriculturalist: Somer Practical Issues. Project Report to USAID BASIS CRSP.

Baxter, V. and Mann, S., 1992. The Survival and Revival of Nonwage Labour in a Global Economy. *Sociologia Ruralis*, 32(2-3), pp.231-247.

Beach, D. N. 1980. *The Shona and Zimbabwe, 900–1850: An Outline of Shona History*, Gweru: Mambob Press.

Beach, D. N. 1994. *A Zimbabwean Past: Shona Dynastic Histories and Oral Traditions*, Gweru: Mambo Press.

Beach, D., N. 1977. The Shona Economy: Branches of Production. In Palmer, R.H and Parsons, N. (eds,) *The Roots of Rural Poverty*, London, Heinemann Educational Publishers.

Beckman, N., 1977. Policy Analysis in Government-Alternatives to Muddling Through. *Public Administration Review*, 37(3), pp.221-222.

Bernstein, H. 2009. V.I. Lenin and A.V. Chayanov: Looking back looking forward. *The Journal of Peasant Studies*, Vol 36, No. 1. 1: 55-81.

Bernstein, H. 2010. *Class Dynamics of Agrarian Change*. Fernwood Press, MA: Kumarian.

Bernstein, H. 2015. African Peasants and Revolution' Revisited. *The Journal of Peasants Studies*, 41(S1), S95– S107

Bernstein. H. 1977. Notes on Capital and Peasantry. ROAPE, No. 10.

Bettison, D.G., 1960. The Poverty Datum Line in Central Africa. *Rhodes-Livingstone Journal*, *27*, pp.1-40.

Bhila, H.H.K., 1982. *Trade and Politics in a Shona Kingdom: The Manyika and their African and Portuguese neighbours, 1575-1902*. Harlow, Essex: Longman.

Bond, P. 1998, *Uneven Zimbabwe: A Study of Finance, Development and Underdevelopment*. Trenton, Africa World Press

Booth, D., 1985. Marxism and Development Sociology: Interpreting the Impasse. *World Development*, *13*(7), pp.761-787.

Bradby, B., 1975. The Destruction of Natural Economy. *Economy and Society*, *4*(2), pp.127-161.

Bukharin, 1973; N. 1973. Imperialism and World Economy. Monthly Review

Press, New York, NY

Bulawayo Sketch plan dated 20 July 1895

Bundy, C., 1977. The Transkei Peasantry, c. 1890–1914: Passing through a Period of Stress. *The Roots of Rural Poverty in Central and Southern Africa*. London: Heinemann.

Bush, R. and L. Cliffe. 1984. Agrarian Policy in Labour Migrant Societies: Reform or Transformation in Zimbabwe? *Review of African Political Economy*, 29, 77–94.

Byres, T.J., 1991. The Agrarian Question and Differing Forms of Capitalist Agrarian Transition and the State: An Essay with Reference to Asia. In *Rural Transformation in Asia*, eds J. Breman and S. Mundle, 3–76. Delhi: Oxford University Press.

Byres, T.J., 1991b. Agrarian Question," in Bottomore, T., L. Harris, VG Kieman and R. Miliband, (eds). *A Dictionary of MarJu'st Thought*, Oxford: Blackwell Publishers.

313

Central Statistical Office 1947. Central Statistical Office Report, Southern Rhodesia

Central Statistical Office. 2012. Central Statistical Office Report, Zimbabwe.

Chambati, W and Moyo S. 2013. Roots of the Fast Track Land Reform in Zimbabwe. In Sam Moyo and Walter Chambati (eds.). *Land and Agrarian Reform in Former Settler Colonial Zimbabwe*, Council for the Development of Social Science Research in Africa, Angle Canal IV BP 3304 Dakar, CP 18524, Senegal.

Chambati, W., 2009, 'Land Reform and Changing Agrarian Labour Processes in Zimbabwe', MM Thesis, South Africa: University of the Witwatersrand.

Chavunduka, G.L., 1982. Report of the Commission of Inquiry into the Agricultural Industry (Zimbabwe).

Cheater, A. 1990: The Ideology of Communal Land Tenure: Mythogenesis Enacted, *Africa*, Vol. 60 (2), pp. 188-206.

Chenery, H.B., 1960. Patterns of Industrial Growth. *The American Economic Review, 50*(4), pp.624-654.

Chidziva Tobacco Company, 2015

Chief Native Commissioner Report, 3 September 1926

Chief Native Commissioner. 1904. Chief Native Commissioner Memorandum to Private Secretary of the Administrator.

Chimedza, R. 1994. Rural Financial Markets. In Rukuni, M. and Eicher, C.K. (eds) *Zimbabwe's Agricultural Revolution*, Harare, University of Zimbabwe Publications.

Chimedza, R., 2006. Rural Financial Markets: Historical Overview 1924-1991.; Zimbabwe's Agricultural Revolution Revisited Edited By: Mandivamba Rukuni, Patrick Tawonezvi, Carl Eicher with Mabel Munyuki-Hungwe.

Chimhowu, A. and Woodhouse, P., 2008. Communal tenure and rural poverty: Land transactions in Svosve Communal Area, Zimbabwe. *Development and Change, 39*(2), pp.285-308.

Clapp, R.A., 1988. Representing Reciprocity, Reproducing Domination: Ideology and the labour process in Latin American contract farming. *The Journal of Peasant Studies, 16*(1), pp.5-39.

Clapp, R.A., 1994. The Moral Economy of the Contract, eds Little, P.D., *Living under contract: contract farming and agrarian transformation in sub-Saharan Africa*. University of Wisconsin Press., pp.78-96.

Clements, F.A. and Harben, E., 1962. *Leaf of Gold: The Story of Rhodesian Tobacco*. London, Methuen.

Cliff, L., Alexander J., Cousins B., and Gaidzanwa, R., 2011. An Overview of Fast Track Land Reform in Zimbabwe: An Editorial Introduction' *The Journal of Peasant Studies*, Vol. 38, No. 5, pp. 907-938.

Cliffe, L 1988. The Prospects for Agricultural Transformation in Zimbabwe, in Stoneman, C. (eds), *Zimbabwe's Prospects: Issues of Land, Class, State and Capital in Southern Africa*, pp309–325 (London: Macmillan).

Cotton Marketing Board. 1992. Cotton Marketing Board Records Annual Report (1991-92)

Cousins, B. 2010. What is a 'Smallholder'? Class analytical perspectives on small-scale farming and agrarian reform in South Africa. Working Paper 16, January 2010. PLAAS, University of the Western Cape.

Cousins, B., 2011a. What is a "Smallholder"? Class-Analytic Perspectives on Small-Scale Farming and Agrarian Reform in South Africa.' In P. Hebinck and C. Shackleton (eds.) *Land Resource Reform in South Africa: Impacts on Livelihoods*, Abingdon: Routledge.

Cousins, B. 2013. Smallholder Irrigation Schemes, Agrarian Reform and 'Accumulation from Above and from Below' in South Africa. *Journal of Agrarian Change, Vol. 13 No. 1, January 2013, pp. 116–139*.

Cousins, B. Weiner D. and Amin N. 1992. Social Differentiation in the Communal Lands of Zimbabwe Author(s): *Review of African Political Economy*, No. 53, pp. 5-24.

Creswell, J.W. and Clark, V.L.P., 2007. Designing and Conducting Mixed Methods Research. California Sage Publications.

Creswell, J.W., 2009. Research Design: Qualitative and Mixed Methods Approaches. London: Sage Publications.

Cusworth, J. 2000. A Review of the UK ODA Evaluation of the Land Resettlement Programme in 1988 and the Land Appraisal in

1996.' In T. A. S Bowyer –Bower and C Stoneman (eds). *Land Reform in Zimbabwe: Constrains and Prospects*. Aldershot, UK: Ashgate.

Davis, D.R., 1998. Does European Unemployment Prop up American Wages? National Labour Markets and Global Trade. *American Economic Review*, pp.478-494.

de Janvry, A. 1981. *The Agrarian Question and Reformism in Latin America*. Baltimore, MD: The Johns Hopkins University Press.

De Schutter, O., 2011. How Not to Think of Land-grabbing: Three critiques of large-scale investments in farmland. *The Journal of Peasant Studies*, 38(2), pp.249-279.

De Soto, H. 2000: *The Mystery of CAPITAL: Why Capitalism Triumphs in the West and Fails Everywhere Else*, New York, NY, Basic Books.

Deininger, K. H. Hoogeveen H and Kinsey B. 2004. Economic benefits and costs of land redistribution in Zimbabwe in the early 1980s. *World Development*, 32(10), 1697–1709.

Dekker, M. and Kinsey, B. H. 2011. Contextualising Zimbabwe's Land Reform: Long-term observations from the first generation. *The Journal of Peasant Studies*, 38(5), 995–1019.

Delgado, C., Hopkins, J., Kelly, V. 1998. *Agricultural Growth Linkages in Sub Saharan Africa*. IFPRI Research Report No.107. Washington, DC: International Food Policy Research

Department of Agriculture 1929. Department of Agriculture, Report of the Secretary

Dey, I. 1993. *Qualitative Data Analysis*. London: Routledge

Diang'a, S.O., 2011. Regularizing Informal Settlements for Sustainable Housing Development for the Urban Poor: The Case of Nairobi, Kenya PhD Thesis, University of Kwa Zulu-Natal, Durban.

Ellis, F. (1998) 'Survey Article: Household Strategies and Rural Livelihood Diversification', *The Journal of Development Studies* 35 (1): 1-38

FAO 2009. Special Report: FAO/WFP crop and food security assessment mission to Zimbabwe, 22 June 2009. Rome: Food and Agriculture Organization of the United Nations; Rome: World Food Programme.

FAO, 2008. Special Report: FAO/WFP Crop and Food Security Assessment Mission to Zimbabwe, 18 June 2008. Rome: Food and Agriculture Organization of the United Nations; Rome: World Food Programme.

FAO, I., 2015. WFP. 2015. *The State of Food Insecurity in the world.*

Foster, J.B., 2015. The new imperialism of globalised monopoly-finance capital: An introduction. *Monthly Review, 67*(3), p.1.

GAIN Report 2010. Zimbabwe: Sugar Annual. Global Agricultural Information Network (GAIN). USDA Foreign Agriculture Service.

GAIN Report, 2012. Zimbabwe: Sugar Annual. Global Agricultural Information Network (GAIN). USDA Foreign Agricultural Service.

Gavian, S. and Ehui, S., 1999. Measuring the Production Efficiency of Alternative Land Tenure Contracts in a Mixed Crop-Livestock System in Ethiopia, *Agricultural Economics,* 20, 37-49.

Gibbon, P. and Ponte, S., 2005. *Trading Down: Africa, value chains, and the global economy.* Temple University Press.

Glover, D. and Kusterer, K., 1990. *Small Farmers, Big Business: Contract farming and rural development.* London, Macmillan Press Ltd.

Gonese, F. and Mukora, C., 2003. Beneficiary selection, infrastructure provision and beneficiary support. *Delivering land and securing rural livelihoods: post-independence land reform and resettlement in Zimbabwe.* Harare and Madison, Centre for Applied Social Sciences, University of Zimbabwe, and Land Tenure Centre, University of Wisconsin-Madison.

Government of Zimbabwe (2001a. Land Reform and Resettlement Program. Ministry of Lands, Agriculture and Rural Resettlement. Harare: Government Publications.

Government of Zimbabwe 2001. Millennium Economic Recovery Programme (MERP).

Government of Zimbabwe 2001a, Millennium Economic Recovery Programme (MERP).

Government of Zimbabwe, 2003. Second Poverty Assessment Study Survey 2003. Training and Field Manual. Government Printers, Harare.

Government of Zimbabwe, 2015. National Budget Statement, presentation by Minister, Patrick Chinamasa, Harare.

Greene, J. C., Caracelli, V. J. and Graham, W. F. 1989. Toward a Conceptual Framework for Mixed-method Evaluation Designs. *Educational Evaluation and Policy Analysis*.

Grossman, I. S. 1998. *The Political Ecology of Bananas: Contract Farming, Peasant and Agrarian Change in the Eastern Caribbean*. University of North Carolina Press, Chapel Hill.

Guba, E.G. and Lincoln, Y.S., 1994. Competing Paradigms in Qualitative Research. *Handbook of Qualitative Research*, 2, 163-194.

Gunning, J., Hoddinott J., Kinsey, B. H. and Owen, T. 2000. Revisiting Forever Gained: Income Dynamics in Resettlement Areas of Zimbabwe, 1983–1996. *Journal of Development Studies*, 36 (6), 131–54.

Haggblade, S., Hazell, P.B. and Reardon, T. eds., 2007. *Transforming the Rural Non-farm Economy: Opportunities and Threats in the Developing World*. International Food Policy Research Institute 2033 K St, NW Washington, DC

Hanlon, J., Manjengwa, J. and Smart, T. 2013. *Zimbabwe Takes Back it's Land*: Kumarian Press, Johannesburg, Jacana Media.

Hardt, M. and Negri, A., 2000. *Empire: The New World Order*, Cambridge and London.

Haroon Ahram-Lodhi, A. 1993: Agrarian Classes in Pakistan: An Empirical Test of Patnaik's Labour–Exploitation Criterion, *The Journal of Peasant Studies*, 20:4, 557-589

Harrison, G. A. 1964: Ayre's T-piece: A Review of its Modifications. *British journal of Anaesthesia*, 36 (2), 115-120.

Hart, G. (1994). The Dynamics of Diversification in an Asian Rice Region. In Koppel, B. *et al* (eds.) *Development or Deterioration: Theories, Experiences and Policies*. Oxford and New York: Oxford University Press.

Harvey, D. 2005: *The New Imperialism* Oxford: Oxford University Press.

Hatendi, D.T., 1987. *The Political Impact of Foreign Capital (Multinational Corporations) in Rhodesia, 1965-1979,* Doctoral Thesis, University of Oxford.

Haugerud, A., 1989. Land Tenure and Agrarian Change in Kenya. *Africa, 59* (01), 61-90.

Herbst, J.I., 1990. *State Politics in Zimbabwe,* California, University of California Press.

Higginbottom, A. 2009. The Third Form of Surplus Value Increase," Paper presented at the Historical Materialism Conference, London, November 27–29.

Hobsbawn, E., 1994. *Age of Extremes. The Short Twentieth Century. Michael Joseph, London.*)

Hodder-Williams, R.1983: *White Farmers in Rhodesia,* London: Macmillan.

Hume, I.M., 1978. A Preliminary Essay on Land Reform in Rhodesia. *Zimbabwe' (Salisbury: Whitsun Foundation,* unpublished mimeo, 1978*).

Institute. Denzin, N. K. 1978. *The Research Act: A Theoretical Introduction to Sociological* Methods. New York.

Johnson, R. B., Ownwueguzie, A. J and Turner, L. A. 2007. Toward a Definition of Mixed Methods Research, *Journal of Mixed Methods Research*, Volume 1, Number 2, April 112-133.

Kamidza. R. 2013. Zimbabwe's Trade Negotiations with the European Union: State Shortcomings and Civil Society Advocacy, 2000-2013 Doctoral Thesis, University of KwaZulu-Natal, Durban.

Kauskty, J. H. 1988. *The Agrarian Question,* 1st edition, London: Pluto Press.

Kay, C., 1999. Rural Development: From Agrarian Reform to Neoliberalism and Beyond. *Latin America Transformed: Globalization and Modernity*, 271-302.

Kinsey, B. 2003. Comparative Economic Performance of Zimbabwe's Resettlement Models. In M. Roth and F. Gonese, (eds). *Delivering Land and Securing Rural Livelihoods: Post-independence Land Reform and Resettlement in Zimbabwe.* University of Zimbabwe and University of Wisconsin-Madison, Harare and Madison, WI.

Kinsey, B. H. 1999. Land Reform Growth and Equity Emerging Evidence from Zimbabwe's Resettlement Programme, *Journal of Southern African Studies* 25 (2).

Kinsey, B. H. 2004. Zimbabwe's Land Reform Program: Underinvestment in Post-Conflict Transformation. *World Development* 32 (10) 1669-1696.

Kitchin, R. and Tate, N. 2000. *Conducting Research in Human Geography: Theory, Methodology and Practice,* Prentice Hall, Harlow, England.

Kitching G. 1982. *Development and Underdevelopment in Historical Perspective: Populism, Nationalism and Industrialization,* London: Methuen.

Kuusinen, O.V., 1928. The Revolutionary Movement in the Colonies. *Inprecor,* VIII, 68.

Lahmann, E., 1986. *Heavy Metals: Identification of Air Quality and Environmental Problems in the European Community.* Commission of the European Communities.

Landau, S. and Everitt, B., 2004. *A Handbook of Statistical Analyses using SPSS* (Vol. 1). Boca Raton, FL: Chapman & Hall/CRC.

Lenin V, I., 1967. Imperialism: The Highest Stage of Capitalism, in *Selected Works,* Volume 1, trans. Moscow: Progress Publishers

Lenin, V. I. 1964: *The Development of Capitalism in Russia.* Trans. Moscow: Progress Publishers.

Lenin, V. I. 1966. New Times and Old Mistakes in a New Guise, *Collected Works,* trans. Vol. 33 (Moscow, Progress Publishers.

Lenin, V.I., 1968. *Selected Works,* Moscow, trans. Progress Publishers.

Lenin, V.I., 1986. *Lenin's struggle for a revolutionary International: documents, 1907-1916, the preparatory years.* Trans. Monad Press.

Lenin, V.I., 1996. Report on Red Army Pogroms, with Lenin's Reaction, 17-18 October 1920. Trans. *The Unknown Lenin: From the Secret Archive, by Richard Pipes.*

Lenin, V.I., 1967 [1899]. The Development of Capitalism in Russia: The Process of the Formation of a Home Market for Large-Scale Industry. In *Collected Works,* Vol. 3. Trans. Moscow: Progress Publishers.

Lincoln Y.S. and Gobi E.G. 1985. *Naturalistic Inquiry.* Beverly Hills, C.A.

Loney, M., 1975. *Rhodesia, White Racism and Imperial Response* (Vol. 41). Penguin Books.

Luxemburg, R. 1968. *The Accumulation of Capital.* London: Routledge & Kegan Paul.

Luxemburg, R., 1951. *The Accumulation of Capital*, trans. *Agnes Schwarzchild, intro. Tadeusz Kowalik* (London, 2003), 350.

Malaba, S.M.T 2014. Catalyzing Agriculture Value Chain Finance, Paper presented at the 2nd edition of the Agro-Business Conference, H.I.C.C, Zimbabwe, 27th August 2014.

Mamdani, M. 1996. *Citizen and Subject: Contemporary Africa and the Legacy of Colonialism* (Princeton NJ: Princeton University Press.

Mamdani, M., 1987. Extreme but Not Exceptional: Towards an Analysis of the Agrarian Question in Uganda. *The Journal of Peasant Studies, 14*(2), pp.191-225.

Mann, S., 199 Marongwe, N., 2011. Who was allocated Fast Track land, and what did they do with it? Selection of A2 farmers in Goromonzi District, Zimbabwe and its impacts on agricultural production. *Journal of Peasant Studies, 38*(5), pp.1069-1092.0. *Agrarian Capitalism in Theory and Practice*. UNC Press Books.

Mao, Z., 1967. *Selected Readings from the Works of Mao Tse-Tung*. Peiking, Foreign Languages Press.

Marongwe, N. 2008: Interrogating Zimbabwe's Fast Track Land Reform and Resettlement Programme: A Focus on Beneficiary Selection. PhD Thesis. University of the Western Cape.

Marongwe, N., 2011. Who was allocated Fast Track land, and what did they do with it? Selection of A2 farmers in Goromonzi District, Zimbabwe and its impacts on agricultural production. *Journal of Peasant Studies, 38*(5), pp.1069-1092.

Marx, K. [1859] 1971. *A Contribution to the Critique of Political Economy*, Trans London:

Marx, K., 1973. *The Revolutions of 1848* (Vol. 1). Allen Lane; Trans New Left Review.

Morse, J.M., 1991. Approaches to qualitative-quantitative methodological triangulation. Nursing research, 40(2), pp.120-123.

Marx, K. 1977. *Theory of Revolution*. Vol. 1. Trans Monthly Review Press.

Marx, K., 1981. *Capital*, Vol. 3, trans. David Fernbach. London: Trans Penguin, 117 (127), p.466.

Marx, K.1967. *Capital* Vol, 1, Trans Moscow: Progress Publishers.

Masakure, O. and Henson, S., 2005. Why do small-scale producers choose to produce under contract? Lessons from nontraditional vegetable exports from Zimbabwe. *World Development*, *33*(10), 1721-1733.

Masst, M., 1996. The Harvest of Independence: Commodity Boom and Socio-economic Differentiation among Peasants in Zimbabwe. PhD Dissertation, Roskilde University.

Matibiri, A. 2013. Overview of Tobacco Production, Marketing, Harare, TIMB, National Annual Report.

Matondi, P., B., Khombe, T.C., Moyo, N., R., Matondi, M and Chiweshe, M. 2008. The land reform and resettlement programme in Mangwe district, Matebeleland South Province. University of Zimbabwe: Centre for Rural Development.

Matondi, P.B. 2012. *Zimbabwe's Fast Track Land Reform Programme*. London: Zed Books ed.

MB6/1/3, Mining Commissioner, Bulawayo, Report for year ended 31 Dec. 1907.

McMichael, P., 2012. The Land Grab and Corporate Food Regime Restructuring. *Journal of Peasant Studies*, *39*(3-4), 681-701.

Mining Commissioner. 1907. Mining Commissioner Report, Bulawayo.

Ministry of Agriculture, Mechanisation and Irrigation Development, 2012. Second Round Crop Assessment Report. Government of Zimbabwe. Harare: Government Printers.

Ministry of Agricultural Engineering, Mechanization and Irrigation 2009. Agricultural Engineering Mechanization and Irrigation Strategy Framework: 2008 – 2058.

Ministry of Agricultural Engineering, Mechanization and Irrigation), 2009. Agricultural Engineering Mechanization and Irrigation Strategy Framework: 2008 – 2058. Draft.

Ministry of Agriculture Mechanisation and Irrigation Development, 2010. Second Round Crop and Livestock Assessment Report, Harare.

Ministry of Agriculture Mechanisation and Irrigation Development 2016. Second Round Crop and Livestock Assessment Report, Harare.

Ministry of Agriculture, Mechanisation and Irrigation Development 2010a. Second Round Crop and Livestock Assessment Report. 9 April 2010. Government of Zimbabwe. Harare: Government Printers.

Ministry of Agriculture, Mechanisation and Irrigation Development 2010b. Agricultural Statistical Bulletin, 2010. Government of Zimbabwe. Harare: Government Printers.

Ministry of Agriculture, Mechanisation and Irrigation Development 2011. Second Round Crop and Livestock Assessment Report. 14 April 2011. Government of Zimbabwe. Harare: Government Printers.

Mkandawire 2013: Neopatrimonialism and the Political Economy of Economic Performance in Africa: Critical Reflections, Publikationsår: Institutet för Framtidsstudier arbetsrapport 2013:1.

Binswanger-Mkhize, H. and Moyo, S., 2012. Zimbabwe from Economic Rebound to Sustained Growth: Note II: Recovery and growth of Zimbabwe Agriculture. World Bank, Harare.

Mkodzongi, G., 2013. New People, New Land and New Livelihoods: A Micro-study of Zimbabwe's Fast-track Land Reform. *Agrarian South: Journal of Political Economy*, 2(3), pp.345-366.

Moore, D. 2003. Zimbabwe: Twists on the Tale of Primitive Accumulation. In Malinda Smith, (ed). *Globalizing Africa* (Trenton: Africa World Press, 2003), 247-269.

Morris Carter Commission (ZAH 1/1/4),

Morse, J. 1991. Approaches to Qualitative-Quantitative Methodological Triangulation. *Nursing Research, 40*,120-123.

Mottier, V., 2005, May. The interpretive turn: History, memory, and storage in qualitative research. In Forum Qualitative Sozialforschung/Forum: Qualitative Social Research (Vol. 6, No. 2).

Moyana, H., V. 1984. *The Political Economy of Land in Zimbabwe*, Gweru, Mambo Press.

Moyo S. 2015: Agriculture and Structural Transformation in Africa, A Peasant Path, Unpublished.

Moyo, S. (2006). Emerging Land Reform and Tenure Issues. African Institute for Agrarian Studies Monograph.

Moyo, S. 1986. The Land Question, In I. Mandaza (ed.), *Zimbabwe: The Political Economy of Transition,* 1980-1986. (Codesria: Dakar).

Moyo, S. 1991. *Zimbabwe's Agrarian Reform Process: Lesson or Domino Strategies,* Zimbabwe Institute of Development Studies, Harare.

Moyo, S. 1995. *The Land and Agrarian Question in Zimbabwe.* SAPES Books. Harare.

Moyo, S. 2000: *Land Reform under Structural Adjustment in Zimbabwe: Land Use Change in the Mashonaland Provinces.* Uppsala: Nordiska Afrikainstitutet.

Moyo, S. 2001. The Land Occupation Movement and Democratisation in Zimbabwe: Contradictions of Neo-liberalism. *Millennium Journal of International Studies,* Vol. 30, No.2, 311-330.

Moyo, S. 2011a: Three Decades of Agrarian Reform in Zimbabwe. *The Journal of Peasant Studies,* 38(3), 493–531.

Moyo, S., 2011b. Land concentration and accumulation after redistributive reform in post-settler Zimbabwe. Review of African Political Economy, 38(128), pp.257-276.

Moyo, S, Chambati, W, Mazwi F and Muchetu R 2014. Land Use, Agricultural Production and Food Security Survey: Trends and Tendencies, 2013/14. African Experiences, African Institute for Agrarian Studies, Eastlea, Harare.

Moyo S and Chambati W. 2012: Unlocking the Economic Potential of Communal Land: Regional/African Experiences African Institute for Agrarian Studies, Eastlea, and Harare.

Moyo, S, Jha, Praveen and Yeros, P. 2013. The Classical Agrarian Question: Myth, Reality and Relevance Today, *Agrarian South,* 2(1), 93–119.

Moyo S. and Nyoni, N. 2013: Changing Agrarian Relations after Redistributive Land Reform in Zimbabwe. In Sam Moyo and Walter Chambati (eds.), *Land and Agrarian Reform in Former Settler Colonial Zimbabwe,* Council for the Development of Social Science Research in Africa, Angle Canal IV BP 3304 Dakar, CP 18524, Senegal

Moyo, S. and Matondi, P 2000. Conflict Dimensions of Zimbabwe's Land Reform Process. Unpblished paper

Moyo, S. and Yeros, P. 2005: The Resurgence of Rural Movements under Neoliberalism, in S. Moyo and P. Yeros, (eds). *Reclaiming the Land: The Resurgence of Rural Movements in Africa, Asia and Latin America*, London and Cape Town: Zed Books and David Philip.

Moyo, S. and Yeros, P. 2007: The Zimbabwe Question and the Two Lefts, *Historical Materialism*, Vol. 15, No. 3.

Moyo, S. and Yeros, P. 2009. Zimbabwe Ten Years On: Results and Prospects, *MRzine*, 10 February. (http://mrzine.monthlyreview.org/2009/my100209.html).

Moyo, S. and Yeros, P., 2011, The Fall and Rise of the National Question. In S. Moyo and Yeros, P., eds., *Reclaiming the Nation: The Return of the National Question in Africa, Asia and Latin America*, London: Pluto Press.

Moyo, S. Chambati, W., Murisa, T., Siziba, D., Dangwa, C., Mujeyi, K., and Nyoni, N. 2009: *Fast Track Land Reform Baseline Survey in Zimbabwe: Trends and Tendencies, 2005/06*. African Institute for Agrarian Studies (AIAS). Harare.

Moyo, S., 2011c: 'Changing Agrarian Relations after Redistributive Land Reform in Zimbabwe', *The Journal of Peasant Studies*, Vol. 38, No. 5: 939–66.

Moyo, S., 2013. Land reform and redistribution in Zimbabwe since 1980. In Sam Moyo and Walter Chambati (eds), *Land and agrarian reform in Zimbabwe: Beyond white-settler capitalism* (pp. 29–78). Dakar: CODESRIA.

Moyo, S., P, Jha & P, Yeros. 2012. Imperialism and Primitive Accumulation: Notes on the New Scramble for Africa. *Agrarian South: Journal of Political Economy* 1(2), 181-203.

Mtapuri, O. 2008. Developing a Poverty Index for Mrican Economies using the Consensual Approach: The Case of Mashonaland West, Zimbabwe, PhD Thesis in Development Studies, University of KwaZulu Natal, Durban.

Mtetwa, R., 1975. Political and Economic History of the Duma People of South-Eastern Rhodesia', PhD Thesis, University of Rhodesia.

Mugenda, O. and Mugenda, A.G., 1999. *Research Methods*. Nairobi. African Centre for technologies studies Press.

Muir, E., 1981. *Civic Ritual in Renaissance Venice*. Princeton University Press.

Muir, K. 1994. Agriculture in Zimbabwe. In: M. Rukuni and C.K Eicher, (eds). *Zimbabwe's Agricultural Revolution*. Harare: University of Zimbabwe Publications.

Müller, M., 2011. Doing Discourse Analysis in Critical Geopolitics. *L'Espace Politique. Revue en ligne de géographie politique et de géopolitique*, (12).

Munck, R. and O'Hearn, D., 1999. *Critical Development Theory: Contributions to a New Paradigm*. Zed Books.

Murisa, T. and Chikweche, T., (eds.) 2015. *Beyond the Crisis: Zimbabwe's Prospects for Transformation*, Weaver Press. Harare.

National Archives of Zimbabwe (N3/33/8)

Neocosmos, M. 1993. The Agrarian Question in Southern Africa and 'Accumulation from Below': Economics and Politics in the Struggle for Democracy. Uppsala: Nordic Africa Institute Research Report, No. 93.

Neuman, S.B., 2006. The Knowledge Gap: Implications for Early Education. *Handbook of early literacy research*, *2*, 29-40.

Nigel, G. 2008. *Researching Social Life*. Third edition, SAGE USA.

Nyakazeya, P. 2009. Manufacturing sector needs major rebuilding. Zimbabwe Independent, Harare, Zimbabwe, http://www.theindependent.co.zw/, accessed on 5 May 2010.

Okoth-Ogendo, H.W.O., 1991. *Tenants of the Crown: Evolution of Agrarian Law and Institutions in Kenya*. ACTS Press, African Centre for Technology Studies (Nairobi, Kenya).

Palmer, R and Parsons, E. 1977: *The Roots of Rural Poverty in Central and Southern Africa*, London, Heinemann.

Palmer, R. 1990. *Guns and Rain: Guerillas and Spirit Mediums in Zimbabwe*. Los Angeles and Berkeley: University of California Press 1990.

Palmer, R.H., 1977. *Land and Racial Domination in Rhodesia*, (Vol. 24). Heinemann Educational Publishers.

Patnaik, P., 2012 (forthcoming), 'The Peasant Question and Contemporary Capitalism: Some Reflections with Reference to India', *Agrarian South: Journal of Political Economy*, Vol. 1, No. 1.

Patnaik, P., 2014. Imperialism and the agrarian question. *Agrarian South: Journal of Political Economy*, *3*(1), pp.1-15.

Patnaik, U. 1976: Class Differentiation within the Peasantry: An Approach to the Analysis of Indian Agriculture, Economic and Political Weekly, Vol. XI, No.39, 25.

Patnaik, U. 1987: Peasant Class Differentiation: A Study in Method with reference to Haryana, Delhi: Oxford University Press.

Patton, M.Q., 1987. *How to use qualitative methods in evaluation* (No. 4). Sage.

Pender, J., Nkonya, E., Jagger, P., Serunkuuma, D. and Sali, H., 2004. Strategies to increase agricultural productivity and reduce land degradation: evidence from Uganda. *Agricultural economics*, *31*(2-3), pp.181-195.

Petras, J and Veltmeyer 2001. Are Latin American Peasant Movements Still a Force for Change? Some New Paradigms Revisited, Journal of Peasant Studies, 28 (2): 83-118.

Phimister, I. 1986: Commodity relations and class formation in the Zimbabwean countryside, 1898-1920, Journal of peasant studies, 13(1), 240-257.

Phimister, I.R., 1977. A note on labour relations in Southern Rhodesian agriculture before 1939. *South African Labour Bulletin*, *3*(6), pp.94-104.

Phimister, I.R., 1988. *An economic and social history of Zimbabwe, 1890-1948: Capital accumulation and class struggle*. Addison-Wesley Longman Ltd.

Place, F. and Otsuka, K. (2002), 'Land tenure systems and their impacts on agricultural investments and productivity in Uganda'. *Journal of Development Studies, 38(6)*, pp. 105-128.

Ploeg, J.D. van der. 2008. The New Peasantries: Struggles for autonomy and sustainability in an era of empire and globalisation. London: Earthscan.

Raftopolous, B. 2003. The State in Crisis: Authoritarian Nationalism, Selective Citizenship and Distorting of Democracy in Zimbabwe. In Hammar, A; B. Raftopoulos and S. Jensen (eds.) (2003): *Zimbabwe's Unfinished Business*: Rethinking Land, State and Nation in the Context of Crisis, Harare: Weaver Press, pp 217-241.

Ranger, T. 1985. *Peasant Consciousness and Guerrilla War in Zimbabwe: A Comparative Study: London,* James Currey.

Ranger, T., 1977. The People in African Resistance: A review. *Journal of Southern African Studies,* 4(1), pp.125-146.

RBZ, 2007a. The Launch of Phase 1 of Agricultural Equipment Acquired under the RBZ Farm Mechanisation Programme', 11 June 2007, Reserve Bank of Zimbabwe

RBZ, 2009, Exchange Control Directive Rk:39, issued in Terms of Section 35 (1) of the Exchange Control Regulations Statutory Instrument 109 of 1996', 23 February 2009.

RBZ, 2011. Monetary Policy Statement, January 2011. Reserve Bank of Zimbabwe.

RBZ, 2012. The National Budget. Sustaining Efficient Inclusive Growth with Jobs. Harare, Ministry of Finance.

Rennie, J.K., 1978. White farmers, black tenants and landlord legislation: Southern Rhodesia 1890–1930. *Journal of Southern African Studies,* 5(1), pp.86-98.

Reserve Bank of Zimbabwe 2016. Mid-Term Monetary Policy Statement Walk The Talk To Restore Trust And Confidence.

Rhodesian Authority, 1920. Rhodesia Before 1920.

Richardson, Craig (2005). The loss of property rights and the collapse of Zimbabwe, *CATO Journal,* 25(3), 541–65.

Riddell, R., 1981. *Report of the commission of inquiry into incomes, prices and conditions of service.* Govt. Printer.

Riddell, R.C., 1978a. *The Land Problem in Rhodesia; Alternatives for the future.*

Roach, S. 2004. Outsourcing, Protectionism, and the Global Labour Arbitrage, Morgan Stanley Special Economic Study, 2003, http://neogroup.com, 6. Roach (2004)

Robinson, W.I., 2004. *A Theory of Global Capitalism: Production, Class, and State in a Transnational World.* Baltimore, Johns Hopkins University Press

Rodney, W., 1972. *How Europe Underdeveloped Africa.* Washington, DC: Howard.

Roemer, J.E., 1988. *Analytical Foundations of Marxian Economic Theory.* Cambridge, Cambridge University Press.

Rossman, G. B. and Wilson, B. L. 1985. Numbers and words: Combining quantitative and qualitative methods in a single large-scale evaluation study. *Evaluation Review, 9,* 627-643.

Rubert, S.C., 1998. *A Most Promising Weed: A history of tobacco farming and labour in colonial Zimbabwe, 1890-1945,* Ohio, Ohio University Press.

Rukuni, M and Eicher, C.K. 1994. *Zimbabwe's Agricultural Revolution.* Harare, University of Zimbabwe Press.

Rweyemamu, J. 1993. *Underdevelopment and Industrialisation in Tanzania,* Oxford: Oxford University Press.

Sachikonye, L.M., 1989. The State and Agribusiness in Zimbabwe since Independence. PhD Thesis, University of Leeds.

Sadomba, W., 2008. War Veterans in Zimbabwe: Complexities of a Liberation Movement in an African Post-colonial Settler Society. PhD Thesis, Wagenigen University, Netherlands.

Saul, J. and Woods, R., 1971. African Peasants. *Peasants and Peasant Societies* Harmondsworth, Penguin Books Ltd.

Schwandt, T. 2006. Opposition Redirected. *International Journal of Qualitative Studies in Education, 19,*803-810.

Schwandt, T. A. 2000. Three Epistemological Stances for Qualitative Inquiry. In N. K. Denzin & Y. S. Lincoln (Eds.), *Handbook of Qualitative Research* (2nd ed), Thousand Oaks, CA: Sage.

Scoones, I., Marongwe, N., Mavedzenge, B. Mahenehene, J., Murimbarimba, F., and Sukume, C., 2010. *Zimbabwe's Land Reform: Myths and Realities,* Suffolk, Harare and Johannesburg: James Currey, Weaver Press and Jacana Media.

Screpanti, E. 2014. Global Imperialism and the Great Crisis, New York: Monthly Review Press, 2014, 51–53.

Selby, A. 2006. Commercial Farmers and the State: Interest group politics and land reform in Zimbabwe. Oxford University.

Shivji, I, G. 2009: *Accumulation in an African Periphery.* Dar es Salaam: Mkuki na Nyota Publishers, Ltd.

Shivji, I.G., 1992. *The Roots of an Agrarian Crisis in Tanzania: A Theoretical Perspective.* Tanzania, University of Dar es Salaam.

Sklair, L., 2001. *The Transnational Capitalist Class,* (Vol. 306). Oxford: Blackwell.

Stavenhagen, R. and Unies, N., 1996. *Ethnic Conflicts and the Nation-State,* London: Macmillan.

Stoneman, C. 1988. *Zimbabwe's Prospects: Issues of Race, Class, State and Capital in Southern Africa.* London, Macmillan.

Stoneman, C., 1981. *Zimbabwe's Inheritance,* (Vol. 1). London, Macmillan.

Stoneman, C., 1981a. The Economy. *Zimbabwe's Prospects. London: Macmillan.*

Takavarasha, T., 1994. Agricultural pricing policy. *Zimbabwe's Agricultural Revolution.* In Zimbabwe's agricultural revolution, eds. M. Rukuni and C. K. Eicher. Harare: University of Zimbabwe Press.

TIMB, 2015: Tobacco Industry and Marketing Board

TNDP, 1983. The Transitional National Development Policy. Prefix by Robert Mugabe,

Tshuma, L. 1997. *A Matter of (In) Justice: Law, State and the Agrarian Question in Zimbabwe,* Harare: SAPES Books.

Ulin, P. R. Robinson, E.T., Tolley, E. E., and McNeill, E. T. 2002. Qualitative Methods: A Field Guide for Applied Research in Sexual and Reproductive Health. Family Health International Research Triangle Van Onselen, C., 1976, *Chibaro: African Mine Labour in Southern Rhodesia, 1900–1933,* Johannesburg: Ravan Press.

Watts, M., 1994. Epilogue: contracting, social labour, and agrarian transitions. *Living Under Contract. Contract Farming and Agrarian Transformation in Sub-Saharan Africa,* pp.248-257.

Watts, M. J. 1994. Life under Contract: Contract Farming, Agrarian Restructuring, and Flexible Accumulation. In Peter D. L. and M. J. Watts (eds.), *Living under Contract: Contract Farming and Agrarian Transformation in Sub-Saharan Africa,* Madison, WI: University of Wisconsin Press.

Weiner, D. 1988. Land and agricultural development. In: Stoneman, (ed). *Zimbabwe's Prospects: Issues of Race, Class and Capital in Southern Africa.* London: Macmillan, pp 63–89.

Weinrich, A.K.H., 1975. *African Farmers in Rhodesia.* Oxford University Press.

World Bank, 2006. Agricultural Growth and Land Reform in Zimbabwe: Assessment and Recovery Options. Report No. 31699-ZW. World Bank

Yeros, P., 2002. Zimbabwe and the Dilemmas of the Left. *Historical Materialism, 10*(2), pp.3-15.

Yin, R. 2003. *Case Study Research: Design and Methods.* Thousand Oaks, Sage.

Zamchiya, P. 2011. A synopsis of land and agrarian change in Chipinge district, Zimbabwe', *The Journal of Peasant Studies,* 38(5): 1093 – 1122

Zamchiya, P. 2012. *Agrarian Change in Zimbabwe; Politics Production and Accumulation,* Oxford University.

Zimbabwe Tea Growers Association, 2010, Tea and Coffee Production Data.

Zimstat 2016: Zimbabwe Statistics Office, Agricultural Production Statistics.

ZimSTAT, (2013). Poverty and Poverty Datum Line Analysis in Zimbabwe 2011/12

Zinyama, L.M., 1988. Farmers' perceptions of the constraints against increased crop production in the subsistence communal farming sector of Zimbabwe. *Agricultural Administration and Extension,* 29 (2), pp.97-109.

In-depth interviews
(All interviews by the author)
Agritex Officer, Hwedza Growth Point, 25 March 2016
Chipo, Chimbga, Hwedza, 27 July 2016
Chipochashe of Mashonaland Tobacco Company, Harare, July 2016
Farai Vheru, Hwedza District, July 2016
Robert Mwade, Hwedza District, 15 July 2016
Tapiwa Mapinga, Hwedza District 10 July 2016
Mr Obert Mataruse, Wagoneka Village, Hwedza Communal Areas, 5 July 2016.
Simbisai Manungira, Fair Adventure, 15th, July 2016
Gabriel Musiiwa, Zviyambe, 10 June 2016
Getrude Mhande, Sengezi ORA, 4 August 2016
Tapiwa Mapinga, Hwedza District 5 May 2016

Masimba, Ministry of Agriculture, Agriculture Extension Department, 15 June 2016

Kudzai, Tobacco Industry Marketing Board, 17 July 2016

www.ingramcontent.com/pod-product-compliance
Lightning Source LLC
Chambersburg PA
CBHW050626280326
41932CB00015B/2543